Lucky 13

Canadians in Battle Series

HUGH GODEFROY

Stoddart

Published in 1987 by
Stoddart Publishing Co. Limited
34 Lesmill Road
Toronto, Canada
M3B 2T6

First published in 1983 by
Canada's Wings, Inc., Canada
in co-operation with
Croom Helm Ltd., U.K.

Canadian Cataloguing in Publication Data

Godefroy, Hugh Constant, 1919-
    Lucky thirteen

ISBN 0-7737-5102-5

1. Godefroy, Hugh Constant, 1919-   . 2. Canada
Royal Canadian Air Force — Biography.   3. World War,
1939-1945 — Personal narratives, Canadian.
4. World War, 1939-1945 — Aerial operations,
Canadian.   5. Fighter pilots — Canada — Biography.
I. Title.

D792.C2G63 1987   940.54'4971'0924   C86-095037-9

Cover illustration by Peter Mossman
Cover design by Brant Cowie/Artplus
Printed and bound in Canada.

PROLOGUE

Thirty years have passed since I was dangling from the cockpit of my Spitfire, and conjured up the strength for one last kick to get me free. Oblivious of those intervening years I feel the suddenness of silence that comes with slow relentless tumbling free in space, for all the world a weightless celestial thing; the stark awareness that I must be falling; the moment spent looking at the rip cord in my hand, the jerk as weight is once again restored, the purring, snapping of the silk like a spinnaker before the wind, the channel tossed by an eight-knot wind, perforated by a large green hole, the bubbling grave of my burning Spitfire, the hopelessness that came with realizing that I could give no Mayday and likely would become a piece of flotsam to be tossed aimlessly upon shore. This, my oft repeated nightmare, had come to pass. I was grateful I'd been spared the fire. I had feared so often, now, how strange, I feared no more.

By chance a boat was there that chased and plucked me from the waves, returned me to a world with time and space to think of rational, rewarding things, not war. And now secure these thirty years from threats of death it seems incongruous to imagine that this was I.

Since then two generations have come to swell the population, and trumpet their demand for change, and champion each new and fashionable cause, while I have plodded on, and worked to find a place and reputation unrelated to my former self.

It seems less painful now to tell a tale of youth that the new generation might understand.

1

THE OUTBREAK OF WAR

In June 1940 I was thirty miles out of Sudbury, Ontario, working on a geological survey. I had gone there the moment final examinations were over at Toronto University. It was the first steady summer job I had been able to get. Two dollars a day with bed and board; good money. Civil engineering did not allow passing-grade students to play hockey and football. Despite having studied day and night, I was sure I had flunked spherical trigonometry. Walking to and from street cars had been my only exercise.

The foreman was a mean little man with one advantage over the rest: he could speak patois French. Up to my arrival he had been supervising the work of a gang of French Canadian Boucherons. To wring a day's work out of a flabby kid like me was much more challenging. Each day he sent the rest to do some job and left them unattended. He knew better than to try to tell them how to do — he had seen them sullenly sharpening their axes every night, but he would show this college upstart exactly what a day's work was. From morning until night he stayed on my back.

I slept in the bunkhouse with the rest. Despite ten years of French I could not understand a word they said. After I had been up there long enough for the pain and soreness to leave my arms and groins, I developed the habit of taking a stroll after supper in the bush. Returning to camp one evening, I was standing by the cookhouse wondering if I was tired enough to sleep. It was twilight, when the night-hawks climb high in the sky, then dive purring down upon their insect prey. The supply truck pulling up in a cloud of dust. With a grunt the foreman tossed me a letter. I recognized my mother's handwriting.

She opened with her usual preamble, hoping that this found me well, then stunned me with the unbelievable news that I had passed, even spherical trigonometry. Then followed two pages of inconsequential chitchat before she dropped the bombshell. She had answered my call-up letter from the Air Force telling them that I was in civil engineering, working in the field, and would not be interested in joining up. I made them take me to the nearest place where I could telephone collect. Mother didn't seem surprised to hear me and gave no argument

3

when I told her to write back and tell them that I was on my way.

When I told the Manager why I was leaving, he said: 'Called up by the Air Force? There's no conscription! You bloody young fool! You must have volunteered. I was a pilot and got shot down in 1918. It has taken me twenty years to recover. I'm just beginning to see the light.' I thanked him for the job saying that I was going anyway.

I shed no tears as I boarded the train at Sudbury. From the moment I had clapped eyes on that rocky moonscape I had felt a little sick. Not a blade of grass, not a tree, everything burnt by forest fires and the acid fumes that vomited from the stack at Copper Cliff.

'Smells like money to us,' they said when I complained. For me I had never been quite that hungry.

The clatter of the train wheels got faster as we moved south. The sound intensified the tickle of excitement that was within me. The scenery was all too familiar, a few abandoned mining camps and mile after mile of burnt-over country sprouting secondary stands of birch and poplar. It was like the bush at Grandpa's silver claim at Cobalt. I wondered how Old Gauthier was. Albert Napoleon Gauthier, the prospector who owned the adjoining claims, had heard the sound of our axes when we were making the log cabin. He had ended up doing a large part of the work, flattening the split logs with his broad-axe to make the floor. The mosquitoes, that had almost driven me mad that summer, didn't seem to bother him at all. He had the stories to tell, veteran of the gold rush and four years in the trenches. A perpetual optimist, he *knew* there was a big silver vein there. He would find it and strike it rich! God, his pancakes had tasted good with the maple syrup that he'd made by boiling maple bark. I would never forget his rugged face, the tears rolling down his cheeks as he played 'Ave Maria' on his mandolin. He could recite Robert Service by heart. He learnt all he wanted to know about the outside world from Liberty Magazine. He could die there in the bush! Nobody would know about it until his $15.00 Veteran's Burnt-Out Pension cheques started accumulating at the Cobalt Post Office. People had offered him lodging for the winter, but he'd refused. Too proud, he'd never taken a hand-out — he'd rather die in the bush first! I hadn't written him in a long time. As soon as I got home, I would drop him a line and tell him the news. He at least would be proud I had joined up.

As I looked out the window, I found myself recounting the turbulent events of the last few years. I thought again of what the man had said who had picked me up while hitch-hiking from Noranda this time a year ago. The Nazi Party, he claimed, was a fixed and popular movement in this land. Ultimately it would sweep the country. He knew for certain that Hitler had come to Canada to lay the groundwork for the organization. The network of 'fifth column' was already well established. It was only a question of time until National Socialism would overthrow and liquidate the capitalist classes and restore the power to the people. I remember how shocked I was when I mentioned this conversation after I reached Toronto. Nobody believed me. I wondered where that fellow was now.

I remember the sense of pride when Canada followed Britain with its declaration of war. The next morning came Hitler's ruthless retaliation. He ordered a U-Boat to sink the defenceless ocean liner 'Athenia'. Peggy was on the Athenia. Her widowed mother and sister were returning to Canada from a holiday in Scotland.

On the front page of the Toronto Globe and Mail was the two-inch headline: 'ATHENIA SUNK!' Galvanized with horror I had read the sparse account. For the two preceding years I had been escorting Peggy Hodge. Shock had been followed by a blinding fury. That very day John Weir, Jim Jordan, Jim Scott and I signed up for flying duty. I recalled again how surprised we all had been to find the formalities and paperwork such a time-consuming business. When it finished with the ritual of swearing allegiance to King and country, there was no doubt in our minds that we had taken a step of a definite nature.

When the deed was done, I remember how we congregated on the steps outside, uncertain how this news would be received at home. We had all decided to go first with John. Colonel Gordon Weir, D.S.O., M.C., would surely understand.

When Colonel Weir came home from the office, the four of us were sitting in his living room. His uniformed portrait hung above the fireplace. As we got up, he took one quick suspicious look at us and said: 'All right, sit down — all of you. Whatever it is, let's have it.'

I remembered how his neatly clipped moustache seemed to bristle as his jaw clamped shut, and how his unblinking gaze was fixed on John.

'I haven't got all day, John!'

'We've all signed up in the Air Force, sir.'

Without a word he had slowly turned towards the fireplace and for a long time stared down into its depths. After a while he looked at each one of us in turn before he said softly:

'We thought the last one was sure to be enough. God help you all. I'm proud of every one of you!'

It had been a warming experience with a man we all respected. It made the job of going home so much easier for me.

But my father was different. He was a Dutch Huguenot, raised in a land of peace by a family which for generations had been steeped in European culture. At thirteen he spoke four languages and could quote passages of Shakespeare, Byron and Goethe from memory. Under the influence of his father he was then made to concentrate

5

on more serious things — the wonders of science. Here he found a discipline which gave a logical explanation for the nature of things. He followed his father's footsteps to Delft University in mining engineering.

On graduation, his father had sent him to Canada for post-graduate studies in hard rock mining. There he had married Permilla Maude McLachlin, my mother. I had always felt sure that this must have been accomplished without the blessing of Grandpa McLachlin. He had little use for foreigners.

My father was then recalled and sent to the Dutch East Indies. It was there my eldest brother and I were born. Upon the insistence of mother we were taken to Canada instead of Europe for our education.

When I was six and my brother nine, we went to boarding school at Upper Canada College in Toronto. The holidays we spent at my grandfather's house where every opportunity was taken to make good McLachlins of us.

I remember how disappointed my father was, on taking early retirement seven years later, to come to Canada and review the results of privileged education. I remember him saying:

'Maude, nothing in their heads but violent, senseless sports. What have we got to show for the thousands of dollars we have spent? A handful of first team caps and a boxing mug!'

It was far too late for him to have much influence on my brother Bill. He was a McLachlin now, through and through. He had acquired as well the posh ideas of a semi-military Canadian prep-school and the values of upper class Toronto society.

Although similarly tarred, at fourteen, I was struggling through the uncertainty of budding manhood. Being of a reflective nature, I was fascinated by the depth of my father's mind. With him I had found myself compelled to argue logically and look far beyond the limits of what a book said. But I could not give up sports! It was the only acceptable sublimation for my ever-rising masculine aggressiveness. Having been given a moderate complement of natural athletic ability, it supplied my only accolade. At sixteen I flunked a year. Miserably aware of my inadequacy and the cost of my education, I had found a job in the Bank of Nova Scotia. For a year I lived the life of an impoverished bank clerk at the annual stipend of three hundred and fifteen dollars. It gave me a chance to see the hopelessness with which others viewed their dead-end prospects, and the hand-to-mouth existence that the small businessman in the depression contended with from day to day. I gained some comfort from playing hockey for the bank. I had caught the eye of a talent scout by scoring the first goal of the season, and was invited to practice with the Marlboros. This was a valuable piece of education. I played amongst the scintillating stars who were going up, and the scarred has-beens dropped from the majors coming down. We played with the knowledge that if we were hurt we would be abandoned. It was then that I gave up all hope of finding a place on the Toronto Maple Leafs — and returned to school.

My mind sped on, and I thought again of that first encounter with my father after leaving Colonel Weir.

'Join the Air Force! Monumental stupidity!' I knew he would say that.

'Stop a career in engineering to become involved in the violence of this senseless war — what are you thinking about, Hughie? The Germans, after all, are intelligent people. The Netherlands, of course, will stay neutral, and the Germans will certainly not invade Holland. This is none of our business.'

I had always found it hard to counter his point of view. He knew I had no desire to become a prancing, swashbuckling soldier. I had argued too often with brother Bill about the futility of the war games we had practiced at 'The College.' But it would hurt to tell him that in those seven years at school I had been greatly influenced by my grandfather whose only son, Hugh McLachlin, had spent four years in the trenches in 1914. Loyalty to the British crown and Empire was the price a McLachlin paid for being a Canadian. These values were part of me now. When Hitler bludgeoned the Dutch army in two days, and the Luftwaffe mercilessly gutted Rotterdam, my father was speechless with horror.

I had learned to love my paternal grandmother who had come to stay with us in 1936. At 80 her regal personality dominated the household. Her feminine European charm was a sharp contrast to Dad's practicality and Mother's Scots conservatism. It was she who told us about the Godefroys. Our line could be traced back to Godefroy de Bouillon, Duc de Lorraine and leader of the First Crusade that took the City of Jerusalem in 1096. In the seventeenth century, after the family had become Protestant Huguenots, they fled from France to Holland to escape religious persecution. Dad's seal ring bore the family crest, she said, the shield of the three boars' heads crowned by the Crusaders' face mask.

When we asked Dad why he had never told us, he replied: 'You are not great because your ancestors were great; what you make of yourself is what is important. You must forget about all that nonsense and think only of what you yourselves can contribute.'

Where was she now? Was she at this moment dead, a helpless victim of Hitler's oppression? Uncle Paul, Dad's brother, had been afraid to come to North America for a visit. It was too full of gangsters who kidnapped children like the Lindbergh child. Now where was he and his family?

To produce the Master Race, Hitler would dictate that there should be only one language and one culture, if it took a thousand years.

With tears in his eyes my father said:

'What do you want me to do?'

I did not answer him, but Bill and I knew what we were going to do.

The evacuation of the British Expeditionary Force from Dunkirk took place during my final examinations in engineering. France had fallen while I had been in Sudbury. John Weir had been the first to be called, and now I would be the next to go. Was Canada's contribution going to be 'too little and too late'? If it was, France, Holland, Belgium and Britain would become parts of the Third Reich.

2

BASIC TRAINING

After two days at R.C.A.F. Manning Pool, Toronto, I thought that I would never get to England in time. It was total comic chaos. The Air Force had taken over the Agricultural Building of the Canadian National Exhibition. It was packed with hundreds of men in every variety of civilian clothing, from all over Canada, the United States, and the islands of the Caribbean. Gormless looking groups wandered from one place to another or sat, wooden-faced, in the gallery of the 'Bull Ring' like lost souls. In the first five days we never left the building, we spent hours in groups of sixty, in the ring either at attention or at ease. I had always found the Rifle Company drill deadly dull. Now to find that I had volunteered to expose myself to this did seem, as Dad had put it, 'monumental stupidity.' There were endless roll calls, endless queues as bits of equipment were issued piecemeal. After waiting in line for hours, you often found when you reached the equipment clerk that they had run out.

One day after we had been standing in the bull pen at ease, our cocky little French Canadian Corporal came back to us, roll call in hand. Our spirits rose, something was going to happen. 'All those who know how to handle horses raise their hands.' A number of hands shot up and waved a little in the air lest he might not see them. 'All those with their hands up form in single file here!' he said, pointing in front of him. They all complied on the double and braced themselves in line. With an exaggerated flourish, his face wreathed in smiles, the corporal turned left and with a swagger and a stomping of the feet, fell in at the head of the column. Half turning his head towards the rest of us, so his command could be well heard, he said:

'Horse shit brigade quick march!' Off they marched to spend the rest of the afternoon mucking out stalls to make room for another contingent!

The catering arrangement deserves a comment. It was reported it had been contracted to a civilian cut-rate downtown restaurant for twenty-five cents a serving. Having spent half my life eating indifferently prepared institutional food, I considered myself an expert quality control tester. Also, by necessity, I'd become a basic cook. My mother

9

had spent twenty years in the Far East with a dozen Indonesian servants who did everything. She started cooking for the first time when she returned to Canada after the age of fifty. Needless to say, her efforts left a great deal to be desired. She excused herself by explaining that black water fever had robbed her of all sense of taste.

The Manning Pool staples consisted of glutenous oatmeal, watery mashed potatoes, half-cooked white beans, woody last-year's turnips and limp cabbage. One day we breakfasted on bread fried in rancid dripping, and one overdone fried egg with the edges brown and wrinkled. There seemed to be only one type of meat, a stringy corned beef. I survived for the most part on the tinned apple sauce and the prunes. My most generous estimate was that they were making a clear twenty-three cents profit a plate.

Suffocating boredom must have its release. One day after the noon meal a gang of new recruits still in their civilian clothes were found standing in the middle of the bull ring in two lines facing each other with their pants and underwear wrapped around their ankles. Someone with a flair for acting (who had already received his uniform) posing as a disciplinarian had marshalled them in this order. He had ordered them to stay there until the medical officer arrived for a short-arm inspection. After an hour of enduring the laughter of the passersby, they realized that they had been had!

Our billet was the 'Hog Pen.' This enormous room was filled with hundreds of double-decker iron beds placed side by side. I thought I was smart to grab a lower bunk but soon discovered how wrong I was. Exhaled smoke rises, but every other aroma exuded from the orifices and pores of the human body sinks to the floor. The fellow in the bunk above me had the worst smelling feet I had ever encountered. He spent most of his spare time in the evening sitting with his feet hanging over the side, quietly discharging flatus.

Each night after lights out you could always rely on someone shouting: 'Anybody from the West?' Invariably some lonely new arrival would answer in naive expectation: 'Yeh, I'm from Regina!' Fifty voices would answer in unison: 'Fuck the West!'

On the fifth day we had, of all things, a pay parade. Each of us got a cheque for seven dollars and thirty-five cents. That night my wallet was stolen even though I had taken the precaution to put it under my pillow.

Then came the I.Q. tests. They were so insultingly basic that I handed in a blank paper. In the mathematics tests I could see from the questions of the others that I knew a great deal more mathematics than the average. (At least there were some advantages to 'privileged education'!) I calculated that this move was to select navigators and possible instructors. I purposely flunked.

In 1940 no Canadian had ever seen an Air Force uniform. Prior to this all service uniforms, with the exception of the navy, were khaki. Ours was the RAF blue. Once the uniform was issued we were told we could never go anywhere again without it. Permission to wear 'civies' had to be obtained in writing from the station commander. Invariably we drew the stares of people and the inevitable comment: 'Who are those fellows — St. John's Ambulance Corps?'

My uniform did nothing for me. The tunic, which fitted my shoulders, had a forty-inch waistline. The pants were too short in the leg, giving undue prominence to my size twelve black boots, which squeaked. My wedge* seemed to have starch in it and would blow off in a light breeze or as I ran. The thickness of the uniform was suitable for the Arctic and had a coefficient of resistance of light sandpaper. It didn't help that Toronto was at the time enjoying a heatwave.

In the ten days I spent at Toronto Manning Pool I never ventured outside the Exhibition Grounds, sure that I would immediately run into friends and become an object of ridicule.

At last I was posted with five hundred other souls to Number 2 Initial Training School at Regina.

Once on the train, we were not allowed off until we reached our destination. There was nothing to read, I didn't have a pencil or a pen, I hated cards and I was ashamed to admit that I didn't even know how to shoot craps. West of the Lakes was particularly dull; a limitless horizon and mile after mile of nothing but endless wheat fields.

The high points of the day were the meals. The CNR served us with their characteristic excellence just as if we were regular paying customers. Imagine the reaction after our bout with Manning Pool food. With the frequent delays on railway sidings it took us two days to reach Regina.

We were the first course to arrive there, and the curiosity of the Reginians roused us to a semblance of military posture. Through some sections people lined the streets and gave us a round of applause. Further on, we passed through another section where we got nothing but hostile indifference. We Easterners were soon to find out why. When we reached our home-to-be for the next seven weeks, we were given an orientation lecture. We were informed that Regina had a large German population, many of them retaining a strong national loyalty. We were forbidden to become involved in any way or do anything that might precipitate an 'incident.' This announcement caused some eyes to glisten, to provoke many a sly malevolent grin. To this gang it was a provocation! At the first opportunity, groups purposely walked through the German districts, eager for a fight.

The first parade at Number 2 ITS was a short-arm inspection. Each
_____
*Fore and aft forage cap.

flight was marched in turn to the corner of the parade square. Our sergeant was a World War I Irish veteran and self-styled Robert Service poet. He drew us up in single file in front of the seated medical officer, then took his place beside him at ease. Each of us in turn had to undergo the undignified procedure of dropping our trousers in front of the medical officer while he searched through our pubic hair for 'crabs.' I had never seen a crab. To my horror one was found on the man in front of me. Between finger and thumb the doctor raised it in the air to get a good look at it, his nose wrinkled with distaste, then dropped it to the ground. Our sergeant snapped to attention, made a smart half-turn towards the physician and stomped it with his foot. With this I began to itch, and my imagination produced myriads of insects crawling around my vitals. Wriggling with discomfort I submitted to the examination.

Next came the inoculation parade. All inoculations were combined in one shot, injected into the shoulder of your saluting arm. For the next week the site was red, swollen, acutely tender, and painful to raise. There were always one or two who, in anticipation of this shot, would fall to the ground in a dead faint. Tall men were particularly susceptible. A big chap in front of me dropped, and as he revived, he shouted:

'Give it to me now, Doc, while I can't feel nothing!'

At least once a week we got a lecture on VD illustrated by the most revolting movies. They were obviously borrowed from the American Army. The actors wore American uniforms, and the ladies of easy virtue were far too Hollywood to be a Canadian brand of whore. The movies undoubtedly dampened the ardour of many an enthusiastic amateur. They dispelled any preconceptions about the purity of the 'gentler' sex. When I peeked wistfully at a pretty girl, I could not help wondering if that chic jumper was hiding a crop of venereal warts or syphilitic chancres.

The depression of the thirties had torn many shakily integrated families apart. Teenagers left home by necessity — get work or starve. The father in many cases had already left. Thus, there was a large migration of young men wandering the countryside in search of work and food. These lads grew up quickly. They lived in the hobo jungles, 'rode the rods,' wandered the sleazy ghettos of each town in idleness, and settled for soup and bread on a farm in exchange for dawn to dusk hard labour. They had been starved, drunk, laid and beaten to a pulp at least once before the age of eighteen. They were the experts on living, the barrack room lecturers who informed the rest of us how life really was.

The urban greenhorn usually came from a household with strong family ties. Their parents, with initiative and ingenuity, had managed to find some sort of work to keep the young men busy, and at home. Groups of families shared entertainment, transportation and acted as spotters for odd jobs. A paper route was a highly valued possession which could be shared; a car to wash was a plum.

Then there was the rural greenhorn. Keith Copeland was a good example. Keith was born on a farm fifty miles north of North Battleford, Saskatchewan. His people were homesteaders of deep religious conviction. Judgment Day was in the offing and the Lord would cast all sinners into the fires of eternal damnation. Where he lived there wasn't a neighborhood store or a school within fifty miles. Keith had senior matriculation and never sat at a school desk. His entire education was through correspondence, studying at night by the light of an oil lamp. From dawn to dusk he worked the farm like the rest of the family. Keith had never been given a chance to 'dabble with no hussy.' He'd never seen one. He had bred hogs, though, and he knew what *that* was all about! I was with Keith the morning after he had been seduced, and saw his reaction to having spent a night of 'wickedness.' The depth of his remorse made him cry out to the Lord to throw him into Hell. I was witness to the answer to this prayer. Keith went down in an incandescent ball of fire over Gris Nez.

One night when the 'experts' had run out of yarns, they banded together and began roaming between the bunks looking for a tormentable greenhorn. They settled on an introverted Jamaican boy.

'Take your filthy hands off me!' he shouted.

He was promptly called a son of a whore.

In an instant the Jamaican was on his feet, switchblade in hand, lunging at his tormentors.

'He's got a knife!' someone shouted.

In an instant ten hands had pinned the Lion to the floor and the knife had been torn from his grasp. He fought like a tiger, choked with fury, his eyes flooded with tears of rage. His was a display of emotion foreign to the Canadian youth of the time. Nobody tried to hurt him, and his tormentors kept repeating their apologies until he stopped struggling. Slowly they let him go and just stood and looked at him in stunned silence. He got up slowly, threw himself on his bunk, face down, and wept. Everybody went back to their bunks grateful that the affair was over.

This incident succeeded in reducing the frequency of infringement on one another's privacy. The forced togetherness and regimentation was to no one's liking. We all had submitted to it for one purpose: to fly. The common realization that everybody hated the route marches, our skin flaking off in the dry heat of the prairies, our winter uniforms soaked with sweat, the reveille at six, the corporal walking through the barracks shouting, 'Rise and shine'; the punishment pack drills for boots and buttons; the deadly dull orientation lectures, welded us into a bond of mutual tolerance.

I particularly remember the lecture on 'Appreciations, Orders and Reports.' It was a sweltering day. Not a breath of air moved in the classroom. In came the most insipid looking officer on the station. The very weight of his sheaf of papers seemed a burden. His voice was high-pitched and nasal. In a somniferous monotone he read as follows:

'General considerations. The appreciation of the situation, whether written or unwritten, is simply a logical process of reasoning, the object of which is to determine from facts known or surmised the best course to adopt in any given circumstances.'

I caught Bill Fogarty's eye, his face a mask of disbelief. We both erupted, stifling as best we could our sniggers. It became contagious and a light titter went through the classroom. The lecturer stopped, and in a voice cracking with hurt indignation said:

'You may be tested on this, you know.'

With silence he continued:

'To this end, all relevant considerations must be methodically, progressively and logically reasoned out and a definite solution arrived at therefrom. The elemental form of an appreciation is therefore . . . .'

His voice droned on, he was no longer interrupted. Every eye in the class had a glazed look. The three-hour morning route march, the dry still stifling atmosphere, and his monotone had put 'B' Flight sound asleep.

Life at No. 2 ITS Regina was not all drudgery. After a bit, we were allowed to go to a tailor to get our uniforms fitted properly. This did a lot for our ego and generally improved our deportment. We were all issued white half-circles of felt to be worn in the peak of our wedge caps. This was to signify that we were aircrew trainees. Years later, when everybody was fascinated by stories of the Japanese Kamikaze pilots wearing the Japanese flag around their heads, I couldn't help but wonder if this wasn't one of the early ideas stolen from us.

At Regina we got another Medical Examination. As the Medical Officer was examining my ears, nose and throat, he exclaimed:

'You've had a mastoidectomy! That will prevent you from being considered for Pilot Training.'

My heart sank.

'Why, Sir?'

'The inner ear is the balance mechanism of the body; a mastoidectomy could interfere with its function, giving you an increased chance of vertigo while flying an airplane.'

'I have never had any dizziness in my life, sir; I've had my head pounded around in boxing, was part of the University of Toronto Gym Team; I've done tumbling, giant swings on the high bar, and never experienced dizziness. For God's sake, Sir, give me a chance! Test me by all means, but don't knock me out of Pilot Training just because of that.'

They put me through a whole series of special tests. Besides checking my hearing, they squirted water in my ear and put me in a special chair which whirled me around, first in one direction, then the other. When it was all over, to my great relief they had to admit that my inner ears were functioning normally.

Often we were allowed out in the evening and groups would head for the shops and cafes for some common purpose. For a few, it was alcohol and women; others were just contented to sight-see. I remember being with a group of the latter that included an English boy. This lad ended up organizing the rest of us, and talked us into going into a tea-room which advertised a fortune-teller who read teacups. The fortune-teller was appropriately garbed in a long gypsy skirt, shawl and a turban headdress. The English lad became very excited, and wanted us all to get our teacups read. Because of my background, I would not part with the twenty-five cents demanded for this hocus-pocus. She started with the Canadians, finishing with the English boy. There were predictions of romance with dark-haired beauties, and marriages producing large and boisterous families, and strangers who would come from distant lands to warn of impending danger. When she got to the English boy and finished the ritual of turning his cup three times, she looked at it. Immediately her face paled and her eyes widened with alarm. Seeing her reaction, he said:

'You're not going to tell me that I will be killed, are you?'

Obviously quite agitated, she clammed up then; mumbling vaguely worded warnings to be careful, she surreptitiously took her leave. Premonition of death was written all over the lad's face. He eventually dismissed it in a jocular fashion. Much later, I too was to experience the power of suggestion but at a critical time.

Some of the more forward and garrulous airmen wangled invitations to dinner in local homes. They all returned with glowing reports of dinner tables groaning with food and the warmth and generosity of western hospitality. It was just a few days before I left that I got my chance. A message was left for me to call a number. Dying of curiosity, I complied. A very pleasant female voice answered, saying they had heard through the family grapevine that I was half McLachlin and thus a distant cousin. I was invited to dinner. Mother had taken us once to Arnprior in the Ottawa valley to the old McLachlin home. To our amazement, we found that we seemed to be related to half the town. My brother and I found them openly warm and friendly, not at all like the rather aloof Toronto society to which we were accustomed. Instantly I recognized the remarkable similarity between my western cousins, the Hills, and my relatives in Arnprior. The daughter Alice was my age and very pretty. Heretofore, I had never been impressed by the beauty of the female members of my family. Now not only did I

15

waddle back to the barracks stuffed with goodies, but tingled with the anticipation of further encounters with this lovely girl. I have happy memories of the last few days, and understandably it was with considerable regret that I left Regina. Although we corresponded, our paths never crossed again.

Just before the seventh week, Air Marshal 'Billy' Bishop, the highest scoring Allied fighter ace of the First World War came to inspect us. The thrill of seeing Billy in the flesh was reduced somewhat by the hours we had to spend in the sweltering heat of the parade square. Scores of airmen dropped to the ground and were dragged to the back.

The end of that seventh week is a period I will never forget. Suddenly we were told that all of us were not going to be pilots — one-third would be pilots, one-third observers, and one-third gunners. The anger and disappointment of the unlucky could only be measured by the following incident:

At evening parade our sergeant arrived with a large list. Standing before us he said:

'The following airmen take one pace forward, James-Smith. . .' and he read out about a dozen names.

'All of you will be gunners. Gunners left turn. Gunners dismiss.'

The rest of us looked at them in stony silence, 'The poor bastards, condemned to sitting in the rear turret of a bomber to shoot back at the Messerschmitts.' As they stomped off in silence, he kept us at attention until they were out of earshot. It was total agony waiting for him to read the next list. I knew it would be the observers.

'The following airmen one pace forward.'

I held my breath and closed my eyes. The list seemed endless, and I thought he would never stop. My name was not among them. He waited what seemed an eternity. Suddenly it occurred to me that maybe these were the pilots. My heart sank again. Not a man moved.

'All these men are observers. Observers left turn. Observers dismiss.'

The performance was repeated while the rest of us trembled stiffly at attention about to explode. The sergeant's face gradually broke into a wide grin as pensively he reviewed us in silence.

'Now, you lucky bastards, you've been chosen to be pilots. Pray God you'll be worthy of the honor that has been bestowed upon you. The very lives of those others may be resting in your hands. God bless you and God help you. Pilots left turn. Pilots dismiss.'

I couldn't help it. I broke into a run, not to the barracks but to the fence. I wanted to be alone. If I had not been chosen as a pilot, I think I would have died. I ran, sweating, round and round the perimeter until I thought I could act like a human being.

When I got to the barracks, the inevitable had happened. One thoughtless lad selected as a pilot had run straight to the barrack room on the third floor. Most of his barrack mates were already there and most of them were gunners.

'I'm going to be a pilot, I'm going to be a pilot,' he sang out gleefully.

The others listened in silence for about two seconds, then, unable to endure it any longer, they pounced on him and dragged him to the window.

'Okay, fly boy, let's see you fly,' they shouted as they threw him out.

From the third story he wasn't killed, but both legs were broken. We had suffered our first casualty.

This is the way it was for the first class of No. 2 ITS in the greatest aircrew training scheme the world had ever seen. From the tip of Newfoundland to Victoria, station after station was started up in the forests, on the plains, in the mountains, with a handful of permanent force and a host of volunteer recruits and civilians. First hundreds, then thousands of men of the Commonwealth were turned from civilians into the most resilient air force the world had ever known. Canadians, Australians, New Zealanders, South Africans, Norwegians and Dutch had joined in common purpose. For Canada, there was only one nationality — Canadians. There was no east or west, no French or English; Canada had forgotten its petty problems and set about as one to live its finest hour.

Years later after the war, Walter Luff, a close friend who was an experienced fighter pilot shot down in a Messerschmitt over North Africa, told me something that I had always suspected. He said that German fighter pilots felt insecure when they knew they were up against pilots from the former British colonies. The British, like the Germans, tended to do the same thing each time in an orderly manner, but the colonial pilots could never be depended on to do the same thing twice.

3

LEARNING TO FLY

Sid Graham and I were the only two members of B Flight of 'ITS Regina' to be sent to the Pilot Training School Limited, Windsor, Ontario. This was a civilian flying school. Besides us, the only other air force personnel on the station was one corporal disciplinarian and two R.C.A.F. Flying Instructors, Flying Officer Ledeaux and Flying Officer Ferguson. It was a very new station. They hadn't had time to get the bugs out of the plumbing system, let alone the Fleet Finch Model 16 aircraft. This elementary flying trainer had been found to have the disconcerting tendency to go into an inverted spin resistant to every known recovery manoeuver. With this prospect to confront us, the parachute packing instructor had no trouble in keeping our attention.

The barrack room was spacious compared to Regina's, with just twelve fellows on the course. We were pleased to find that the sweeping and mopping of the floor was not our responsibility. Doby did that. Doby, a bleary-eyed, bald-headed man in his early fifties with baggy pants tightly belted over a fat tummy, welcomed us, broom in hand. We soon discovered that his appearance was misleading. He was a sly old devil with a wealth of information. He was in the happy position of being part of no establishment and thus content to do his task for board and lodging and enough money to buy booze and cigarettes. What comforts he couldn't get by scrounging were freely provided by a widow who lived nearby. Once we had gained his trust and confidence he became our most valuable ally. The kitchen was run by local civilians who consistently produced good home-cooked food in ample quantity.

One of the first parades was a visit to the quartermaster stores for flying equipment. We were issued helmets, goggles, baggy work overalls, summer and winter flying suits and fur-lined boots. We were made to sign for all this on our individual equipment sheets. Due warning was given that these articles could only be replaced if they became unserviceable or if they were lost in the course of legitimate service duty. If it could be shown that they were lost or damaged by carelessness, the cost would be charged against us. Equipment would be subject to inspection without notice to ensure that it was being maintained in serviceable order.

Years later after bailing out over the channel, I was saved from abject penury by a British equipment officer. I was applying for an RAF issue wristwatch to replace the one I had lost in the channel. He had my equipment record, and before listing the watch, he became absorbed in reading it.

'Sir,' he said, 'May I make a useful suggestion?'

'Please do,' I replied.

'Do you by any chance have any of these articles in your possession: Airmen's boots black — airmen's flying boots, brown, fur — brass shield, buttons — navigator computer Mark III — gauntlets, leather brown — gauntlets, leather heated electric. . .'

'Stop,' I said. 'No, I don't have that stuff. I don't remember where or when I lost it, and I don't particularly care at this point.'

'But, sir, they are charged against you. May I remind you that your most recent unfortunate adventure affords us a unique opportunity.'

'What's that?' I asked.

'May I, on your behalf, list all this equipment down to watches Mark II aircrew for the use of, as having been lost at sea.'

'My God, I would have to have been flying a Lancaster.'

'Sir,' he replied, 'for your information I am not required by KR and ACI* to list the mode of transport, and hopefully another occasion like this may never arise.'

Equipment officers as a group may have been guilty as charged with centuries of undetected crime, but they were one of us and God bless them, every one!!

Windsor was indeed a welcome relief. To all intents and purposes our entire training was conducted by civilians. From the instructors to the cook in the kitchen, they took pride in doing their job while insisting on their prerogative of not being subject to air force regulations. They were contracted to deliver us back to the air force with sufficient ground and flying training to meet the dictates of an R.C.A.F. Service Flying School. It was Flying Officer Ledeaux's job to decide when they had accomplished this.

The instructors did a remarkable job. Between August twentieth and October the eighth, 1940, they taught us to fly, read a map, and transcribe twenty words a minute in Morse Code. They gave us a smattering of the theory of flight, aerial navigation, meteorology, and airframe and engine construction. As long as we produced, they saw, that we had time off. There was a token roll call at lights out, but God help you if you weren't on deck the next day.

Bert Waite was the only one who ran foul of the system. Bert

*King's Regulations and Air Crew Instructions

came from Prince Edward Island. He was a lovable, naive boy, brought up with prohibition. Bert had no idea how to handle liquor, and knew nothing about women, except what he had seen in the movies. There was nothing wrong with his sexual motivation, but he was possessed with an overwhelming shyness. He persisted in trying to dissolve it in alcohol. Bert's predicament became the social responsibility of the entire flight. When confined to barracks, we gave him lessons in dancing, small talk, table manners, female anatomy and seduction. Whenever we were released, we were released together, and we all went out together. Our favorite place was Thomas' Inn. At Thomas' they welcomed us with open arms. There was a bar, music and girl 'drop-ins.' If all else failed, there were the slot machines and a reasonable midnight snack.

Time after time we went out, determined to get Bert what he so desperately needed.

'There's a toothsome piece over there, Bert,' we'd say. 'Have a go! Ask her to dance first, Bert.' He would blush, and twist and shrink up in his chair, before he exclaimed:

'I'm scared. Get me another drink! Maybe then I'll be able to do it.'

Bert never made it. Before he could get the courage to speak to one of the girls, he was giggling drunk. One night in this condition he asked me to take on one, and while I was making love to her, see if she would let him work on her armpit. On one of our visits to Thomas' we discovered that Bert had passed out with his eyes open. We carried him home and laid him face up on his bunk. By reveille next morning he still hadn't moved a muscle, his bloodshot eyes still open. At ten o'clock the corporal was sent to find him.

'Waite! What are you doing in bed? You're supposed to be in ground school. Any complaints?'

'Puking and headache, sir.'

Sid Graham and I got K.B. Wilson as flying instructor. K.B. was an old bush pilot. He had black straight hair, a square prominent jaw, and as Bert so aptly put it, walked 'as if he had a poker up his arse.' As we stood at attention before him, he circled us in silence as though he were buying horse flesh. Finally, looking Sid in the eye, he said:

'What's your name, you?'

'Graham, sir.'

'Godefroy, sir.'

'Do you know how to put on your parachutes?'

'Yes, sir,' we replied in unison.

'Okay, Godefroy. Put it on, and get your arse in the front seat of that aircraft.'

He finished his cigarette before throwing his leg over the back seat and climbing in.

'Got your safety harness fastened?'

'Yes, sir.'

'Okay, plug in your ear tube in the connection between your legs.'

I complied.

'Can you hear me?' his voice boomed in my ear.

I nodded my head.

'Now if you want to talk back, speak into the funnel-tube by your left hand. Understand?'

I nodded again.

'Now keep your hands and feet off the controls.'

This time he shouted to the mechanic waiting by the prop.

'Switches off and primed! Turn it over!'

The mechanic pulled the prop through about three times, and then stood back.

'Switch's on?' he barked.

'Switch is on,' said K.B.

The next pull the engine started with a roar.

As the engine warmed up, K.B. went through a cockpit check in my ear. He made me look at all the control surfaces as he moved them through their full range. He ran up the engine and tested the magnetos. With the engine idling, he again waved to the mechanic who pulled the chocks away, and we were off. I had had one previous joy ride in a Piper Cub.

Wilson climbed straight ahead to three thousand feet without saying a word.

Once again his voice came back in my ear, this time slowly and deliberately.

'Now here we are at three thousand feet, I'm going to show you spins, how you get into them, and more important, how you get out of them.'

He closed the throttle. It sounded as if the engine had stopped.

'Here we are at fifty miles an hour just on the stall. I pull back the stick — back — back — back, and I kick on rudder and. . . .'

My stomach dropped.

With a swooshing, whirling motion, the aircraft spun. Everything in my visual field turned into a blur as I held onto my seat.

There was a cool indifferent quality to his voice as he continued:

'Here we are in a spin — nothing to be afraid of!'

Each shuddering whip seemed to get closer to the last.

'So what do we do? We put the stick fully forward and give opposite rudder like that.'

With a snap, we were in a dive, aimed straight to the ground.

'We gently pull the stick back . . . open the throttle . . . and we're

21

straight and level. See?'

I fumbled around, found the speaking tube, and in a voice that was annoyingly high-pitched replied:

'Lovely, sir. There's nothing to it!'

We returned to the base in silence, landed, and he took up Sid Graham for the same treatment. That was all for one day, and that was enough. We both had a good idea how much quarter we were going to get from K.B. Wilson. From that day until we left the station, K.B. Wilson was constantly in my thoughts. Everyone else on the station, save Doby, is rather hazy to me now, but not K.B. Wilson.

As all pilots know, steering an airplane is done with the feet. Once in the air the stick that comes up between your legs, when pushed forward, makes you go down. Pull the stick back, and you go up. Hold the stick over to one side or the other and the aircraft rolls slowly in a horizontal plane to that side. As K.B. put it:

'It's so bloody simple! Any ass with an ounce of coordination could do it.'

Let me tell you, for some people it's not easy, and I was one of those 'some people.' For one thing, as all we left-handers know, it's a right-handed man's world. To fly this type of aircraft, the left hand is kept on the throttle and the right hand on the stick. I had to learn to fly with the hand the Lord meant for me to keep behind my back. That wasn't my worst problem. I was also 'ham-footed.' 'Chief Lead Foot' K.B. used to call me. Before you get the wretched thing into the air, you have to open the throttle with your left hand, get the tail off the ground by pushing the stick forward with your right hand, while steering a straight course across the field with your feet. This was one of the hardest things I had to learn in flying. For what seemed like the longest, I had the sinking feeling that I would never learn. I was the cross that K.B. had to bear. On the other hand, Sid Graham was a smooth, coordinated, cool right-handed boy with an even, quiet temperament.

'It's a pleasure to teach that boy,' K.B. would say, as if to himself. 'My God, if they would give me a few more lads like him, I could send them something that would end this bloody war.' His eyes would fall on me.

'Oh, my God, for a moment I'd almost forgotten. This shouldn't happen to a dog. Come on, Lead Foot, get your arse into the front seat.'

His face would screw up and with a pained expression:

'Now, let's try and see if you can treat those rudder pedals a little less like a football, will ya?'

He sent Sid off solo in about six hours. He suffered through a good eight-and-a-half before he would take a chance with me.

When K.B. Wilson stepped out of the back seat that fateful day and secured the empty safety belts in the back, my heart came up in my mouth. Slowly he turned to me and looked me squarely in the eye. For a second his eyes softened and his leathery face broke into a wry smile.

'Now — see if you can get it down so that you can walk away from it, will ya!'

I had got it up and down with K.B. in the back. What would I do when I was alone? I wondered if I was going to be one of those who took so many shots at the field that they ran out of fuel. To my great relief, I made it on the second attempt.

'Why didn't you put it down the first time, Lead Foot?'

'I thought I would take just a practice run first, sir.'

'Was that bounce part of the practice?'

'Just testing the under-carriage, sir.'

The day K.B. sent me to do solo spins is unforgettable. General instructions had been issued that if anybody got into an inverted spin, he was to bail out. I didn't do my first spin from three thousand feet like K.B. I climbed straight ahead to six. With my stomach churning, I finally got up enough nerve and kicked the left rudder. As the left wing dropped, it seemed to put me right on my back. There was none of this K.B. stuff of letting it wind up to ten to twenty turns. I had enough with three, and kicked the opposite rudder and jammed the stick forward. 'IT CAME OUT, BY GOD!' I was elated. I climbed up and spun it down the other way. I spun it till I was intoxicated with the mania of conquest.

It had been a perfect day, clear as a bell, and now it was one hour before sundown. There was Lake St. Clair.

'Put it on your left and follow it back to the aerodrome,' I said to myself. As I watched the sun's reflection on the water, I thought of K.B. Whenever he had a student in the air, he'd be pacing up and down in front of the hangar, smoking one cigarette after the other, kicking the stones.

'I'll show the old bastard,' I mumbled.

'I know this time I'm going to grease it on the grass, and he'll have to say something good about me.'

I followed the lake, occasionally throwing the plane into a steep turn just for the hell of it. I was startled to find that no matter how loud I tried to sing I couldn't hear my own voice. A half hour went by. No aerodrome. I saw nothing that seemed familiar. Oh, well, I must have gone farther down the lake than I thought.

'Keep it on your left, and you can't miss.' I checked my watch. I had been airborne an hour and thirty minutes, and my fuel was down to half. The sun was down, and dusk was falling.

'Hooray,' I thought. 'I must be lost; now I'll have to do an emergency landing.'

My twelve hours flying time had not included instructions in forced landings. 'Just pick out a nice flat field,' I said to myself, 'and put it down.' There was a nice one right beside the railroad track, and there was a train.

'Casey Jones ta ta ta ta tee ta,' I sang to myself. 'Lay down some smoke so I can see which way it blows.'

The smoke was floating down the centre of the field. I made a couple of low passes, an exhilarating excuse for low flying. 'Stubble field, smooth air with dusk, fence at both ends, no tall trees. Have a go.'

I had never landed an airplane at less than seventy miles an hour, the prescribed speed for coming into the home field.

I went well back and took a long run at the near fence. At seventy miles an hour, I came as close to it as I dared. Once over, I pushed the stick forward and the wheels were on the grass. I was down. I applied the brakes. Nothing happened. I looked down. My tires were sliding in the dew-laden grass. I seemed to be going faster than when I was in the air.

'My God, I'm going to go through the fence!' Bracing myself, I clenched my teeth.

There was a tremendous crash, pieces of prop flew in all directions, and the engine screamed for a second before it hit the dirt as I rolled over on my back. Hanging upside down in the straps, for the first time I heard the plaintive bleating sound that a hot engine makes when it is buried in cool ground. It was like a wounded stag.

I hung there for a minute, stunned. Not thinking of the consequences, I pulled the release pin on my Sutton safety harness and promptly dropped three feet into the ditch on my head. I got up and walked around the airplane in absolute misery. I could see myself in the center of the parade square, with K.B. Wilson cutting the buttons off my uniform to the roll of drums. Quite suddenly I became aware there were two men standing open-mouthed, gawking at me as if I had just landed from Mars. I took a quick look around. Cars on a nearby road had stopped and people were streaming across the field. Further back there was a cloud of dust being kicked up by two more cars speeding to the scene. I could just hear them:

'Come on! One of them yellow air force planes has just gone and crashed in John Brown's field.'

I could see it now. In five minutes this gang of souvenir hunters would pick my machine as clean as a flock of vultures. I turned to the two men still staring at me in stony silence. In my best Gary Cooper drawl I said:

'Okay, you two, in the name of King George I command you to guard this airplane with your lives. It contains secret equipment vital to the outcome of this war. Any person taking anything off this aircraft will be punished by death by firing squad. Where's the nearest telephone?

'John Brown yonder has got one,' said one pointing to a nearby house.

'Okay, you're in charge!'

When I found out where I was on the map, I could see what I had done. I had climbed six thousand feet from the airdrome, straight towards Lake Erie. In the anticipation of doing solo spins, I had looked neither to right nor left. I had never seen Lake Erie from the air. When I found that I had survived the first spin, in exhilaration I had flitted around the sky like a barn swallow. When the vapors left me, I had taken Lake Erie to be Lake St. Clair, and now I was halfway to Niagara Falls.

It was hours before Aimsley, the chief flying instructor, and Wilson arrived to pick me up. I sat between them in the front of Aimsley's car. Neither one of them said a word to me all the way home.

First thing the next morning, K.B. Wilson had me in the air doing precautionary forced landings. He had me flying the airplane in a shuddering stall until my teeth hurt. I think I dragged that tail over every fence within a radius of fifty miles. Just as I was beginning to become confident in doing power on precautionary approaches, he went to emergency dead stick landings. He did this by suddenly closing the throttle at the most unexpected moment in any altitude of flight.

'Okay, you got a dead engine, get it into the field.'

This meant trimming the airplane to fly by itself in a gliding altitude, followed by a quick search for the cause of engine failure. Fuel starvation was the most likely cause. He would have already turned the fuel off. The drill was to turn the fuel back on but continue to land as though you still had a dead engine. Instantly you had to select a good big smooth field with no surrounding trees within easy gliding distance. The next essential thing was to discover the direction of the wind. Smoke from trains gives no true indication of the direction of the wind. It was carefully pointed out to me that a train's smoke moves in a direction which is the resultant of the forces of wind, its own velocity and the turbulence created by the train. If I had applied my knowledge of dynamics, I should have figured that out by myself. But, like most people of twenty, I was rarely inclined to use my head.

To become proficient at these emergency exercises takes practice and a certain amount of judgment. With K.B. in the back seat it took a lot more. He wouldn't just turn the fuel off once. He'd turn it off three or four times or while going into a loop.

On one occasion when he cut the engine, the only available field large enough to get into had trees on the upwind side. I manoeuvered for

25

landing position all right, and I caught him the first few times he turned the fuel off, but he cut it off again just as I was making my last turn into the field. This time I missed it. He sat there as usual humming to himself as if he had nothing else to do but watch the scenery, but he also forgot that he had turned the fuel off. He let me come down to the wheat tops before he said:

'Okay, climb straight ahead!'

When I opened the throttle, the engine cut halfway across the field. In an instant he had control. The fuel was on, and he was pumping the throttle like mad. We were just sinking into the trees at the far end of the field when the engine roared into action, and we were able to stagger over the tops just in the nick of time.

He didn't say anything for a long time, then in a slow deliberate voice he said:

'That was my fault!'

There was nothing small about K.B. Wilson. He made the same mistake with one of the students in a course after us. As a result of the crash, the student sustained a broken nose and K.B. a broken leg.

One of the other instructors got sick, and for a week K.B. had to take on one of his students. On his first outing with this lad, he was told to give him an hour of instrument flying under the hood. For this exercise the instructor sat in the front seat as the blind flying hood was in the back. This was a tall thin fellow who'd always found the safety straps tight over his shoulders. For the sake of comfort he always undid his safety harness while he was instrument flying.

K.B. did not like to be bored, and after a half an hour of sitting in the front seat with a new student trying to master instrument flying, he was bored; besides, he was very curious to know what this lad had learned flying under the other instructor. Quite suddenly he snapped the canvas blind flying hood open covering the student behind him and said:

'Okay, do me a roll.'

Forgetting his straps, the student dove the aircraft down and rolled it over on its back. He promptly fell out of his seat and his head went right through the perspex coop-top. K.B. sat, arms folded, in the front seat, oblivious of the student's predicament. The aircraft, without guidance, continued to fly inverted.

'If you think I'm going to help you, you're wrong,' said K.B. 'You can bloody well roll it out yourself.'

The only thing attached to the student was his earphone tube. The student was terrified to do much struggling lest the perspex coop-top break loose from its runners and drop him out. Finally K.B. heard the student's white-knuckled fingers drumming an SOS on the coop-top and turned around. Only then did he take over.

26

By the time I had thirty hours I was completely hooked. I adored our airplanes. I felt a thrill every time I looked at them. The wooden prop fanning the grill of the stubby radial engine, the whiff of 'dope' from the fabric, and the cross-wires that sang in the wind. On the ground so awkward to manoeuvre, the tail dragging and the nose obscuring forward vision, somehow with flying speed it metamorphosed and became a steed that carried you into a thrilling third dimension. With confidence came the heady exhilaration enjoyed only by a bird in flight.

Except for its refusal to recover from an inverted spin, the Fleet 16 was a beautiful aerobatic machine. The cause of this vicious tendency was discovered by accident.

One evening two of the instructors took off, determined to find a recovery manoeuver. They climbed as high as they could and purposely put it into an inverted spin. All the kicking and the rocking was to no avail. The spin continued. At 3,000 feet they jettisoned the coop-top to bail out. The plane promptly recovered by itself. It was then realized that in an inverted spin the coop-top was shielding the rudder and elevator.

In the two months I stayed in Windsor, I logged forty-seven hours and thirty-five minutes. K.B. Wilson taught me more about flying in that forty-seven hours than any instructor I had in the next thirty-five years of flying.

Ten days before we left Windsor, a new course of students arrived. The first night they spent in our billet plying us with questions. Happily we basked in their wide-eyed admiration.

'How long did it take you to go solo?'

'Were you scared the first time?'

It was almost impossible to resist the temptation to 'scare the shit out of them.'

'Hughie,' said Bert Waite, 'here is a poor bastard that drew K.B. Wilson.' Catching his cue, I raised my eyes to heaven and deliberately crossed myself. The lad's face paled. By the time Bert had finished with him, it was ashen. This briefing contributed to what happened the next day.

K.B. Wilson took off with this student. As usual he started with his spin test. When the aircraft fell from the sky and started to spin, the lad instinctively shot both feet out against the rudder bar and grasped the stick with both hands frozen with fear.

K.B. couldn't budge the controls. Failing to get the boy's attention with an eloquent barrage of curses, he reached forward and laid him out with the fire extinguisher. They pulled out well below a thousand feet. K.B. was all for 'washing him out.' Flying Officer Ledeaux, knowing Wilson, gave the lad to another instructor.

K.B. wanted to be a fighter pilot as badly as I did. I was told that he disappeared on a flight through the mountains of British Columbia. He was never heard from again. God rest his turbulent soul!

4

THE KING'S COMMISSION

The last week at Windsor was devoted to writing our final examinations in ground school and taking our flight checks. There were no misfits in our course. At Regina, all of us had learned to respect each other's rights and individual differences. At Windsor, we became welded together, all for one and one for all. We helped each other and so there were no wash-outs.

As we looked to our next posting, we learned from our instructors that there were two possibilities: A single engine, or a twin engine Service Flying School.

Twin engine training meant bombers or Coastal Command work. The shortest route to action was single engine training and then into the fighter squadrons of the RAF. Each of us was asked if we had a preference and everybody requested single engine training. When our posting was announced, it was greeted by a loud cheer. The entire course was posted to Camp Borden, a single engine training school.

As we excitedly packed up and prepared to get cleared from the station, we basked in the affection of our civilian instructors now freely expressed. We had lived up to their expectations, and there was nothing more they could do for us at this point. We all chipped in and bought Doby a bottle of gin. As we boarded the bus, even K.B. Wilson showed up to give Sid Graham and me a last 'kick in the arse.'

As soon as we entered the gate at Camp Borden we knew we were back in the Air Force. It combined all the 'bullshit' military establishment plus the growing pains of an Air Force Manning Pool. Outside the permanent buildings lay street after street of temporary buildings, hastily thrown together to house the recruits and 'other ranks.' New construction was in evidence, but it was barely keeping up with the constant influx of partially trained people like ourselves. Besides aircrew, schools all across Canada were producing riggers, fitters, armourers and partially trained personnel who as yet had not been classified. Besides those marshalled in flights, that produced the constant thud of marching feet, there were hundreds who wandered aimlessly from one place to another. We were fed in shifts. The station commander had given up repairing holes in the fence and relied entirely

29

upon patrols of Service Police. Nearby was the Army's huge Camp Borden. In the absence of a visible enemy, men being trained to fight will fight amongst themselves. Inter-service rivalry was a perfect excuse for brawls. If you liked that sort of thing, you could always find satisfaction in some sleazy beer joint outside the gate.

Flying and ground instruction seemed to be equally disorganized. There were just too many students and too few instructors. I had five different flying instructors while at Camp Borden. One of them, Pilot Officer 'Pee Wee' Hunt had fifty hours more than I did. Hunt was a short blond fellow still unsure of the role he was supposed to play as a newly commissioned officer. I have a very clear recollection of one of my days with Hunt.

We were flying a Yale. This was an all silver, all metal aircraft with a fixed undercarriage and wheel pants. It had been made in the U.S., originally for the French Air Force, and all instruments were calibrated in the metric system. Hunt put me through some basic flying sequences and after an hour, decided to get some practice himself.

'I've got control,' he said from the back seat.

It was a lovely evening just before dusk. I folded my arms and proceeded to enjoy my role as passenger. By the time he came back over the aerodrome all the other aircraft had landed except one being flown by an instructor. He was putting on an aerobatic display. I assumed that Hunt had seen him. At two thousand feet we flew straight up the main runway just as the instructor was coming off the top of a loop in the opposite direction. Determined not to appear windy and assuming that Hunt was trying to pull a K.B. Wilson on me, I didn't say a word. Finally realizing that this was going to be too close for comfort, I took a quick look behind me and saw Hunt looking down at the tower. I grasped the controls and pulled the aircraft into a steep turn to the right. We came close enough to the other aircraft to hear the sound of its engine.

'Christ!' said Hunt. 'What was that?'

'I thought you saw him, sir. That was one of the instructors coming out of a loop.'

Obviously shaken, he levelled off too high on his landing and dropped it in from about ten feet with a crunch.

Each morning in the flight room we were treated to a pantomine. It went like this: The Flight Commander would enter looking a little the worse for wear just in time to hear the phone ring.

' "A" Flight, Flying Officer Wilson speaking.'

'Yes, sir,' he said, scanning the serviceability board. 'I've got three Yales and two Harvards serviceable, two Yales on major inspection, and one Yale waiting for a port wing tip.'

There would be a pause, while he listened.

'That one yesterday, sir? That was a write-off.'

Pause.

'I'm alone, sir. Hunt is on leave and Martin is sick in bed.'

Pause.

'I don't know, sir. He couldn't keep a thing on his stomach.'

Pause.

'Only six students showed up. God knows where the rest are.'

Pause.

'Yes, sir. I've already sent Corporal Barnes to look for them, sir.'

Pause.

'Two of them haven't gone solo yet. The other four are solo on Yales.'

Pause.

'What sequences do you want me to have them do, sir?'

There would be a long silence during which he moved the phone from his ear and winced. When he did this, we could hear Squadron Leader Kennedy's voice from where we sat.

'Yes, sir, I'll think of something after I look at their log books. Goodbye, sir!'

He would raise his eyes to heaven as he replaced the receiver. Observing the grins on our faces, he would shout:

'Godefroy, Graham, Evans, take those silly grins off your faces! Get your God-damn parachutes and get into the air! I don't care what you do as long as you're back here in an hour.'

I would be free to go, free as a breeze to twirl and twist that pretty silver aircraft through the puffy cumulus clouds.

At Camp Borden there was only one flying instructor who taught me anything. That was Sergeant Houston. He was the only sergeant pilot instructor I saw on the station. He was a short, stocky, older man who seemed to be constantly preoccupied with a multitude of worries. By the time Houston got me, I'd flown more solo than I had dual. Between what K.B. had taught me, and trying solo what the instructors had told my friends to do, I had done most of the flying sequences by myself. As far as I was concerned, I was a 'whiz.' After my first trip with Houston, he informed me that he didn't think I should be flying. He didn't like the size of my feet, either. I never mentioned K.B. Wilson.

'How in God's name did they ever expect me to get you ready for the next wings test I will never know. Have you ever been up with a senior flying instructor?'

'Yes, sir, Flight Lieutenant Priestley.'

'He obviously didn't know his arse from third base, or he would have sent you back to initial training school.'

He would stomp off leaving me to bring in the parachutes.

31

I had developed a pretty hard skin with K.B. Wilson, but the thing that hurt me most about Houston was that he sounded as though he really meant it.

One day Houston was going to give me an hour's instrument flying under the hood. For this I sat in the back seat. None of the hundreds of aircraft on the station had radios of any kind. I took the aircraft off on the main runway on instruments under the hood. As instructed, I climbed straight ahead to two thousand feet. When I levelled off, Houston said:

'Turn ninety degrees starboard and let down at two hundred feet a minute at eighty miles an hour.'

I complied. In descent, I passed a thousand feet, five hundred feet, to three hundred feet. At this point I noticed Houston slide his coop-top back. I was much relieved, for at least I knew that he wasn't asleep. Through the small crack in the front of the canvas blind flying hood, I could see him poking his head out, first one side and then the other. He let me come down to two hundred feet before he said:

'Okay, climb up straight ahead to two thousand feet, eighty miles an hour, at five hundred feet a minute.'

Houston had long since passed the stage of wanting to be a show-off. Letting me descend to two hundred feet on the instruments was a definite departure from his usual procedure. The only thing I could think was that the 'old bastard' had a girlfriend, and he was getting me to shoot the place up for him.

'Two thousand feet, sir.'

'Turn ninety degrees starboard, and when you're on course, let down at two hundred feet a minute, eighty miles an hour.'

I complied.

He did the same thing. At two hundred feet he again opened his coop-top and poked his head out, first one side, then the other. After K.B. Wilson, and my experience with Hunt, I trusted nobody. Below five hundred feet on the let-down, I watched him through the crack in the hood like a hawk. At two hundred feet, he made me climb up again only to repeat the entire sequence one more time. On this occasion he let me come down to one hundred feet before he said:

'I have control!'

He pulled the release lever which snapped open the canvas hood covering my head, and I was able to see the problem. We were in dense fog, visibility about two hundred feet, and through the mist I could see the tops of trees flashing by the wing tips. He put down the flaps, and at sixty-seven miles an hour we mushed around, dodging treetops. He wasn't even looking at the instruments. With my heart in my mouth I watched the air speed. I knew we were going to spin in at any minute. Suddenly a ploughed field appeared, the near side only visible in the

32

mist.

'I'm going in,' he said coolly. 'Tighten your harness.'

He mushed it down over the fence and plopped it in the field like a winged duck. It was a startlingly soft three-point landing. We ran for about a hundred yards across the furrows until we came to a drainage ditch, then it went on its nose. It balanced on the very tip for what seemed like ages, then gradually it sagged down on the port wing tip, and stayed there.

'Don't move,' said Houston. He didn't have to tell me — I'd been frozen stiff for several minutes.

'I'll get out first,' said Houston. 'If it starts to go over, keep your head down.'

Very gently he slid over the port side of the windshield and slowly let himself down to the ground. As I watched him, I was amazed at how far it was to the ground from the back seat with the aircraft in this bizarre position.

'Okay, Godefroy, easy does it. Don't worry. I'll catch the tail if it comes over,' said Houston, moving to the spot where the tail would hit if it were over on its back. Slowly I undid my safety harness and eased myself over the side and gingerly lowered myself hand-over-hand down the fuselage. It swayed a little this time but never went over. The engine was still bleating out its last moans. I didn't tell Houston that I had heard that sound before. Houston lit a cigarette and with his face a mask of misery, stood in silence looking at the airplane. It had not gone unnoticed by me that he had not forgotten any of the emergency drill. The gas and switches had been turned off before landing.

'Sergeant Houston, may I say something?'

'Go ahead,' he said gloomily.

'You sure scared the hell out of me, but I want to tell you something. That was the finest, coolest piece of work I've ever seen or ever expect to see again.'

'Thank you,' he said mournfully. 'We went into that stuff right after take-off. For once in your bloody life you flew the aircraft smoothly on the instruments. You can see now how vital it is to be able to let down at a constant air speed and a constant rate of descent.'

Even under these circumstances, I thought, he is still teaching. For the first time, as I studied the care-worn lines of his face, I was seized by a feeling of genuine affection for this man. He had probably saved my life, for I would probably have panicked if I had been alone. I suppressed my desire to say something, realizing that there was nothing I could think of that wouldn't sound ingratiating. Finally he mumbled as if to himself:

'You wait, they'll blame me for an accident anyway.'

Later I learned that forty aircraft had become enveloped in this

33

famous Borden fog which had completely blanketed the area. What happened to all the rest I never did hear except that some of them had bailed out. Just as he had said, Sergeant Houston got his log book endorsed with the infamous phrase: 'Pilot error in judgment.' To my great regret I was passed once more into the hands of another instructor and muddled along until the day of my wings test.

I had practiced all the sequences I was supposed to and felt reasonably confident; but the thought of having to do them with Squadron Leader Kennedy in the back seat was a different matter. Kennedy, the Chief Flying Instructor, had the reputation of being tough when he was in a good mood, and murderous at all other times. He was a heavy-set, raw-boned, bulldog-faced brute with the habit of looking through you. When my turn came, he fixed me with a fishy eye, slowly pointed a finger at me, and said:

'You, get in the front seat of that Harvard.'

I obeyed. I'm sure I sat there strapped up and ready, trembling in my boots, for at least half an hour before he climbed in the back. I don't remember the details of the wings check other than I thought I did what he asked me to do reasonably smoothly. I distinctly remember, however, the half hour we both sat in the aircraft after I taxied in and shut down. Through the test he had said very little to me other than barking out one order after another. On the ground he sat there without saying a word while I listened to my stomach gurgling. Finally I took a quick glance around me, wondering if he was having a snooze. He had his head down and was reading my log book.

'Godefroy. How come you haven't got half of these sequences as having been given to you dual?'

'I never got them, sir.'

'What do you mean, you never got them? How did you learn them?'

'Well, sir, I just asked the other fellows what their instructors told them to do, and then went out and did the same.'

'Without permission, Godefroy?' I didn't answer.

'Without permission, Godefroy?'

'Yes, sir.'

'Get out!' I complied. I respectfully waited until he got out, as I did with the other instructors. I started to bring his chute with mine. He spun around.

'Leave it there!'

'Mine, sir?'

'No, you ass, mine.'

'Yes, sir.'

It was some minutes before I got back to the flight office. Kennedy had been there, and was 'eyeballing' the Flight Commander in dead silence when I entered. The Flight Commander's eyes shifted to me for a second and then back to Kennedy. From the look on his face, Kennedy must have just torn a strip off him, and was now staring him down. Slowly Kennedy turned to go out, and said:

'Okay, send me the next one!'

I was in agony. I waited until the door closed behind Kennedy, then went to the Flight Commander.

'Please, sir, did I pass or did I fail?'

Wilson gave a long sigh before he said in a low voice: 'Yes, you passed, Godefroy; but you're going to have to do all those sequences you missed. Why didn't you tell me you hadn't had them, you clot?'

'Didn't I do them right, sir?'

'Yes, Godefroy, by the grace of God, you did them right. This is for the records, the God-damn stinking records! Go on, get out of here and leave me alone!'

At the presentation of the wings all student pilots were to become sergeants, a few conceivably might be given a commission.

With my record to date, I had little hope that I would be amongst the latter. The only thing any of us wanted anyway was our wings. Squadron Leader Kennedy presented them, and in accordance with 'King's Regulations — Air,' he made a speech. What with the Harvards taking off and landing over our heads, I never heard a word he said, except those spoken in front of me. As he pinned the wings on me, he was wearing his characteristic scowl, but this time he said to me softly:

'Congratulations! In the name of King George the Sixth, I have been authorized to elevate you to the rank of Pilot Officer.'

As I stared at him in utter disbelief, for the first time he looked *at* me, not *through* me, and just a suspicion of a smile passed across his face. The next instant it was gone, and he went on to the next one.

5

THE VOYAGE TO BRITAIN

I was given ten days leave to get a uniform, and be ready for embarkation for overseas. I didn't tell anybody at home that we were given the option of remaining in Canada and going to instructors school. I had acquired another reason for feeling obliged to serve overseas. To date, my course through flying training was punctuated by a trail of destroyed aircraft, all ours. I was a little sensitive about this and secretly lived with the belated hope that I could make Corporal Hitler pick up the tab.

For several years I had been going out with Peggy Hodge. She survived the sinking of the *Athenia*, having been picked up by a destroyer. Her only living parent, her mother, was lost at sea. Her father had died of wounds as a result of World War I. The war had brought us much closer together. Under the prevailing circumstances I was in no position, I thought, to consider asking for her hand in marriage. An operational pilot could hardly be classified as a safe job. The last published statistics on RAF fighter pilots was an operantional life expectancy of between fifteen and thirty minutes. The ten days embarkation leave could not be classified as pleasant for one who was too conscious of the fact that a pleasant carefree period of our lives was coming to an end.

Fortunately, I was kept busy getting outfitted. The T. Eaton Company, where I used to get all my clothes at boarding school, gave me a tailored uniform, a greatcoat and all the trimmings in two days. I had to buy another uniform in England when I got there. I purchased that one from Gieves of London. No matter what I did to it, it never looked right. The Eaton suit became my security blanket. By the end of the war I was still wearing it, although tattered and grey, the colour of the wings faded by the sun, the cuffs and elbows reinforced with leather, the buttons replaced by 'escape buttons' that contained compasses and the padding of the left shoulder hid a flexible 'saw' that could saw through iron bars.

When Eaton's downtown store in Toronto called me that my uniform was ready, Mother had the car out doing some grocery shopping. Without thinking, I put on my greatcoat, got on a streetcar and went down. I walked into Eaton's, a leading aircraftsman (L.A.C.), squeaking boots and all, and walked out a pilot officer. I couldn't have felt more self-conscious if I had been naked. I think that if I'd been acting in a play, I could have done it properly.

I tried to remember Bill, my brother, who was an officer in the U.C.C. Rifle Company, when he got his first officer's uniform. He had already understudied the officers class. He'd seen every war picture for the last ten years. He even had the sneer down, like Von Stroheim when he played the U-Boat Commander. He was perfect in the part and liked nothing better than to ham it up. His rendition of 'If you can't come back with honor, come back on your sword' was particularly good.

However, I hadn't rehearsed a thing. It was like stepping out on opening night as the lead without a line. Eaton's downtown just didn't have a back exit from the men's department. It was strictly the elevator or the escalator. I chose the latter; I didn't think I could stand the squeeze in an Eaton's elevator looking like this. By the time I walked up Yonge Street to College, I was able to catch my reflection in enough store windows to get the hang of it. Thank God I didn't see any airmen because I didn't really have the guts to practise saluting to myself in the store windows.

This was my first proper leave since joining the air force. I had been living in close quarters with a bunch of boys who were entirely different from the carefully protected class of lads whom I had known at Upper Canada College. I had made a lot of new friends. Learning to adapt to the dictates of military discipline and flying instruction had brought us very close together and changed us all a great deal. Seeing life through the eyes of others with different backgrounds, and different values, had greatly widened my field of vision.

On the other hand, fashionable staid society had changed very little. The war, and the alarming events in Europe were far away and seemed to have very little influence on party conversation. My friends who had made it to University were fully absorbed and going right on with their courses. Into the service went the ones who had flunked their exams or had not adjusted to the business life. I, on the other hand, had not flunked, but nonetheless had forsaken my place in a secure society and had, of all things, joined in 'the ranks.' Up to this point I had been looked upon with benevolent amusement for my foolhardy brainlessness. On this leave, however, I was a little bit more acceptable socially. I was an officer.

In my absence the Red Cross had become active. Some of the girls had joined and were seen at various social functions in uniform. Service in the women's divisions of the active services had not yet become the thing. Norway had fallen during the summer and a Norwegian Air Force Flying Training Base had been established in Toronto. They, too, wore the RAF blue uniforms and all seemed to be officers. They were popular additions to any social event. They were suave and different and gave the hostesses the satisfaction 'of doing their part.' At the time of my leave they had been prominent enough at parties to create a certain amount of resentment amongst the men, who found the situation just a bit too competitive.

I learned that I had been missed at the Cricket Club as they could have used another left-handed bowler. I would have been a shoo-in for opening batsman at the Old Boys Upper Canada College cricket game and would have played centre between Jack Statford and George Mara at the Old Boys Hockey Game. I expressed my genuine regret at having missed these opportunities, and explained that adjusting to my new environment and activities had given me neither the time nor the inclination to even think of such things. My life and my sense of values had changed so radically in the last few months that all this sounded strangely unimportant. I found myself disinterested in the small talk and limited myself for the most part to Peggy's company. Having survived the horrors of the sinking of the *Athenia*, she was no longer just a pretty girl, she was a realistic woman.

My family was kind. They let me go without a tear. Only my brother Bill seemed restless. Before lunch, on the day of my scheduled departure, out of the blue he said:

'Dad, let's you and I take Hugh down and have a drink with him.'

Dad looked up from his book obviously taken aback, but when Bill with great vehemence insisted, he allowed himself to be led out to the car. Bill drove in silence to the Royal York Hotel. I was not a bit interested in the expedition, but like Dad went along with it for Bill's sake.

There was a tavern on the street floor level of the Hotel with its own separate entrance. It was the popular meeting place for the young men who aspired to making a career in business on Toronto's Bay Street. In the year that Bill had spent as one of the board markers at Thompson and MacKinnon, a brokerage house, Bill had given this place plenty of business. When he parked the car, he led the way to the entrance, his steel-shod Army boots pounding the pavements noisily at the prescribed hundred and twenty to the minute. He led us in looking as if he owned the place. More than half the tables were occupied, and he selected one prominently situated in the middle. He ordered three pints of Black Horse Ale. My father on an appropriate occasion would partake of a social drink. He preferred wine and looked upon beer as boorish. He got no choice, he got Black Horse. When we were all served, Bill, with great melodrama, his face a mask of seriousness, looked at me over the top of his raised glass through eyes narrowed to slits and said:

'To Hugh, Dad, God help him.'

Feeling self-conscious, I tried desperately to change the subject. Bill fell silent. Suddenly he was on his feet, and with one leap he was standing in the centre of a vacant table nearby.

'Quiet — quiet, everybody shut up and listen to me.'

With his best Company Sergeant Major frown he glared at them until they all complied. Pointing his finger at me, he said:

'That is Pilot Officer Hughie Godefroy, my brother. Today he leaves for Overseas. On your feet, every one of you bastards, and raise your glasses.'

In awkward silence one after the other began standing up, and Bill waited until he had them all on their feet before:

'To my brother, may he have Godspeed and a safe return.'

My face red as a beet, I sat there absolutely mortified. I will never forget Bill standing on the platform at the salute as the train pulled out. This time I had no hesitation in saluting him back.

The troop train was in two sections, transporting five hundred men in all. With the exception of about fifty RAF aircrew who had been in Canada on course, they were all Canadians. There were a few tears being shed for the first hour or so, and there wasn't much talk, but soon we jollied up and things got back to normal. At the wings parade everybody had been promoted but quite a few of my friends were not officers. They were sergeant pilots. As we recounted to each other the events of our embarkation leave, it was obvious that something had happened to the 'Esprit de Corps.' Those who were sergeants treated the rest of us with a suspicion of reserve. No matter what we said, it just didn't seem to be the same.

'From now on I'm going to have to salute you, Hughie,' said Sandy Morrison.

'It just can never be the same. You're going to be in your Mess, and I'm going to be in mine. That's two different worlds, boy, two different worlds.'

There was a long silence. Finally Sandy raised his head and said:

'I'll tell you what, Hughie, on this bloody trip there is no way they can divide us. Let's enjoy our last days together and forget it.'

As with all the other troop trains, there were long stretches of time spent stationary in railway sidings or creeping at a snail's pace through marshalling yards. Finally the train came to a halt at the quay-side in Halifax Harbour. As we stepped off, we were met by the cold damp salt breezes off the North Atlantic. I heard one of the RAF fellows exclaim:

'Gad! This is proper 'brass monkey'* weather.'

It was dusk as we shambled across the railway tracks of the siding and assembled on the quay-side, beside a dirty-looking ship. We stood there in the penetrating cold for about three-quarters of an hour, and
* i.e. Freeze the balls off a brass monkey.

then people began to get restless. Someone shouted:

'What in hell is the holdup?'

An embarkation officer with a sheaf of papers in his hand appeared and shouted:

'Everybody back on the train — all personnel back on the train.'

There was a chorus.

'BACK ON THE TRAIN?'

'Yes, all personnel, back on the train!'

'WHAT FOR?'

'You're all under quarantine. The medical officer has found a case of measles.'

'MEASLES?'

'This contingent will be quartered in quarantine at Debert for ten days.'

'TEN DAYS?' came the chorus.

'Get back on the train, will you?'

By the time we were transported to our alternate destination, steady rain had started to fall. Once off the roadbed of the railway siding we found ourselves in a morass of red clay. We were to be the first inhabitants of a new flying school still half-constructed at Debert, Nova Scotia. The hangars and runways were down but no walkways. We trudged through the mud towards a group of wooden buildings that smelled of fresh paint. We made a quick 'recky' and discovered that the plumbing system seemed to be in, but the water was not connected, and there was no heat. In the corner of each room on top of the cigarette butts and the flotsam and jetsam discarded by the construction workers were four double-decker beds, eight mattresses and a pile of blankets. In the few days that I had been on leave as an officer, I had spent the usual amount of time admiring myself in the mirror in my new uniform. I had thoroughly enjoyed the privilege of wearing black Oxfords and thin black socks instead of boots. As it had been snowing in Toronto when I left, I had purchased a pair of tipped rubbers to go over my shoes. By the time I reached the barracks block, having stepped into a hole, I had red clay halfway to the knee of my right leg and lost one rubber. The sergeants were better equipped. They were wearing their issued galoshes and had no problem. I must say that when I reached my officers' quarters I was a little disenchanted. I think I might have lodged a complaint if it hadn't been for the reaction of the RAF officers.

'This is unbelievable! Surely, this is not where '*We*' are billeted. This must be the Airmen's quarters, and not very good ones at that, eh, Reginald? This must be somebody's incredible joke, and in extraordinarily bad taste. Reginald, do you think they realize what we are with this *lot*? *Do* go and see if you can find out *who* is in charge of this outrageous shambles! The clots have probably never heard of RAF Part II of the War Manual. It's all there, under billeting.'

Then later:

'Nothing can be done? *Nothing*? Have you seen the catering arrangements? Why, it makes the N.A.A.F.I.'s tea wagon look like the Savoy. We must report this to Air Ministry.'

At this point, I *had* seen the catering arrangements. The cooks and food handlers were all volunteer civilian women, bathed in sweat, standing over hastily erected steam tables working with a frenzied desire to please. They did their best to give us a little bit of home away from home. They were so grateful to those of us who gave them a little bit of thanks. There was obviously no point in 'bitching.' There was no other choice. It was just another example of the incredible problems facing the Commonwealth Air Training Scheme.

Years later I met an R.C.A.F. Medical Officer whose first assignment was to proceed to Debert and deal with a measles epidemic. Young and keen, he decided that all clothing belonging to a known case had to be sterilized in a hospital autoclave. The pressure and the temperature of an autoclave completely alters the character of wool fibres. Fourteen days after his arrival the medical officer came down with unmistakable measles himself. His own new uniform was autoclaved by his own orders. No matter how many times he sent it away after that to be pressed, it still returned looking as though he had slept in it for a week. His cap was limp and sagged down at the edges. Realizing this was to no avail, he applied to RCAF Headquarters for a new uniform allowance to replace the one lost in the course of the 'front-line duty.' His request was refused. From that day until his discharge in 1945, he never missed a station parade wearing his first uniform in silent protest. Air Force Medical Officers in general were not a happy lot. They had joined up bright-eyed, full of the anticipation of performing miraculous medical and surgical feats at the front line.

In the personnel establishment of each unit, there was always a Medical Officer, whose main function was to handle sick parade. The only legitimate excuse for an airman not being where he was supposed to be was because he was on sick parade. As far as the commanding officer was concerned, a good Medical Officer was one who knew how to make a sick parade a painful alternative. He was a specialist in recognizing and curing '*sick paraditis*.' One of the doctors kept a gallon jug of castor oil on his desk and before asking for complaints gave everyone a tablespoon. Another, frustrated in his desire to do surgery, kept a rusty old scalpel in his drawer. Any airman naive enough to display his haemorrhoids got the same treatment. He was told to bend over in the corner bare-arsed, and the Medical Officer took a swipe at them with his scalpel. Popular treatments for such things as minor upper respiratory complaints, headache, sinusitis was one week confined to barracks. It was the Medical Officer's duty also to keep all personnel well supplied with 'French safes.' As this preceded the time of public preoccupation with overpopulation, the prime purpose of this was the prevention of VD. The antibiotics had not been discovered, and failure to use 'protection' and be unlucky enough to contract a 'dose' at this time meant harsh treatment indeed. Gonorrhea meant the 'hockey stick' treatment, or frequent insertion of a hockey stick shaped dilator in the barrel of the penis. For syphilis you got the 'hot box.' This was described as a coffin-like heated box in which the patient was kept until his temperature was about one hundred and six. Survivors of these treatments from then on took ample precautions to make sure they didn't have another course.

The unit Medical Officer was limited to treating the sort of conditions which a good orderly could easily handle. All real medical or surgical problems were immediately shipped to a local hospital. Thus, it was understandable why they felt that their expensive medical education was going to waste.

Finally the order came through that our internment at Debert had come to an end. We were to re-embark. Like everyone else, I had a sack full of dirty laundry, and my new uniform was blotched with red clay. After another train ride we found ourselves wandering back along the quay-side, and I read the name of the ship up on the bow as we passed: 'Yohan Van Oldenbarnevelt.'

'That's Dutch,' I said to myself.

Once up the gangplank and inside, I instantly recognized a sickening putrid smell.

'Copra.' I even remembered the name. In an instant a peculiar feeling came over me as if I were reliving things long forgotten. I felt hot as though I was in the sulphurous miasma of the Tropics again, and the faint aroma of spices took me back to the Dutch East Indies. A kaleidoscope of memories returned. The bamboo stalls in the market place, the strings of dried fish, hot peppers and lush fruit. The klink-clonk of the wooden shoes on the cobble-stones, and the maddening screech of Chinese music. I heard my voice say:

'Hot Verduma beanyatung codoc!'

Out of the shadows, an Indonesian Yongus rose from the floor where he had been sitting on his heels. Pointing his finger at me with a broad smile, he said excitedly,

'Nederlander, Nederlander!' His dress was just as I remembered it, small brown and white, batik turban on the front of his head with a corner sticking up behind like a feather; the striped cotton jacket, the batik sarong and sandals. The enquiring gazes of my companions made me feel self-conscious, like the first day of boarding school. The master had ordered me to say something in Dutch. I had said those very words, and everybody had hooted with laughter. I was 'Indian Cudy.' That was me.

The others were preoccupied with their new surroundings and passed me by. The Yongus was still smiling broadly. I shot him a furtive smile, and, sensing my feelings, he said no more. They were kind, sensitive people.

This ship had come right off the tropical run between Rotterdam and the East Indies. They hadn't had time to strip it as a 'trooper.' The lounges still had thick Oriental carpets, heavy teak and ironwood furniture and Balinese wood carvings.

We just had time to get ourselves settled in a cabin when a steward gave the first call to lunch. We were seated four to a table, and one of the Yongus produced the menu. At the table, I became the interpreter and ordered everybody hot Indonesian food. I was dying to taste it again.

'How can you eat this stuff, Hughie?' asked Jim Loany. 'I'm burning up.'

I explained that I'd been weaned on coconut milk and rice, and that in the Tropics spices were essential medicines. Their taste and aroma stimulated the non-existent appetite that usually followed a bout of dysentery or malaria.

I had left a huge pile of laundry on my bed. Just as I expected, it had disappeared. The cabin boy had taken it to wash.

'I bet you don't get it back, Hughie,' said Wallie Murray, my roommate.

'You wait and see, Wallie, I will,' I said.

Sure enough, it was there the next morning stiffly laundered in a neat pile.

In the first few hours on board, everybody was in a pitch of excitement. Jim Loany, who had never been at sea, couldn't stand it inside any longer.

'Come on, Hughie,' he said. 'To hell with the cold, let's get bundled up and get out on deck.'

We donned our great coats and went up on A Deck. Halifax Harbour in winter can be a dreary place, and in wartime it was even worse. Above, a leaden grey sky; in the mist, grey and black camouflaged ships lay at anchor in the murky, oily water. Occasionally, a dirty-looking seagull would skim across the water, lighting to pick up a piece of floating garbage.

But nothing could dampen Jim Loany's ardour. He darted around on deck, thrilled by everything. We had just arrived in time to see the tugs pushing us away from the quay-side, headed for mid-harbour. Finally

43

they gave us a farewell blast on their whistles and left us to move off under our own steam. The battleship HMS *Royal Sovereign* led the way, and we followed leading the other three troop ships in line ahead through the anti-submarine nets. We were just in the outer harbour when Jim Loany, his back to the railing, said to me:

'Hughie, are we rolling?'

'Look along the edge of the deck while watching the horizon, and you can tell,' I said. After a few minutes he said in a very subdued voice:

'Hughie, I'm going back to my cabin. I don't feel well. Maybe it was lunch.' From that moment until we reached the Clyde ten days later Jim never left his bunk, except to hug the commode. I thought it was particularly unkind when one of the fellows, passing the bathroom, saw Jim on his knees again and shouted:

'Strain it through your teeth, Jim, and when you come to the brown ring, swallow it. It's your arsehole.'

The last six months had confirmed for me the ancient adage that war is long periods of boredom punctuated by short periods of acute excitement. I had developed the habit of always having something to do during such periods. I brought two articles with this in mind, a balsa wood model airplane kit, and a new diary. The airplane was a model of the Westland Lysander, a graceful gull-winged airplane in service with the RAF. Two days before the end of the voyage, I was lying in my bunk with the lights off. I had just finished the model. With a wing span of three feet, I was wondering what I was going to do with it. Wallie Murray answered my problem. He stumbled into the cabin 'under the influence,' fell on top of it, and broke it into a thousand pieces.

My diary was a much more durable purchase. It was a well-bound book with plain lined sheets. I had graduated from the stage of forcing myself to make daily entries. I would record only events that I thought might be worth remembering. Before the war was over, I had to buy a companion volume.

U-boats were already having a field day in the peaceful waters of the Eastern Seaboard. From the outset, each ship changed course every five minutes. The second day out found us pounding into the teeth of a North Atlantic gale, with wind speeds reported at 100 miles an hour. I had seen just such a storm in the Indian Ocean when we were being brought to Canada to school. I watched this one just as I had the other, through a porthole overlooking the fo'c'sle. The waves were mountainous, dwarfing the ship. Out of the valleys it would struggle up the face of the next wave, which looked for all the world like a slope of Mount Everest. We always managed to reach the summit before the peak would crash upon us. As it plunged forward down the other side, our propellors would break water and the whole ship would shudder from the strain. As the crest would go over the bow, the hurricane-force winds drove the spray horizontally, lashing the masts and the funnel. Torrents of water streamed across the decks with such force that it seemed it would sheer the superstructure flush with the decks. The storm raged all night abating mid-morning of the next day. Bent and twisted portions of the steel superstructure gave evidence of the ferocity of the gale.

With the improving of horizontal visibility we found that we were alone. There were no troopships and no *Royal Sovereign*. At this period of the war the German pocket-battleships had broken out into the North Atlantic for the purpose of preying on convoys such as ours. It was reported that the *Bismarck* was lurking about the North Sea lanes through which we would have to travel. During this period of loneliness without escort there was plenty of 'twitch' on board, and despite the weather the decks were lined with airmen, scanning the horizon. I was in the lounge trying to think of something else when somebody rushed in and shouted:

'There's a tripod mast to port!' In an instant the lounge was empty as everybody ran up on deck.

'It's the bloody *Bismarck*,' a cockney voice behind me shouted. Then another voice said:

'Did you hear that? It's firing.'

'Get on with it, "Tigger." It's *not* bloody-well firing, that's your heart pounding in your bloody ears again. That's the *Royal Sovereign*, or I'm a monkey's uncle.'

Several minutes passed as we all peered over the railing in silence. A man with field-glasses said:

'It's flying the white ensign, thank God. For once in me life I'm glad to see the ferkin' senior service.'

'It's about bloody time, Cock.'

Gradually the deck cleared again, and I was left with a member of the ship's crew. He had heard the remarks of the others and after a while he said wistfully:

'It's a damned good thing that *wasn't* the *Bismarck* firing at us. All it would take is one shell into this ship, and we'd all be blown to hell.'

'Why?' I asked.

'The hold is full of anti-aircraft shells.'

'Well, isn't that nice?' I said as I left for the comfort of the lounge.

The next event was the organizing of anti-aircraft gun crews. We had lots of gunners on board, most of them RAF. Tigger was one of them. He was on the first watch, and I was in the lounge when he came off duty, blue with cold.

'Get this, lads, you were right, old Lewis guns, and not a single sight on the lot.'

Somebody shouted:

'Have you got tracer ammo?'

'Ball, if you please, blinkin' old ball. With that lot, I couldn't even get a Gerry's attention.'

'Never mind, "Tigger," you wouldn't hurt him no matter what you 'ad. You couldn't 'it Saint Paul's Cathedral with Big Bertha.'

Before I was six years old, I had travelled two-and-a-half times around the world. I had been on many ocean liners, even the *Olympic*, a four-funneller reported to be the biggest ocean liner of her time. I remember that even it wasn't large enough to prevent the frustrations of confinement on a long sea voyage. This trip was no exception. The constant zig-zagging of the convoy made us feel we were getting nowhere. The arrival of the light cruiser *Edinburgh* to join the escort provided some diversion. On the third time change, the observers calculated that we must be four to five hundred miles out.

At this time we were all called to the lounge for an address by the executive officer. Like many tall people, he walked with a slight stoop, and on this occasion his leathery lined face was shrouded in gloom. His precise English with a Dutch accent made it even more dramatic. The gist of his message was as follows:

We were now in U-boat infested waters; the escort vessels in all probability would be dropping depth charges; the concussion from these had been known to break dishes. We were, therefore, to take appropriate precautions. He emphasized that he must insist on implicit obedience to all orders from the bridge. The survival of the ship's company might depend on it. All personnel were to sleep in their clothes *and* life jackets until further notice. At the end of his epistle, he waited an appropriate time for questions, gave a short bow, a sigh, and slumped away.

There was a babble of conversation as soon as he was out of earshot.

'He's a bright little ray of sunshine, ain't he?' from the fellow sitting beside me.

It all had seemed a little too melodramatic, but we were soon to discover that the Royal Navy was concerned about our safety. Destroyers began to appear on the horizon, and before nightfall there were four. They turned and twisted around the convoy, sometimes veering so sharply that they heeled over to about thirty degrees. The blockade run was on.

During the night the convoy turned north, and in a space of two hours the ship was turned into a veritable icebox. This ship was fitted for tropical water, and not for the north Atlantic. All water had to be shut off as the sea was well below freezing. This was the sort of conversation in the corridor near the lavatories:

'Close the bloody door, mate, that's a good chap.'

'Not bloody likely, cock, I don't want to asphyxiate myself. Have you been in here lately? This *can't* be human!'

I was having lunch with a dapper blonde RAF Flying Officer who sported a handsome handlebar moustache. I was hoping to pick up a few pearls and the latest 'Gen.' He was at the point of preening himself with his table napkin when I heard my first air raid siren.

'There goes the air raid siren,' I said excitedly and started to get up.

'Sit down, man,' he said. 'If you jump up every time you hear "Moaning Minny" in the UK, you'll be clapped out before you get operational. We haven't had our coffee yet. It's the only decent thing on the menu. I noticed you seem to have some influence with these wretched "wogs." See if you can fetch us one, there's a good chap.'

I didn't want to appear 'windy' so I gave in to his request. The coffee was served, and I dutifully choked it down. I was itching to see what was going on and finally made the excuse that I needed a 'breather.' I donned my cap and greatcoat and went on deck. There I was met by a thrilling sight. There were twelve destroyers in addition to the cruiser *Edinburgh*. The *Royal Sovereign* was no longer to be seen. There was no doubt from the look of this formidable escort that Churchill wanted every ship in this convoy. Each escort vessel had a hackle of guns pointing skywards. I searched the sky, and saw nothing. Somehow I had expected to see the sky black with Stukas and Condors.

Pensively I watched the destroyers for hours, knifing through the water, their bows streaming a huge bow wave, the aft deck all but invisible in the wake. I couldn't help but wonder as I watched, if we could be worth all of this in the end. We could never be compared with Frederick's Prussians, the Guards or Napoleon's *Grande Armée*. We were just a bunch of rawboned, half-trained, undisciplined Canadians. As yet we had not acquired a hatred for the Hun from the constant crump of bombs, levelling our homes and liquidating our loved ones. We were a naive, wide-eyed curious group of young men, with an established respect for the formidable enemy and his awesome reputation for unchecked omnipotence.

I opened my porthole next morning early. The sky was clear, and the sea melted into low-lying mist obliterating the horizon. In the distance a mountain of rock loomed above as though floating on a blanket of cloud. It was Ailsa Craig, and beyond it the hazy outline of the rugged coast of Scotland.

6

WARTIME LONDON

It was a glorious day when we disembarked at Greenock. The 'bonny banks of Clyde' were dotted with granite houses along the water's edge, and the hills formed a majestic background. Above, three fighters in V formation laid their smoke trails across the sky like rockets.

The convoy proceeded slowly in a well stationed line ahead. It just happened that I was looking at the *Dempo* ahead of us, when there was a thunderous explosion, and a fountain-like water spout shot up on its port side. The *Dempo* heeled over to starboard to about forty-five degrees.

'Gor blimey!' exclaimed a voice at my side. 'I'll bet that gave them a bit of a start.'

It was a loose mine that must have floated in on the incoming tide. If it had been thirty feet closer to the centre of the channel, it would have sunk the *Dempo* with five thousand troops on board.

We were given little time to admire the scenery. As soon as the anchor was down, we were whisked by tender onto a boat train bound for London. The coaches seemed minute compared to their Canadian counterparts, but the seats were well cushioned. No sooner was the train loaded than we were off. The local Scots, having seen the arrival of the troop ships, lined the tracks or hung out of the windows of the adjoining houses, waving and cheering us on our way.

We travelled all night and were to pass through several air raids. The train always slowed to a crawl when aircraft were directly overhead, and on one occasion came to a stop altogether. As we listened to the throb of heavy engines overhead, the conductor came to the car and stuck his head in each compartment, saying,

'Make sure the blackouts are down. Make sure those blinds are down.'

We all sat staring at the dull blue bulb, the only light in the compartment, as we listened to the conductor's voice getting fainter as he repeated the message to the others behind. Although it seemed ridiculous, we all kept silent as though we were afraid they would hear us. Slowly the sound of the aircraft engines became fainter, and then the train proceeded on its journey.

It was seven-thirty in the morning when we arrived at Uxbridge just north of London. Stiff and grimy, we were glad to stretch our legs and walk to the station. Uxbridge was an aircrew manning pool, and it was here that we got our first exposure to the RAF 'Admin' types. They epitomized the word 'organization.' Every moment of one's day was planned. Every stiffly clipped order was worded in such detail that one couldn't help but gather that they must look upon us as gormless half-wits. We let ourselves be led around in subdued silence until we were all gathered in a lecture room for the 'orientation and discipline lecture.' This was given by an administration officer with a neatly clipped moustache. His hat was flat on his head with the peak pulled well down on the forehead, his shoes and buttons glistening, and a pair of brown gloves held tightly in the left hand. He stood before us the very model of RAF deportment and dress.

The general text of his message was that we were now in the RAF. Carelessness, or slovenliness of dress, such as unbuttoned tunics, or tardiness would not be tolerated. Failure to carry our newly issued gas masks and steel helmets was a punishable offence. They were to be carried, slung over our right shoulder, strap adjusted to place them exactly behind our left hip — 'just so.' London, he told us, was patrolled by RAF Service Police. They were on the lookout for any infringement of RAF orders of good conduct and deportment. They were at liberty to stop and take the names of all offenders regardless of rank. Fraternization or interference with the members of the WAAF* on duty was 'frowned upon.' After a further series of similarly worded orders, he finished with,

'Have I made myself perfectly clear?'

There was a sullen silence.

'Are there any questions?'

A Canadian aircrew sergeant, his face flushed with irritation, raised his hand.

'Yes, sergeant?'

'Have we done anything wrong yet?'

'Sergeant, you will from now on address all officers as "sir." In answer to your impudent question, NO! YOU HAVE NOT DONE ANYTHING WRONG. THESE REMARKS ARE ISSUED BY WAY OF FAIR WARNING LEST YOU MIGHT BE TEMPTED. If there are no further questions, all ranks will proceed to room four at the end of the hall. There you will be issued an advance of pay. All ranks are then released from the station until 0600 hours tomorrow morning.'

This sort of thing did nothing for us so-called 'colonials.' During the operational training phase of our lives in England, these 'types' plagued us like blowflies. Saddled with a difficult task of trying to maintain

* Women's Auxiliary Air Force.

49

discipline, they were constantly at odds with the aircrews, and from here on they would be disdainfully referred to as 'wingless wonders.'

In my conversations with RAF fellows on the ship, I had gathered that rationing had not yet affected the restaurants in London to any degree. I was told that they were crowded, however, and reservations were essential. When I asked for the names of restaurants with good cabarets, the Cafe de Paris consistently topped the list. Jim Lowney had now decided that he was going to live, and had developed a ravenous appetite having lost fifteen pounds at sea. It wasn't difficult, therefore, to get him to join Al Harley and myself for dinner. I called and made reservations for three and off we went by tube for London. By the time we got out of the tube station and into a cab, it was pitch dark, and we had the first rather eerie experience of being in an enormous, bustling city totally blacked out. The headlights of all cars were masked and had a few horizontal shaded slits that gave just sufficient illumination to see immediately in front. In the taxi we heard our first London air raid siren wails. It started from a low frequency growl, then built gradually to a maddening scream and then, just as slowly, fell back to the low pitched moan again. It was repeated so often that we felt like crying out:

'We hear you, damn it! Stop!'

At first I felt as though I should be crouching down. The driver continued on as if he hadn't heard anything. At the last minute he turned the cab sharply over to the curb almost in its own length. The door was opened by a doorman in a scarlet tunic to the knees, brass buttons, and a black silk topper.

'Good evening, sir,' he said. ' "He" seems to be about again. Shouldn't imagine it will be as bad as last night, though. Mind the step, sir.'

A few nights later the 'Cafe de Paris' received a direct hit from a delayed action bomb. It was reported there were no survivors.

We passed through the door into the red carpeted foyer and were relieved of our coats. We were directed to a broad carpeted stairway which led to the cabaret below. From force of habit we fell into step with one another. To the left of the stairway was a bannister beneath which was a raised platform for the orchestra. As we started down the steps, the all-Negro orchestra in orange jackets was playing to a full dance floor. Glancing up, the conductor saw the Canada flashes on our shoulders, stopped the music he was playing, and switched to 'Oh Canada.' Crimson with embarrassment, we reached the floor to a standing ovation. The smiling maitre d', large menu in hand, beckoned us to a front row table. I was instantly struck with the incongruity of the setting. Outside the defences of London were fighting a fierce battle, the whole skyline lighted with the flash of guns and the flicker of burning buildings. The air was reverberating from the crash of bombs and the deafening defiant answer of our ack ack. Down here we were relieved of these sounds. We were listening to the music of London's social life which drifted on unperturbed.

Being the sort of chap who slips into the last pew at church, I felt uncomfortable at a front row table. Happily the waiter occupied our attention, and we found ourselves saying yes to all his suggestions. The standard Canadian fare we were accustomed to included soup, main course and dessert. Here we found ourselves wading through hors d'oeuvres, soup, a fish course, then pheasant under glass washed down with a nice bottle of wine. This was followed by three more courses, the sweet, savory and the coffee. I refused the brandy and the cigars.

We were sipping our coffee with its strong chicory flavor when the band played for our attention and the cabaret began. Twelve leggy, voluptuous girls burst onto the floor, and danced a sort of can can in flawless synchrony. This bobbing routine gave a dazzling emphasis to their arresting figures. Throughout they surveyed us with such confident amusement that I found their gaze a little disconcerting.

At the end of their first number they skipped from the floor, each returning with a wooden horse. After arranging them in line, they sat on them, and, to the music, demonstrated how they could be advanced along the floor by rocking them back and forth. While I was still wondering what the point of this was, they jumped from their horses and ran between the tables. Now, I had been particularly impressed with a tall Nordic looking blonde and my preoccupation with her had obviously not gone unnoticed. To my alarm she came straight for me. Before I could collect my wits, I found myself dragged to the floor and placed on a horse with a half a dozen other shanghaied members of the audience. The girls lined up on a designated finishing line opposite their choice, and off we went. It took a certain amount of dexterity to make any progress, but by paying attention I soon began to move. I found that if I allowed myself undue preoccupation with the cleft between the bosoms of my prize, my progress slowed. By thinking obtusely I advanced and won a bottle of champagne and a dance. Even at close range she was striking.

It was a delightful evening, and it was with considerable regret that we took our leave in time to catch the last train back to Uxbridge. When the door slammed shut behind us at the Cafe de Paris, we once again faced reality. We walked to the nearest tube station in 'the nightly hate.' On the underground platform of the tube station a sight met our eyes that made us stop and stare. Against the wall was a row of double-decker beds each occupied. Around the beds on the floor as far as the eye could see were men and women lying in every conceivable attitude, some on blankets, and some on just brown paper laid on the bare concrete. There was one couple asleep in each other's arms. Children slept between their parents on makeshift beds or blankets. This was just one of the underground stations, and we knew they all must be the same. These were the bombed out people of London, many having returned to their homes to find them a heap of rubble, with a pair of blankets perhaps the only thing not burnt or stolen.

There was a rush of air as the train approached through the tunnel. It built up to a roar before it appeared at the entrance of the tunnel, and with a hiss of brakes it shuddered to a stop. Only the children stirred in their sleep. We stepped on board, the doors clanged shut, there was a jerk, and we were soon rocketing away into the inky darkness. The scene was gone, but I found it difficult to forget. I remembered that instinctively I'd looked at the sleepers in search of a familiar face. How silly, I thought, the faces familiar to me were protected from this agony by a thousand miles of water.

7

TRAINING FOR WAR

We were only two days at Uxbridge before we were posted to an Operational Training Unit. Al Harley, Wally Murray, Sid Graham, Keith Copeland, and I were sent to Suttonbridge to train on Hurricanes. We were told this would be the last formal training we would get before we tackled the Huns. Suttonbridge was on the east coast of England close to the mud flats of the Wash. It was flat midland country infiltrated by a network of narrow inlets and salt marshes, and mud left by the changing tides. The mess was a drafty wooden building with only one warm place in its stark interior, in front of the fire. Socially, it was depressing. Staid 'wingless wonders' stifled any camaraderie with their prissy men's club rules. I rarely stayed there for more than an hour at a time.

High tea was served every afternoon, and, as we soon discovered, it was classified as one of the main meals of the day. Later, a scanty unappetizing supper was served. I never managed to get one of the cucumber sandwiches. By the time I could get myself to the table, all that was left were a few wrinkled up pieces of bread sparsely buttered with Marmite. The first time I tasted Marmite, I was reminded of my father's story about George Bernard Shaw asking his Canadian host what Oka cheese was made of.

'Horse shit,' whispered the host from behind his hand.

'Oh, I can taste that,' said Shaw, 'but what else?'

I was billeted at the home of a widow about forty years of age who lived a mile and a half from the airdrome. She was a kind rather timorous soul, with grey hair and a high colour to her cheeks. She always wore a sweater coat, tweed skirt to mid-calf, lisle stockings and woolly bedroom slippers. Her hands looked red and a little swollen. The fingers were beaded with arthritis. She kept a clean house tastefully furnished, and I was given an upstairs bedroom with a high turnpost mahogany bed and a feathered mattress. I had never slept in a feather-bed. The temperature of the room was always about forty-five and damp. At first, I found it took a certain amount of teeth chattering courage to take your clothes off and even more to get between the damp sheets. In the featherbed I invariably ended up in a little nest in

53

the middle with the mattress all around me. Each night my good hostess would put a stone pig in the bed. For those who have never encountered one, a stone pig is a fat sausage-shaped crockery receptacle filled with boiling water to warm the bed clothes. For the first four nights I burnt my foot on it every time. Each morning at six o'clock she would shyly tiptoe into my room with a cup of tea.

'Good morning, time to get up. Here is a nice cup of tea.'

Just towards the end of my stay I managed to remain awake long enough to drink it before it turned cold. Having taken all night to get the bed warmed there was very little incentive to dress. The only thing that got me out on time was the thought of flying Hurricanes.

I can't say that I enjoyed the one-and-a-half-mile walk before breakfast. As I plodded my way to the station, my shoes became wet from the morning dew. I always seemed to be facing a damp penetrating wind off the fens. The frosted glass effect of the dull grey morning fog would finally be broken by the misty silhouette of the sentry box. You couldn't tell from a distance, but it was always manned. Each morning we had the same little game. How close could I get to the box before I would be challenged?

'Halt, who goes there?'

'Password.'

He always startled me, but stop I must or have a volley of bullets at my feet.

When I first was warned of this, I asked if that wasn't an unnecessarily aggressive response. I was promptly told that England was full of spies and that a Luftwaffe pilot who had escaped from his guards boldly walked into a fighter airdrome posing as a Polish pilot early one morning. The sleepy orderly officer became suspicious when he discovered that the man had left the washroom of the Officers' Mess through the window. He caught him sitting in a fighter trying to fathom the starting procedures. This was the famous Von Werra, who later escaped from a Canadian prisoner-of-war compound. He slipped across the border into the U.S.A. which was still officially at peace with Germany. He was feted at the German Embassy in New York before being returned to the Reich to a hero's welcome. Von Werra was later killed on the Russian Front.

Frankly these lads on guard duty had my sympathy. I couldn't think of a job more likely to produce smouldering resentment than guard duty on an airdrome on the Wash. As one would suspect, Suttonbridge was notorious for little battles between the guards. From fear or fulminating frustration, one of the guards would fire at a shadow and startle the others. For the next half hour bullets would be flying all around the perimeter.

Now breakfast at Suttonbridge was an interesting experience. It was here that I was introduced to my first kipper. To us Canadians it was a poor substitute for bacon and eggs, and as a hungry Scot so sagely put it, 'There's nae much eatin' in a kipper.' I filled up on the toast, the jam and the tea. The coffee was undrinkable.

Each time I came to the Dispersal Hut and saw the Hurricanes, I got a thrill. There was something exciting about the sputtering and crackling of a Rolls Royce Merlin engine running up. These tour-expired machines, with the paint flaking off, their sturdy metal wings, the fabric stretched tightly over the ribs of the wooden tail with the patched bullet holes, made them the very epitome of the seasoned veteran of the line. I had a hundred and seventy-six hours and twenty-five minutes flying time when I took off in a Hawker Hurricane. There were no two-place Hurricanes. Therefore, there could be no dual. One was given a pre-flight briefing of what to expect and off you went.

When flying any single-engined propeller-drive fighter, if you opened the throttle fully without touching the rudder pedals you would go around in a circle on the ground. The reason, of course, was the enormous torque produced by their powerful engines. The Hurricane was no exception. The drill, therefore, was in opening the throttle slowly, while countering the torque by putting the right rudder pedal against the stop. We were warned that it was tail light, so too much forward pressure on the stick would put the plane on its nose. We had been trained on aircraft with hydraulic brakes activated by toe pressure plates attached to the rudder pedals. The Hurricane, on the other hand, had compressed air brakes, activated by a single lever on the control column. Squeezing this hand brake with the rudder pedals straight across caused each of the wheels to receive equal braking. To produce more braking on one side or the other, one compressed the desired rudder pedal. At low speed, we were told, it was very light on the ailerons and had a nasty tendency to drop a wing. To get the flaps or wheels up or down, it was necessary to switch the control column from the right to the left hand, then reach well forward with the right to an H-shaped switch-box with a single lever. From one side of the neutral position the flaps could be put up or down, from the other, the wheels. The British would never dream of designing a fighter that was easy to fly. That wouldn't be sporting.

There was a characteristic appearance to a Hurricane taking off under the control of an inexperienced pilot on his first solo. Once airborne, it flew half-way down the field as though it were following a horizontal wavy line, then it rolled over on its side, while the pilot put the undercarriage up. The Hurricane landed almost in flying position so there was a natural tendency at first to drop it on the ground tail first. At best this would produce a hippity-hop dance before it sat down; at worst, it broke the wooden back of the airplane. All in all, a

Hurricane was a bit of a challenge for an inexperienced pilot.

I distinctly remember the first time I became air-borne in one. I got the wheels up without rolling over on my back, but when I slipped the coop-top forward over my head, the thing seemed to take off at a frightening velocity. The engine sounded like a gigantic buzz-saw, and before I had a chance to even think of turning, I was miles from the airdrome in the murky haze. It was like being on a runaway horse. Gradually I got the feel of it, and after half an hour I thought I was in control. Feeling that I was ready to try a landing, I came back across the airdrome. Looking down, I counted seven Hurricanes 'pranged' on the field, an eighth on final approach with flaps and wheels down. The fire truck shot a red flare arching in the air to make him go around again. I had no intention of trying to bring this juggernaut in for a landing unless I could see a nice wide long piece of grass into wind. The other Hurricane and I went round and round the field for about half an hour while they cleared away the debris. Finally, I got a green light from the watch office and with plenty of air speed on the clock, I put my flaps and wheels down. I managed to bring the brute back onto the ground, as KB used to say, 'so I could walk away from it.'

The student trainees at Suttonbridge at the time were a multi-national group. Besides Poles, Czechs, Free French and ourselves, we had the first contingent of the American Eagle Squadron. Some of the latter group had rather exaggerated their previous flying experience. The RAF let them 'have a go' anyway.

With practice, I soon became the exhilarated master of my machine. With a flick of my wrist I could soar a thousand feet in the air like a gull on a fresh breeze, or make the horizon spin in a roll. As most of us had never been exposed to radio transmitters and receivers, the ground training for the most part was devoted to learning RAF Radio Transmission or R/T Procedure. This meant hours spent committing to memory the code words and the proper phraseology in the procedure book. Along with this, they attempted to teach us how to pronounce these words of the English language. In the air no departure from correct usage was tolerated. We Colonials had to admit that the British manner of speaking was particularly well adapted to transmitting a message at 'strength two,' not much louder than a whisper.

In the course of 'listening out' on a receiver of an aircraft at OTU, many amusing conversations could be heard in those days. I particularly remember one. An Eagle Squadron pilot, who had successfully soloed a Hurricane, was discovered by the RAF Flight Commander to 'never having done any aerobatics in his bloody life.' After telling the pilot what he thought of his previous instructors in no uncertain terms, the Flight Commander told him how to do rolls and loops and sent him up to do them. With reticence and foreboding, the pilot climbed to ten thousand feet and braced himself for a roll. He'd been told it was 'a piece of cake' in a Hurricane. I was in the air at the time and heard the following conversation between this fellow and 'Founder,' the Suttonbridge controller:

The pilot, voice high-pitched and full of alarm,

'Hello, Founder, corset one six, I am in a spiral dive, and I can't pull out. What will I do?'

The controller's voice sounded devilishly calm and unimpressed, and in replying he omitted none of the recommended R/T procedure.

'Hello, corset one six, corset one six, Founder answering. Your message received and understood. Stand by. I will have a word with your Flight Commander.'

The Yank, obviously unnerved and devastated by Founder's lack of concern, replied almost in a whimper:

'Christ, Founder, there's no time for you to argue with the Flight Commander now. My air speed is three hundred, and I can't get this crate under control. If something doesn't happen in the next few seconds, I'm bailing out.'

Still unimpressed, the controller replied:

'Hello, corset one six, corset one six, please use R/T procedure and stand by. Your Flight Commander's line is busy!'

Dead silence followed. I could imagine what the pilot was saying to himself. On his own, the pilot got the aircraft under control and landed it. As he rolled to a stop he still didn't know what was wrong. He shut down in the middle of the field, unwilling even to taxi it. In the RAF all non-commissioned ground crew were referred to affectionately as 'erks.' The pilot, while still sitting in the cockpit attempting to recover his composure, suddenly found an erk standing on his port wing.

'There's something wrong with this crate,' he said.

'I should bloody well think so, Sir. Have a look.'

When the pilot stood up and looked back, he saw the cause of his trouble. All the fabric from the cockpit back had peeled off like a giant banana skin and was now wrapped around the tail. It took the Flight Commander several days to coax the pilot into another Hurricane.

In our Flight there were two Poles who didn't speak a word of English. They had flown in the Polish Air Force defending Warsaw. The Flight Commander, in desperation one day, said to me:

'Godefroy, take these two Poles up for an hour's formation, there's a good chap.'

'They don't understand a word I say, Sir.'

'I'm not surprised,' he said, 'but go on, do the best you can, you do all the nattering with Founder. At least these fellows understand the standard hand signals, that's a start, isn't it? Get cracking then.'

I took the two Poles over into a corner, and after elaborate exchanges of courtesy, I tried to get down to briefing, confining myself to hand signals and grunts. Surprisingly enough, we seemed to establish complete understanding so we got into our Hurricanes and taxied out.

I felt a little conspicuous with them taxiing in formation on me: We took up half the field. I turned around into wind and stopped. They crossed over behind me and stationed themselves in V-formation about two-and-a-half wing spans out. I waved to them to come a little closer. They both turned around and, this time, came in so close that our wings overlapped their props ticking over frighteningly close to my wing tips. There was only one way out of this mess, I thought, straight ahead. I briskly opened my throttle in the hope of leaving them behind. To my alarm, I found that they had managed to stay with me, their props still turning a hair's breadth from my wing tips. At first, I was afraid to do anything but go straight ahead. Gradually I started turns, shallow at first, and then into a full ninety degree bank. They were there, as if bolted to my wing tips. Finally, I came back across the field down wind and gave them the horizontal half-circle wave that means 'break off and land independently.' They never budged. I did several circles of the field while pointing down and repeating the signal. They still didn't budge. At this stage of my career I had never landed in formation. Hoping that they would understand, I put my wheels down. So did they. I led them around until I was on final approach and put my flaps down. Still attached to my wing tips like a couple of lampreys, so did they. At this point, I was thoroughly unnerved. Aware of my own limitations, I realized that if I didn't land smoothly straight ahead, we would all end up in a chewed up pile of rubble. Fortunately for me it was one of my 'greasers.' When I stopped rolling they were still in formation with me and proceeded to taxi with me back to Dispersal in the same order. When we got out they came over to me with broad grins, and nodding their heads, said: 'Good?'

'Too good,' I said.

One day two pilots of the Eagle Squadron were reported overdue having been sent on 'familiarization cross-country flights.' The Observer Corps reported one of them had crashed. The pilot was dead. We heard nothing from the others for hours. Finally a call came to Dispersal from the pilot. He had succeeded in landing safely in a field and gave his position. Greatly relieved, the Flight Commander dispatched an instructor in a Miles Master to pick him up. The instructor found the field, which was very small, but there was the Hurricane intact with the pilot standing beside it. The Miles Master was a two-place single-engine fighter-trainer less powerful and vicious than the Hurricane. The instructor made a precautionary approach to the field. When he touched his wheels on grass, he realized that he was going too fast to stop and went around again. He didn't want to look like a fool in front of this 'sprog pilot' who had obviously managed to get a Hurricane into this field. On his second attempt he brought his aircraft in hanging on the prop and waddled into the field and plopped down. He promptly went straight through the fence at the other end and over on his back. When he got out, he was absolutely livid.

'How the Hell did you get that kite into this field?'

'Well, sir,' drawled the Yank, 'I did it different. I was trying to get into the field behind this one, bounced and went over the fence.'

The instructor bought the beer in the Mess for the next week.

At Suttonbridge, I managed to get thirty-five hours. In order to make room for the next course, we were passed out as 'Operational.'

FIRST ACTION

Al Harley, Keith Copeland and myself were posted to 401 Squadron. Sid Graham was posted to 402 Squadron. Both squadrons were stationed at Digby in Lincolnshire and formed the nucleus of the first Canadian wing in England. Gordon McGregor, DFC, was made Wing Commander Flying. My squadron Commander, Dean Nesbitt, and one of the Flight Commanders, Jack Morrison, met us at the train station. For the first time in our Air Force career we had the pleasure of being spoken to like pilots instead of brainless trainees.

The first person I saw when I walked in the door of the Mess was John Weir. For some reason I expected to see a terrific change in him, but he was the same old Johnny. The very sight of him rekindled memories of our happy irresponsible days at school.

'Are you still late for everything, Johnny?' I asked.

'Godefroy, you have never been on time for anything in your life and from the moment I met you neither have I. God, and I was beginning to reform. Now it's hopeless.'

We both laughed, and as he took me along to my room, we both reminisced about old friends at home. He stopped at the door and said, 'This is it, Number 13, this is where you hang out; I'm just across the way. This used to be Paul Henderson's room. You remember him, don't you?'

'Yes,' I said, 'where is he now?'

'Oh, he "pranged" himself the other day. Too bad! He was a nice fellow. See you in the mess, Hughie.'

Paul Henderson? It seemed such a short time ago that we had been in school together. Oh, well, I thought, I'll have to get used to this. Room 13, that will be my lucky number from now on. Having been inseparable friends since boyhood, I knew John well. He had passed the subject off a little too quickly. But I was not superstitious, and finding someone who was, had always made me want to prove them wrong. I felt at the time as though I had accepted a wager, a wager which I was sure I would win. In my enthusiasm, I was so certain that I felt genuinely sorry for the rest.

When they found out that we could not formate very well, had

60

never flown in cloud, nor practised dog-fighting, they set up a little flying school under the command of Flight Lieutenant Ed Rino to bring us up to full operational efficiency. It came to be known as Rino's Flying Circus. Ed Rino was no K.B. Wilson. He was a nice guy who 'knew his stuff,' and he knew how to get respect and cooperation. He had us flying day and night unless the weather was hopeless. I would often return to my room, flop on my bed to think the day over and fall fast asleep before supper.

One day I spent doing nothing but cloud flying. We had to master the technique of fighting the vertigo which plagues pilots flying on instruments. In the early days often I found myself sweating. I felt as though I were spinning in a spiral dive. One had to say to himself, 'The instruments are right, and I am wrong.' Finally I would break cloud, and find to my great relief that I was flying straight and level. We never worried in England at that time over what else might be flying in the same cloud. We never gave it a thought.

It had been an exhausting day, so I ate dinner early and went straight to bed. The moment I switched out the lights, I fell fast asleep and began dreaming. I was flying my Hurricane in an azure blue sky, below was a solid bank of white fleecy clouds which stretched forever in all directions. I dove and for a while rocketed along a few feet off the dazzling blanket. For the last few seconds before I sank into its depths, puffs of white flashed over my wings and my aircraft began to bump gently. As I penetrated more deeply, the light faded, and I lost all sense of speed and position in space. Gradually I was aware of the disturbing sensation that I was slowly turning in space. The air became rougher. Rain peppered the wind screen and a fine spray penetrated the cockpit. As I made myself concentrate on the instruments, my field of vision seemed to narrow as though I were looking through a tunnel. Suddenly I felt I was spinning, and my aircraft seemed to shudder as I went down. With a start I sat bolt upright in bed. In the pitch darkness I could see nothing. A second before I'd been spinning in my aircraft, and I felt certain I was still there. In a cold sweat I groped for the throttle, the controls, and the hood above me. I was spinning in a vacuum. Suddenly my hand hit something. There was a crash and the lights went on. I had hit my table lamp, and it had gone on. I was crouched in the middle of the room bathed in sweat, quivering in every muscle. The sudden violent exertion made me feel faint and exhausted. I flopped into bed. With my heart pounding and gasping for breath, I relived the dream. Gradually the shivers left me, and I fell asleep.

One G is the downward force or weight of any object subject to the influence of gravity. This force increases whenever a moving object is turned away from a straight course, and the increase varies directly with the rate of change of direction multiplied by its velocity or speed.

You couldn't cavort around the skies in an aircraft designed to withstand the speeds of a fighter without experiencing G. In our training, Ed Rino would ask one of the operational pilots to test us out in a dog-fight. I was very flattered to be sent out to dog-fight with Moose Fumerton. As his nickname suggests, Moose was a massive man, slow and deliberate. He had a sharp-eyed penetrating gaze that surveyed life unperturbed with mild amusement. You soon discovered, however, there was nothing slow about his wit or his reflexes. He had the reputation of being a most formidable opponent in a dog-fight. He was destined to become one of Canada's night-fighter Aces. Now by this time I was turning a Hurricane tight enough to have the force of G drain the blood from my brain and give me the feeling of greying out. With Moose I had my first black-out.

At first, he playfully wound and twisted me around the sky. With the constant struggle against G, I was soon bathed in sweat. In the first three-quarters of an hour he must have got on my tail in shooting position at least ten times and had convinced me that I was still an amateur. In the end, he let me get on his tail, and just as I was closing, he flicked over on his back and went straight down from ten thousand feet. I followed him, my engine 'balls out.' As my speed built up, the aircraft began buffeting and shuddering and the ailerons stiffened until they were almost solid. The last thing I remembered was Moose beginning to pull out with white vapor trails streaming from his wing tips. I woke up with the exhausted unreal feeling one gets after losing consciousness. I was looking at clear blue sky. I was in a Hurricane with the prop still turning, but there was no engine sound and no horizon. I wondered if I was dead. Slowly before my eyes a swirling earth appeared, and with a crackling roar the engine screamed back to full power. My aircraft had pulled out by itself and gone straight up until it stalled and spun; now it was spiralling straight down again. Instinctively, I took over the control and gently pulled out of the dive. Feeling useless, sick and tired, I returned to the base and landed. Finally one day Ed Rino said,

'Okay, lads. I want to put on a formation show for the boys. If you look good enough, you'll be passed out as Operational. Copeland, I want you to lead. Harley and Godefroy will fly in number two and three positions, respectively.'

We took off in formation and then split up and did individual aerobatic displays and dog-fighting over the field. Finally, 'Copy' waggled his wings to signify to Harley and me to return to V-formation. When we were in tight, he led us through a series of steep turns.

When aircraft are flying in V-formation and doing a turn, to maintain position the aircraft on the inside must go slower than the leader, and the man on the outside faster. It is essential in tight formation for the wing men to look at nothing but the leader concentrating on maintaining position.

While doing a turn to the left with me on the inside, Copy raised his hands in signal to put down our undercarriages. With my eyes on Copy, all I could see beyond was Al Harley and sky. Still in this position he put his hand up again to signal flaps down. Concentrating on looking at Copy, I had no idea where the ground was or what my air speed was. Suddenly I felt myself mushing and my controls felt awfully sluggish. I took a quick glance in front and saw that I was close to the ground and sinking like an elevator. Ignoring my position in the formation, I opened my throttle to check my descent. I managed to level off and hit hard on three points, then bounced into the air. My port wing dropped and hit the ground. With my throttle wide, I roared across the field in a gradual turn to the left, with my right rudder pushed in with all my strength in an attempt to get the wing tip off the ground again. I almost made it, but about halfway across the field my port wheel cover caught the ground. I cartwheeled from nose to wing tip to tail to wing tip. There was a series of tearing, rending, snapping sounds as pieces of metal were torn from the aircraft and the wooden tail snapped like a handful of dry sticks. Despite my harness I was thrown around the cockpit like a dice in a box. Finally the aircraft came to rest balanced on the nose and one wing tip. For a second I thought it was going over on its back. It teetered momentarily, but then fell back right side up. As the Merlin was a liquid-cooled engine, its last agonal moans were different from those of air-cooled engines I had crashed. A hissing sound was added as the coolant burned and vaporized on the hot metal. As before, I sat in the cockpit stunned, smelling the pungent vapour of burning glycol. My aircraft was a complete wreck, the wing tips and the undercarriage were gone and so was the prop. With the back broken, the tail was twisted around and pointing in the opposite direction. As an erk helped me out, I was conscious that my shoulders and back hurt. I was so afraid they would stop me flying that I swore that I hadn't an ache or a pain.

I was very worried this would delay my becoming an Operational, but Ed Rino assured me this would not be the case. He did not consider this was my fault. Copy, through lack of experience in leading formation, had brought us in too slow to keep me, the inside man, from stalling. I was sent straight off in another Hurricane for an hour's local flying.

But the accident was reported through the 'usual channels' to 12 Group Headquarters. The Air Officer Commanding decided that, as an aircraft had been destroyed by accident, somebody had to be punished. As my aircraft was destroyed, and I was captain of the aircraft, I got my log book endorsed 'Pilot error in judgement.' I felt very hard done by.

It was May, 1941, when I first took my place on readiness. Great Britain stood braced and as ready as it could be for Hitler's invasion. In the occupation of Holland it had been reported the German army stopped at railway stations, took down the advertising notices, and found printed on their back full scale maps of the various locales. This had been the pre-invasion work of the Dutch Fifth Column. In England the precaution was taken to remove all railway, highway and street direction signs. This made no difference to the local who knew his way around anyway, but to the Allied and Commonwealth servicemen, it created an irritating problem.

The news broadcasts offered what seemed to be nothing but a series of disheartening events, adding to the aura of invincibility of Hitler's War Machine.

A special broadcast by the BBC announced at this time that the *Bismarck* had been sighted in the North Atlantic by a patrolling Catalina and that units of the North Atlantic Fleet including the battle cruiser HMS *Hood* had been dispatched to intercept.

It was a carefully kept secret that the Catalina was an American patrol aircraft piloted by a U.S. Naval Ensign.

As I listened, I remembered the pictures I had seen in boys' magazines of the Hood and the Nelson with their long foredecks and heavy front gun turrets. It was claimed that they were unsinkable. Now, I thought, the pocket battleship had met its master. As we waited excitedly for further news, a second broadcast was issued. The Admiralty regretted to report that HMS *Hood* had been sunk with all hands. The *Bismarck* had scored a direct hit with its first salvo, and the *Hood* had blown up. We were thunderstruck.

The walls of our dispersal huts were papered with posters of German paratroops, dripping with hand grenades and armed with Schmeissers, the German Tommy guns. Squadron personnel were issued pikes, not too sturdy sticks with sharp metal points on their ends, to be used in the defence of the airdromes in case of paratroop attacks.

Rudolf Hess, Hitler's Deputy Reichsmarshal, bailed out of a Messerschmitt 110 over Scotland. He claimed to have come to try to negotiate a last-chance peace. His efforts were coldly ignored as 'preposterous.'

There were frequent dismal announcements from the office of Lord Woolton in charge of food rationing; repeated pleas were made for increased domestic food production. All this added some credence to the extravagant claims of Lord Haw Haw, the Irish-born news announcer who read the nightly news release from the German High Command. Astronomical claims were made about the ship tonnage sunk weekly;

the U-Boats and the Luftwaffe, he claimed, had virtually closed all
supply ports but the Clyde, the Mersey and Bristol. It was only a matter
of time, he would sneer, before Britain's lifeline would be severed and
we would be starved into submission.

Having wanted so much to take my place on readiness, I soon found
it boring drudgery. 12 Group, the second line of defence of the south
of England, was too far from the front line. Any Hun who managed to
penetrate had either been shot down, or taken refuge in cloud where we
couldn't see him.

But even in 12 Group, despite the rationing, the fighter pilots fared
well. We had bacon and eggs a couple of times a week, a fair proportion
of meat, but, like the rest, had to fill up on staples like cabbage and
beans and sparingly sweetened desserts smothered in custard. The
'banger,' the fat sausage filled with cereal flavoured with meat, was a
regular part of the menu. For those who wanted it, there seemed to be
plenty of rum in the bar and a good supply of lime juice which made it
more drinkable. There was no room for Canadian cigarettes in the holds
of ships, so smokers were limited to British Players; when these ran out,
Woodbines. At this time, when I neither drank nor smoked, I was
constantly hungry, and, having been trained to eat everything, always
left a Lord Woolton's plate. I even ate the boiled onions. I found,
however, after eating these meals and being scrambled and sent to
twenty thousand feet my stomach became distended and hard as a
kettledrum. I had constant heartburn. On questioning the seasoned
pilots, who lingered at the table puffing a cigarette, I found that none
of them shared my complaint. I had to do something. I tried an after-
dinner cigarette, and it seemed to help.

Costly lessons had already been learnt about land and air warfare.
The battle of France and Dunkirk showed the futility of engaging in land
battle in the absence of aerial superiority. Luftwaffe bomber units
unopposed in daylight in this campaign were devastating but in the face
of RAF fighter defence in the Battle of Britain sustained incredible
losses. Goering had the task of bombing England into submission. He
was forced to restrict his bomber force to individual intruder sorties
with cloud cover or to night blitzes. It was vowed that every city in
Britain would be reduced to ashes like Coventry in November 1940.

Churchill in his last radio broadcast to the French had promised to
return. There was no way he could do so with the Luftwaffe in control
of the skies of northern Europe. So began the war of attrition for aerial
supremacy. Fighter Command's 11 Group that had defended London
was launched on offensive sweeps over the French coast. Squadrons of
12 Group like ourselves were used to swell their ranks. I have good
reason to remember the first time my squadron was ordered to
participate.

That evening before dinner, Dean Nesbitt told the Flight Commanders to post a lineup for squadron formation to take off at first light. We were to join the Wing at West Malling for a sweep over France. There was a buzz of excitement amongst the pilots. Everyone was greatly relieved at the prospect of something besides defensive readiness. Here was a chance at last to redeem myself. Determined to get on the show, I sought my Flight Commander, Norm Johnson. As I approached him, I tried to appear cool, and calm and keen.

'Good evening, Norm. Have a drink,' I said.

'No, thanks, Hughie,' he said, 'I've got one.'

'By the way, Norm, what time do you want me in the morning?'

'You can sleep in the morning, Hughie. I won't need you.'

'Oh, gosh, Norm, look who's been doing all the readiness lately. Surely that's earned me a chance to be on this thing.'

'Hughie, don't be in such a hurry. There will be lots more sweeps. Besides, there are dozens of fellows who've done much more readiness than you.'

I could see that I was wasting my time. Bitterly disappointed, I stalked off. I had been labouring under the impression that my flying had so greatly improved that I was well up to standard and definitely able to pull my weight. I had to face it. I was still looked upon as a 'sprog' pilot.

The only people left in the Mess after first light were the wingless wonders, the medical officer, Freddy Watson, and myself. Freddy had been grounded because he had a bad cold. To make matters worse, I was made orderly officer. This meant being saddled with an irritating series of administrative functions that I considered unbecoming to an Operational Pilot. I had a wretched day. That evening I came into Mess shrouded in gloom. I picked up a magazine and sat down to wait for dinner. Freddy Watson, an experienced pilot, was standing at the bar with a drink in his hand and had witnessed my truculent entry.

'What's the matter, Hughie? You look as if you've lost your last friend. What you need is a drink. Have a rum and lime.'

Up to this point I had found life so exciting that I had had no desire to dull my perception with alcohol. I had had ample opportunity to observe the effects of over-indulgence. On the few occasions I had been talked into a drink, I found I didn't like the taste of it. Thus, I had nursed every drink I had been given and consumed so little that I had felt no effect.

'No effect, eh?' said Freddy. 'This I want to see. You're on, Hughie. You drink 'em, and I'll buy 'em.'

While I went on reading my magazine, Freddy turned to the bar steward and mumbled something. The next thing I knew there was a glass sitting on the table beside my chair, and Freddy standing there confronting me with a whimsical smile. I picked up the glass and sniffed it. Finding the pungent odor of rum particularly offensive, I gulped the whole thing down in one swallow in the hope this would get Freddy off my back. I had no sooner got back to my reading when there was Freddy again putting another glass beside me. I distinctly remember the second glass didn't taste as bad as the first. In a muse of detached indifference I continued to drink the contents of the glass at my elbow. Suddenly, to my annoyance, I remembered that I was supposed to be at the 'Ops' Room for another inspection. I jumped up, got my cap and went out through the blackout doors of the mess into the inky darkness.

Sticking to the gravel walkway, I plodded my way towards the central Ops Room. I passed airmen and WAAF's coming off duty. Suddenly, as if struck by a haymaker, I lost my sense of balance and coordination. Ashamed and mortified to be seen by 'other ranks' in this condition, I fought desperately to maintain a straight course. Finally I was challenged by the guard on the Ops Room door.

'Halt, who goes there?'

'Password!'

'Puna,' I said. 'Orderly Officer, reporting for evening rounds. Anything to report?'

'The only thing so far, is that I think that the Orderly Officer is a bit the worse for wear.'

'Somebody's given me a bloody Mickey Finn,' I cursed, 'I don't drink, you see.'

'Oh, I can see that, sir, but I suggest you go back to the Mess. If the Squadron Leader Ops sees you, you'll be C.B. for the duration. I'll report that you've done rounds.'

'Thanks very much. Sorry about this. I think I'll follow your suggestion.'

I stumbled back along the path to the Mess, desperately trying to get my forward lurches longer than my backward ones. It was with a sense of overwhelming relief that I finally pushed open the blackout doors of the Mess. The rest of the night was complete oblivion. Apparently, I had been flippant with Doctor Porter, the Medical Officer. To give vent to his frustration, he was given to make snide remarks. I took umbrage apparently and tossed billiard balls at him. Freddy Watson finally put me to bed.

Next morning Padre Cochran had been summoned to take my last will and testament. I was sure I was going to die. With careful nursing, counsel and prayer, in two days I was back on deck, a wiser and repentant man. Only then did I discover that Freddy had managed to get seven triple rums and limes into me.

News of the war elsewhere was equally depressing. In February, General Wavell in North Africa had been wading through the Italians, and it seemed as though the desert would soon be secure in British hands. In March, General Rommel was appointed General in Command of the Afrika Corps and with just two armoured divisions proceeded to out-fox Wavell. If it hadn't been for the heroic stand of the Australians, he would have taken Tobruk by April.

In May, we heard through German news broadcasts that a large paratroop force had made a successful landing in Crete. By June an intrepid Sunderland pilot evacuated the last remnants of British troops from the island. Lord Haw Haw heralded this as another brilliant German victory. On yet another front, Hitler's armies in the Balkans had had major success. Rumania and Bulgaria had 'bellied up' and accepted German 'protection.' The valiant Yugoslavian army finally capitulated, and Greece, too, was now in German hands.

In view of the experience gained in the successful invasion of Crete, the next seemingly logical thing for Hitler to do was to eradicate the last remaining pocket of resistance, the British. The United States was still preoccupied with isolationism. She was nationally not convinced that this war was her business. Soviet Russia, under the iron heel of Joseph Stalin, was still struggling with the internal problems. Her sympathies, if any, seemed to lie with the Germans as Stalin had signed a non-aggression pact with Hitler. Having seen the tools we were expected to use to resist an invasion, I had a sneaky feeling that if Hitler launched the full might of his German war machines by land, sea and air, we would lose.

Instead Hitler turned his attention to Russia and ordered a massive attack on a two-hundred-and-twenty-mile front. By the time I did my first offensive sweep, German divisions were pouring like a tidal wave across Russia.

We took off in squadron formation at dawn to fly to West Malling on the south bank of the Thames. The air was smooth as silk at first light, and there wasn't a cloud in the sky. The valleys were marked by pools of mist and to the east the sky was crimson with the first flush of dawn. Ahead to the south the horizon was obscured by the industrial haze of London. It was a glorious sight from the centre of this tightly packed formation, each aircraft seemingly bolted to the next. A great sense of pride welled up at being a member of this team. The formation epitomized to me aggressive and disciplined attack. As we roared over the great city of London, hundreds of silver balloons lay gleaming below us in the bright sun, all pointed into wind like a great convoy on a sea of haze. Barges moved up and down the Thames leaving a shimmering wake behind them. Suddenly, below us, the grass field of West Malling appeared with dozens of Hurricanes and Spitfires parked around its perimeter.

We peeled out of formation in fours and landed on the grass. As we rolled to a stop, a dozen erks ran out and waved each one of us to a dispersal point. I was impressed with the split-second timing and organization of this front-line fighter station. It was obvious that I was not the only one who had been stimulated by this early flight. Eleven young keen Canadians in their yellow Mae West's, their pants tucked in their black flying boots topped with white sheepskin, rallied around Dean Nesbitt. He was the only pilot in the formation who had already withstood the baptism of fire. With his slow, languid Westmount drawl, he marshalled his exuberant flock to proceed to breakfast. A large truck pulled up with its canvas-covered top open at the back. We all piled in and off we went. We 'keen types' stared out of the back as it skirted the perimeter of the field. We passed squadron after squadron of dispersed Hurricanes and Spitfires. One spotlessly clean Hurricane marked with a Wing Commander's pennant had twenty-five swastikas painted on its side. It belonged to our Wing Leader, the famous Robert Stanford Tuck, D.S.O., D.F.C. and two bars. Very excited, we wandered into the Mess. The place was filled with pilots, most of them RAF. There was a smattering of Poles. The Free French were distinguishable by their darker blue uniforms. All of them had the top button of their tunics undone. Since the Battle of Britain, this was the tolerated habit of fighter pilots. There was an impressive number of these wearing well-worn ribbons of the Distinguished Flying Cross. The breakfast left nothing to be desired, as much bacon, eggs, ham and sausage as our stomachs could tolerate.

As soon as we had eaten, we were whisked off to the 'Watch Office' for the briefing. The long briefing room was filled with chairs, and had a raised platform at one end. Behind it was a wall map of the entire south coast of England, France and Holland. Different coloured ribbons leading from the fighter stations surrounding London were pinned on the map, indicating the course that these units would fly. On one corner of the wall was a blackboard, and the intelligence officer was standing on a stool in front of it making last-minute corrections in the weather report. Watching him, with an air of detached boredom, was Wing Commander Tuck, an impressive array of decorations below his wings. I expected him to look like a youthful version of Winston Churchill. Instead, Tuck made me think of Leslie Howard's portrayal of the Scarlet Pimpernel. He was a slim man with carefully groomed hair and a neatly clipped moustache. Rather foppishly, he held a long cigarette-holder between two fingers. The only thing about him that suggested violence was a long scar down the side of his cheek. In his left hand he had a long wooden pointer which he handled as though it were a staff. He soon tapped it on the floor for silence. It was as if we were watching a play. I was too preoccupied with the atmosphere to remember much of what he said. I noticed, however, as he laid down the plan of action and indicated where he expected we would be engaged, that his eyes flashed and the scar became whiter and more obvious. I did hear the word 'Dunkirk.' Just before dismissing us to our dispersal points, he ordered us to synchronize watches.

There was dead silence while we all looked at our watches.

'In ten seconds, chaps, it will be five minutes to the hour. Five, four, three, two, one. There you have it. We'll press tits in half an hour.'

We were driven back to the dispersal hut close to our aircraft where we underwent a short briefing by Dean Nesbitt. Dean told us that we were to fly a wide, loose-V formation in sections of two. These sections were to stay together regardless. This was a formation the squadron had used in the Battle of Britain. When we reached the French coast, he would dispatch one of the sections to fly a line astern figure of eight behind the arms of the V to keep a lookout. As these aircraft would be expected to use more fuel than the others, he would send another section later to replace them. If he did a turn, the leaders of the section composing the V would slide underneath him and take up the same place on the other side. We were to maintain strict R/T silence until we reached the French coast and at ten thousand feet we were to turn up our oxygen to twenty-five thousand. I was flying No. 2 to John Weir. At the last Dean said:

'Freddy, your section will take the first roving search. Start your search as soon as the Wing Commander breaks R/T silence. Are there any questions?'

Nobody said a word. Then, Dean, looking down at his watch, said:

'All right, lads, you've just got eight minutes before we press tits. Let's go.'

We all rushed out excitedly, donned our parachutes and strapped ourselves into our aircraft. I had time to do my cockpit check a dozen times before anything happened. At exactly five minutes to, I saw the prop of the Wing Commander's Hurricane turning over and, in a cloud of smoke, his engine started. Then the propellors of all the aircraft on the field began to turn and soon the aircraft were taxiing out. One after the other each squadron took off.

We climbed slowly in good order into a cloudless sky over the sparkling ultra-marine blue of the English Channel flecked with white caps. With butterflies in my stomach, I saw for the first time the pointed bill of Cap Gris-Nez, and to the west of it, the curved jetty sticking out into the channel from Boulogne Harbour. We levelled off at twenty thousand feet and for the first time R/T silence was broken by Bob Tuck:

'Okay, chaps, keep your eyes open.'

70

We settled down into a wide V formation and Freddy's section began to weave behind us. Looking around, I was startled at the number of aircraft in the formation. Above us were the Spitfires, a squadron at every thousand feet up to twenty-seven thousand. The top squadrons were making smoke trails, and at this distance their dihedral wings made them look suspiciously like '109's.' Below us, like a mother hen with its brood, was a single four-engined Stirling bomber surrounded by squadrons of Hurricanes. Once we crossed inside the French coast, everybody in the squadron seemed to be weaving. John and I were at the tip of the V and every now and then I would be scared out of my wits seeing an aircraft on my tail, only to find after a quick turn that it was either one of our own doing the roving search or a Spitfire from God knows where. On one of these violent breaks I inadvertently pushed the stick forward and my engine cut. It seemed to stay out for an unbearably long time. Suddenly people began reporting enemy aircraft.

'109, seven o'clock!'

While I was looking at seven o'clock, the squadron turned, and I went sailing straight ahead. In an instant, I was miles from my squadron now on their way home. With my throttle wide I gave chase, kicking my tail out of the way from time to time to check the blind spot beneath it. Excited reports of diving 109's buzzed in my ear, and I felt sure that everyone was warning me. From high above an aircraft slowly spun down on fire, leaving a long black snaking trail behind it. Around me on all sides were black puffs from exploding heavy ack-ack shells. They looked so completely harmless in the brilliant sky. Up there I knew must be Messerschmitts, but to save my life I couldn't see them. It seemed as if I was hardly moving, and yet from the scream of my engine I knew I was 'balls out.'

Suddenly the distinctive voice of Bob Tuck came over the R/T, now languid and indifferent,

'We managed to get a brace or two. We'll be back in twenty minutes. Do put on the tea, we're simply parched.'

I thought: 'Tea. I'm glad you're all right. What about me?'

The last thing in the world I wanted at that moment was a cup of tea. After what seemed to be an eternity of weaving and searching, I crossed over the French coast, but not until I was over Dover did I draw abreast of my squadron.

It was all over, but to me it had been a complete shambles, a nightmare of whirling airplanes. When I landed, Dean Nesbitt came over and said sternly:

'Hughie, you're damned lucky to be back. What the hell were you doing trailing behind like that? You were a sitting duck.'

'Well, sir,' I explained, 'when the squadron turned, I was looking at seven o'clock where a 109 was reported, and as a result, I went straight ahead. After that, I was flat out trying to catch you. If you'd only done a turn, I could have cut the corner and caught up.'

Dean shook his head and drawled,

'Hughie, I've got a squadron to worry about. I have to leave stragglers to fend for themselves.'

As I hung my head dejectedly, he said softly:

'You're going to have to keep your eyes open, laddie.'

To us 'Sprogs,' Dean Nesbitt was the benevolent father figure. In mild amusement, he gently protected us from the wrath of the higher-ups. I knew he was right, but just the same it made me feel very much on my own.

Hart Massey, son of High Commissioner Vincent Massey, was a pituitary dwarf. I had known him at school.

As a man of twenty-five, Hart Massey was no taller than a boy of ten, but in other respects was perfectly proportioned. He was commissioned in the Air Force as an Intelligence Officer. His Air Force uniform was specially made, even the buttons in proportion. His first duty was to interrogate the pilots returning from this sweep.

Freddie Watson had never seen Hart and walked into the Dispersal Hut hot and weary. Hart approached him and said:

'What did you see on the sweep?'

Freddie Watson, seeing a little boy in Air Force uniform, said:

'Get lost, son, I'm tired. Why don't you run away and play with your blocks?'

When I told Freddie who Hart was, he was mortified and apologized profusely. Hart was used to this sort of thing; it just rolled off his back.

I was given a forty-eight hour leave. Usually John and I were released together, but we were short of operational pilots so I had to go alone.

We got the RAF scale of pay. As a Pilot Officer, I got twenty-two pounds a month. At Digby, my extra messing bill was thirteen pounds a month. Half the time I couldn't afford even to leave the station. As I had saved a little, I decided to get away anyway. I was tired of wandering around Nottingham cathedral. I felt like a little fresh air, so I decided to explore Skegness-on-Sea.

I threw some things into a bag and boarded the bus. A fine drizzle was falling when I arrived, and by the time I found a place to stay I was good and wet. I found a room at the Marine Hotel, and I was pleased to see that across the road in front of it just fifty yards inside the sea wall was a swimming pool. Determined to take advantage of all the facilities in spite of the rain, I donned my swimming trunks and went out to take a dip. On the first length of the pool, I got a mouthful of the chlorinated salt water. It almost made me throw up. The chilling breeze off the sea made me soon decide that I had had enough.

After dressing and finding that the rain had stopped, I set out to try to get to the beach. I found it a maze of barbed wire, studded with cement and iron obstructions erected in case of invasion. I took a stroll therefore down the avenue that bordered the sea. The souvenir shops had only the off-season choice of trinkets, so I sent Mother a holiday postcard. I soon discovered that Skegness had an RAF Initial Training School. Most of the pedestrians were aircrew trainees with the white flash in their caps, ever anxious to practice their salutes. After an hour of pretty solid saluting, I ducked into a movie.

It was pitch dark when I came out and steady rain was falling. The only sign of life was the occasional car that loomed out of the inky darkness, the masked headlights emitting a shimmering reflection on the wet pavement as it passed me by. Seeing no alternative, I decided on dinner, and, turning up my collar, set out for the Marine. I was the only occupant of the dining-room and after partaking of its indifferent fare, I went to my room and rolled up with a book.

I awakened next morning to a grey misty day. After breakfast, I concluded that this was a hopeless waste of my precious money, so I packed up my things, paid my bill and left. As I started down the waterfront road to the bus stop, a flight of sixty airmen rounded the corner and headed towards me. I took refuge in a pub. The bar was open and behind it stood the proprietor chatting with a small bald-headed man casually dressed in an open-necked shirt, sport trousers, and soft rubber canvas shoes. He had a large pint of beer at his elbow. With an expansive wave and a benevolent smile, he invited me to join him for a pint. Glad to have somebody to talk to, I gratefully accepted. Forthwith I was given a review of the life of Mr. John Johnson of Skegness. He was a self-made man, and proud of it. He had owned a few properties and had made a few quid in his day. Even now, he was doing pretty well. He was the owner of a chain of Fish and Chips shops in Skegness, the best in the country, and from these alone he was able to pocket a 'hundred quid a month.' He had travelled and been very impressed with the America's. I asked him if he would have a drink on me. On this occasion he said he would, ordering another pint of 'ruff.'*

Now happily committed to entertaining me, he rambled on. He had a son studying architecture at the University, and a daughter studying music. When he found that I had no firm plans, he insisted that when we finished this 'session' I go to lunch at his home.

I was taken to a modern-looking, two-story house with a central entrance. Once through the swinging gate, the walkway leading to the front door passed through a well-kept rose garden. Inside, Mr. Johnson proudly introduced me to his family. Frank, his son, my own age, was

* This I discovered was half bitter and half mild ale.

a very likeable friendly fellow. His precise Oxford accent was in sharp contrast to his father's Lincolnshire brogue. His daughter was no beauty but greeted me with warmth. She spoke with the same articulate precision as her brother. From the back reaches of the kitchen Mrs. Johnson appeared, whisking off an apron as she came at a busy pace in her woolly flat-heeled slippers. A few wisps of grey hair escaped from the bun at the back. As she welcomed me with a warm smile, her cheeks flushed even more, unprepared as she was for an unexpected guest. She insisted that it was no trouble, all she had to do was put on a few more potatoes. She invited me to spend the rest of my forty-eight-hour leave with them. This appeared to fit in perfectly with Mr. Johnson's plans; he was organizing an 'eeling' party and another hand would be welcomed. I inquired at lunch about eeling, and I was told that it was an age-old sport complicated to explain but easier to demonstrate as would be done later.

During the afternoon, I had a chance to become more acquainted with the Johnson family and the facilities of the house. At ten-thirty that night the eelers arrived. There was Mr. Muckleston, an old friend from Nottingham: Bill, an employee of Mr. Johnson's, and his red-headed, vacant-looking son, Ronnie. Bill and Ronnie had been working all afternoon preparing the tackle. They were old hands. Mr. Johnson supplied a sack of beer, and we were off.

We walked for about half an hour through wet grass to the edge of a stream. Mr. Johnson stationed us along the bank at intervals on little stools. Everyone but Mr. Johnson was supplied with a rod, a line, and a 'bab,' which consisted of worms threaded on strings all tied together. The idea was to lower the bab until it touched the bottom, and then with a gentle bobbing motion, raise and lower it a few inches up and down at that depth. We would be informed of a nibble by the gentlest of tugs. You had to raise the rod very, very gradually but steadily so as to land the catch. Too quick a pull would allow the eel to slip off. I asked the obvious question why not a hook. I was informed 'that would not be sporting.' Nothing happened for an interminable period of time. Mr Johnson, nursing the beer, acted as supervisor. Mr. Muckleston didn't take the job too seriously either, but Bill and Young Ronnie sat silently and methodically babbing. Frank and I relieved the boredom with whispered conversation. Frank had just remarked sarcastically that it was very peaceful, when Bill yelled:

'I got one, I got one, by gum.'

Something silver shimmered in the moonlight. Like a well-disciplined team, Bill and Muckleston dived at the spot where they had seen it fall. There was the sound of a struggle in the darkness, and yells of 'Look sharp.' 'Here he is.' 'Hold him.' 'I got him.' 'Oops!' with Mr. Johnson whimpering in the background, his speech now slow and slurred.

1 P/O H.C. Godefroy in flight in 401 Squadron Hurricane II
2 P/O H.C. Godefroy by his first Hurricane

3

3 S/L A. Deane Nesbitt, CO of 401 Squadron in Hurricane cockpit
4 401 Squadron pilots relax at a game of horseshoe

5   F/O E.L. Neal, P/O Ian Ormston
6   F/L R.W.A. Ivermee, the Adjutant of 401 Squadron

4

7   F/O H.A. Sprague of 401 Squadron

8   F/L Bruce Handburg and F/O "Moose" Fumerton

9   Practice scramble during a simulated gas attack — 401 Squadron

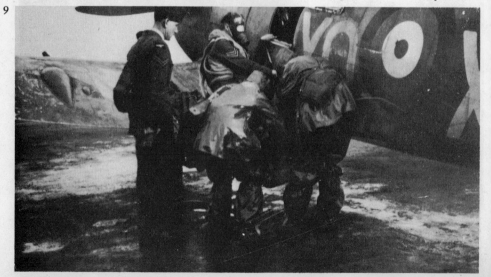

10 P/O H.C. Godefroy, 401 Squadron
11 Sgt Stan Thompson, 401 Squadron (killed 27 October 1941)

12 Spitfire VB of 401 Squadron testing guns

13

14

15

13 Device to carry groundcrew on Spitfire wing
14 F/O H.A. Sprague with his 401 Squadron Spitfire
15 Don Blakeslee, an American member of 401 Squadron who became a famous fighter leader and ace with the USAAF

16 P/O Ian Ormston and his 401 Squadron Spitfire
17 P/O Godefroys Spitfire VB, YO.R

18 P/O Godefroy points to bullet hole in his Spitfire

19 Godefroy's Spitfire — tail wheel repair

'Don't let 'im get away! Don't let 'im get away!'

For a moment I saw Bill's silhouette, hands upraised with the eel a wriggling flash of silver in the moonlight. The next instant it shot into the air like a wet cake of soap and fell only to be pounced upon by Muckleston. Soon Bill came up with it again. This time he threw it down and picked it up, threw it down and picked it up. In front of him was Muckleston on his knees, hands outstretched, mouth open, his head following the catch like a spectator at a tennis match. After numerous repetitions, it lay stunned. In a flash Muckleston grabbed it and threw it into the mouth of the bag that Ronnie had been holding open all this time with patient expectation. There was silence but for the sound of heavy breathing. Then Mr. Johnson:

'Well, lads, this ruff didn't get us drunk for nowt.'

After a while I got a few bites, but I either pulled too hard or not hard enough. It was an amusing evening, but I was glad when I finally got to bed having dutifully admired the catch wriggling in the kitchen sink while Mr. Johnson finished off the last of the beer.

Next morning I was treated to a hearty breakfast of bacon and eggs, a rare treat in wartime. Mr. Johnson explained that he had 'connections.'

My time was up, and I was obliged to bid farewell and many thanks to my host and hostess. I rumbled my way on the bus through the Lincolnshire countryside looking out the window. In this short time I had been lulled into the tempo of a middle-class Midland family. The pace was like that plodding of Clydesdale ploughing a straight furrow or the young woman with the baby carriage chatting with a neighbour at the garden gate. The lulling purr of the engine of the bus was abruptly drowned out by the crackling roar of a Merlin engine. A Hurricane zoomed over our heads and disappeared into the haze beyond. I was back. The bus ground to a stop, and the driver shouted:

'Digby, Sleaford.'

Jarred out of my reverie, I grabbed my bag and stomped off in front of the main gate. As I made my way to the Mess, it seemed I had been away forever. I quickened my pace as I felt a tickle of excitement. What had happened in the interval? It wasn't long before I discovered that I had really missed something.

The squadron had been on another sweep. One of the new pilots, Sergeant Jeff Northcott on his first sortie had had a terrifying experience. Flying as a Number 2, his aircraft was suddenly riddled by cannon and machine gun fire. One bullet opened up a V-shaped tear in his helmet. With a dead engine, streaming glycol, Jeff glided back across the Straights of Dover and landed in a field. It was rough terrain and the aircraft flipped over on its back pinning him in the cockpit, and burying his head up to the ears in mud. He struggled in vain to extricate himself and in the process strained his back. He was obliged to listen to the hissing of liquid dripping on the hot engine. He was sure it was petrol that would catch fire at any moment. He had pulled out his revolver to shoot himself at the first sign. After an agony of waiting, a farmer who had seen the crash dug him out.

Unaware of Jeff's predicament, the squadron had returned and landed at West Malling. Two pilots were missing, Jeff Northcott and Jeep Neil. There had been a lot of heavy flak, and nobody had seen any enemy aircraft. It was assumed, therefore, that they had been shot down by flak. It was after the squadron had returned to Digby and these two pilots had shown up later that the true facts of the engagement were brought to light. Jeep had been the only pilot to see the 109 that had hit Northcott. At the end of its attack it had pulled up in front of Jeep who gave chase. In the process he became separated from the formation and due to lack of fuel had landed at the nearest base, Manston, just inside the cliffs of Dover. When I heard all this, I button-holed Jeep Neil to get a first-hand account.

'Jeep,' I asked, 'what did he look like?'

'It was a 109F, Hughie, with the biggest black crosses that you've ever seen in your bloody life.'

'Did you get a squirt at him?'

'Yeh, I had a long squirt, but he rolled over on his back and went straight down. Let me tell you. There's no way you can catch a 109 in a dive with a Hurricane. Wait'll we get our Spitfires. We'll show the bastards.'

'Are we getting Spitfires?'

Jeep furtively turned to see if anybody was listening, then out of the corner of his mouth he said:

'You're goddam right, Hughie, and if you'll keep your mouth shut, I'll tell you something else. Inside of a month not only will we have Spitfires, but we'll be going South.'

Spitfires and a posting to 11 Group. I couldn't wait to get my hands on a Spitfire.

It was at this stage of my life that I gave in to the impulse to own a motorcycle. I rationalized that undertaking indebtedness to get some cheap transportation was justified. Visiting historic places of interest in England would keep me out of trouble. I bought a second-hand BSA machine with a pillion. It was free of oil and grease and looked in mint condition. When I inquired about the slack chain, I was told that all motorcycles that were well broken in had sway slack chains.

'Copy' and I were released on a forty-eight-hour leave. He offered to pay half the transportation costs. With one bag between us, we took off. We chose a secondary road in a northwesterly direction hoping that it would miss Lincoln. With no road map and all signs removed,

God only knows where we went. By dinnertime we found ourselves in a medium-sized town with a reasonable-looking pub. We decided to stop and spend the first night there as they had a double room.

After washing and brushing the road dust off our uniforms, we went down to the bar. As I had signed the pledge, I ordered a ginger ale, and Copy a pint of 'pony piss,' as we called the watered-down wartime draft beer. We took a table in the corner and settled down to observe. The regulars had already taken their favorite seats, and a young unattached buxom redhead was holding forth. She engaged us immediately in conversation. She kept up a steady stream of chatter while strutting about displaying her wares. We had dinner and returned to the bar. By this time the innkeeper was playing the piano, and two or three couples were dancing. The redhead button-holed me and got me out on the floor. While dancing, she told me that she too stayed at the inn and occupied the room three or four doors down the hall from ours. She whispered she would go to her room as soon as the bar closed and would leave her door unlocked, so I could get in if I wished.

In the course of the evening, she also managed to get Copy up on the floor despite his insistence that he couldn't dance. She took it upon herself to teach him. Finally the innkeeper called, 'Time, Gentlemen, please.' I told Copy that I was going to get a little fresh air before turning in. I felt very righteous that I had abstained. As I walked in the invigorating night air, I began thinking about the redhead. I had earned a little bit of comfort, and with this arrangement, if I walked quietly, I could accept the invitation without Copy finding out about it. I walked for a good three-quarters of an hour, then tiptoed upstairs and down the hall to her room. I opened the door to a darkened room, but with the hall-light beaming on the bed, I was able to make out the naked bodies of Copy and the redhead. Copy looked very uncomfortable.

The next morning I was a witness to Copy's soulful outcries of remorse. Nothing I could say seemed to console him. To add fuel to the fire, he had not used any protection. This was the way the Lord would punish him for his sin, he was sure he'd get a 'dose.' Finally, he agreed to get dressed and go to the nearest Service First Aid Station. We travelled to the centre of the town where I parked to make inquiries. We were given directions to a nearby Army Post that had a Station. At this point all attempts to start the motorcycle failed. Exasperated, we set out in search of a garage. We found one with a mechanic who agreed to help if we would bring the machine to the garage. When I returned to my motorcycle, a Bobby was standing beside it writing out a parking ticket. He refused to listen to any explanations. It cost me ten bob to get the motorcycle started, and it took the rest of the morning to get Copy treated. He wanted to get out of the place as quickly as possible, so we checked out and returned to Digby.

One month later a summons arrived ordering me to appear in Court to answer charges. Dean Nesbitt let me take my aircraft to the nearest RAF Station to argue my case. When I got to the Station, I discovered that RAF transport was non-existent, and the next bus to the county seat would arrive an hour after I was due to be in Court. Completely thwarted, I flew back to Digby. A week later, I received notice that the judge had fined me one pound in absentia. To add to my misery, while riding my motorcycle to the Dispersal Hut, the chain broke. I got rid of it, losing ten pounds in the process. I have never been tempted to own one since.

At dawn the following morning we took off for West Malling, for another sweep. It was a repeat performance of my first one, twenty-one squadrons of Spitfires and Hurricanes escorting six Blenheims. I was determined this time not to get detached from the squadron. Once again over France the formation turned into a confused blur. Suddenly Wing Commander Tuck's voice broke R/T silence:

'109's – six o'clock – BREAK!'

As I followed Johnny in a shuddering turn to the left, I saw below me a Hurricane streaming a long trail of glycol. The next second it burst into flames. I had to concentrate on staying on John's tail, which gave me very little chance to look around. The incident was soon forgotten, intent as I was on maintaining station.

After counting heads at West Malling, we found Copy was missing. The Wing Commander reported that he had seen him hit in the cockpit and later the plane burst into flames. Only then did I recall seeing the lone Hurricane streaming glycol, and realized who it must have been. Why had I not seen the attacker? That 109 must have been very close to me. Was I one of those people who just couldn't see? If this was the case, it was only a matter of time for me.

One evening in August, the BBC reported another piece of depressing news. Douglas Bader, the famous legless pilot, had failed to return after a sweep over northern France. The loss of the leader of the Tangmere Wing was a bitter blow indeed. Shortly afterward, a report came through Intelligence that for the first time the Luftwaffe had communicated with Fighter Command by radio: Bader was alive and safe on St. Omer Airdrome, and they would permit an aircraft carrying his spare legs unchallenged passage to drop them. Once more we were ordered to join the Wing at West Malling. We were to act as secondary cover to the formation that would drop the legs. As we waited in the briefing room, a different sort of optimism prevailed. For the first time, the Germans had done something similar to the acts of mutual respect that fighter pilots on both sides carried out in the First World War. German pilots at least seemed honourable men after all. I was

78

still enjoying this image of our adversaries when the briefing started.

Bader's legs would be carried by six Blenheims. After dropping the legs, the Blenheims were to bomb the airdrome.

'Oh, Christ!' a voice from the back exclaimed.

As if in answer, the order read

'This is total war, not a game of cricket.'

The Luftwaffe stuck to its word, but the Blenheims dropped their bombs anyway. I felt ashamed and mortified.

It was decided that Digby was becoming too congested and that the squadrons would have to be more widely dispersed. We were sent to a new satellite field nearby that would be called WC2 Wellingor. Formerly it had been a large farm centred around an ancient brick farmhouse. It had gabled windows and a red-tiled roof, a cobblestone yard separating it from the brick out-buildings. These structures were all contained within a high stone wall. The gate was closed by huge wooden double doors. The out-buildings became the airmen's quarters, and the farmhouse the officers' mess. We were to sleep in tents erected in a small apple orchard beyond the yard. A dispersal hut was constructed on the edge of the field around which our Hurricanes had to be dispersed each night. Refuelling was carried out by hand from twenty-five-gallon tins of petrol. A reserve supply of tins was stacked in the corner of the field.

An Army platoon guarded the field. The regiment was made up of draftees from the ghettos of Liverpool. Shortly after we moved to WC2, one of the guards stuck his bayonet through every petrol tin in the stack. A week later a bricklayer and helper from the 'Works and Bricks' department started building a twelve-by-twelve building to store the petrol cans. Despite the war, their union forbade them to lay more than one thousand bricks a day. We never saw the finished building. These two seemed to be having a perpetual tea break. All maintenance other than daily inspections was carried out at Digby.

We found it took a certain amount of ingenuity to be comfortable in a tent in the dampness of the Lincolnshire countryside. However, more casual forms of dress were allowed and complete freedom from the bullshit that was inescapable on permanent 12 Group stations like Digby. We were issued with collapsible camp beds, heavy canvas sleeping bags and canvas wash basins mounted on wooden tripods. Hot water was available in pails from the mess, and we washed and shaved over our canvas basins under the apple trees. The English had not imported the black fly, and their mosquitoes were comparatively civilized. Gnats were our only problem.

At Wellingor we were made to work hard. When not on sweeps as part of the West Malling Wing, we were on twenty-four-hour readiness. One flight of six pilots stayed in Dispersal from first light to noon when the other flight took over to finish at dusk. The sun rose about four-fifteen in the morning and set about eleven o'clock at night. Every second or third day the flights exchanged their period of duty, which meant that one flight at this time would come off duty at eleven only to be awakened at three in the morning so as to be dressed and fed and ready to work at four-fifteen.

If it hadn't been for Le Boeuf, our French Canadian batman, we would never have made it. Le Boeuf was a dark-haired determined little fellow who never smiled. He was stuck with the job of getting us out of bed. He was up to all our *'maudit naisiere.'* If the first warning didn't work, Le Boeuf resorted to brute force. When it was discovered that he was consistently managing to get John Weir and me on readiness on time, he was given the additional task of handling Bud Connell. The other batman had given up on Bud. Connell had had a longer exposure to military life than the rest of us; he was a graduate of RMC. He was not the usual swashbuckling RMC type. He liked to live well and relax. He always enjoyed a few good snorts when he came off readiness at night, and as soon as he finished his dinner, he would fall asleep. By 3.00 in the morning the only sign that suggested that he was living was shallow respiration. Le Boeuf took on his new task with a vengeance. Each morning he started by getting John Weir and me on our feet in the damp grass; then he would brace himself and stride into Connell's tent. Immediately there would be the sounds of a furious struggle.

'Get up, Goddamn hit!' Le Boeuf would be heard to shout as he burst through the flaps of the tent breathing hard, carrying Connell's sleeping bag. He would dive back in muttering to himself, and would come out dragging Connell by the feet. After he had rolled him two or three times in the dew, Bud would begin to move. When he finally got him sitting up, he would invariably exclaim with satisfaction:

'Tiens! Nobody beats Le Boeuf, not even Goddamn Connell.'

One morning John and I had wakened with Le Boeuf's rude treatment. After putting on our damp clothes and dousing the sleep from our eyes in our washbasins, we stumbled over to breakfast. We flopped in the back of a panel truck which rattled and bumped its way to Dispersal. Norm Johnson, the Flight Commander, while writing names on the readiness board said:

'Weir and Godefroy on first readiness.'

This announcement brought both of us to life. We ran out of the door to our aircraft where the riggers had dispersed them the night before. We taxied them back in front of Dispersal, put our helmets over the stick. Having plugged in the cord to the radio and the tube to the oxygen outlet, we hung our parachutes over the leading edge of the port wing with the straps hanging down, then ran as fast as we could for the Hut.*

The reason for our haste was that there were only five beds. Six pilots were on readiness. The last one in had to sleep on the floor.

We arrived back at the Dispersal Hut at the same time, and were fighting over the last bed when the 'Tannoy' blared out, '401 Squadron Red Section scramble.' John and I bolted out still half asleep, blaspheming the controller. One minute later we were roaring across the field in formation. The first indications on the controls that I had reached flying speed always made me forget any complaint. Smoothness of the air in early morning invariably cleansed my mind of everything but the consciousness of flight. The controller's voice sounded quite cheerful as he gave us a vector, and his clear precise order somehow emphasized the fact that we had the sky to ourselves. Ahead of us a grey blanket of cloud melted with the greenish blue line of the horizon. Ordinarily a formation leader like John would have had a chance to get the letters of the day before taking off. These letters were changed each day and were used by pilots to identify themselves as friendly aircraft if challenged by ground or sea forces. If challenged, the formation leader was to tap the letters out in Morse Code on the identification light on the belly of his aircraft. It was rare to be challenged by anybody but the Navy. As these letters of the day were top secret, they could not be transmitted by radio as our radio transmissions were monitored by the Huns. John was airborne without them.

In silence we followed our vector which took us straight to the east coast and out over the sea. The water was like a sheet of glass with a few patches of early morning mist here and there. Twenty miles out we passed a stationary vessel gently rolling in the swell. Beyond it the horizon merged with low cloud and haze. We must have gone about sixty miles when shapes began to appear. They were ships, hundreds of them, large and small, freighters, tankers, and large armed merchantment. Around this enormous convoy, turning and twisting were the ever vigilant destroyers, their guns bared suspiciously following us as we circled. It gave one an eerie feeling seeing all those ships quietly stealing through the mist on a breathless sea.

John looked over at me and said,

'Have you got them?'

I shook my head. He raised his eyes to heaven. At that moment we got a challenging series of flashes on the aldis light from the lead escort vessel. John did a gentle turn away from the convoy and gave them a belly side view of us, then hesitatingly reached to his light key and gave a couple of dots and a dash. Immediately he raised his hands to his ears,

---

* As you were expected to be airborne in a minute and a half, all these preparations were essential. Our best time from lying down in Dispersal to being airborne was forty-five seconds.

and ducking his head, closed his eyes. Every armed ship in the convoy opened up. In an instant the sky was full of black puffs, and enough curving orange Bofors shells and tracers to look like the twenty-fourth of May. The escort leader was taking no chances and had no intention of letting us come anywhere near the convoy without giving the letter of the day. John had only one recourse. We had to fly back to Digby and land and get them.

The first time I did a convoy patrol, I was very excited. I searched diligently, expecting at any moment to see a German raider. But after I had a dozen, each one-and-a-half to two hours long, with nothing to see but ships and sea, it became deadly dull.

As promised, every industrial city within the range of the German bombers took its turn at being blitzed. The ack-ack and the night-fighters were not hacking down enough, so we were sent up in Hurricanes to see what we could do.

The Hurricane was never designed for night-fighting. At eye level at night, there were two blue glows from the flaming exhaust stacks in front. A metal baffle-plate was designed to shield this light. It made very little difference. They sent twelve of us to fly singly over cities like Manchester during a raid. They would have a Hurricane circling at every five-hundred-foot level from eight thousand to perhaps fourteen thousand feet. One of our newer replacements was a lad named Tourney. On several occasions I had the misfortune of flying in the section behind Tourney in daylight formations. He was all over the sky, his slip stream constantly making it difficult for me to stay in formation on my leader. Every time I was sent on one of these night patrols, I found that I had Tourney either directly above me or directly below. I spent most of the time worrying where Tourney was. One night in this state of mind, I saw my first Hun. With my eyes feeling as though they were sticking out on stems, I was peered over the nose of my Hurricane past the flickering exhaust. A huge black cross flashed in front of me, and for a second I heard the sound of twin engines. I had narrowly missed colliding with a German bomber, God knows what type. It was a pitch black moonless night. I did a quick turn, but he was gone.

Wellingor was used as the night operations field. It was thought unwise to illuminate a flare path on the main station at Digby lest it attract intruders. Each night, a dim flare path was laid out on the grass at Wellingor, and on the upwind side a thing that was called a 'Chance' light. This light looked to me like an old mobile search light. The beam was directed horizontally down the flare path. Upon requesting permission to land, the flare path was turned on, and on final approach on came the chance light.

Now Squadron Leader Bon Corbett was stationed at Digby. Two of his younger brothers had been to school with me at Upper Canada

College. Bon had been shot down one time in flames, and burnt rather badly about the eyes. It had been rumoured Bon didn't have particularly good eyesight to start with, and the fire had not improved it. It was traditional in the RAF to tolerate the idiosyncrasies of anyone who had more guts than sense.

One night Bon was circling Wellingor, having finished a fruitless search for bombers over Manchester. Upon his request to land, the flare path was turned on. What Bon didn't know at the time was that a Junkers 88 was also in the circuit. On his final approach Bon called for the chance light with the Ju 88 in shooting distance behind him. The 88 pilot held his fire for Bon to become nicely silhouetted against the beam of the chance light, but he hadn't reckoned with Bon's night landing technique. As usual on his first attempt, Bon bounced thirty feet into the air and went around again. The 88 pilot, frustrated at finding that his target had disappeared before his very eyes, opened up with cannon fire. The only casualty was the poor little erk who was manning the chance light. He ran so fast for cover that he broke his leg. Oblivious to all these goings on, Bon serenely completed his circuit and bounced his way into a successful landing.

All mail from Canada came by boat. With the losses at sea there were often long periods of silence followed by stacks of mail all at once.

About this time, John Weir and I heard from home that the two cronies whom we had signed up with, Jim Jordan and Jimmy Scott, were in England. One day John and I on our way to West Malling for a sweep, ran into bad weather, and had to land instead at RAF Station Stradishall. By sheer chance we had landed where Jordan was stationed, and while waiting to be refuelled, who should walk up but Jimmy. In the course of our jubilant reunion, Jimmy told us that Scott was an observer in Coastal Command and stationed at St. Eval. They had regularly corresponded, but Jordan's last two letters had been unanswered. He was worried. We promised to try to wangle a trip to St. Eval to find out what was going on.

Some time later we managed a trip, and from Jimmy Scott's squadron mates discovered that his crew had been missing after a daylight torpedo attack on the battleship *Gneisenau* in Brest Harbour. The thought of flying into Brest Harbour at zero feet in a Beaufort torpedo bomber seemed like sheer suicide. With the battleship *Scharnhorst* in Brest as well, the Germans had converted Brest into a flak fortress. The chances of penetrating with an old Beaufort seemed slim indeed. Jimmy's pilot's name was Campbell. Years later I read that Campbell had been awarded a posthumous Victoria Cross, and that the French underground reported that a blond Canadian's body lay beside the body of the skipper, at the controls of the Beaufort that attacked *Gneissenau*.

9

SPITFIRES

It was an exciting day when it was announced we were to start picking up our Spitfires. First, each of us in turn was sent solo on an old Spitfire Mark II. Once we were familiar with the aircraft, we were sent to ferry in one of our new Mark V's which would have our squadron letters painted on them.

Unlike the Hurricane, the Spitfire Mark V was all metal. After the Hurricane, everything about the Spitfire seemed small and delicate. By comparison the wings seemed thin as razor blades, and the narrow undercarriage as sturdy looking as a couple of toothpicks. A door on the left folded down to allow access to the cockpit. With the seat in the up position, with the door locked closed, my shoulders touched each side of the cockpit, and to close the perspex top I had to lower the seat. A crowbar was provided, secured on the folding door to 'jimmy' yourself out in case of emergency. To get my eye level with the gunsight I had to lower the seat about as far as it would go. In this position, looking through the gunsight in front and the one-inch bullet-proof windshield, one saw the seemingly endless cowling covering the long liquid-cooled engine. Two twenty-millimetre cannon protruding from the leading edge of the wings provided visible evidence of its increased firepower. The additional four machine guns in the wings were not visiblé from the cockpit. Each cannon contained a hundred and fifty rounds of ammunition, giving six seconds of fire, and the machine guns had sufficient ammunition to give an additional six seconds. All the guns were mounted outside the arc of the propellor and were synchronized to provide a cone of lethal density between two and four hundred yards ahead of the gunsight.

When the engine was properly primed and switched on ready to start, a push on the starter button fired a cartridge which turned the engine over. There were four cartridges in the starter drum, and if you failed to start with the fourth cartridge, the drum had to be reloaded by the ground crew. The small landing flaps were activated by compressed air. They had two positions, up or down. As in the Hurricane, the undercarriage lever was on the right side of the cockpit. Because of space limitations in the cockpit, the ring grip control column was hinged just above the knees to give the lateral movement needed to activate the ailerons. The Spitfire Mark II had fabric ailerons but the Mark V had metal ones that considerably improved the rate of roll at high speed. It was even more tail-light than the Hurricane on takeoff. Because of the small rudder surface the Spitfire had a rudder trim that had to be put in the full right position on takeoff to keep it straight. To prevent the aircraft from skidding in flight, thus throwing the bullets off the line of sight, the rudder trim had to be adjusted at different speeds. Compared to those of the Hurricane, the beautiful elliptical wings looked so delicate that at first you wondered if they would snap off in a pullout. They were stressed to withstand a sustained nine G's, and a short snap of up to twelve. The aircraft would shudder very noticeably well in advance of a stall, useful when flying by the seat of your pants in combat. Because of the very small coolant radiator, the Spitfire was very prone to heating up when taxiing or idling on the ground. This had to be taken into account when planning formation takeoffs so as to get all the aircraft into the air before the engine temperatures went off the clock. Providing you made allowance for its peculiarities, once into the air with the wheels up, the Spitfire was superlative.

Shortly after we were re-equipped, the adjutant received a message that in two hours we would be inspected by His Royal Highness, the Duke of Kent. As bad weather had been predicted, the CO and both Flight Commanders were off on forty-eight-hour leave. F/O Blake Wallace was in charge. Blake's front partial plate was broken, leaving a great gap in his upper jaw. As a result, his lean features took on a sinister quality when he smiled, accentuating his need of a haircut. What with the twenty-four-hour readiness, punctuated by convoy controls and sweeps, we were all tired. Blake decided that the Duke of Kent would have to take us as he found us. As predicted, at eleven hundred hours camouflaged limousines arrived with Air Officer flags flying from their front fenders. Out in front of an unruly gaggle of unshaven Canadians in battle dress and 'Mae West's,' Blake Wallace welcomed His Royal Highness with a toothless grin. The handsome Duke, impeccably dressed in Air Commodore's uniform, was in sharp contrast to this motley gang of rogues. I noticed he took care not to let you get a good grip on his hand. He was accompanied by a covey of heavily-braided officers including the Air Officer Commanding Twelve Group, Air Vice Marshal Saul. They all looked at us with evident disapproval. The only ranking Canadian Officer among them was Group Captain Campbell, who nervously tried to promote light conversation. After a brief visit to the Dispersal Hut, the Duke announced that he would 'see the men's quarters.' Blake showed him the men's quarters, and the Duke opened every door in the two-story brick building in which they were housed. He caught one fellow with his pants down sitting on the 'john'. Not knowing what else to do, the man stood up with his pants still at half-mast. It seemed to Blake that he must be looking for something, and being thirsty himself, at an appropriate moment whispered to the Duke:

'Sir, would you like a drink?'

The Duke's eyes twinkled.

'That's a very good idea.'

In the Officers Mess, over a few drinks, the mood of our visitors improved appreciably. On leaving, the Duke commended Blake warmly for his state of preparedness. The whole squadron was stood down and given a forty-eight-hour pass.

Herbie Norris, the Chief Canadian Administration Officer at Digby, had more contacts in London than Mackenzie King. He reserved the entire sixth floor of the Park Lane Hotel for the squadron.

Just at this time I received a letter from Peggy Hodge informing me she had received a proposal of marriage from a very nice American boy with farms. On the recommendation of her guardian, she had decided to accept. This news came as a shock. The last remaining connection with my carefree boyhood days had been severed, the umbilical cord which still carried happy memories of a distant land undisturbed by this life-and-death struggle. I had to admit it was the sensible practical thing to do, for a mere girl, orphaned by two great wars, and a survivor of a U-Boat sinking at sea. I consoled myself she could now live in peace and security. I wrote, giving her my best wishes and hopes that she would be blessed with a long productive marriage. The squadron 'bash' in London was a welcomed diversion.

The bar at the Park Lane was a popular London meeting place. A group of us decided to have a glass of sherry before lunch. Most of the places at the bar were already taken, and seeing a gap beside a blond Flying Officer, I squeezed in. As I did, the officer turned, and I saw his face. It was a twisted mass of scar tissue. I did my best to pretend that I hadn't noticed. Somebody at one of the tables shouted:

'Hillary.'

'Yes.'

'Do come and join us. I want you to meet a friend of mine.'

[Later I discovered that this was Richard Hillary, the fighter pilot who had been so badly burnt, and the author of the splendid book, 'The Last Enemy.' Granted his request to return to action, Hillary was killed in a night fighter.]

As if by way of contrast, his place at the bar was taken by the most striking girl I had ever seen. She ordered a glass of sherry. She had blonde hair casually tossed in loose waves, and large limpid eyes. She had a faultless peachy complexion and full sensuous lips. She was dressed in a smartly tailored suit over a white silk blouse open at the neck. She wore tan gloves which matched the high-heeled spectator pumps.

The girls from England whom I had met in Canada had left me less than interested. Any family adventurous enough to leave the 'realms' for our rugged country seemed to me to produce the same kind of girl. Straight hair, usually cut in a boyish bob; dressed, if anything, to hide rather than accentuate her sex; the strong-armed, piano-legged captain of the field hockey team at Bishop Strachan school was typical. Having never expected to be interested in English girls, I was completely surprised by the girls of London. Despite the severe wartime restrictions limiting the production or importation of fineries, they always looked titillatingly piquant. This girl stood out among her kind and caused my nostrils to flare and sent the blood coursing to the groins. To the amusement of my mates, my naive advances were coldly ignored.

When I joined my friends at a table, I was told that this was the celebrated London 'Blackie.' She would take you for everything she could get and leave you the moment she found it to her advantage. There was no use trying to ply her with liquor; she had hollow legs and hadn't met the man yet she couldn't drink under the table. I was advised to leave her alone no matter how much I might be tempted. Looking at her, I found this almost impossible to believe.

The sixth floor of the Park Lane Hotel was well suited to our Squadron needs. All the rooms had interconnecting doors which we left open. It was easy therefore to find the centre of activity by walking through the suites without going out into the hall. The arrival of an entire squadron of pilots in London was rather unusual in 1941, and it had not gone unnoticed. Whenever we ventured out into the hall, we encountered fashionably dressed women, usually in pairs, who claimed to have an engagement with someone whom the desk clerk thought might be up here. After being told that there was nobody up here but us, and being invited to join our party, they demurely accepted.

Between those girls and the ones that were special guests of the more seasoned veterans, we were soon outnumbered. Nobody asked whom you knew, what school you had gone to, your religion, whether you were married or footloose and fancy free. Nobody had any name but their first. None of the girls encouraged anyone to become too curious about where they came from either. One amusing incident particularly stands out in my memory.

Johnnie McCall, a chunky slow-talking deliberate sort of fellow, had taken his tunic off and left it over the back of a chair in his room. Having been where the action was, he wandered back through the interconnecting doors to his own room badly in need of a 'squirt.' There he found a girl all by herself. She instantly began telling him how handsome he was. In his wildest dreams Johnnie had never thought of himself as being handsome. He had rugged pudgy features with an unmanageable mop of black hair and a heavy beard. He always looked as if he needed a shave. He took a look around the room and noticed that his tunic was not in the same position as he had left it. Without a word he walked over to his tunic, pulled out his wallet and found it empty.

He carefully rearranged his tunic, stuffed his empty wallet in his hip pocket, walked to his bag and extracted his Smith and Wesson .45. Slowly he approached the girl and fixing her with his beady little eyes, said:

'I'll give you five.'

Nervously she stated that she had never been so mortified in her life. Did he think for one minute that she would take something? This would certainly have to be reported to his Commanding Officer.

'One.'

'How dare you threaten me, you brute.'

'Two.'

By the time Johnnie got to four she handed over his money.

With his revolver hanging over his trigger finger, he carefully counted his money, and finding that it was all there, he carefully laid down the gun, took the girl firmly by the arm and, leading her to the door, said:

'Make tracks, chippy.'

After my recent experience with hard liquor, I warned everyone that nothing would pass my lips stronger than sherry or light lager. In company like this I felt definitely over my depth. Painfully aware of my inexperience, and being cold sober, I decided on the following strategy: I was not going to become involved.

I would get a glass, which I could nurse while walking with one hand behind my back and making noncommittal remarks.

I was just beginning to enjoy my new role as a detached man of good will, when the party settled down to more serious things. The crowd thinned, and I found myself alone with an attractive blonde called Penelope.

'I've never been up on this floor before,' she said. 'This is an awfully attractive room. What sort of room did you get?'

Not thinking of the consequences, I replied,

'Oh, very nice really; would you like to see it?'

'I'd love to,' she said.

When we reached my room through the interconnecting doors, she exclaimed, 'Oh, isn't this cozy! Do you mind if I use your facilities?'

'Please do,' I said.

With increasing uncertainty, I noticed that she closed and locked the interconnecting door.

I waited nervously while she was in the bathroom, painfully aware that I had overplayed my role, and I was anything but the suave confident blade that I had been portraying. While I was still wondering what to do with the wretch, she suddenly emerged from the bathroom stark naked. As I stood there panic-stricken, she happily proceeded to remove my clothes. I was relieved to find that she found me physically adequate. Before I had a chance to catch my breath, we were in bed. I needn't have worried about not knowing what to do. She showed me. I had always prided myself in keeping myself reasonably fit. My father was a health nut, and had all of us doing exercises in the morning before breakfast. The only thing that ever brought me to the point of total exhaustion was rowing in an eight in the Canadian Grande Challenge. But this was something else again. She had an unending repertoire of sexual gymnastics. I was in bed with what I concluded must be a nymphomaniac in the pink of condition. She had a nice even set of teeth, and from time to time she had the alarming habit of baring them in a vicious grimace as if she was about to take a large bite out of some part of my anatomy. At the last moment she would fall short of it and give me a series of little nips as though she were de-fleaing me.

After what seemed like hours, when she had me feeling as though I was about to black out, she said:

'Isn't this fun! I could go on like this forever. Let's see if I can't jolly us up once more.'

I didn't think I could stand anybody to touch me down there with a feather. I made the excuse that I was just convalescing from a bout of double pneumonia, and the doctor had warned me not to overtax my strength. I expressed the hope that when my recovery was complete I might be in better form. With that she condescended to put on her clothes and leave.

When I looked at myself in the mirror the next morning, I was not pleased. Through two bloodshot eyes I studied my pale waxy features which made me think of the portrait of Dorian Grey. Any nice girl who clapped eyes on me would be able to know instantly where I had been and what I had been doing. I spent a long time that morning polishing my shoes and buttons, and brushing off my uniform. Even after a good long soak in the bath, I still seemed to reek of Penelope's perfume. I doused myself all over with after-shave lotion, got dressed and went down to breakfast. When asked where I had disappeared to last night, I replied that I had gone to bed.

Al Harley, a classmate who had joined our squadron, was older than I, married, and always seemed to have something productive to do with himself through the long hours on readiness. He had already suggested that I take up photography. I had had a pretty good course in photography at Engineering School but knew nothing about the practical aspects. Harley had obtained permission for us to use the equipment in the station photographic lab where he had shown me how to develop film and print enlargements. He had told me what sort of camera he thought I should get to start off with, but up to this point I had thought I couldn't afford it. Now I realized the wisdom of his suggestion. After breakfast, I set out in search of a camera shop. In Regent Street I found a shop that specialized in everything from spectacles to the most sophisticated German cameras. Inside, everything was so highly priced that at first I thought I had better limit myself to a pair of dark glasses. I tried a pair. I looked like one of the triggermen in the current George Raft gangster movies. Finally, one of the attendants noticed me and informed me that they did have good cameras that were not as expensive as the ones on the purple velvet. He produced just the thing, a box-like secondhand camera in guaranteed perfect working condition. It had an F 3.5 lens with the capability of accurate focusing, with a good range of shutter speeds. Yes, it came with a leather case with a shoulder-strap attachment. It looked much better on me than the glasses, so I took it. I was afraid to buy film as I still had to pay my hotel bill. I spent the rest of my forty-eight-hour leave walking around pretending to take pictures of bombed-out buildings. I was glad to leave London behind me and return to the simple comforts of my tent under the apple trees.

Strangely enough, Cecil Beaton was waiting for us on our return. Cecil had made a name for himself with his unusual portraits of the Royal Family. He took some of them they say while standing on the mantelpiece. He had been appointed Court Photographer. His portraits lacked the regal formality of previous studies, and had a cleverly composed 'folksy' quality about them. Al Harley and I were fascinated with the man. He was much more interested in photographing the lowly sergeant pilots. Unlike many Englishmen with aesthetic interests, he was easily approachable and friendly. There was a dithery sort of flair about the way he worked.

'Oh, please,' he might say. 'Don't button up your Mae West. I want to take you just as you are.'

He insisted he knew nothing about photography. He preferred to think of himself as an artist. He concentrated on composition and went to endless trouble to catch the character and mood of his subjects. When he realized how interested Al Harley and I were in his work, he invited us to visit his studio in London.

My name came up on the list as Orderly Officer again. This meant that for twenty-four hours I was grounded. On this occasion, an additional chore was added. I was to act as Adjutant of a funeral parade. A sergeant pilot from 402 Squadron had gone straight in, and the remains had been reported as a shovel job. At the appointed hour I took command of the funeral parade, marshalled it in standard order and handed it over to an RAF Squadron Leader 'Admin' Officer. Besides Flight Lieutenant Cochran, our Padre, and the deceased, I was the only other Canadian in the outfit. As we set off slow march to the beat of a muffled drum, a light drizzle began to fall. Ahead, behind the commander of the parade, a flag-draped coffin was carried on the shoulders of six airmen. We were led to a fenced-in plot on the perimeter of the station where a few wooden crosses marked it as the station burial ground. As we marched along, I began wondering if I'd ever seen this lad before. I had not recognized his name. When we got to the entrance, the Squadron Leader opened the gate to let the parade through, closing it again behind us. When we were assembled at the graveside, I noticed a single little WAAF outside the gate. With cap in hand she peered through the fence, her hair wet and straggly from the rain. I caught the Padre's eye and gave a quick nod of my head towards the gate. When he looked around and saw her, he closed his Bible, walked solemnly over and led the girl tenderly by the arm to the graveside. Every eye was on her as she sobbed softly through a tightly held handkerchief, her eyes red and brimming with tears. She was the only person there who gave a damn. From the start of the service, the Padre seemed to be totally oblivious of military protocol. In a soft reassuring voice he spoke directly to her, his tone full of compassion and sympathy. The service seemed such a stark contrast to this military order. When the Padre finished speaking, the sharp staccato voice of the Squadron Leader barked out an order and, as the coffin was lowered beneath the ground, the rifle contingent fired a twenty-one gun salute. Again the Squadron Leader's voice rang out, each word enunciated precisely and sharp as a pistol shot:

'Right turn, in column of route, by the left quick march.'

Off we went through the gates to the beat of an unmuffled drum, leaving the Padre and the little girl standing by the graveside in the misty rain.

As it drew closer to the time when our Squadron would join the Biggin Hill Wing, excitement mounted. It was decided to have a dinner dance at the Mess 'Canadian style' in our honour. Herbie Norris took charge, and by judicious scrounging produced a dinner menu fit for the gods. A full dance orchestra was also procured. Partners were going to be imported from London.

I had had my fill of London girls, so I was determined to make different arrangements. The young girl who had the job of station master at the local railway station seemed to be a well brought up, unsophisticated little thing. I thought that squiring her around would be a sure way of staying out of trouble so I asked her to come.

She seemed quite pleased with the invitation and phoned her father straight away to get his permission. I was now faced with the problem of how to get her there and back. Service transportation for a Pilot Officer was out of the question. George Elliott had bought himself a little sports car. After I discovered he was not taking anybody and was going to play the field, I pleaded with him to let me borrow it. After much coaxing, he finally agreed.

With my boots and buttons gleaming, and my newly cut hair slicked down, I set out in George's car with the pleasant anticipation of an uncomplicated evening. I met the girl's parents, and on our departure I found it pleasantly reminiscent of earlier days when her father informed me that he expected me to have her back before midnight.

'I certainly will, sir,' I said.

She looked pretty as a picture. She had on a long dress of a sheer material with an open neck, gathered at the waist. When she was doing the job at the station, she usually had her hair pulled back out of the way and held in a pony tail with an elastic. On this occasion her hair fell around her head in loose soft curls. Her mother threw a white lacy shawl over her shoulders, gave her a kiss, and off we went. Fortunately it was a nice warm evening, and rain was not predicted. In the half hour that it took us to drive to Digby, she excitedly plied me with questions about the arrangements. It was refreshing to be with somebody again naive enough to look at this sort of thing with anticipation.

As soon as we stepped into the dining room where the dance was to be held, we were surrounded by the fellows on the stag line. All the pilots knew her. At one time or another, you had to go through Sleaford Station, if you were at Digby. I didn't mind people like Johnny Weir and Al Harley, but there was Freddy Watson with a big grin on his face, and Rocky St. Pierre, of all people. He was supposed to be training on night fighters. I should have known he wouldn't have missed a party like this. There he was, salivating at the mouth as usual, methodically undressing her with those big black lecherous eyes. Determined to protect her from these scoundrels, I stood by her in close attendance.

'What'll you have to drink, my dear?' asked Freddy Watson.

Before I had a chance to say I would look after that, she replied,

'I'll have a Singapore Sling, please.'

'What in God's name is that?' I interjected.

'I don't know really; I read it in a book, and it sounded so romantic.'

'I'll get it,' said Freddy, striding towards the bar.

While I was watching Freddy, painfully remembering what he had done to me some time ago, Rocky St. Pierre slipped in beside her and asked her to dance. As I watched them on the floor, it was very obvious that she was a good dancer. For the rest of the evening they never left us alone for a minute. I managed to get only a couple of dances with her, and each time someone cut in. She was much more popular than the imports from London. Knowing Freddy, I thought she'd had enough to drink after the first one, so I purposely avoided offering her any more. Not so with the rest of them. Each time she finished a dance, there was somebody standing with another Singapore Sling. I tried to interest her in a little food, but she said she wasn't a bit hungry and was having far too good a time to stop for that.

By 11:30 she was well relaxed and conscious that she was the centre of the stage. Each time she was on the floor she made a real exhibition of herself to the delight of all. Realizing that somehow I had to put a stop to this, I said,

'I'm terribly sorry, but we'll have to go. I promised your father I'd have you back before midnight, and it's a good half hour's drive from here.'

'Oh, don't be a killjoy,' she remonstrated. 'I haven't even had a chance to dance with Freddy yet.'

It was almost midnight before I got her to come. At first, I drove in silence, wooden-faced with righteous indignation.

'Hughie, I've had a simply marvellous time. Thank you very much indeed,' she said softly.

My mood softened. After all, she had done no harm and obviously had enjoyed herself. As I followed the narrow twisting road between the hedgerows, I began telling her about the various fellows and what part of Canada they came from. Suddenly the engine stopped, and I was forced to pull over to the side into a bye.

'What in God's name is the matter with this thing?' I blurted out.

With an impish grin, she giggled:

'I'll tell you what's the matter. I've got the keys,' and she jingled them in front of me.

'What did you do that for?' I growled.

'Because I want you to make violent love to me right here.'

'Has anybody ever made love to you before?' I asked.

'No, but there's got to be a first time, and this is going to be it!'

Before I knew what was happening, she threw her arms around me and smothered me with moist kisses.

The moment I had a chance to come up for air, I said: 'I'm not going to do anything of the sort. The only reason you're saying that is because you're tiddly. Besides, I haven't got any protection.'

'What do you mean, "protection"?'

'There, you don't even know what you're doing. Never mind, it's far too complicated to explain. It's bad enough for me to be bringing you home in the state you're in, let alone your father finding out in six months that you're pregnant as a yard dog.'

Finally, when she realized I meant what I said, she gave me the keys back, and we continued on our way. When I pulled over in front of the garden gate, I gave her one last kiss, and with her long dress flowing behind her, she ran up like an excited little girl to the front door.

'She is a cute little thing,' I thought to myself. 'I wonder if her father will ever let me take her out again.'

I had no intention of waiting around to find out, and took off in a cloud of dust.

Next morning, being in much better shape than the rest, I was put on first readiness. At about 11:00 the telephone rang, and I was told that someone wanted to speak to me.

'Pilot Officer Godefroy speaking.'

An angry English male voice shouted, 'What did you do to my daughter last night? I want to see you outside the front gate in half an hour, young man.'

With a crash he slammed the receiver down in my ear.

Not knowing what to make of it, I asked to be relieved from readiness, saying that I had to meet someone. As I walked toward the old wooden gates of Wellingor, I wondered to myself what on earth she had said to her father when she got home. I knew one thing. I had used every bit of self-control I had, and I had done everything I thought was humanly possible to comply with her father's instructions. I felt bitterly disappointed in the wretch. I could only think he had blamed me for keeping her out late, plying her with liquor, and for all I knew, trying to rape her. I was determined to set this matter straight. I waited in front of the gates for a full hour, and nobody showed up. Finally, I went back to the Mess. Nobody seemed to be interested in where I had been, and I didn't volunteer any information. In my own mind, I knew one thing for sure — I would never ask that girl out again as long as I lived.

[Fifteen years later I was talking to one of the pilots who survived the war, who was in the Squadron at the time. In the course of our reminiscing, he asked me if I had ever discovered who it was that called me that day. When I told him that it was the girl's father, he burst into laughter. 'No, it wasn't, you ignorant clot, it was Bill Ivy!' Bill Ivy was our Adjutant who had emigrated from England before the war and had joined the RCAF. He spoke with a strong English accent. What a prude she must have thought I was.]

That part of the summer of 1941 which the Squadron spent at Wellingor has left me with many happy, carefree memories. In preparation for going south, the complement of pilots was built up to the maximum. The arrival of people like Omer Levesque, Jimmy Fiander and others brought a new sparkle to life. Omer thought about nothing else but flying, and talked about it constantly in half English half

French. Jimmy Fiander was a quiet meticulous sergeant pilot who looked about seventeen. Dean Nesbitt was the catalyst who blended us into happy unity. With a well-balanced combination of discipline and reason, he saw to the training of all the new pilots and made them an integral part of the unit.

Not all the Squadron would be coming with us to Biggin Hill. Le Boeuf the batman, Gallagher the cook, and Phillip the barman, had to stay behind. Only the pilots, the ground crew, the Adjutant and the Engineering Officer would move. The personnel at Biggin Hill would supply us with all other services. At this point a signal arrived awarding Dean Nesbitt the Distinguished Flying Cross, and to everyone's disappointment, he was posted home for a rest. Norm Johnson was promoted to Squadron Commander.

To add to the uncertainty resulting from this change of leadership, Prime Minister Mackenzie King paid a visit. We had all been ashamed of his middle-of-the-road policy on conscription. We felt we needed someone who could convince all Canadians that this was not just another British imperialistic war but a last ditch struggle for the survival of every country in Europe. Safe within the tight security afforded to a Commonwealth leader, he seemed to us to have come for no other reason than morbid curiosity. He made a bellicose speech in the British House of Commons which won him a standing ovation. He said exactly what the British and our other allies wanted him to say. We looked on it as nothing but a series of hollow promises from the Peace Tower in Ottawa, protected from bombs by two thousand miles of sea. We were relieved when he went home and left us alone.

10

BIGGIN HILL

With us at Biggin Hill were two experienced RAF fighter squadrons, 609 and 72. Our wing leader was Jamie Rankin, a Scotsman from Edinburgh. One of the first people to walk into our Dispersal Hut after we landed was Moose Evans. Moose, now the only Canadian in 609 Squadron, had been on the same course with me at Borden. The only other Canadian in 609, Larry Robillard, had just gone missing. Moose told me that his parents had been scared out of their wits reading a report in the paper. It told of the hair-raising adventures of one of the fellows with us at Borden who had just returned from the war-torn skies of Northern Europe. This lad had copped out on his first sweep. In an interview upon arriving home, he told of many blazing dogfights. During one, he said, he had seen Moose Evans go down in flames. It took Moose several telegrams to reassure his parents he really was alive and well.

At first, mess life at Biggin Hill reminded me of boarding school. With the exception of Jamie Rankin, who spoke to everybody in his soft Scottish brogue, the rest of the mess could be divided in two groups, the Sprogs and the Old Guard. We were the Sprogs, and everybody else was in the sixth form. The polite reserve with which they mingled with us bordered on aloofness. They had their own private jokes and jargon that went right over our heads.

Our sleeping quarters were dispersed at some distance from the mess. Initially, we spent most of our time there. I found that I had an English batman all to myself. Giles was a most unmilitary-looking, bald-headed man of about forty-five. He had been in service as a 'Gentleman's Gentleman' before being drafted. He remained with me the whole time I was with the Biggin Hill Wing. Never in my life, before or since, have I been looked after with such meticulous care. He was not only a personal servant, he was a secretary, a purchasing agent, and an expert scrounger. My personal effects ceased to be my things, they became 'our things.' Worn-out socks, and underwear either disappeared and were replaced, or repaired without my saying a word.

From the point of view of organization, the moment you touched down at Biggin Hill, you knew you were on a front line operational station. Everything was stripped for action. There was only one objective — to control, maintain and cater for fighter squadrons. Every member of the team was proud of the Wing, and it came first. There was no time wasted. The first day we arrived we went out on a sweep. I was in on it, but before I arrived at the coast my engine packed up, and I had to limp back to base. After a long impatient wait, the Wing returned, and I was able to hear of the various combats. The Squadron had drawn its first blood — Blake Wallace had destroyed one and damaged another.

Further action was interrupted by the weather; but the Squadron, having contributed to the Wing's score of victories, had come up in the eyes of the others. An invitation was issued to play rugger. Having played a lot of Canadian football, I turned out in spite of knowing nothing about the game. Bill Igo, a controller, was the team captain. He explained the rules to me. When my questions became too long and complicated, Bill said:

'Never mind, Godefroy. Just tackle the fellow with the ball.'

After the first fifteen minutes of play, he came over to me and said, 'Godefroy, for God's sake, when you tackle a man, you're not supposed to kill him. When you bring a man down, he has to drop the ball, and you're supposed to let him go. If you keep on like this, you're going to be sent off.'

A trap shooting competition was organized. Sergeant Stan Thompson stole the show. He was an expert duck hunter from the Midwest and gave a faultless performance shooting clay pigeons holding the gun with one hand. They discovered that Hughie Merrit, a short, burly ex-policeman was a good snooker player. Another of the controllers was the Mess champion, and he challenged Hughie to a game. The whole Mess turned out to watch. Volunteer snooker was decided upon, and the champion offered to break. He scattered the balls all around the table. Before he had a chance to get another shot, Hughie Merrit scored 90 points. By the time the week was up we were looked upon as part of the Wing.

Jamie had been very anxious to get his new squadron into action, but it wasn't until 27th October that the weather became sufficiently fine for a wing sweep. Most of the potential targets on the French coast were obscured by low cloud, making it useless to send out a bomber force. After much pleading from Jamie, Eleven Group authorized a single sortie by the Biggin Wing.

A new battle formation had been designed which was thought to be more suitable to offensive operation. In climbing towards France from England, the squadrons flew in three lines of four aircraft. On reaching our designated altitude and while flying a straight course, each section of four was to fly a loose formation with the fourth man in each section on the outside. This lent for better visual coverage of the blind spot astern. If the leader wanted to make a sudden turn all aircraft in each section followed their leader in line astern. The section on the outside of the turn crossed over the top of the lead section, and the section on the inside crossed underneath. The best place from which to attack is from out of the sun. At twenty thousand feet on a clear day it is almost impossible to look directly into the sun for long. So that each squadron would be looking into the sun from a different angle, the squadron which was flying top cover had to station itself above the lead squadron on the side away from the sun; the squadron flying bottom cover stationed itself below and near the sun. This formation was used until the end of the War.

As this was to be a casual 'saunter' over enemy territory, Jamie just called up our Dispersal and said we were to be airborne as a Wing in ten minutes. For a short time panic reigned. However, a list of pilots was soon posted, and we all managed to get off on time.

Over England the weather was clear and behind Jamie Rankin, we climbed towards the French coast. Just before we reached our destination, Norm Johnson, our new Squadron Commander, and Jeff Northcott both had to turn back because of engine trouble. Bud Connell, the designated Deputy Squadron Commander, took over. We were flying the top cover position. Before we reached the French coast, the controller departed from the usual form of letting the Wing Leader break R/T silence. He called up reporting fifty plus over Ostend, fifty plus over St. Omer, and fifty plus over the Pas de Calais. In spite of having logged a fair amount of operational time, I still hadn't seen a Messerschmitt. I had often heard the unruffled voice of the controller reporting large gaggles of enemy aircraft in this manner, so I wasn't impressed. Besides, I was flying with a highly experienced Biggin Wing and didn't have to worry. As we passed over Dunkirk we got a few puffs of red marker flak that could be seen for miles.

'Okay, chaps,' said Jamie, 'On your toes. There's the marker flak. They must be about.'

He did a turn into the sun but Bud Connell didn't cross over soon enough so we got behind. In order to catch them, we all had to fly line astern with our throttles wide open. Suddenly I began to feel uncomfortable. It was as though a sixth sense suddenly told me that all was not well. Looking out to the right I saw what I thought were sparks coming out of my engine. This was a fine time for something like this to happen, I grumbled. For a moment I watched them, listening for a sound of malfunction. Then suddenly I realized that the sparks were going forward not backward! 'TRACER!' I pulled the stick back in a wild break out of the formation. Looking back, I was just in time to see Brian Hodgkinson behind me roll slowly over, flames pouring from his engine, and a Messerschmitt pass below me within yards of my tail, his nose and wings rippling with fire. Ten voices scream on the R/T at once:

'For God's sake, break, 109's!'

'I'm hit. I'm on fire.'

'Bail out, you fool.'

'My tail's gone. I'm bailing out.'

It was complete pandemonium, but it lasted only for a minute. I was in a tight turn, and I was alone. Looking up, I saw above me fifteen 109's all circling like a flock of vultures. Looking behind there was one trying to turn inside me, shooting fingers of tracer. Beside me was another in the process of going by, fishtailing to try to slow down to get behind. The ones above came down in pairs, one taking over where the other left off. Turning and twisting, I kept firing at everything that went in front. Two peeled off from above and attacked head on. I flew straight at them, firing back. They went by on either side like rockets spitting flame. With my thumb on the button I heard the sickening hiss that indicated that I was out of ammunition . A cold sweat broke out all over. For an eternity I turned and twisted avoiding attackers. With the tendency to hold my breath while watching tracers reaching for me with the constant force of G in the shuddering turns, I was forced to gasp for breath. I was getting nowhere: I had to try to get out. Another was coming down behind. I turned my aircraft tighter and tighter to keep ahead of the tracer. Then just when he was about to break off his attack, I pulled the stick back into my guts and kicked my aircraft into a spin. From twenty-five thousand feet I let it wind K.B. Wilson style. On the way down I opened and closed the throttle to give black puffs of smoke to make my pursuers think I was on fire. At about fifteen thousand feet I brought it out of the spin, but continued down in a spiral dive, balls out. As the speed built up, the aircraft began buffeting and shaking as if it were going to fall apart. At ten thousand feet I started a pull out and pointed towards England. I could feel the blood draining from my head from the G. I levelled off at wave top height and ran for home. The balloons and the cliffs of Dover looked like the pearly gates. As I throttled back and made my way to Biggin, for the first time I began wondering how the others had fared. I recalled again Brian Hodgkinson going down in flames, then I remembered the screams on the R/T. There must have been more.

As I taxied over to the Dispersal, I could see that two other aircraft had landed before me, Bud Connell and Al Harley. Harley was just walking into Dispersal with his parachute over his shoulder. As I shut down, my rigger jumped up on the wing and asked excitedly: 'Did you get any, Sir?'

'I don't know for sure,' I said pensively. 'I fired at least at a dozen. Did I pick up any holes?'

He jumped down and went over the aircraft carefully.

'Not a one.'

I sat in the aircraft for a long time, benumbed. It was unbelievable that so many could have shot at me without putting a single hole in the aircraft. As I relived the moment of combat, hackles prickled my scalp and the sweat felt cool on my back. A hurly-burly of black crosses and swastikas flashed before my eyes with gleaming yellow spinners spewing tracer that clawed at me on every turn.

This was no joust bound by the rules of chivalry. I had never witnessed such persistent savagery. They were out to kill us by any means possible. No quarter, it was either us or them. But now I had seen and knew the enemy. I could turn inside them and outmanoeuvre them. Hopelessly outnumbered, using the tricks that I'd been taught with cunning, I'd survived. Gradually the warmth of a renewed confidence came over me. I climbed out, threw my parachute over my shoulder and strode off to Dispersal.

I found Al Harley's experience resembled mine almost to the letter. In the engagement he had hit one 109 good and hard but couldn't stay in one position long enough to watch it crash. He had been credited with one probably destroyed. We sat down and waited for the others. Fifteen minutes went by, half an hour, and finally an hour. At this point the ground crew from A Flight came in and sat around in dead silence. None of their aircraft had returned. When the telephone rang, everybody jumped to answer. It was the Ops Room. Stan Thompson had been killed trying to bail out over Dover; the Observer Corps on the Cliffs reported that they could see a pilot walking around on the Goodwin Sands just off the coast, a boat had been dispatched to pick him up. An army unit on Dungeness had Jeep Neil who had crashed there in a riddled craft. It had to be assumed now that all the rest were lost. The ground crew from A Flight, without saying a word, quietly left. The place was like a morgue. We had lost Wally Floody, Johnny Small, Blake Wallace, Stan Thompson and Brian Hodgkinson. As the rest of us hung around in silence hoping there might be another late report, I began thinking of all those lads, Hodgkinson, Small and Floody, all on their first sweep. Rugged Stan Thompson, knowing him and how he could shoot, I knew full well that he must have taken a few with him. But now, nobody would ever know. The ringing of the telephone interrupted my thoughts. It was the controller again. He suggested we pack up and come to the mess. He said that if it made us feel any better, the last count of enemy plots on the board showed three hundred plus in our area. The Biggin Wing had been alone in France and 401 Squadron was the only squadron heavily engaged.

He suggested we all come up to the mess and have a drink. With some reticence, we got our caps and piled in the back of the truck.

'I want to go to my quarters,' I said.

'So do I,' said Al Harley. 'There's no way I could stomach a drink right now. I'm afraid we haven't got much to celebrate.'

My batman was waiting, and as I began undressing in silence, he respectfully withdrew.

'Your bath is drawn, sir.'

'Thank you,' I nodded. 'I'm going to need one.'

Even the comfort of a nice warm tub couldn't make me stop thinking. It had been a disaster. How could we face the other pilots of the Wing in the mess after this? As I lay back and pensively soaked in the warm water, it suddenly struck me. Tomorrow was my birthday. I would never be carefree twenty-one again.

I was saddled with the unhappy task of gathering Wally Floody's personal effects to be shipped home. His room had to be made ready for his replacement, and nothing could be left. A Petty drawing from Esquire on the wall, an empty bottle of Dimple Haig he was saving to make a lamp in the wastebasket, the rabbit's foot in the suitcase. It seemed such an infringement of privacy to sort through his personal effects. Hidden sides of the man were revealed in all their childlike nakedness.

All leave for the ground crew was cancelled. They had to work day and night on seven new aircraft. Acceptance inspections, squadron letters painted on, and the guns butt-tested. The entrance of a pilot from 401 Squadron in the mess had an instant dampening effect. Out of sympathy, jocularity ceased and not knowing what to say, they fell silent. One was conscious of the furtive glances and the whispered conversations. It made you finish eating quickly and get out.

John and I had been invited by the Stevens family to spend a forty-eight-hour leave at their home. Major Stevens was a friend of Colonel Weir's, and John and I had put in for the leave together some time ago. John was to be posted to A Flight which had sustained the heaviest losses, so this would be the last leave we would have together. We were glad to get off the station.

With Major Stevens' precise instructions, we had no difficulty finding his house in Kensington. The tall rhododendron bushes at the gate were in bloom. We were shown into the drawing room where Mrs. Stevens was at her desk catching up on correspondence. She was a carefully groomed, matronly woman, tastefully attired. She welcomed us warmly and then told the maid to inform Helen we had arrived. Helen was a pretty dark-haired girl with classic features and a smile which emphasized her dimples. Her well-rounded figure was complemented by a smart silk dress. At twenty-one, she had that well protected

101

look of one not yet having lost all of her baby fat. In a break in conversation Mrs. Stevens asked Helen to show us the guest room. She was expecting her husband and Monica at any moment, and lunch would be in half an hour. John and I were given a chance to freshen up for lunch, and I took this opportunity to find out about the Stevens family. Major Stevens had four children. The eldest were two boys recently commissioned in the Army, tied up on manoeuvres. Then came Helen and Monica, the youngest. In spite of being only seventeen, Monica had managed to get into the WAAF and was working in the Ops Room at Fighter Command Headquarters.

As we were coming down the stairs, the front door burst open and in came Monica throwing her hat on the bench in the foyer. Not seeing us she shouted, 'Mummy, have they arrived?'

By the time John and I made our entrance she had already taken off her tunic. She jumped up from her mother's side to face us, her brow wrinkled with concern.

'I'm terribly sorry what's happened,' she said almost in a whimper. 'I'm in the Ops Room at Fighter Command Headquarters. I know all about it. I did my utmost to try to try to convince the controller to turn you back. He wouldn't listen.'

Impulsively, she raised her hand and bit on her finger in anguish. The awkward silence was broken by the entrance of Major Stevens, 'Monica, please go upstairs and get yourself ready for lunch. It should be ready in five minutes.' Then turning to the rest, he said, 'Who's joining me in a glass of sherry?'

From the conversation over lunch, it was evident that they were a very close-knit family: Monica the outspoken non-conformist; Major Stevens giving the impression that he was saddled with the tiresome job of keeping some semblance of order and common sense in his household. He obviously adored his daughters and inwardly took delight in Monica's spontaneity. While we were having coffee he disappared. The conversation was broken by the sound of a sharp whistle.

'Wouldn't you know it,' said Monica. 'There's Daddy calling another air raid practice.'

At the Stevens', time was not allowed to lie heavy on our hands; our day was organized for us. After lunch, a 'rattling good' game of tennis and our first taste of an iced Pimm's cup between sets. In the evening it was the dinner dance at Grosvenor House. After breakfast we were off with a picnic lunch, a motorboat had been hired – at Marlow-on-Thames. Every waking moment of the forty-eight hours we were kept busy by two attractive girls.

When we got back to Biggin, many changes had been made. There were seven new aircraft ready for flight testing. Painfully aware that our lives were dependent upon the perfect function of that engine, we carried out these tests with meticulous care. The engine had to run smoothly from idling to a speed run balls out without a splutter. When trimmed, the airframe had to be capable of straight and level flight with the hands off the controls, and have no unmanageable characteristic in a high speed dive. The guns had to be capable of continuous synchronous fire in every conceivable attitude including inverted flight. Then, and only then, would a pilot breathe a sigh of relief, stroke its side and say,

'Okay, we'll take it.'

There were a lot of new faces in the Dispersal Hut. Some did not last long enough for me to get to know them well. The ones I would have reason to remember were Sergeants Gardiner, Don Morrison, Dean McDonald, Dick Denison, and Pilot Officer Don Blakeslee. It was odd to find I was looked upon now as an experienced pilot. Gardiner made me feel ancient; he didn't look old enough to be on the first football team. At eighteen he still had peach fuzz on his chin. Blakeslee was the opposite extreme. He was a ruggedly handsome, supremely confident native of Florida whose features were marred by sufficient scars and blemishes to indicate that this wasn't the first fight he'd been in. He was the sort of fellow who would swagger into Dispersal in flying boots and fur flying jacket, his hat on the back of his head, slam the door to get attention, then posing feet wide apart, hands on hips, and say:

'Okay, you guys, let's not fuck around. Let me at 'em.'

With the requirement to let our new pilots familiarize themselves with the area, Squadron operations were limited to readiness. As the leader of Green Section, I was scrambled with four aircraft, with Omer Levesque flying as my Number 3.

'Green Section Airborne,' I reported.

Bill Igo, the controller, snapped back coolly, 'Green One, Vector 105 and buster.'

This meant to go at fast cruise three-quarters throttle.

At eight hundred feet we were just touching wisps of cloud in the solid overcast with a visibility over land of three miles. Once over the sea, the horizon disappeared, and the ceiling was down to five hundred feet and periodically we flew through patches of low fog.

'Green 2, in ten seconds, pip squeak.'

This meant that in ten seconds my Number 2 would have to start his pip squeak clock, the device which would emit a signal every sixty seconds. From this, our exact position was plotted.

'Five, four, three, two, one – pip squeak in.'

'Green 1, vector 075 and Booster – bandits five miles.'

I opened the throttle wide. After about another five minutes of flying through the murk, Bill Igo's voice came back on the R/T:

'Have lost contact, Green 1, Vector 250 for Base.'

Feeling frustrated I pulled my throttle back and headed for home. Another wild goose chase. Visibility had deteriorated even more, and my Section tucked in tight around me anticipating I might have to enter cloud. Over the sea, with frequent changes in direction and no landmarks, I hadn't the slightest idea where I was. I began worrying about the balloons at Dover.

Although Balloon Command was never supposed to fly balloons in cloud, it frequently did.

'Green 1 calling. Are the oranges down?'

Oranges was the code word for balloons. Bill Igo sounded slightly indignant as he replied, 'Green 1 continue, vector 250.'

Suddenly we were over the Cliffs and flying through cables.

'Green Section — BREAK,' I shouted, pulling the stick back, and disappeared into cloud. I didn't hit a cable, but I was alone. Just as I had feared, they had brought us straight in over the balloons at Dover, which were still up in the overcast. Miraculously, all of my Section survived, but each had to be vectored back to base independently.

The movie of Hemingway's 'For Whom The Bell Tolls,' starring Ingrid Bergman and Gary Cooper, was playing at the Odeon in London. I tried to interest some of the others. They all thought it was too much trouble, as we had to be in readiness at six in the morning. I was fed up doing readiness and each evening standing around the bar listening to pilots shooting lines, so I got cleaned up and caught the train for Victoria. I had dinner at a Chinese restaurant that had been recommended. The rice was soggy, the vegetables overdone, but in the main it was better than the Chinese chop suey joints in Northern Ontario. It was crowded and the service was slow, so I missed the start. It was a marvellous movie. I sat through some of the second showing so as to see the part I had missed. Still mesmerized by the drama of Hemingway's novel, I wandered around outside in the blackout imagining myself forced to spend the last few hours of my life in the arms of Ingrid Bergman. I lit a cigarette and in the light of the match caught a glimpse of my watch. It was 11.25 and the last train left at 11.35. I spent several feverish moments trying to stop a cab; then, realizing it was hopeless, set off at the double for the station. I arrived on the platform just in time to see the red light on the last carriage disappearing down the tracks. The next train, I was told, left at 5 'bloody' 30 in the morning, the run took forty minutes, and I had to be on readiness at 6.30. The thought of spending the night on a bench in the dampness of Victoria Station was the end. I still had three quid so I decided to go back to the Regent Palace where I had managed previously to get a single room for ten bob. With the bench at Victoria Station as the only alternative, I was willing to blow a pound, if necessary.

'You haven't a prayer, sir,' said the clerk. 'We're full up, and this time of night, I can't think of a single place in town that isn't.'

Faced with no alternative, and with the prospect of killing the next five and a half hours, I turned up my collar, stuffed my hands into the pockets of my great coat and strode out into Piccadilly. Having no particular direction in mind, I wandered aimlessly up Regent Street. I hadn't gone more than a hundred yards when a female voice beside me said, 'Hello, dawling, would you like some company?'

'No, thanks,' I said.

Recognizing my Canadian inflection, she changed from a West End London to a New York City accent.

'Well, hello, Canada. Why don't you come with me to my place for a little fun?'

'Where's your place?' I asked, as she tucked her arm in mine.

'Just around the corner, dearie! You come with me.'

She led me through an arch into a narrow alley, despite my repeating, 'I'm not really interested in this, you know.'

She opened a door right on the alley, and I was ushered in to a dimly lit room with two easy chairs and a large double bed. 'There's the work bench,' I thought.

'Take off your coat, honey, and make your little old self at home,' she said, flopping down in one of the chairs with her legs wide apart.

In the dim light, all I had been able to see was that she was tall and thin with sharp features and in the shadows her deep sunken eyes were invisible. Sitting in this position, she looked particularly unappetizing.

'How much will it cost me to spend the night here?' I asked.

'One pound, honey, just one pound.'

'Well, I'll tell you what I'll do. I'll pay you one pound for the privilege of sleeping in that bed alone. There's nothing personal in this mind you, because I think you're perfectly charming; but I've got to be on readiness at 6.30 in the morning and what I need most at this time is sleep. You see, you'll be letting this room to me, while you can be outside picking up the odd ten bob on a knee-trembler.'

'No go, Canada. If you sleep in this bed, you sleep with me.'

'Well, I'm awfully sorry,' I said, standing up. 'In that case, I'll just have to go.'

As I opened the door to let myself out, she streaked by me into the alley. Screaming like an infuriated banshee, she darted in and out of the shadows at my side, lashing me with the most eloquent stream of abuse I had ever heard in my life. Not a single item of my physical makeup, sexual behaviour, intestinal fortitude, or ancestry was left unmentioned. Without repeating herself, she followed me out into Regent Street, down Piccadilly and a good quarter of the way to Victoria Station. She seemed to be particularly vile when people passed. Realizing the magnitude of the feeling of hatred this poor soul must feel for me made the hackles rise. To contemplate the depth of despair that this creature lived with was horrifying. In spite of my great coat the dampness of Victoria Station entered every bone of my body.

On November 8th, I was on first readiness. We were scrambled immediately to patrol a convoy in the Thames Estuary. By the time an hour and a half had passed the sun had burnt off the last vestige of fog, and it was clear as a bell. When I landed, the truck was waiting to take us to the briefing room for a sweep. Exhilarated by the beautiful weather and confident now that I could see, I listened with anticipation. Our routing was much the same, Cap Gris Nez to St. Omer and then out by the Somme Estuary. We were to fly low cover, and I would be flying No. 3 in Blue Section on the flank. As we crossed the French coast, now knowing where and how to look, I saw coveys of 109's high above us, their sky-blue bellies glinting in the sun. Bent on putting the record straight, I was determined to attack the first aircraft that came within range. I didn't have to wait long. One came down behind on my side, and as he went by, I broke from the formation and went after him. As soon as he saw I was well separated and pursuing him, he pulled straight up. I followed, but by the time I had him in my sights, he was out of range. In my frustration, I pulled up the nose and gave him a long burst until I stalled and had to turn down. I was soon to regret that waste of ammunition. Suddenly I spotted a 109 below me. Hoping to compensate for my impetuosity I flicked over on my back and, with throttle wide, went after him. He, too, had his eyes open, for the moment he saw me committed to my attack, he rolled gracefully over and went straight down into a cloud. When I levelled out, I found myself directly over Le Touquet, and a little ship outside the harbour was throwing up a furious barrage of flak at me. While I was in the process of turning and twisting, dodging the flak, I was 'bounced' by two 109's. They were a well disciplined pair, so stationed that one could take over the attack where the other left off. Soon they were joined by two more. Turning and twisting I took short blind bursts at anything that went in front. It seemed no time before I heard the hiss. I was out of ammunition. I was still over the ship which was relentlessly tracing my course through the sky with its flak. The 109's pressed home their attack with persistent vigour, one coming within fifty yards, firing all the way. Watching his tracer, I found myself trying to climb up on the dashboard. With one shuddering turn after another I was bathed in sweat. I had to keep my head spinning from one side to the other so that I could watch two at a time. Gradually a sickening dread came over me as my strength diminished. On the point of exhaustion, I was ready to give up when all at once they left me alone. Realizing that they too must have run out, I flicked over on my back and went straight down on the sea through a hail of light flak. I kicked my tail out of the way a few times for a quick look, but sure enough, nobody was there. On the ground at Biggin, I carefully went over my Spitfire YOR with my rigger. There was only one machine gun hole, but the flak ship had scored five hits. The rigger concluded no vital structures had been hit, and all the holes could be patched.

Discouraged and weary, I made my way back to Dispersal, and, while turning in my escape kit, the Intelligence Officer took the combat report. When he'd finished, he said, 'Weir and Gardiner are missing. Did you see them by any chance?'

'Weir missing? Have you checked to see if he's landed at Manston?'

'Yes, I've checked, and there's no report of them yet, Blakeslee reported seeing two Spitfires line astern, both on fire.'

I had been so preoccupied thinking about myself that I had completely forgotten about John now that he was in A Flight. It was Gardiner's first sweep.

Somehow, I had just never worried about John. He was always there, he'd always been there since we were in prep school. He had spent a good part of his life trying to keep me out of trouble. I thought of how we used to meet at 5:30 every Saturday morning at the streetcar stop with our hockey sticks and skates over our shoulder on our way to play midget hockey. Half the time, he would forget his shin pads, but would play anyway. Tough as nails and a perpetual clown, I could see him catching that pass I was supposed to throw to somebody else in a football game against St. Andrew's, and how he ran zig-zag all around the field with half the St. Andrew's football team after him while he avoided their tackles with little bursts of speed. It seemed impossible. He was too quick, they couldn't have got him. Two hours later all forward stations still reported nothing. I thought of Mrs. Weir, the chronically impractical product of the roaring '20's. I could hear her say, 'Hughie, now don't forget to wear your rubbers and wash out your hair with egg shampoo.' I could just see her and Fran, John's fiancee, reading and re-reading the telegram.

'We regret to inform you that Flying Officer John Weir was reported missing after action over enemy territory.'

What a heartlessly empty communication. I wished somehow I could be the first to explain. I had done it so many times before when he was late coming home from school. I got out the blue leather correspondence case that Peggy Hodge had given me before I left Canada. The sight of it gave me pangs of conscience. It hadn't had much use. I wrote a letter worded in the more specific language that I had always had to use with Colonel Weir. I could hear him say:

'Okay, give us the facts and forget the trimming.'

When I read it over, I felt like tearing it up, but I couldn't think of anything better to say, so I sent it.

A few days later the Ops Room rang up and told Norm Johnson to get his Squadron on readiness for a sweep. All pilots were to be in the Briefing Room three-quarters of an hour earlier than usual as Air Marshal Leigh-Mallory would conduct the briefing. After the Battle of Britain, a high level shake-up had taken place. Air Marshal 'Stuffy' Dowding had been kicked upstairs because, it was rumoured, the rigours of his responsibilities at his age had softened his resolve and caused him to be too preoccupied with losses. Leigh-Mallory, a younger, more aggressive and ambitious leader had been chosen to replace him as Air Officer Commanding, Fighter Command. The Air Marshal strode into the Briefing Room and took over. Leigh-Mallory looked the epitome of aggressive efficiency. Impeccably groomed, chest full of decorations and a hat heavy with 'scrambled eggs' pulled well down on his forehead. He surveyed us for a moment coldly, hands on hips and his stubble moustache bristling like the hackles on a hog's back.

'The main objective of Fighter Command is to draw the fighter units of the enemy into action and destroy them. On this sortie, Air Marshal Harris will supply us with a few bombers as decoys. Jamie, once over France, I want you to cease operating your units in Squadron order. I want you to split them up in pairs or singles, if need be, to engage the enemy. Do I make myself clear?'

'Yes, sir,' said Jamie, firmly.

'You can all see from the map the routing of your sortie. That is of minor significance compared to the objectives. I will leave the rest of the details to you, Jamie. Are there any questions?'

There was dead silence. Without another word, he strolled out. In the vacuum he left we found ourselves lost in our own thoughts. Then and there I knew I could never be a great General. I wondered how anybody could issue such an order without being prepared to lead the men himself.

I went through the next few sweeps like a zombie, robbed of my closest friend. I wallowed in a state of moral limbo. I did what I was told, went where I was told and remembered little of what happened. On one of the sweeps, for example, Hank Sprag, Jeep Neal, Don Blakeslee and Gilbert all engaged the enemy and were each credited with 'one damaged.' I saw nothing worth noting.

A message was left for me that Air Commodore Chamier had called. I knew at once what had happened. The Chamiers were close friends of the Weirs; Mrs. Chamier, a Canadian, had been a girlhood friend of Freda Weir's. They must have cabled for further information. I was not anxious to talk about the matter, but I returned the call. To my relief, the Air Commodore asked no questions; instead, he invited me to dinner and to spend the night at his flat. I accepted. The occasion solved a problem that worried me. With the job of getting John's things together to send home, I realized that his personal correspondence of interest to his family would be confiscated by the censors. Giving his things to the Chamiers would assure they would one day get there.

They couldn't have made it more easy. The Air Commodore met me alone. When I voluntarily blurted out a full account of all that I knew about John, he listened in silence. Seeing the bag with Flying Officer J.G. Weir printed on the side, he asked:

'Do you want me to take that?'

'Yes,' I said, 'I thought maybe . . .'

And then I was interrupted.

'I don't think you've met my wife.'

Over sherry before dinner we talked about skiing. The Air Commodore had met his wife on a skiing holiday in Switzerland. Discovering that I had had some exposure of dynamics, he confounded me with his formula for designing the perfect sailing hull. He just happened to have three tickets to the premiere of an American movie that had glowing reviews. By strange coincidence, I found that it had nothing to do with war. It was a delightful evening spent with two charming people, finishing with the luxury of sleeping in a soft warm bed and waking up to a substantial breakfast.

As I took the late train from Victoria Station, I felt calm and much refreshed. Air Commodore Chamier in his quiet way had taken over.

I was greeted by a jubilant Squadron. I had missed the best sweep so far. Jamie Rankin had led them on a perfect bounce, and they had destroyed four — one each by Ormston, Blakeslee, Morrison and Levesque. Omer Levesque was also going to be credited with one probably destroyed and four damaged. I was just in time to listen to the debriefing. Don Blakesley was called first and with his usual offhand manner described the details of his victory. Ormston, flushed with elation, described how his had blown up in his face. Don Morrison had chased three off Jeep Neal's tail, sending one of them down in flames into the sea.

'Has anybody else got a claim?' Jamie asked.

Bill Haggarty stood up and said, 'I think Sergeant Levesque has, sir.'

Everybody turned around and looked back at 'Trottle.' He was slumped in a chair at the back of the Briefing Room, his face bathed in sweat.

In response to the silence, he stood up like a frightened little boy and as he searched for words, his lips trembled. He took a deep breath, a long sigh, and said,

'Sir, I should be dead twenty times. I could have been killed without knowing "nutting about it".'

There was a roar of laughter which he didn't seem to notice. Choked with emotion he haltingly gave his report. There was no more laughter. His story had the undivided attention of every pilot in the Wing. He had been attacked by a gaggle of radial engined aircraft faster than anything he had ever seen. He had shot two of them down and after a battle for his life made his escape. With sweat pouring off his brow, he gave a big sigh, and slumped back on his seat. There was dead silence. Then somebody beside me said,

'Boy, he's had it!'

Omer was promoted to Flight Sergeant and sent off on a forty-eight-hour leave, with the full expectation that he would be sent home. After his leave, Trottle came straight to Dispersal. Habitually particular about appearance, he looked neat as a pin with his new Flight Sergeant Crowns up. He had by no means 'had it.' He was not a bit interested in going back to Canada. On the contrary, he planned to stay a long time. He had bought himself an MG sportscar. To the delight of everyone he was his familiar cocky self again. With a swagger he strode over to Dean MacDonald slumped in a chair.

'Sergeant MacDonal'. You see those Goddam crowns? From now on, you show respec' Chris. And smarten up.'

Wreathed in smiles, Dean gave him a limp-handed salute, and Trottle retaliated by grabbing him round the neck. Before leaving, he gave the Intelligence Officer a piece of paper on which he had drawn what he remembered of the shape of the radial engine aircraft. Copies of Levesque's drawing were circulated throughout Fighter Command and proved to be a remarkably accurate picture of the German's new fighter, the Focke-Wulf 190. In his absence other pilots had reported seeing them. One had flown head on into a formation escorting six Blenheims. He had half-rolled and gone straight down on the bombers, shooting one down at 90 degrees deflection; pulled out of the dive below the bombers and had gone straight up through them again shooting down another. He had enough speed to climb five thousand feet for a victory roll before diving back into France. The escorting fighters couldn't get anywhere near him. As some of the aircraft had been hit by cannon fire, it was assumed that they were armed with two cannons only which their hottest pilots could make good use of. From the point of view of speed, flying our Spitfire Mark V, against FW 190's was like flying Hurricanes against 109's. There was only one consolation. At least we could still turn inside them.

Hitler's promised invasion had still to be considered a possibility. Heralding this the Luftwaffe would certainly make every attempt to destroy the big fighter bases in the south of England. In such an event, the squadrons would be scrambled to attack but might have to land on some aerodrome which hadn't been bombed. There, without their maintenance crews, they would be limited. Group Captain Barnwell, Station Commander at Biggin, submitted an idea he thought could keep the flying and ground personnel of the squadrons together. Each aircraft would be supplied with two zipped-up heavy-duty canvas bags made in the shape of half a tear-drop, divided longitudinally. It had to be as long as the body of a man. The flat side had a metal reinforced bottom with leather straps to hold it firmly to the twenty millimeter cannons in the wings of the Spitfire. No sooner had the idea been submitted than the prototype arrived for a trial. We got a couple of the erks to get into the bags to see how they fit. We promised not to take off while they were inside. It was a novel idea, but welcomed with little enthusiasm by the ground crews. They couldn't even get the Poles to try it out. One of the Sergeant pilots attempted one better; he took his WAAF girlfriend out early one morning, put her in the seat of the Spitfire, sat on her without his parachute, and took off. It was an unauthorized flight, of course, but he would have got away with it if his prop hadn't stopped when he landed back on the field. Two people getting out of a Spitfire, one of them in a skirt, was certain to be noticed.

With the predominance of damp misty weather in the month of November, the occasional frustrated pilot sent out to test his guns would fly on and do the job over enemy territory. It was decided to formalize these spontaneous expressions of aggressiveness into planned operations and called them rhubarbs. The Photographic Reconnaissance Units, flying souped-up Spitfires stripped of all guns and carrying a camera, kept up a constant surveillance of the Channel ports and scoured the territory inland watching troop movements. They kept RAF Intelligence supplied with a steady stream of photographs of potential targets. 'Spy,' Biggin Hill's Chief Intelligence Officer, could give you a map showing the position of all light and heavy flak concentrations. I received permission to do my first rhubarb on 30th November. Unfortunately, I had to abort the mission because my wheels would not retract. I would make a speciality of the type of operation in time.

The Englishman considers his daily habits sacred. Wherever possible, planned operations were scheduled so that everybody was back in time for tea. If the NAAFI wagon didn't come round to Dispersal with tea at four o'clock, a complaint would be registered. At Biggin, peace time mess routine went on regardless. There was a Mess dinner once a month with a guest speaker. Most of the Canadian officers, expecting it to be another dreary RAF formality, did not attend. Being more curious, I was an exception. Guest speakers were selected from a list of well-known after-dinner speakers. The guest was expected to sit through a Mess meeting conducted by the President of the Mess with careful adherence to proper Procedure. Complaints about the extra messing charges, or the quality of the marmalade, were duly dealt with. After the Mess Steward would produce the port and cigars, the speaker would be introduced. He would appear to be delighted at having been privy to the inconsequential debates preceding him and often would open with a few ridiculous suggestions of his own. It was different from our ever serious military leaders. We delighted to hear the ramblings of fertile minds.

One day it was announced the next guest speaker would be Edward G. Robinson. The English boys seemed excited with the prospect. The only Hollywood star I had ever seen in my life had been Mary Pickford, the Canadian, who was married to Douglas Fairbanks. She had been invited to inspect the Rifle Company at Upper Canada College. At close range, I discovered that this Hollywood darling had a pockmarked complexion presumably due to constant exposure to make-up. Before her departure in her Cadillac convertible, she had delighted the Corps by throwing her arms around our pious Headmaster and giving him a big kiss. He was thunderstruck. In North America, one expected this sort of thing, but I couldn't imagine the standard publicity-seeking Hollywood actor fitting in with the demands of an RAF Mess like Biggin. The English seemed to hold us accountable for everything that happened on the other side and were constantly asking us to explain North American attitudes and events. Edward G. Robinson, who was best known for his roles as the tough-talking gangster type, for all I knew, might be rendered speechless without a bunch of cue cards. To my great relief and genuine surprise Edward G. Robinson gave a commendable performance and sat down to an enthusiastic round of applause.

As I made the last entries in my flying logbook for the month of November in preparation for the signatures of my Flight and Squadron Commanders, I found it an occasion for reflection. We had been in the Biggin Hill Wing a little less than a month and a half and already we had lost nine pilots on the sweeps I had been on. I had just short of fifty hours in combat, and with sixty-eight hours total time on Spitfires, I had learned to manoeuvre it as though it were a part of me. Norm Johnson and Bud Connell were beginning to look a little care-worn and edgy, but Jeep Neal in command of A Flight was still full of aggressiveness. At the end of the month we had lost Hank Sprag, and the Squadron morale was low. We were flying together to France but once in combat we were on our own and the Devil take the hindmost. Jeep kept having 'Bull sessions' trying to promote unity. It was evident to everybody that what we needed was aggressive leadership and Jeep was our man for the job.

A shake-up was precipitated by the outcome of a sortie in the first week of December. We were scrambled as a Squadron and in five minutes managed to get twelve aircraft off the ground and in formation. When Norm Johnson reported his Squadron airborne, Bill Igo snapped:

'Daring Leader, vector zero nine zero angles ten . . . buster!'

At three-quarters throttle we climbed to 10,000 feet toward the coast. We had just crossed out over the water north of Dover when we heard:

'Twenty plus twelve o'clock Angels Ten harassing Friendly Ducks homeward bound.'

Norm Johnson's aircraft suddenly slowed down causing the two wing sections to go past him. Announcing that he was returning to base because of engine trouble, he turned the Lead over to Jeep Neal. Behind Jeep we continued on. When we reached mid-channel we came across two motor torpedo boats pounding through a heavy sea line abreast. Five thousand feet above us was a ring of 109's. As we took up patrol over the boats, the 109's peeled off in pairs and foursomes diving to the attack. When we turned into them, they took short squirts at us, then continued on down for a shot at the boats. Each time the boats veered sharply away from each other, and just as sharply turned back into line abreast. Jeep ordered us to operate in sections with one objective: to keep them away from the boats. It was a frustrating job taking potshots at 109's rocketing by. Seeing two coming down on my Section, I increased my speed by going into a tight spiral with the hope of getting a better shot as they went by. Convinced that my lack of success heretofore was because of over-preoccupation with what was behind, I dove after one of them hoping to cut the corner and catch him as he pulled out. While concentrating on my target, I began feeling very uncomfortable. I took a quick glance behind, and there was a 109 in my rear blazing away. Pulling my head down behind the armoured plate, I pulled the stick back in my guts and blacked out. I woke up going straight up in the air with two 109's firing at me head on. I contented myself with firing back at them until I stalled.

Returning to a circling patrol of the boats, I discovered that there were only three of us left: Jeep Neal, Dick Denison my No. 2, and myself. There still seemed to be the same number of 109's above us, my cannons were empty, and I was down to a few rounds of machine gun. I had to content myself with preventing them from making attacks on the boats. It wasn't long before I was completely out of ammo, but the 109's took care to avoid our mock attacks just the same. Finally we were ordered to return to Base. My faithful Spitfire YOR had been hit by two cannon shells and one machine gun bullet. She was irreparable.

A signal came through from Headquarters that Norm Johnson and Bud Connell were to cease operational flying and were to be sent home for a rest. The signal didn't designate a replacement for our Leader, but it was assumed that Jeep Neal would be given the job. As the Senior Flight Commander, he assumed acting leadership. Al Harley was put in command of B Flight. Jeep Neal encouraged the buddy system. Omer Levesque had always flown with his friend, Bill Haggarty. When Haggarty went missing, he teamed up with Dean McDonald. Ian Ormston always had to worry about somebody; with John missing, he began worrying about me. We had a lot in common. Ian's father, an Englishman, had emigrated to Canada. Raised in a prep-school atmosphere, he claimed to understand my peculiarities. He professed much more life experience, having been brought up in the cosmopolitan atmosphere of Montreal. He had come to the conclusion that the thing that would get me out of the doldrums quickest was an oil change, under his supervision. He arranged with Jeep for us to get off together on a seven days' leave. He was to make all the necessary social arrangements. If we ran out of money in London, he had a standing invitation to take a friend on leave to his uncle's home at Barrow-in-Furness near Preston. Glad of any change, I let Ian take full charge.

The weekend started with a visit to the bar of a West End Club that had possibilities. As he expected, we found two rather chic-looking girls sitting alone drinking sherry. To demonstrate his savoire-faire, Ian introduced himself. They professed to be waiting for some friends but had no objection to joining us until they arrived. With a flourish Ian called the bar steward and asked him to take orders.

'Give me a double whisky and soda, Dimple Haig, if you don't mind,' said one.

I'll have the same,' said the other.

Realizing that I didn't have the money to last too long at this rate, I asked, 'Ian, what time does our train leave for Barrow-in-Furness in the morning?'

'Ten thirty,' he grinned.

With the third round of drinks, the girls were still cold sober, and their hypothetical company had not arrived. In desperation Ian asked them to join us for dinner. The invitation was demurely accepted. We found they had discriminating but expensive taste, were in excellent appetite, and that it took two bottles of Moselle to quench their thirst. They were very good dancers, and our stock improved somewhat when they discovered we could dance, too. Having estimated and spent our financial resources almost to the last farthing, they invited us to their flat for a nightcap. We accepted. The flat was very tastefully furnished, had two bedrooms, large drawing room, small dining room, kitchen and bath. Ian seemed to have already come to some understanding and disappeared, leaving Jane, the pretty girl, with me. From time to time he very disconcertingly reappeared in his undershorts to

114

sit cross-kneed on the living room floor listening to my timorous advances.

'Do you need something, Ian?' I would ask.

'Nope, just getting a breather,' he'd reply.

After what seemed like an eternity of conversational foreplay, I managed to entice her into the bedroom, and one piece at a time finally got all her clothes off. She had an arousing figure and seemed to enjoy my fondling her principal parts in a detached sort of way. But that, she said, was enough. Then I resorted to the 'poor mouth technique.' I stated that I was in such a pitiful state of sexual frustration that it was definitely interfering with my chance of survival. She seemed favourably impressed with this, and for a moment I thought she might be willing to help.

'How long is it since you've been with a woman?' she asked.

Totally unprepared for the question, I feverishly searched for an interval that might be too long for an experienced lover.

'Two whole weeks,' I said.

'You are a pig,' she said. 'I don't care what you do with yourself, but I'm going to sleep.'

There was no point in arguing. I had blown it. I spent a frustrated, fretful night.

We bade farewell in the morning and set out for Lloyd's Bank. In spite of having been in England the best part of a year, our pay records from Canada had still not caught up with us. Lloyd's Bank kept body and soul together by giving us advances of pay. Feeling much more secure with a few crisp pound notes in our pockets, we caught the train for Glasgow.

Ian's uncle lived in the country. He was the Chief Naval Architect for Vickers' vast ship-building works that operated 'round the clock' producing submarines and ships of all kinds. He spent most of his time in his office while Ian and I were being thoroughly spoiled by his wife. In an atmosphere devoid of temptation, we got plenty of rest, good food and exercise. On the last day of our leave, he took us on the rounds of the ship-building yard that was feverishly trying to keep pace with the appalling losses of ships at sea. We witnessed the christening and launching of a submarine by a Naval Commander's wife. Ian remarked that he could think of better use for a bottle of champagne, but his Uncle assured him that he would taste some before the day was out.

As I watched this ritual, it was evident that those involved in the building of ships took this very seriously. If the bottle broke the first time it hit the bow, and it slid smoothly into the water, and floated away proudly, they all breathed a sigh of relief and vented their feeling with a loud cheer. As we walked to the limousine that would take us to the reception, I felt strangely out of things as I had once at a Jewish circumcision party. We were taken to a rambling mansion used solely by Vickers for entertaining and ushered by a butler into a palatial drawing room.

Here, our select little group patiently awaited the return of the ladies, who had been given an opportunity to freshen up. Rejuvenated and evidently grateful to be relieved of the constant din of hammers and the rattle of the rivet guns, they engaged us in relaxed conversation. The butler appeared again with a large silver salver full of sparkling glasses of champagne. Behind him came a steward with a plate full of canapes. I had my first exposure to caviar and smoked salmon.

Ian's uncle then presented the Commander's wife with a beautiful diamond brooch. I had admired such dazzling pieces in West End jewelry shops in London. Thinking of my mother, who had never acquired such luxuries, I had gone in and asked to have a look at one. I was astonished to find that the pound sterling price ran to three figures. Even Ian and I were presented with mementoes, handsome cigarette cases. The whole experience was an astonishing insight into the workings and customs of the men who stood behind the embattled British Fleet.

On my arrival at Biggin, Giles told me that Air Commodore Chamier had called. Feeling certain that he must have news of John, I anxiously returned it. Through the International Red Cross in Switzerland, he had word that John was alive. He was in hospital recovering from unspecified wounds. At least he was alive.

Only after the war was I able to hear John's full story. He had been shot down in flames with the result that his eyelids had been burnt off. He spent the rest of the war in the dust bowl of Stalag Luft III. He had kept his fertile mind alive working on making his escape. A tireless digger in the tunnels, he had earned himself a place amongst the first who were to break out so vividly described in the book, *The Great Escape*. Shortly before the fifty-man break, John was sent to hospital for further plastic surgery. A British surgeon obtained permission from the Germans to graft some eyelids on him. There was one stipulation: He had to do it without anaesthetic. John had both his eyelids grafted on 'rawhide.'

11

CHRISTMAS 1941

On the 7th December Pearl Harbor was attacked by Japanese carrier-based aircraft with devastating results. America was shocked out of its ambivalence and complacency as events moved quickly. Hitler declared war on America, dispelling any doubts that the Axis was bent on world conquest. It was impossible for us then to visualize the impact that our new Allies would make in this life and death struggle. For us Canadians, the time would come when we would thrill with pride at the sight of Armadas of aerial formations produced and manned by our cousins from below the border, flying with us into battle. It was with a sort of wistful envy that we heard that a joint session of the American Congress had voted unanimously to order national mobilization and conscription and the whole nation solidly stood behind them.

At Biggin, life went on unchanged. With dreary weather we did a lot of readiness, convoy patrols, and covered mine sweepers clearing the Thames Estuary. To the regret of every pilot in the Wing, it was announced in December that we would lose Jamie Rankin. Jamie had earned the affection and respect of everyone. His leadership was the backbone of the Wing. To soften the blow, Jamie was allowed to hang around awaiting the arrival of his replacement, Wing Commander Bob Tuck. Bobbie, who had led us from West Malling, was just finishing a stint in the United States as an Air Attaché, duty familiarly known as being on the 'cocktail circuit.' Due to the presence of a Canadian squadron in the Wing that could not go home, Jamie announced that there would be no special Christmas leave for anyone.

The thought of Christmas made all of us a little homesick. It prompted those who had fond memories to relate the method in which they celebrated the occasion. We resigned ourselves to the fact that there would be no Christmas this year. A spontaneous movement started amongst the English boys bent on showing us a jolly good time anyway. A holly-picking sortie was organized. It was an odd sight when these pilots poured back into the Mess, each with an armful. They split into prearranged teams, each responsible for decorating a room. While one stood on a chair in front of the mantelpiece, the leader stood in the middle of the floor with arms folded pensively watching. It seemed

117

so totally out of character to see a highly respected veteran pilot in his scratched up black flying boots, and thread-bare uniform, pointing to the picture over the mantelpiece with a holly branch and saying:

'Now I want one more piece in the middle, Christopher, with plenty of berries.'

A Christmas dance was planned, and on the eve of the party the squadrons were 'stood down.' Some of our pilots had decided to skip the party and have their own celebration in their quarters. Jeep Neal was holding one of his flying bull sessions in his room, and everyone had gravitated there.

'Ormston,' I said. 'I'm going to the party. What about you?'

'I'm with you,' he said. 'Let's go.'

We both got cleaned up and donned our best blues. As we strolled toward the Mess, Ian announced that he was determined to get his hands on some woman and give her the Ormston treatment. We pushed through the double blackout doors of the Mess together. There, just off the dance floor was a pretty little blonde WAAF Officer whom neither of us had ever seen before. Ian made a lunge for her, but before he had a chance to get there, I grabbed him by the arm and spun him around so as to get in front.

'I wouldn't have anything to do with that chap,' I told her. 'He's a thoroughly bad type. May I have this dance?'

'He's a dull fellow. He lacks finesse and savoire faire,' said Ian. 'Why don't you dance with me?'

Obviously unfamiliar with this abrupt and informal behaviour, the girl looked thoroughly confused. Finally she laughed, 'Well, *he* asked me first,' pointing at me.

She was an excellent dancer, and all the while she maintained a stream of nervous chatter, in a soft Scottish brogue. The canny way in which she answered each of my questions, I found most refreshing. Being from Edinburgh, she knew Jamie Rankin and his family well. The reason we had never seen her before was because she was one of two Cipher Officers from the Ops Room. She worked twenty-four hours on and twenty-four hours off. With these hours she had few occasions to come to the main Mess, spending most of her time in the WAAF Officers' Mess, close to her quarters.

As the music stopped, our conversation was interrupted by the entrance of Jamie Rankin and some of the pilots of 609 City of Edinburgh Squadron. She obviously knew them all and, being on much more familiar ground, accepted Jamie's invitation to join them for a drink in the bar. Evidently considered almost a part of this famous outfit which enjoyed the special privilege of wearing a crimson lining to their great coats, she was the centre of attraction. Feeling definitely out of it, I withdrew to a corner armchair with a drink.

In the bar was a girl whom I had seen on many previous occasions as a guest of different pilots in the Wing. She was in a particularly skittish mood. Conscious of the fact that she looked very titillating in her revealing long evening dress, she flaunted her favours amongst all and sundry. Seeing me alone in the armchair she impetuously came over and sat on my lap and began teasing my hair. The young WAAF Officer looked very disapproving and to my amusement, came over and said, 'I like the tune the band's playing. I'll have that dance now.'

Delighted, I quickly excused myself and led her to the floor. For the greater part of that evening I remained her steady companion. Her name, I discovered, was Connie Helm. Her ability to follow me through all the dance routines I knew did not go unnoticed by Jeff Northcott. Jeff, a Westerner, was rather shy and uncertain of himself with English women. Seeing that Connie seemed to be satisfied to dance with a Canadian, he came over and asked me if he could have a go. Unbeknownst to everybody, Jeff was an expert at the Big Apple and proceeded to swing Connie through the full routine. Nothing like this had ever been seen at a dance at Biggin and soon they had the floor to themselves as everybody watched. When the music stopped, there was a roar of applause, much whistling by the Canadians, and calls for 'encore.' The orchestra cooperated by striking up a suitable tune and off they went again. News of the performance spread to the bar, which emptied as everybody came to watch. The music kept going until sweat was pouring from Jeff's brow, and at the end they acknowledged the ovation with an elaborate bow and curtsy.

It was a marvellous party, and, as I escorted Connie back to her quarters, she informed that in Scotland New Year's Eve was celebrated with more vigour than Christmas. The Scots considered it good luck if a dark-haired man crossed the threshold to share in the celebrations. I had the appropriate colouring, so she made me promise to visit the WAAF Officers' Mess at ten-thirty on the evening of the 31st for what she called 'First Feetin' (footing).

It didn't disturb me that the January weather left few opportunities for operations. At the end of each day I had something special to look forward to, a pretty little Scots girl who preferred my company and whose lack of sophistication matched mine. She showed me the things of London she had learned to love. We saw good plays, pantomimes and variety shows. She introduced me to the celebrated rum cocktails at the Salted Almonds Bar at the Savoy Hotel, and the excellent Scottish smoked salmon and steak and kidney pud' at her favorite pub in Bromley. We had long walks through the countryside of Kent and regular exercise on the tennis court at Biggin. Her zest for life was contagious. She loved her work and took the responsibilities as an officer very seriously, but when she was off, she organized me so

119

that we took every advantage of each moment of leisure. Regardless of the dull weather, my mood at Dispersal improved immensely.

Al Harley and I had had an application in to do a rhubarb for some time. Finally, permission for it was granted. We were at the point of making last minute plans before taking off when in strode Bob Tuck. Bobbie had been like a caged lion in this long period of bad weather. As he entered, he said, 'Okay, you two get the shillings out and toss for it. One of you is going to stay behind, because I'm going. I can't stand this inactivity.'

Al won the toss and off they went together. I waited anxiously at Disperal for their return. An hour later, a single Spitfire came back in the circuit. It was Harley. When I got to his aircraft, he was outside inspecting his radiator to see if there were any branches stuck in it. He had flown through a tree dodging flak. He had seen Bobbie stream a long trail of glycol when they were engaged by the flak batteries of Boulogne. Harley's last view of Bobbie was of him turning back into France.

It was a bitter blow for Fighter Command. Now experienced Wing Leaders were in short supply. Bader and Tuck were gone. Jamie Rankin was on a rest, so at this stage it was decided to try to stiffen the backbone of the Biggin Wing by introducing some of the career officers who had been trained at the Officers' Training School at Cranwell. Instead of 401 Squadron going to Jeep Neal, Squadron Leader Douglas was put in command. A New Zealander, Wing Commander Masterman, with no previous experience in leading fighter wings, was made Wing Commander Flying.

I was in Dispersal on readiness one day when Connie unexpectedly phoned up and asked to speak to me. When I got to the phone, she said to me icily, 'If you were tired of me, why didn't you just jolly well tell me, instead of doing something like that?'

'Like what?' I said

'You volunteered for Malta. Your name is on a list of thirty pilots posted to Malta. There is only one way it could have got there — you must have volunteered.'

'Oh, my God!' I said. 'I forgot all about that; I put my name in after John went missing.'

'Well, you can't get out of it now; you've all got to report for injections for the Middle East and be ready to leave within forty-eight hours.'

I was bitterly disappointed. For the first time in a year in England, I was really beginning to enjoy myself. There was nothing I could do. I got my shots and made ready to leave. Forty-eight hours later a second signal arrived cancelling the draft. Connie phoned me at once, as she got all the signals.

'If you really want to stay, you'd better call the Admin Officer and tell him to take you off the draft.'

In the last few months of 1941 and the early months of 1942 the German pocket battleships in Brest Harbour were kept under close surveillance. There were strong indications they were preparing to break out. All units became involved. Besides the torpedo bombers of Coastal Command, even Bomber Command Wellingtons were sent off to lay mines. These Wellingtons flew into Brest Harbour at zero feet at night. A rear gunner in one of these Wellingtons, Bud Fitzgerald from Toronto, bailed out of his riddled aircraft near Biggin returning from one of these sorties. He told me that on his approach to the target at zero feet the flak was coming down on them from the surrounding hills. They then had to climb to eight hundred feet into the flak to drop the mines so that the parachutes on the mines could open.

Jamie Rankin had led us to the area in support of a daylight bombing attack before he had gone on his rest. For us it was uneventful except for the one-hundred-mile-an-hour headwind that we had to face on our return. The Eagle Squadron had flown with the Wing that day and got separated in cloud. The entire Squadron failed to return. It was reported they landed in the Channel Islands thinking that it was Land's End.

The opportunities for 'togetherness' during the month of January and the Malta affair, caused a rapid maturation of the relationship between Connie and me. A certain magnetism possessed us. It was heightened by the necessity to live one day at a time. It was then that Connie told me that she was engaged to a dear friend who had known and loved her since childhood. He was older than she, gentle and kind of nature. Because of a boyhood illness he was crippled and unfit for military service. He was a barrister. With me Connie could look forward to nothing but insecurity. Even more than before I felt obliged to continue to fight this war to the bitter end. Logically, to break her engagement and marry me would be senseless. As I fell silent, the loneliness and aimlessness that had haunted my life in England settled once more upon me. Sensing my feelings, she lifted my spirits by telling me that she realized she had never really loved anybody before. She was faced now, however, with the unhappy task of telling her fiancé. She was aware of the odds facing a fighter pilot, she said, but because she felt that we had been blessed with each other we had something to live for and had to look to the future with optimism. She asked me to go with her to Scotland to meet her family and help her explain her feelings to her fiancé. I agreed with some reluctance. We put in for seven days leave together in the first week of February.

With inclement weather in the month of January, life in Dispersal was dull. For the most part, the events were eclipsed by my preoccupation with Connie. One of the pilots did a rhubarb and, to our horror, his combat film showed a woman pushing a baby carriage being sprayed by bullets. We all turned around and looked at him in stony silence. Unconcerned, he said, 'They told me to hit anything that moved. I couldn't have got that truck behind in any other way.'

The number of Squadron victories gradually mounted through the tenacious efforts of Blakesley, Ormston, Omer Levesque and Don Morrison. Morrison quietly announced at a debriefing that he had got two.

At last the day came for our seven days leave in Scotland. I booked a table for the dinner dance at Grosvenor House and Connie reserved two compartments on the Flying Scot that night for Edinburgh. We took a taxi from Victoria and travelled to our destination with the familiar accompaniment of the air raid siren. Inside Grosvenor House, out of earshot of the nightly hate, we were shown to our table by the Maitre d'. When the orchestra struck up 'Begin the Beguine,' I found it particularly hard to concentrate on my menu and the items that the waiter was pointing out on it with his pencil. With Connie's restraining influence, I impatiently sat through the hors d'oeuvres. To accompany the main course, the waiter with a flourish of his napkin produced the iced bottle of Moselle he had recommended. With great deliberation, he handed me the cork and guided me through the ritual of sniffing the bouquet and mouthing a sip of this excellent vintage. Mindful of my father, I raised my glass to Connie and said, 'Prosit.'

Preoccupied with studying Connie's happy smile across the table through my shimmering glass, I was jostled back to reality when someone called out,

'Hello, Hughie.'

As we both turned around, I looked into the lecherous eyes of Penelope. As she danced away from the table, she gave me an inviting smile. Conscious of my extreme embarrassment, Connie asked suspiciously, 'Who, may I ask, was that?'

'Oh, that was just one of the girls who came to a party when we were at Digby.'

'By the way she spoke to you, she seems to know you very well.'

'Oh, she's just one of those wretched name droppers who takes pride in calling everyone by their first name,' I said.

I was flabbergasted. How was it that this wretch just happened to be having dinner at the very same place in this enormous city on this occasion. With my Presbyterian background I had a well-established free-floating sense of guilt never too far beneath the surface. I had the disquieting feeling that Providence was trying to tell me something. The rest of the evening was hell. Every time we got on the dance floor, there was Penelope, flashing a big grin. By this time, Connie seemed to be enjoying the whole affair, and tortured me with questions that were painfully close to home. To my great relief, we finally had to leave to catch the train. This prelude to my visit to Edinburgh did nothing for my confidence.

We were met by Connie's fiancé, whom one couldn't help but like and admire. He had all the desirable features a girl could ask for in a suitor: Good-looking, forthright, humble, patient, and obviously her devoted slave. I couldn't imagine my ever being able to develop such an impressive set of sterling qualities. He was accompanied by a British Indian friend, an equally nice chap. I chose to walk with the friend as we strolled along Princes Street. I set a brisk pace nattering nervously in order to leave Connie with an opportunity to tell of her change of heart.

The seven days leave was illuminating and rewarding. Contrary to my expectations of being viewed as a trifling presumptuous outsider, I was welcomed into the home of Dr. Herbert Robbie, Headmaster of the Bathgate High School with a genuine warmth. Effie Robbie, Connie's sister, a graduate of the University of Edinburgh, shared with her husband the exacting responsibilities of leadership in community education. She ran the spacious two-story granite Headmaster's residence with great care. The furnishings betrayed the Scottish emphasis on quality and practicality. Adjacent to the school, the house was the daily meeting place of the heads of departments. They brought and ate their lunches together in the drawing room.

Dr. Robbie did his fair share of the teaching, besides filling the exacting job of School Administrator. Although he had to resort to corporal punishment on occasions, he preferred to reward wrong-doing with appropriately selected extra school work. I was struck by the dedication with which these two worked together for a common purpose. They seemed to be chosen heads of every cultural endeavour in the community as well. If they had a spare moment, it was spent maintaining the large vegetable garden in the back.

Herbert, renowned for his dry wit, was one of the principals of the local Robert Burns Society. Effie's patronage was required in this association which promoted Scottish dancing. We spent one exhausting evening doing eightsome reels. The scream of the pipes seemed to have a galvanizing effect on its listeners. Ladies of every shape and age were drawn to the floor. By the end of the evening, I was drenched in sweat and wondering why some of my more lymphatic partners had not had heart failure.

At the end of the seven days leave, with Herbert and Effie's blessing, Connie and I announced our engagement. I left Edinburgh glowing from the warmth with which they seemed to accept me.

When I got back to the Mess at Biggin, I discovered I had missed 'the big one.' The battleships had broken out of Brest, steamed through the Channel, escaped into the North Sea and now would be able to operate from the Norwegian fjords. Group Captain Barnwell had been the first to sound the alarm. In spite of the body cast he wore because of a broken back he had sustained crash landing a Spitfire, Barnwell had the habit of doing his local flying over the Channel. At ten o'clock, on February 11th, just off the Somme, he sighted a large destroyer force steaming along the coast towards Gris Nez. Circling in the misty rain was a swarm of Messerschmitts. He nipped into cloud and reported his discovery. Every available aircraft capable of carrying a torpedo was scrambled to the attack. The mine laying units of Bomber Command were dispatched to lay a carpet in the path of the flotilla.

A squadron of Swordfish, the pitifully obsolete torpedo launching bi-plane of the Fleet Air Arm, landed at Manston to refuel. They attacked as a unit and every one of them was shot down.

The Biggin Wing was scrambled to work in pairs on the German fighter cover. Omer Levesque and Dean McDonald had flown together. As Omer had already made a name for himself, Dean flew as Number 2. Apparently, without looking to right or left, Omer had lunged to the attack. In no time Dean discovered that he had not one Messerschmitt on his tail but three. As he turned into their attack, he warned Omer, who took no heed. Dean's last view of his friend saw him scoring hits on one 109 with two more on his tail. Don Morrison was also missing. With one of his legs blown off, Don Morrison had bailed out of his crippled Spitfire. His courage earned him great respect from the Germans. He was one pilot the Germans allowed to return to England via the Red Cross in Switzerland.*

On the thirteenth of February while we were on a sweep starting at the North Foreland to Dunkirk and thence to Gris Nez, a 109 streaked down from high above us and came in to attack on the quarter. After warning the Squadron, I turned into the attack. At $90°$ deflection the 109 pulled his nose up and took a long burst at me. Once again, I heard the rattle of metal as my aircraft was sprayed with machine gun bullets. As he went by my tail, he flicked over on his back and streaked for the ground. Back at Biggin it was found that one of the bullets had damaged the main spar and the wing would have to be changed. Connie knew all about it. Working at the nerve centre of the Fighter Station, she received instant reports of every detail regarding aircraft service ability and flying personnel. She was in a position to know before I did who had given a mayday. The Chief Controller had apparently suggested she stay in the Cipher Office during sweeps, as she was making some of the plotters nervous.

* At a special investiture King George presented him with the Distinguished Flying Cross before he was repatriated to Canada.

We lost another pilot in a strange way. Blakeslee was caught by a WAAF Flight Sergeant fondling a toothsome plotter on her bed in the WAAF billets. I was in the bar when the Station Commander was discussing the matter with the Wing Commander Flying.

'There's not a thing I can do with her; the Queen Bee is being beastly and insists on pressing charges. That means an automatic court-martial.'

'I must say I admire his taste,' said a voice from the back.

'I agree,' said the Group Captain. 'The only inexcusable thing is to allow yourself to be caught. What a brainless thing to do. I'd just put him and Ormston up for a DFC.'

'May I make a suggestion, sir?' proposed Spy, the chief intelligence officer, 'It will take at least three weeks to prepare a court-martial. Blakeslee's an American. Why don't you suggest that he transfer to the U.S. Army Air Corps? One of the main objectives of their advance party over here is trying to recruit expierienced pilots. They'd take him in a second.'

'Jolly good suggestion, Spy. Contact U.S. Army Headquarters in London immediately and see if you can arrange it.'

Blakeslee was transferred to the U.S. Army Air Corps. By the end of the War, Blakeslee was a 'Bird' Colonel, leading one of the most successful long range fighter escort groups in England. He led one of the first wings of fighters to fly the Pacific, refuelling in the air.

The first sweep Wing Commander Masterman led he chose 401 as Lead Squadron. I was given the job of flying as his No. 2. I never worked so hard in all my life. Throughout the entire sweep he kept opening and closing his throttle, and whenever enemy formations were reported, he would make a sharp turn in that direction. As a result, the Squadron and the Wing were strung out all over the place.

Ian Ormston, who was leading Blue Section, suddenly began flying in a bizarre manner. In an excited voice he began reporting imaginary formations of enemy aircraft while dodging all over the sky. We were above twenty thousand feet. Obviously he was having oxygen failure. The Section tried desperately to get him to fly down and out, without success. He continued to fly crazily around the sky at this level. It was impossible for anyone to stay with him. On the return, Blue Section reported being short of fuel and landed at Manston. In dribs and drabs the rest of the Wing limped back to Biggin. I was the last to enter Dispersal. With my uniform drenched in sweat, carrying my parachute, I stomped through the door and said, 'That was an utter bloody shambles. The Wing CO jerked his throttle all the way through the sweep and flew around the sky like a bumble bee.'

Turning to our new Commanding Officer, Squadron Leader Douglas, I said, 'Sir, do you think you could diplomatically say something to him?'

There was a long pause as Douglas fixed me with a cold stare.

'Godefroy, don't let me ever hear you make critical remarks about your Wing Commander Flying. The only thing that is demanded of you is to follow your leader wherever he goes. Do I make myself clear?'

There was an audible silence.

'Yes, sir.'

An hour later, the other three members of Blue Section landed at Biggin and gave us the full story about Ormston. While they were waiting to be refuelled at Manston, a lone Spitfire dived into the circuit downwind, did a stall turn, put flaps and wheels down and came in and landed. Realizing from the markings that it was Ian, they all ran out when they saw that his prop had stopped. They found Ian slumped over the controls unconscious. They dragged him out and laid him on the grass. The ambulance was summoned and he was taken to the hospital, babbling. For several days Ian remained incoherent. Finally normal responses returned and after a week he was allowed to return to the Squadron. He remembered absolutely nothing after reaching our designated altitude of twenty thousand feet. How he managed to land his machine was a miracle.

To avoid the possibility of the Biggin Wing being rendered inoperable by a surprise attack on the airdrome, it was decided that 401 Squadron should operate from the satellite field at Gravesend. As Giles would follow me, I wanted Connie to meet him before we left the Station. He was packing our things when I brought Connie unannounced into my billet. Taken by surprise he fussed around at first straightening up the room, but when he realized the purpose of our visit, he beamed with pleasure, evidently flattered.

'Madam, since hearing about the announcement, I have been most anxious to make some changes in our quarters. With your permission, may I dispose of these?' he asked, pointing to Peggy Hodge's portrait and the centrefold Esquire Petty drawings on the walls.

'You certainly may,' said Connie, with great deliberation.

He pulled down the Petty drawings and carefully tore them up in small pieces and threw them in the wastepaper basket. Then he removed the photograph from its frame and methodically treated it likewise.

'I've always thought this frame was in rather good taste, Madam; would you be good enough to supply me with a suitable replacement?'

'Giles,' I said, 'I want you to instruct her how best to look after me.'

'I would prefer to be of service to both of you, sir. That's really the sort of thing that I've been used to,' he replied.

When the Ground Personnel had been transported and fully entrenched at Gravesend, we flew our Spitfires to the grass field. Without aircraft dispersed around and the camouflage, it was rather hard to find. I had flown over the area many times and never suspected that it was a landing strip. A portion of Cobham Hall, Lord Darnley's estate, had been commandeered as the Officers' Quarters. Although we never saw him, Lord Darnley still occupied one wing of the building. A long winding driveway led from the entrance gate past beautifully tailored lawns shaded by huge gnarled trees spattered with moss. Unperturbed by our presence, deer grazed contentedly on the lawn. Giles met me at the entrance and conducted me past the drawing room with deep leather easy chairs flanking a fireplace. He led me through a door covered in leather and studded with brass tacks to a long hall. There was a musty smell about it and, to the hollow sound of our footsteps on heavy oak floors, I walked by one large regal portrait after another. The only one I had recognized was King Henry VIII.

'This is to be your room,' said Giles, opening the door to a bedroom with high ceilings and a large mahogany four-posted bed. A small fire-place faced the bed, and to one side a door that led to the private bath. There was a strange coldness about this rambling mansion house that somehow seemed to inhibit the light-hearted levity so characteristic of a Fighter Mess. The thick walls cloaked the place in such silence that it came as some relief when it was broken by the crackling roar of a Merlin engine. The pilots of one Squadron and a few RAF Admin types were lost in such expansive quarters.

Routine defensive and offensive operations continued, but were unworthy of note until the 28th of February. The Wing was ordered to operate as part of the Fighter Force on a sortie with the code name of 'Circus.' This indicated that a light bomber force would be escorted to bomb the docks at Ostend. Before taking off, Squadron Leader Douglas informed us once again we were to split up into pairs to seek out and engage the enemy. At twenty-three thousand feet we got right to the Ostend area before the Controller broke R/T silence reporting strong formations in the vicinity. I saw two 190's about twenty miles inland at my level. Putting my throttle through the gate I broke from the forma-tion and went after them. They saw me coming and split up, one diving away while the other climbed up into the sun. I followed the latter. In spite of being blinded, at three hundred and fifty yards, I gave him a long burst. He flicked over on his back and went straight for the ground. Looking around, I saw another inland and gave chase. He too saw me coming, and dived away. Looking around, I found I was alone, a straggler well behind the Hun coastal patrols. I began a shallow dive for the coast and at six thousand feet two miles inside Boulogne I found myself in a solid block of flak. I turned back inland in the hope of coming out somewhere else, but the barrage of flak had given me away, and already I noticed a 190 five thousand feet above, following. I turned out once more aiming for Cap Gris Nez. Out in front, just off the water, I saw a lone Spitfire. He was weaving hopelessly with two 190's on his tail and two more standing by. I had the sickly feeling that at any moment I was going to witness his destruction. As I dived to his rescue, the 190 above came down behind. With my head spinning from back to front, I continued my dive and took a long burst at the ones in front out of range. They broke off their attack. I made a wild break just in time to see the 190 spitting tracer rocket beneath my tail. A wild dog-fight ensued. As usual, the 190's followed each other in well-timed persistent attacks. They were good marksmen. One took a burst at me from 90° deflection, and I heard the rattling tattoo of machine gun bullets going through my aircraft. Just off the water, one pressed home his attack to within about twenty-five yards, and I heard the sound of his cannons firing. Just on the point of stall, in desperation I did a barrel roll, and the 190 slid underneath my tail, and I ended up on his. At this speed I was mushing, and I realized that if I fired my guns, the resultant loss of twenty miles an hour in air speed would make me spin into the sea. It was infuriating, but before I had time to get sufficient air speed to fire, he was out of range. Gradually we worked ourselves farther and farther out to sea. Finally they gave up. Flat out, line abreast, we headed home.

Having had my throttle through the gate for the greater part of the sortie, I was low on fuel. As we crossed in over Dover, I had the first opportunity to study my companion's aircraft. It had the YO identification letters of our Squadron but was not one of the aircraft in my flight. With his mask on, it was impossible to tell who the pilot was. In his port wing root was a huge hole through which I could see daylight. I called the Controller and reported that we were landing at Manston. When we had taxied in, the pilot removed his helmet. It was Slim Cosburn, one of our new replacements in A Flight. Having not seen the hole in his port wing, Slim almost put his foot through it getting out. It was his first sweep.

Hughie Merritt also landed at Manston. Flying in my Section, he had seen a 190 flash under my tail and had gone after him. In the process of scoring visible strikes, he heard a tremendous explosion behind. When he broke, he discovered there was a 190 chewing on him from behind. Unaware of the extent of the damage, he'd elected to land at the first base. His oxygen bottle behind had stopped a cannon shell, exploded and blown a hole in the fuselage. It was large enough to put your head through. He was credited with 'one damaged.'

In spite of my opulent quarters, for me Gravesend proved true to its name. It was too far away from Biggin for me to be able to see Connie. We kept in touch by judicious use of the direct telephone line from the Mess to the Ops Room. With the rapid turnover of flying personnel, I had shied away from becoming too friendly with anyone. On a few occasions I took relief by visiting the Leather Bottle, an interesting old pub in the area.

Lucky Thirteen

In the last week of February, I spent a forty-eight-hour leave with Connie as the guest of her brother the Reverend Tom Helm at Tunbridge Wells. The town, renowned as a health spa and for its mineral water, nestled in the heart of Kent only an hour's train journey from Victoria.

In this household I was a misfit. Tom, a saintly man dedicated to his calling, willingly accepted the hardship of living on a pitifully small stipend. In the hope of compensating for the difficulties that this imposed on his wife and two children, he combined frugality with personal denial to obtain the niceties that might make life more pleasant for them. First light found him in his study preparing himself for his services, then he was away on foot to visit the sick. Each night he took his turn on duty as a volunteer policeman, with a steel tommy hat to protect him from the shrapnel. His only other passion was flowers. Every spare moment he spent working in his garden.

These exposures to Connie's family made me aware of their sharp contrast to me. Raised by men in a prep school and by a family which emphasized the practical, I had joined in the RCAF a group of men from every walk of life on the North American continent. Air Force language was ingrown with four-letter words. For the past two years, I had lived and breathed flying. When the day was done, we thought of nothing else but how to satisfy our immediate needs. I had stifled the aesthetic part of my nature. I had become a part of them. The only way I could remain inconspicuous in this family was to keep my mouth shut.

The first week of March was devoted to making arrangements for the wedding. In obedience to the dictates of Auntie Jessie, the self-appointed matriarch of the family, I was not to be allowed to clap eyes on Connie until we were in the 'Kirk.' Having absolutely no experience in such things, I was grateful to be left completely out of this.

It is not uncommon for the principals of a marriage ceremony, faced with the full significance of the vows, to experience a sense of uneasiness. What had been planned as a simple ceremony seemed now to require hours of organization. As the day drew near, Connie was engulfed in a maelstrom of activities as one requirement was added to another. All this produced in me a creeping uncertainty that began to border on panic.

With the demands of flying there was no time for a wedding rehearsal. On the day I was given a five-minute briefing on procedure as I entered the Kirk. I had asked Jeep, the senior Canadian, to be my best man. He had never been known to leave a fellow in the lurch. Being a good Catholic, however, he hadn't set foot in a Presbyterian church and didn't know anymore what to do than I did. Al Harley and one other pilot were released from duty to allow them to attend. They looked pretty lonely by themselves in the third row, the only occupants of my side. Herbert and Effie sat down beside them to even it up a little. Jeep and I had to sit in the first row in front of them, a pew I had never occupied in my life. To avoid the blank inquisitive stares of the choir, I nervously studied the ceiling.

Suddenly I was frightened out of my wits by a hand on my shoulder. It was Herbert. Tom who was conducting the service had been trying to catch my eye to get up. Connie was halfway up the aisle. A blue funk enveloped me obliterating the memory of most of the details of the proceedings that followed. I tried to speak loud enough to be heard at the back of the church, but my throat was so dry my voice cracked.

All I could think of on the way to the reception was Connie's glowing description of Herbert's wedding speech. Not only was I totally unprepared, but my mind was a complete blank. I began worrying about what Jeep would say as master of ceremonies. I was given no opportunity to slip off. I could have used something to moisten my lips and loosen my tongue.

To my great relief and suprise Jeep did a very polished job and kept a civil tongue in his head. I would have enjoyed Herbert's dry wit as he proposed a toast to the bride if I hadn't had to answer him. I rose to my feet hoping to convey how happy I was. I got so tangled up in my remarks that my audience concluded that I was utterly miserable. Connie was visibly relieved when I sat down. The agues left me on the train to Victoria. Connie had been granted only two days leave so we had decided to make the best of it. We were shown into a magnificent suite at the Savoy with tall French windows over-looking the Thames. A bottle of champagne in an ice bucket with two shimmering glasses on a silver salver awaited us. The valet and the chambermaid meticulously attended to our every need. Unlike us they were prepared for rice and French safes to fly out of my bag. They disposed of the rice, untied the knot in my pajamas, and put the safes in the dresser drawer.

The champagne was the panacea. Totally relaxed, we stayed at the dinner-dance to the small hours of the morning. Finally, when we returned to our suite, we found our bed turned down, our night clothes laid out, and the heavy drapes drawn over the windows. An air raid was at its height. As I doffed my tunic, a stick of bombs came down, each deafening explosion louder than the last. One couldn't help but feel that the next one would blow us to eternity. Connie suggested we go down to the air raid shelter. I adamantly refused. Having paid for this, I intended to enjoy it regardless. The building shook as a land mine exploded with an ear-splitting blast.

'Oh, dear,' Connie shuddered. 'This is a really nasty one. We can't possibly get undressed. We may have to get out of here at any moment.'

Fully clothed, we settled on the bed while I held on to her tightly

With each crash I felt her wince and gave her a little squeeze. Gradually as bomb bursts became less frequent, and the sound of the guns more distant, we fell asleep.

I dreamed that I was in my aircraft in a wild dog-fight. With horrifying reality there was a tremendous explosion and the cockpit became a cauldron of fire. With a convulsive leap, still dead asleep, I landed in the middle of the floor. I woke up weak and dizzy from the exertio.

'What on earth's the matter?' Connie exclaimed with alarm.

Still not awake, I said, 'I'm just bailing out.'

I was awakened by the sound of a boat whistle and getting up, I tiptoed to the window and peeked out between the heavy drapes, squinting with the brilliant sunlight. It was a glorious morning without a cloud in the sky. A river barge was pushing its way under the bridge crawling with traffic. The daily life of London was going on as if nothing had happened. Gradually, I drew the drapes apart. With the room full of light Connie opened her eyes and sleepily joined me by the window. Pensively, we watched the pedestrians winding their way along the footpath below. A pair of Coldstream Guardsmen while passing an Army Officer braced and snapped a salute. Languidly, the dapper Captain acknowledged by tapping his leather-covered stick on his cap. Interspersed amongst servicemen were the men of Whitehall, with their black Homburgs, striped trousers, briefcases and umbrellas.

After a while I ordered breakfast. In what seemed like no time there was a gentle tap on the door and the waiter wheeled in a table and stationed it between the two chairs by the window. A substantial breakfast was served piping hot from the silver-covered servers on the preheated plates. I had my first taste of croissant, mouth-watering when adding a dab of butter and marmalade. With special permission from the Station Commander, Connie had been granted the right to wear 'civvies.' I was not permitted to look until she was fully dressed in a smart London suit she had purchased as part of her trousseau. The corsage I had given her for the dinner-dance was not wilted and added a bit of flair.

My struggle for survival once again commanded my attention. By 13th March, I was back in the groove, reflexes taut and ready for the prospect of the sweep ahead. As usual, five minutes before 'press tit' time, conversation at Dispersal had tapered off. I was preoccupied with stuffing my escape kit and envelope of foreign money in my Mae West and pulling my heavy Red Cross socks over my knees, when one of the new replacements came up to me and asked:

'Do you know what day it is?'

'No,' I said.

'It's the thirteenth!'

'So what? I'm not superstitious.'

'I've been reading your log book. Have you noticed how many times you've been hit on the thirteenth?'

As the thought sank in, it seemed I heard a crackling sound in my head such as static electricity makes in the open before a thunderstorm, the prelude to mortal fear. What he said was true, and I was one of the last who had come from Wellingore. In a voice husky with emotion I said:

'I told you, I'm not superstitious.'

But the seed of doubt had been planted, and, as I strapped myself into my cockpit, every nerve in my body was tingling. This was 'it.' With shaky hands, while fumbling around doing my cockpit check, I saw the prop of the Squadron Commander turning. Soon we were all taxiing out. Brimming with anxiety, I took off. Slowly we climbed to the coast to make our rendezvous with the bombers which would bomb Hazebrouck. For the first time I hoped for some malfunction that would force me to turn back. It didn't come. Above twenty thousand feet, in spite of the cold, I felt the sweat cool on my back and forehead. The sky was a brilliant azure blue and the Channel an icy green flecked with white caps as we crossed over Dungeness. For the first time since Prep School, I prayed the only prayer that I could remember:

'Now I lay me down to sleep, I pray the Lord my soul to keep.'

Inside the coast, a Focke-Wulf 190, its yellow nose glistening in the sun, went by on my side. In level flight at high speed the 190 flew with nose down. The prop appeared to be barely turning, as though the pilot had throttled back to wait. It seemed as if he was looking at me with a hooked nose and a malevolent sneer. I couldn't stand it. I had to get it over with. Banging the throttle through the gate, I peeled out of the formation and went after him. He was the sucker bait, and, as if he was thumbing his nose, he rolled gracefully over and streaked for the ground. I was where they wanted me, a − l − o − n − e. In an instant, two more came rocketing down from above with the leading edge of their wings rippling with fire. As they split up and took turns attacking, a wave of nausea came over me. Determined to sell myself dearly, I took chances on longer bursts as they went by. The shudder of my guns maintained my spirit but I knew that soon my six seconds of fire would be up. The next time I pressed my thumb I heard that sickening hiss. I was out. Gasping in my mask as I strained with the G., I worked myself towards the Channel. Doggedly they kept after me. By the time I had managed to get ten miles off shore I felt myself greying out with exhaustion. I was ready to give up. Another was coming in. I levelled out, flew straight towards England and closed my eyes. After what seemed like an eternity, I opened my eyes and looked.

On my port side was a 190 slowly going by. For a moment we looked at each other eye to eye. The next instant he was in a climbing turn and went diving back into France. I was alone. I dived down on the waves and went 'balls out' for Dover. As I crossed in over the cliffs with the balloons all riding gently into the wind, I felt as though I had awakened from a nightmare. With ten gallons of fuel I circled Manston for a landing.

When I had landed and shut down, I just sat in the cockpit. Pensively, I surveyed the bullet holes in my wings, contemplating the folly my emotions had allowed me to engage in. I had flown like an accident prone clot. I'd allowed myself to be influenced by the young pilot. Like the English lad at Initial Training School with his tea leaves, I had allowed suggestion to give me the kiss of death. The fact that I was back was a clear indication of the stupidity of such a reaction. I swore to myself that never again would I allow this to happen. It would not be such events as these that would dictate the hour for me to go.

Sitting on the grass in the warm sunshine beside my aircraft waiting to be refuelled, I found my attention drawn to a lone Spitfire making a circuit. As he turned into the wind, I noticed that his wheels weren't down. A red flare arched in the air from the Watch Office. Oblivious to the warning, the aircraft ground in on its belly in a cloud of dust. I recognized the Squadron letters to be the same as those of the Polish Squadron Leader and his two mates who, like me, were waiting to be refuelled. As the pilot in the aircraft on the field stood up in the cockpit, the three Poles ran to assist him. From a distance, the pilot appeared to be unhurt, and from the way he was moving his hands he was evidently recounting an engagement. His three Squadron mates gave a synchronous shout of triumph and threw up their hands. With his arm over the shoulder of the pilot the Squadron Leader led his men back to Dispersal jabbering in Polish. As he passed me, I asked:

'Was he shot up badly, Sir?'

'No,' he replied, in a tone as if I'd asked a stupid question.

'Why didn't he put down his wheels?'

'Oh dat, he just forgot! What matter, he killed two German.'

With a wide toothy grin and a convulsive grunt, he stomped his foot emphatically. I was very envious.

The rest of the month of March, we were kept very busy. I was given no opportunities to see Connie, and in one sense I was grateful. I had steeled myself to face each day with a new resolve. I didn't feel I could relax to think of the gentler things of life. I wanted to cleanse my mind of the demoralizing influence of fear, and I felt I could do it best without her anxious eyes upon me.

The only sweep of note was my last one at the beginning of April. It was a pure fighter sweep, rendezvousing over Manston. The tentative plan was to sweep the area from Mardyke to St. Omer and come back over Dungeness. The squadron was bounced by twenty Focke-Wulf 190's and a furious skirmish broke out. I got in behind one and got in a long sustained burst, feeling sure I hit him. Unfortunately I observed no strikes. Tired and disappointed, I went back to my room at Gravesend, threw myself face down across my bed and fell asleep. I was wakened by the gentle hand of Giles.

'Your bath is drawn, sir.'

'Thank you, Giles,' I said, sitting up and pulling off my flying boots and my uniform.

There is nothing more soothing than a hot bath, and I took full advantage of it. When I came out, I found the boots and clothing I had removed were gone. In their place, Giles had left my best blue, the tunic with the buttons gleaming was over the back of the chair, the pants across the seat; socks, underwear, shirt, collar and tie, neatly arranged on top of the pants, and a shining pair of Oxfords at the foot. He was nowhere to be seen. Giles had done it again. But for him I would have stayed in bed and not gone down to dinner. The meal was nothing to write home about, but it was food, and I felt the better for it. I had just lit a cigarette hoping that it would improve the flavour of the coffee when Giles informed me that Connie was on the telephone.

Somewhat impatiently, I went and listened to her preamble. Finally I interjected.

'Okay now, that's enough; You've obviously got more than that to tell me — what is it?'

'Guess,' she said excitedly.

'I haven't the slightest idea.'

'I just got a signal about you.'

'About me? Not Malta again. I took myself off the draft.'

'I'll read you the signal — the 4th of the 2nd, '42, 1700 hrs. stop, Eleven Group Headquarters to Officer Commanding 401 Squadron Biggin Hill stop.'

'Never mind the unimportant details. Get down to the message.'

'PO H C Godefroy J3701 posted from 401 Squadron to AFDU RAF Station Duxford stop.'

'What the hell does all that mean?' I said.

'Darling, you've been taken off Ops; AFDU I've discovered stands for Air Fighter Development Unit. They test all new aircraft before they're put in service. They also are the one with the German Circus. The Squadron Leader Ops tells me you're damn lucky. It should be a lot more interesting than being on an OTU.'

'I don't need a rest.'

'Don't argue with *me*, dear. I'm just telling you what the signal says. I know you're disappointed to leave your friends, but I do think it's right; you have been getting a little testy lately, I hate to tell you.'

To me this was the final straw. After a long series of unproductive encounters, I had finally been 'turfed.'

'I don't want to talk any more. I'll call you later.'

I felt incredibly lonely and bitterly disappointed. I was just beginning to feel my efforts should be rewarded. In a state of dejection, I opened the door of my room to find Giles turning down my bed.

'I'm posted,' I said.

'I know, sir,' said Giles softly. 'Madam was kind enough to phone and tell me. It won't be for long, sir; they say they never keep you longer than six months.'

'Six months? That's a bloody lifetime.'

'It will pass quickly, sir. I believe we must have our things ready by 0800 hours in the morning. I will see to it. Is there anything else, sir?'

'No thanks, Giles. I'm going to turn in.'

Next morning I got the final blow. Giles had told me he would come wherever I went. This had all been changed; they were short of batmen, and he would be going back to Biggin. In Dispersal I was no longer one of them. Everyone was preoccupied with the prospect of the sweep ahead. Douglas allowed Dick Dennison to fly me to Duxford in the Miles Magister.

12

POSTED

Wing Commander Campbell-Orr was a tall pear-shaped individual with long spindly legs, and jowls that shivered a little when he shook his head. He spoke with the precision of a Cambridge Don. Charming, and used to the finer things of life, he was the perfect man to command this Unit that had a steady stream of VIP's. He was a pilot with sufficient experience to delegate the more tiresome strenuous flying to somebody else. He seemed to be of a slightly bilious nature, for whenever he got excited he had a tendency to belch a little between words.

I found him in the Dispersal Hut warming his backside by the pot-bellied stove. Hoping that he was unaware of my posting, I said:

'Sir, I'm Pilot Officer Godefroy from 401 Squadron at Biggin. For some unexplained reason I was told to report here. I can only think that someone has got their signals crossed.'

For a moment he looked me up and down, his lips pursed and his nostrils quivering with indignation.

'You "Fightah boys" can be so terribly tiresome. As if I didn't have enough to do. My dear fellow, I regret to say that you will be with me a minimum of six months, and I would be grateful if you would try to be as little bother as possible. Smith, your Canadian!'

Squadron Leader Smith was a small unobtrusive man. I soon discovered that he was the brains behind the organization. Content to be relieved of the public relations, he was able to let his inventive mind concentrate on the job. The primary objective of Air Fighter Development Unit was to test all the latest aircraft and report on the best way of making use of them operationally. Secondly, as the War progressed, and enemy aircraft were downed in a reparable state, AFDU got the job of flying and testing these aircraft, reporting on their capability and comparative performance.

The other permanent flying member of the Organization was Flight Lieutenant Clive. Clive was a tall blond fellow with a carefully preened handle-bar moustache. He professed to being a fighter pilot. Given to swashbuckling behaviour, he acted the part convincingly. I didn't learn much flying from Clive, but I did have the opportunity of observing a master of the art of 'brownnosing.' An Air Vice Marshal would never have a chance to tap his cigarette more than twice on his thumb before Clive's lighter would flash in front of him invariably lighting on the first flick. He treated his immediate superiors with affable benevolence and condescension. Every effort was directed towards undermining their self-confidence and convincing them that they were hopelessly disorganized. Wing Commanders and above received his special attention. While insidiously damning everybody else in the organization with faint praise, he worked on giving them the impression that without him everything would be utter chaos.

The rest of the flying personnel were transients, tour expired operational pilots. From Bomber Command, there was Squadron Leader Jock Murray, DFC, a Scotsman, and Pilot Officer Walker. From Fighter Command came Flight Lieutenant Sewell, DFC, Squadron Leader Scruffy Haywood, Pilot Officer Thorne, and Pilot Officer Scott, an Australian. There were also two Poles. The only one I got to know well was Sergeant Teddy Kulczyk. I was advised that the other, a Pilot Officer with the British DFC and the highest Polish decorations available, wanted to be left alone. He was a big fellow, with high cheek bones, a rugged jaw and a prominent gold tooth. He spent most of his time brooding, slumped in a chair in Dispersal. In the company of these men I was to learn to appreciate some different approaches to life and how to get the most out of an airplane.

It is surprising how quickly a person, adapted to service life, can adjust to new surroundings. Despite the Canada flashes on the shoulders, I found it required little effort to blend harmoniously with my confreres. With one tour under my belt, I had something in common with all the operational pilots in this Unit. There were dozens of different airplanes I had never flown, everything from a Gladiator, the obsolete single-seater bi-plane which had seen service before the War, to Lancasters and Halifaxes that would become the workhorses of Bomber Command. From the Luftwaffe we had a flyable Junkers 88 and a Messerschmitt 109E.

There was also a Fiat CR 42, one of the bi-plane fighters that Mussolini had sent into the Battle of Britain. A dozen such aircraft had been in the Italian formation and all of them had been shot down but this one. The pilot had landed it intact in a farmer's field. It was a magnificent aerobatic airplane when it was in the air, but because of its lack of speed and fire power, it had become long since obsolete. It had no flaps and a fixed undercarriage. At sixty-eight miles an hour it would fall out of the sky, and at seventy-two with the throttle closed, it would float the full length of the airdrome without sitting down. If I expressed the desire to fly a certain plane, whether single or multi-engined, I was given five minutes verbal instruction, shown where the tits were to start it, and off I went. I took full advantage of this privilege. By the time I left this Unit, I had flown forty-seven different types of aircraft.

With a healthy complement of operational pilots, and some 'odds and sods' from the Fleet Air Arm, it was a spirited Mess. Besides the WAAF Officers we even had a Canadian WRNS* Officer. Having become accustomed to hearing women speak in an English or Scottish accent, listening to this girl was refreshing. Frequently we banded together to defend our point of view. As a Canadian, I found myself being much more critical of her behaviour than of other women.

Living among these tour expired pilots, each from a different walk of life, I found there was one rather contagious attitude. Faced with the threat or promise of another tour, they lived each day to the full. Thorne and Walker openly admitted they had had enough. Thorne could see only one way out: Remaining as a permanent Test Pilot with AFDU. His whole energy was devoted to impressing his Commanding Officer with his suitability. Walker studiously avoided work of all kinds. Denying any fragment of 'keenness,' he was content to pass the rest of his days at Dispersal, puffing on his pipe through his tobacco-stained moustache.

To Scottie, the Australian, Walker had all the characteristics he found so distasteful in the English. A perpetual free-loader, Walker would sit wooden-faced at the bar nursing a half pint of beer until somebody offered to buy a round. Such an announcement would bring him smartly back to life and with moustache twitching he would respond:

'Don't mind if I do. I'll have a pint of mild.'

To add to Scottie's misery, wretched as he was here, separated from the rest of the 'cobbers,' he had been made to share a room with Walker. He repeatedly accused him of using his toothpaste and his after-shave lotion. He never brushed his teeth without feeling the brush to see if it were wet. He 'wouldn't put it past the bastard to use even that.' More than once, after a couple of beers failed to get any reaction, with a tirade of insulting remarks Scottie would challenge Walker to 'put up your dukes and settle this like a man.'

The whole matter came to a head one night when Walker returned to the Mess 'in his cups.' He had had his regular visit to the village for a few pints on 'Doris' and the comfort of a knee trembler from her outside the main gate. He staggered down to his room to find Scottie asleep with the lights out. Having been threatened with bodily harm if he dared to put the lights on when Scottie was asleep, he wisely stumbled in in the dark. Feeling an irresistible urge to empty his bladder he decided to use the wash-hand basin. He groped around until he ran into something that felt like it and with a sigh of relief began to void. Scottie was awakened from a dead sleep with warm water squirting

* Women's Royal Naval Service.

in his face that had the distinctive odor of urine. A terrible fracas started, but in the darkness Walker made his escape. When Scottie threatened to call the Australian High Commissioner if he weren't moved, the President of the Mess condescended and gave him other quarters.

Connie managed to get a forty-eight-hour leave, but with the time required to travel back and forth by train there was just enough left for us to spend one night together in a pub at Cambridge. She came with exciting news, however. She had applied for a posting to RAF Station Debden, the nearest Fighter Station to Duxford. The Controller felt certain that he could wangle it. If I could find digs somewhere between the two Stations, for the first time we'd be able to live like man and wife.

I spent the next week, after hours, pedalling my issue bicycle up and down the countryside, searching. I was directed to the sleepy little village of Saffron Walden, seven miles away. On the approach from the North, it is hidden from view behind a hill. On reaching its crest, one has a panoramic view of the village with its church spire and narrow cobblestone streets nestled in a valley below. Resisting the temptation to explore, I got straight down to ringing doorbells. After many fruitless calls, I was given the name and address of a Mrs. Clitherow who 'might be able to help.'

I found Mrs. Clitherow hanging out the wash with her five-year-old son. She was at the stage of pregnancy which made her walk like a bass drummer with her maternity dress gaping a little in front. At first she listened to my plea sympathetically. Interrupting me, she asked if we could continue the discussion upstairs where we could sit down over a cup of tea. She was the wife of an RAF Sergeant Armourer stationed at Duxford and was having quite a time making ends meet. The upstairs flat had been the only thing available and financially was a bit over their heads. Apologizing for the humble furnishings, she offered to let me have a room with kitchen privileges. It was simple, scrupulously clean, and perfectly adequate. After agreeing on financial arrangements, she offered to make new curtains for our bedroom.

As promised, Connie was posted to Debden. It was the Fighter Station occupied by the Eagle Squadron. Connie, being a person who felt a little squeamish at breakfast each morning, reacted strongly to the Americans' table manners. Impressed by their forthright generosity and friendliness, nonetheless she had great difficulty eating while watching the pilots smear jam on their bacon and eggs. She quickly made arrangements to move into our new digs. By timely use of a little charm, she managed to wangle some transport and didn't have to put in for a bicycle. Seven miles is not far on a bicycle, but I soon found that the brisk penetrating wind that faced me on my way to work in the morning often faced me on my way back at night. When one added rain, the ride could be particularly tiresome.

As soon as we had synchronized our days off, we went exploring in the village. In the narrow winding back streets we didn't see a soul. Our footsteps echoed on the cobblestones as we strolled between old Tudor houses with swayback wooden beams. The silence seemed to cry out in protest when it was broken by the crackling roar of an aircraft flying low over the chimney pots. Finally we traced our way back to the High Street. We went into a few shops as much from curiosity as anything else. Each time there was some delay before the tinkle of the bell on the entrance would bring the shopkeeper from the depths of the dark storeroom at the rear. We would be engaged in a pleasant conversation about anything but the business at hand. Making a sale seemed to be the last thing that interested them. The predominant wish was that they could render us service. Money was accepted almost with reluctance, accompanied by profuse apologies for the dreadful price of things these days.

We came across an attractive little tea shop called the 'Copper Kettle.' The door was wide open. On either side were large plateglass windows which enabled one to see everything and everybody inside. Centrally located behind one of these windows was a table in the middle of which was a large tarnished copper kettle flanked on either side by baskets filled with freshly baked cakes and scones. The place was crowded, and as we entered, we had to make our way around a table littered untidily with papers and pencils and a tin box full of change. Excusing ourselves repeatedly, we had to step over several pairs of feet and a few dogs to reach the last two remaining seats. The shop was run by four art students who seemed to enjoy their work. The cooking and washing was done in the basement and hauled noisily up in a rickety dumb waiter. The girls shouted back and forth at each other through the hole. A congenial informality pervaded the place encouraging us to be more garrulous and converse with the total strangers who shared our table.

Inadvertently, we had become members of a tea party. The girl who brought the tea and cakes broke right into our conversation. If amused, she threw back her head and made the rafters ring with laughter. Over a good cup of tea we had a pleasant chat with the elderly couple who shared our table. As we took leave we found ourselves marvelling at our good fortune in finding a place in the bosom of this peaceful little village.

Connie's cooking instructions had been terminated after she burnt her first piece of toast. She had never read a cookbook or seen a civilian ration card. With eggs, bacon and butter in short supply, filling me up with something edible was a problem. Having learned to do a little cooking because of the lack of talent on my mother's part, I found myself at first offering suggestions. These were not appreciated. I kept body and soul together by taking larger portions at lunch at the Mess. After a while she began to get the hang of it by mastering a few foolproof filling recipes like macaroni and cheese and shepherd's pie.

Every third night she was on duty and would get home after I left in the morning. It wasn't long before we discovered that Mrs. Clitherow was a person who promised little and did much. A soiled shirt, for instance, would disappear and the next day I would find it on the bed neatly washed and ironed. Rather than let me muck around in the kitchen when Connie was on night duty, she insisted on feeding me, claiming that she had plenty for all of us. I refused to continue accepting her hospitality until she promised to let us pool our rations and let me pay half the grocery bill. With some reluctance she agreed.

One cannot wander the back roads of rural England in peace or war without making the acquaintance of somebody who has a litter of new puppies. Cycling on the road each day I had met an Alsatian female who was very friendly. After I started bringing tidbits for her from the mess, she met me every day on my way home. The friendship was soon noted by the owner who, seeing that I loved dogs, stopped me and asked me if I were interested in one of her pups. There had been five in the litter and all of them had found homes except one female. They would have to destroy her if she were not placed because of the shortage of food. When I saw this soft furry thing, tail wagging furiously, clawing at its enclosure pleading to be picked up, and held it in my arms licking my face, I was hooked. With the reservation that I would have to bring her back if Mrs. Clitherow objected, I happily accepted the offer. When Mrs. Clitherow saw the look of excitement on her little boy's face, any reservations she might have had disappeared.

'Spitty' became my constant companion. At first I had to carry her most of the way to the Station on my bicycle, but as her legs lengthened she was soon running beside me on a leash. Connie had no objection, as long as I promised to clean up if she made any mistakes. She was an intelligent little thing and soon became house trained. The only real boob she made was chewing the heel off one of the mules that Connie had bought as part of her trousseau. This pair of brocade shoes with gilt soles had been her prize possession. Food was no problem; I got plenty of scraps for her from the Mess.

From time to time, Connie and I would get the day off together. When the weather was fine, our favourite pastime was visiting Cambridge. We would hire a punt and spend the afternoon poling on the river through the backs of the colleges. Some of the buildings bordered the river which is spanned at several places by gracefully arched bridges. On one bank, the buildings are at some distance, partially hidden behind tall trees that give shade and shelter to the lawns that lead to the water's edge. Drifting in a punt on a warm day, dabbling one's fingers in the cool still water, soon made one forget that this country was locked in war. The utter peace of these surroundings was mesmerizing, inviting one to fall silent and listen to the sound of the birds and be perfectly content to do nothing more energetic than watch the travels of a bumblebee. Invariably, we would be brought back to reality by Spitty falling out of the boat after trying to sniff her image mirrored in the water. A puppy shaking herself within the confines of a punt quickly interrupts any reverie. These were pleasant days.

AFDU received all operational combat films, and had a special laboratory with equipment to assess possible hits. A report was sent back with each film which could confirm or deny each claim made. I made a careful study of this equipment. With unrestricted access to Spitfires with camera guns, I spent hours practicing shooting at any target that became available. I did all my own assessments. Gradually, but surely, I learned to estimate range and the angle off. With painstaking practice, I finally reached the point where I knew exactly when to fire, where to put the bead in relation to the target and how long to keep my finger on the button. I swore that never again would I run out of ammunition without having the satisfaction of knowing that what I had expended had met its mark.

In bad weather, we hung around Dispersal sitting in the easy chairs circling the potbellied stove. The conversation inevitably got around to shop talk. There was a difference between these sessions and the ones we used to have at Biggin. The participants came from every operational Command in the RAF. They had all had experience that was sufficiently unpleasant that they didn't want to think about it. Conversation was limited to the various strengths and weaknesses of the different aircraft. In a bomber, what was needed was the ability to carry a big bomb load and be able to fly in spite of having sustained enormous damage. The Whitley, the flying boxcar that rumbled along nose down, and the Wellington with its geodetic construction that twisted and bent its way through an explosive atmosphere, were spoken of with affection. Both were capable of flight with enormous chunks of their anatomy missing. Speed was of no importance.

The Coastal Command boys who swept the sea lanes of the Atlantic, the Bay of Biscay and the Mediterranean wanted aircraft with reliable engines and enough fuel to fly forever. Cloud was their security blanket in case of attack. A bomb bay full of depth charges over target was their raison d'etre. For the anti-shipping boys the Beaufighter or the Mosquito was all that one could ask for. Fast and manoeuverable with four cannons in the nose and a few bombs or a torpedo, they were capable of doing damage and still looking after themselves. A pilot going to a second tour in any of the Commands had to face a common statistic: Surviving the first five sorties was hard. Once accomplished, however, there was a good chance of finishing the tour. For the Bomber Command boys, a tour was 30 trips. The last one was made in the face of dreaded odds, a good enough reason for apprehension.

We were sitting around the stove engaged in just such talk one day with the ceiling five hundred feet in misty rain, when the Wing Commander came in. Wosnyk, the Polish Officer, or 'Warsaw' as Sewell called him, had his favourite seat in the corner and was ignoring the conversation. Campbell-Orr handed him a letter, saying, 'This seems to be a personal letter that arrived somehow in my mail.'

When Warsaw saw the handwriting, he grabbed it and sat up with a start, tearing it open eagerly. We all fell silent as we witnessed the first sign of enthusiasm we had seen on the man's face. His mouth moved silently, and as he read feverishly, a large tear began rolling down his cheek. With a deep grunt he jumped to his feet with a maddened look in his eye and lunged out the door.

'I think it's from his wife,' said Campbell-Orr quietly, leaving the room.

With a crackling roar a Spitfire started up.

'What's he doing?' Sewell wondered going over to the window.

I reached the window just in time to see a Spitfire with the tail up and the coupe top closed streaking across the airdrome. With a jerk the aircraft was off the ground and the wheels snapped up as it rolled over on its back in the wisps of low cloud. For three quarters of an hour we were treated to an incredible performance of low aerobatics. It was done with such violence that I expected at any moment he would spin in and crash. Finally, to our relief, he put his wheels down and came in to land. Respectfully, nobody said a word. Teddy Kulczyk told us later that Warsaw, after two years, had received word that his wife and child were still alive in Poland.

Bomber Command and Coastal Command were sustaining very heavy losses from Luftwaffe fighter attacks. AFDU was asked to work on flying tactics that would reduce these losses. The result was a report recommending the corkscrew technique. It had been discovered that if an aircraft being attacked by a fighter starts a continuous series of diving and climbing turns making it follow a corkscrew track through the sky, the attacking fighter is faced with a continually changing deflection shot. This greatly increased the difficulty in scoring hits. The Wing Commander was ordered to form a Fighter Affiliation Unit. This Unit was to be dispatched to all Operational Stations in Bomber and Coastal Command to demonstrate this technique. A large part of the time I spent with AFDU was taken up doing this work. One of the other Fighter Pilots, Jock Murray, and myself operated as a group. In six months we visited seventy Operational Stations throughout the length and breadth of the British Isles. Most of our attention was directed to Bomber Command. Air Chief Marshal 'Bomber' Harris, or 'Butch' as he was referred to by some pilots, took over Bomber Command in late 1941. His relentless aggressive policy was in full force by 1942.

We helped in the training of the crews which participated in the first daylight raids. In the month of August we observed the formation of the Bomber Command's Pathfinder Force. Having previously been equipped with Whitleys and Wellingtons, the Bomber Command Squadrons were undergoing conversion to Stirlings, the Halifaxes and the Lancasters. Night bombing had been disappointingly inaccurate. So as to give the bombers an instant 'fix' in bad weather, a device called the Gee-box was invented and put into service. This instrument was designed to pick up pulse signals from three widely separated parts of the British Isles. From these it automatically computed a fix. Like radar, these signals followed a straight line of sight and thus the range at which the Gee-box would work was dependent upon the distance from the transmitter stations and the height of the aircraft.

Visiting Bomber Command Squadrons at this time was an unforgettable experience. Like the weather of the Midlands, a depressing gloom seemed to hang in the atmosphere. In the crews fortunate enough to have a skipper with some semblance of leadership, a healthy measure of camaraderie existed. In others, if there was no such person, the crews acted like robots. On many occasions the courage of a rear gunner or an observer would come to the fore in a crisis, and stimulate the crew to complete their mission and work together so that all might survive. They thought of themselves as part of a crew, not a squadron. They ate, drank and flew together, and when their number was up, they died together. It was a nightly occurrence for a Bomber Command aircraft to limp back across the inhospitable expanse of the North Sea with a dead or dying buddy on board. He was immediately replaced.

When a crew was stood down, it left as a group to 'get the hell off the Station' and headed for the pubs, drab as they might be. Many of these had little signs on the wall: 'Walls have ears.' 'Is your journey really necessary?' It was often said that the proprietor of the local knew what the target was before the crews took off. With the exception of a handful of wingless wonders, the Messes seemed to be empty most of the time. The crews were either sleeping, having just come back from a raid, or trying to sleep before going out on another.

On one of these junkets, which often kept me away from home as much as a week, I found myself sitting in a Bomber Command Mess all by myself. It was the Home Base of an RAF Squadron composed of a mixture of British and Commonwealth fliers. A group of Admin types wandered in and congregated at the bar to order drinks. It was obvious from their conversation that they enjoyed pretty exclusive use of the Mess. At this point a scruffily dressed, short, unattractive civilian entered, walked up to the bar and ordered a drink. He listened intently to their conversation then broke in, expressing his views in some detail. This was obviously resented by the officers. To my amusement he appeared to be totally immune to cold shoulders and snubs. Oblivious to it all, he kept barging in. Finally, to the relief of the others, he announced that he had to spend a penny and left.

'What an insufferable, insensitive boor that fella is,' said one. 'Who on earth is he?'

'One of those damn technical narks,' said another, with irritation. 'Have you ever seen such gall?'

At this point the Mess Steward came over to tell me there was a lady on the telephone who wanted to speak to any Canadian.

'I'm not in this squadron.' I countered. 'I am a transient.'

'I have already explained that, sir, but apparently that doesn't seem to matter. She seems very persistent. Would you mind, sir?' he implored.

With considerable reluctance, I went to the telephone. Over the wire came the sound of a Canadian woman's voice in considerable distress. I listened to a long involved story about how she had managed to get to England to marry her fiancé, who was a member of this squadron. She had arrived just in time to be informed that he had gone missing. She had found no one who would take the slightest interest in her dilemma and she was desperate. I expressed genuine sympathy for her in these circumstances and then explained that I was not a member of this squadron and could imagine no way in which I could possibly help. She pleaded with me to get on the bus and come the seven miles to the village where she had found digs. To talk to anybody from home would be a great comfort. After listening to such pleading, I finally agreed. If it hadn't been for the pleasing experience of hearing a female Canadian voice again, I think I would have refused. She was to meet me at the bus stop and would be wearing a crimson flower on her dress.

The more I thought about it as I travelled through the dreary Yorkshire countryside, the more uneasy I became. I took comfort in the fact that she did not know what I looked like, and if I saw a woman with a red flower on her dress who looked dangerous, I could stay on the bus and keep on going.

I arrived at the village to find the street empty. I tried my best to look inconspicuous as I disembarked, painfully aware that I was the only Canadian airman to do so. As I tried to walk quickly away from the bus stop a girl with a red flower on her dress burst from a tea shop close by and came straight for me. She didn't look a day over eighteen, with pretty features marred by too much makeup. She wore a black shiny blouse drawn tightly around a narrow waist, that placed eye-catching emphasis on her full breasts. Feeling guilty at having this tarty looking girl thrust her arm in mine, I led her out of range of the amused gaze of the occupants of the bus.

Despite her gaudy appearance, she was articulate and chattered away happily. I twice walked her around the block unable to get a word in. She did not mention her predicament. Finally I asked if we might get a cup of tea and sit down to talk about what she should do. She led me to the shop from which I had seen her emerge. She didn't seem anxious to talk about serious business. I became more and more uneasy as she plied me with questions, while studying every detail of my features. In the hope of discouraging her, I said that I was married. She wasn't a bit disturbed, saying she knew a lot of people in Canada of Scottish descent. Contrary to popular belief, they were most generous. She felt sure that Connie would be happy that I was taking the time to help a countryman. In this instance, knowing Connie, I wasn't a bit certain that she was right.

Anxious to get down to business, I said I had given the matter a lot of thought and that the best thing for her to do was to go to London to the Canadian High Commission and ask for their help in getting back to Canada. She stated flatly that she didn't want to go back to Canada, she wanted to stay here. In that case, I suggested the only thing to do was to get herself a job in one of the war production factories or join one of the Services. I assured her the country needed all the hands it could get. She seemed satisfied with this, so I paid my bill stating that I would have to make my way back to the Station. Outside the tea shop, the bus schedule was posted. I discovered that the next bus back was ten o'clock that night. She jumped up and down with delight. 'Now you'll have to stay with me for a while; come, I want you to meet the people I'm staying with; they're so kind and hospitable.'

With some misgivings, I allowed myself to be led through narrow back streets to a group of one-story adjoining country houses. The entrance door of her digs opened directly into one large room. In front was a sofa flanked by two easy chairs. Peat smouldered in the small fireplace, and behind the sofa was a small dining table and four chairs. Evidently at home, my young friend skipped through the door at the back calling to her landlady. After some delay she emerged with a woman in her middle thirties who eyed me with obvious approval as she wiped her hands on her apron.

'He's a fine lad, Mary,' she said, and then to me,

'Take off your coat, love, and 'ave a coop of tea.'

I found myself being relieved of my coat as I nervously explained that I couldn't stay long. She paid little attention to me and, turning to Mary, said, 'Put it in your room, Mary; you might as well. Settle down Canada, I know what you need. Mary, get him a bottle of Guinness.

You'll find it in the pantry.'

After a few good pulls on my glass of Guinness by the fireplace, I began to feel a little less ill at ease. Mary sat down disturbingly close beside me on the sofa, and as she did, her blouse puffed open revealing the cleft between her prominent bosoms.

'Now tell me more about yourself, where are you stationed?'

Glad to have something else to think about besides sexual awareness, I told her I was a tour expired fighter pilot who had been sent up here to teach the bomber pilots how to avoid getting shot down. I babbled on about the heavy losses and the morale of the Bomber crews.

'What do they have to do to avoid getting shot down?' she asked, examining herself in a hand mirror.

Her question brought me sharply back to reality. I thought of those signs in the pub. For the first time I looked at her in an entirely different light. How old was this woman really? Long since, I had come to the conclusion that I was hopeless at guessing women's ages. I remembered once at a house party becoming particularly enamoured of a tall willowy girl and dancing with her all evening. Later, a friend told me that she was only thirteen. I remembered also the time I had spent at eighteen trying to get my hands on a toothsome voluptuous blonde, only to discover that she was a thirty-year-old divorcée. I had fallen for this girl's story; but it could be a lie. For a moment the thought came to me that maybe it was my duty to get on with the business of seducing her, and by devious means find out exactly what she was up to. I could see myself trying to explain my actions to Connie. I was in a fix. The only smart thing to do was to leave. I did it in the only way I knew how. I jumped up and said, 'I've got to go.'

Ignoring her pleading in silence, I got my hat and coat and left. Once more I felt as though the Hand of Providence had intervened on my behalf, for as I reached the bus stop I was just in time to catch the last bus back to the Station. The ten-thirty bus had been cancelled, and the new schedule had not yet been posted.

Next morning at breakfast I found that I was the only aircrew officer in the Mess. The flying personnel of the Squadron were having a rest. Three of the officers I had seen in the bar the night before were finishing their morning tea when a fourth who apparently worked in the Watch Office came in, excited, and said,

'I say, do you remember that scruffy little squirt who made such a nuisance of himself last night? He was one of our agents. The Squadron Commander dropped him by parachute.'

Like a chain reaction, the eerie feelings I had had the night before came back to me. I tried to remember all the things I had said when Mary asked me about Operations. With a sense of relief, I realized that I hadn't said anything that would be of any use to the enemy, but it was my duty to report the whole stupid incident to Intelligence. I was relieved to find that the Intelligence Officer took the matter quite seriously, commending me for reporting it. Late that afternoon we left for RAF Station Scampton, and I never heard what happened to Mary.

We got a very cold reception from Wing Commander Guy Gibson, DFC and Bar, at Scampton. He obviously had no use for fighter pilots and didn't think there was anything we could teach his squadron. He felt the proposed exercise was a complete waste of time, and that once again Headquarters was demonstrating its capability of bungling up his schedule. With great reluctance he agreed to give us one crew to participate in this 'silly business,' but informed us there was no way he could lay it on before the following afternoon. I left his office feeling I would welcome the opportunity of showing him how smartly a fighter could send him down in flames. Grumbling to myself, I wandered up to the Mess and got myself a room. I had a nice long soak in the bath, got dressed and went downstairs. I was curious to know if the morale of his flying personnel differed from that of the other squadron I had visited in Bomber Command.

The bar at Scampton was at one end of a long rectangular common room flanked with easy chairs and divided by a leather sofa in the middle. At the other end was a large fireplace. Standing in front of it with feet wide apart was Guy Gibson with a pint of beer. In one corner slept one of the biggest Alsatians I had ever seen. It was a striking-looking animal with sharp pointed ears and a thick honey-coloured coat. There were a few aircrew officers sitting reading and a couple more leaning on the bar. As I ordered a beer, I remarked to one of them, what a beautiful animal it was and asked if it was friendly.

'I'd suggest you don't go near him, Cock. He's a one man dog that's particularly unfriendly at the moment. He belonged to one of the Flight Commanders who went missing last night, and he's not happy. If you want a dog to play with, play with this one,' he said, patting the head of a Labrador puppy that had sidled up to him wagging his tail and panting.

'Watch this,' he said, taking an old tennis ball that had been sitting on the bar, and throwing it over the sofa.

In a flash, the Labrador vaulted the sofa, retrieved the ball, vaulted back again, bringing the ball to hand. The dog was just about to fetch the ball for the third time when there was a ferocious growl from the corner. With hackles raised, and bared teeth, in one bound the huge Alsatian was standing over the Labrador. Everyone watched as though paralyzed. At any moment we expected to see the Labrador torn to ribbons. With an angry growl, Gibson lunged into action. In two long strides he was over the Alsatian, grasped it with both hands by the skin of the back and threw it in the corner. The Labrador slithered away to the protection of his friend by the bar. For a moment, Gibson stood glowering at the disgruntled brute. With its hackles still raised and with its eyes fixed it gave a low growl as if it was about to attack.

'Lie down,' he said, pointing to the corner, 'and bloody well stay down, do you hear me!'

In the utter stillness not a person moved. Without taking his eyes off Gibson, the dog obediently went to the corner and put his head down on the floor facing him. Without another word, Gibson walked non-chalantly back to the mantelpiece and picked up his beer. Gradually quiet conversations began to be resumed as though nothing had happened. This experience gave me an insight into the character of Gibson. As I returned to the bar for a refill, my friend whispered to me out of the corner of his mouth:

'That's the way he does everything. If anybody else tried to do that, they'd have had their arm taken off. You can be bloody sure I wouldn't have tried it.'

Before leaving Scampton I knew what the bomber crews thought of their Commanding Officer. They had the greatest respect for him, but he was unrelenting and unapproachable.

'All I can hope,' said one of the gunners, 'is that I can finish my thirty bloody trips without being sent to be his next rear gunner.'

The extraordinary flying career of Guy Gibson has been well documented. His fearlessness will stand as an example for all time.

Next in priority was Coastal Command. The units catching the worst 'packet' were those stationed on the East Coast of England and Scotland. Their prime mission was attacking shipping off the Norwegian coast. Because of early successes in these sorties, Luftwaffe single engine fighters had been stationed in Norway to give fighter protection for the ships. They were giving the Coastal Command boys a hard time. For the most part these Squadrons were equipped with Beaufighters.

The Beau Mark I had two Bristol radial engines and clean lines. This model was the most manoeuverable and forgiving of the Beaufighter family. With these qualities and the range of a medium bomber, it was particularly suited to this work and much preferred by the anti-shipping Coastal Command boys of that time. A Mark II Beaufighter was also produced. It was not a replacement for the Mark I for doing this job. The Mark II, reputed to be faster with its two Merlin engines, killed quite a few before it was discovered that it had some vicious flying tendencies. The Beau II was converted to a night fighter. Painted black, bulging with air-borne radar equipment and antennae protruding from its nose like the feelers of a fly, this model became the workhorse of the night fighter squadrons. As a result of these modifications, the Beau II lost twenty miles an hour of its top original flying speed.

At RAF Station Dyce near Aberdeen on the east coast of Scotland we found an aggressive, optimistic Coastal Command squadron. Unlike Bomber Command, this outfit welcomed us with open arms. Knowing that our Spitfires were more manoeuverable than their German counterparts, these pilots were anxious to practice dogfighting with us. With combat experience under their belt, it was remarkable how these lads could throw their Beaufighters around. With four twenty-millimetre cannons that could fire along the line of sight from the nose, it was a dangerous adversary. At Dyce, we spent many an hour shuddering around over the water trying to get decent shots at these lads. To avoid an attack from below where the attacker could not be seen, they preferred flying low over the water, concentrating on manoeuvering into firing position on a Beaufighter with condensation trails streaming from its wing tips a couple of feet off the water can be dangerous business. Without a horizon in the prevailing conditions of mist and haze, a small miscalculation of height, and you can be into the sea.

I remember one particularly good pilot who timed his turns so perfectly that I never had anything but a 90° deflection shot. He manoeuvred his aircraft with such violence that he seemed to have contrails continuously streaming from his wing tips. He did everything with that big twin-engine aircraft but a flick roll. After landing back at Dyce, he came over to my aircraft as I was getting the film magazine out of my camera gun. Wiping the sweat from his brow with a broad grin, he said, 'Get it assessed, Canada. I'll wager a round of drinks that you didn't score one decent hit.'

He was right, and this was one wager I didn't mind losing.

From Dyce we went to Speke where we received an equally enthusiastic welcome.

The most northerly Station we visited was Sumburgh in the Shetland Islands above latitude 60, which goes through the tip of Greenland. It was a grey and misty morning when we took off, with a solid overcast at fifteen hundred feet, and visibility about three miles. With Jock Murray flying the Boston and Scottie and I formating on him, we headed north. The cold grey sea melted with the mist and cloud, denying us the comfort of a horizon. I found myself listening intently for any irregularities in my engine and wondering how long a body could last in that icy water. After a while we were whisking along through wisps of low cloud at eight hundred feet. As I watched Jock in the cockpit of the Boston, bobbing very gently up and down beside me, he didn't appear to be the least bit concerned behind his two engines.

'I hope for our sake, you know where you're going, Jock,' said Scottie.

With a grin, Jock put his mask back on and said,

'Get some bloody sea time in, Cobber.'

Knowing that at this height and this distance we were probably out of range for giving Maydays, I couldn't help wondering how easy it would be to miss the Shetland Islands. Beyond that there was nothing but sea and the Arctic circle. With nothing to do but fly formation I found myself carefully watching the fuel gauge and thinking that we had been a long time out of sight of land. There's something mesmerizing about flying low over mile after mile of open sea with the green water corrugated by a regular pattern of waves. After a while it produces a sense of resigned indifference. Because of the decreased horizontal visibility, I was jerked out of this reverie quite suddenly by the sight of a line of foam on the horizon where the waves finished their travel and lashed upon a rocky shore. In a few minutes we were over Sumburgh, the RAF's stark outpost in the Shetlands. There seemed little else to the Station, as we circled, but two runways coming to a Vee, carved out of the solid rock.

'Watch for the hills,' warned Jock.

'You're the one that'll have to watch it, with your Bomber Command approach,' said Scottie.

A white T lay on the rocks between the runways, indicating the one in use, and beside it a tattered windsock flew with its tail straight out. At one end of the main runway was a mound of rock rising to eight hundred feet. The other end was shielded by a forbidding mountain that rose to a thousand.

One would have thought that a Boston and a couple of Spitfires, rarely if ever seen at a place like Sumburgh, might have generated some interest. We landed, taxied in and shut down by the Watch Office before we saw the first sign of life. A baleful looking erk wandered out and asked us if we needed refuelling.

'How would you like to do your next tour up here, Jock?' asked Scottie.

'I'll go back to Scampton right now if need be. This is the bloody end.'

While Jock and Scottie went inside to make contact with the squadron, I stayed outside to supervise refuelling. Loving wild open country, I was fascinated by the place. There was something solid and majestic about those hills covered with bracken, gorse and heather with a few shaggy sheep grazing peacefully. The cool salty breeze smelt clean and made one want to draw in a deep breath. Above, two seagulls circled lazily gliding on the wind. I would have given anything at that moment to strike off along the paths of the sheep and climb to the summit of that mountain to see what I could see.

'What a wild and beautiful spot this is,' I said to the erk. 'You must love it.'

'It's not my cup of tea, mate. There is nothing up here but bloody sheep. Half of the time you can't hear nothing for the 'owling of the wind. Last week a shot-up Beaufort came in at night in the pouring rain, blew a tire and ended up on them rocks. The lads on the crash truck who were trying to put the fire out saw the glint of a torpedo and ran for their bloody lives and told the chap in the Watch Office. He got on the Tannoy and called, "All personnel to proceed a fourth of a mile from the crash." Everybody thought he had said 'four miles' and it took them a week to get the blokes back out of the 'ills. For my money, they should have left this place to the bloody sheep.'

From the point of view of fighter affiliation, it was a fruitless trip. There were no spare aircraft, they were all unserviceable. So, with a break in the weather, we took off for our return journey to Duxford. We came back via the West coast past Ailsa Craig, stopping to refuel at Prestwick.

On my return, I discovered that Connie had been keeping a little secret. For several weeks she had suspected that she was pregnant, and in my absence she had gone to the Medical Officer who confirmed her suspicions. Pregnancy was one of the few ways that a WAAF Officer could get her release from the Service. The RAF did not cater to such frills as Married Quarters and she could not expect to be posted with me to my next Station. Since our marriage, the few moments that we had been able to spend together had only succeeded in giving us a taste of the stability that married life can provide. With the separate demands that service life made on each one of us, it was impossible to satisfy the longing that we had to establish roots. Out of the service, she would be able to follow me and be able to enjoy some semblance of domestic life.

During our absence from Duxford, Bomber Harris had stood down a Lancaster squadron to be trained for a low level daylight attack on a special target deep in enemy territory. AFDU was to help. To avoid radar detection, the formation was to fly at zero feet. A formation had to be devised that would allow twelve four-engine bombers to keep station on the lead aircraft while providing good cross-fire from the rear turrets. The crews of RAF Bomber Command had had no training in low flying and hadn't the slightest idea how to formate. Used to operating singly on night bombing missions, they were mainly preoccupied with navigation. On the deck, the new Gee Box would be of no value as they would be out of range of home stations. They had already started their own training. It consisted of long range navigational exercises flying around the Midlands of England above the treetops in a gaggle. Flying above them on these practices, I was convinced a Staffel of 190's would have everyone of them in flames in half an hour. It would be easy: pick off the stragglers, then nibble away at the aircraft on the flanks. They flew far too far to the side to get any help from the gunners in the middle of the formation. The crews seemed to be so exhilarated by authorized low flying that they didn't even listen.

Word came from Bomber Command Headquarters that they would have only enough time for one last practice before the sortie. We decided to fly with the crews on this occasion in the hope of teaching them some semblance of formation flying. I was in a Lancaster piloted by a young English boy. I chose to sit in the front turret so as to get a commanding view. It wasn't long before I regretted that decision. I spent three hours with my teeth clenched, with two white-knuckled hands locked on the controls of the gun turret. I found myself moving the guns upward in the hope of getting the aircraft over the next grove of trees. If the pilot got behind, he opened all four throttles and the next minute we were going by underneath the leader. As I watched the props on the leader aircraft turning over above my head, I felt at any moment they were going to go through the perspex. I would find I had my right foot pressed hard against the floorboards as if to put rudder on to skid off to the side. He didn't pay the slightest attention to my instructions and every time he came to a grove of trees while pulling the stick back he gave a little squeal of delight. Realizing I was getting nowhere, and not being able to stand it another second, I went back and got into the co-pilot seat. Here, at least, I would be able to intervene by getting on the controls. When I showed him how to keep station, he ignored me and struck up a conversation with the Flight Engineer behind him. Finally, to my great relief we returned to Base and prepared to land.

On final approach I was puzzled to hear the Flight Engineer calling out the air speed. Looking around, I found the entire crew standing in the passage between the two pilot seats. With a bounce that shook every rivet in the aircraft, he thumped it down on the runway, ran over onto the grass on the right, gave a burst of his starboard engines which swerved us back on the asphalt and across on the grass on the other side. After a vigorous application of brakes, we finally found ourselves running down the centre of the runway. Suddenly, a chorus of voices behind me shouted, 'Good show, Skipper, you got it down again.'

Flak and fighter were obviously not the only hazard this crew had to worry about.

I was in the Watch Office with one of the Intelligence Officers the night they took off for their sortie. Their target was a munitions factory deep in enemy territory at Le Creusot. Take-off was timed so they would reach the enemy coast at first light. With a sense of foreboding, I listened to the din made by forty-eight Merlin engines running up, and the crackling spitting noise as they taxied out with their navigation lights on. In silence we watched as one after another took off. As the drone of the formation faded in the distance, I turned to the

Intelligence Officer and said:

'They'll be lucky if any of them reach the target. The only ray of hope they have is if the Jerrys are taken completely by surprise and no airborne craft with a radio happens to spot them.'

'Don't you think you're being a little too pessimistic? Don't forget some of you boys were shot down by the return fire in the Battle of Britain.'

'That's all very well,' I said, 'but the Luftwaffe bombers flew in formation so that their rear gunners could provide cross-fire. This will be like a herd of cattle swimming a river full of piranhas.'

'Well,' he said, 'you might as well go back and see if you can get a little shut-eye. It's a long time before breakfast.'

By an amazing coincidence, eleven of the twelve aircraft returned. They had been right on course, avoided all fighter bases and, fifteen miles from target, had climbed to eight thousand feet, spread out and bombed individually. The one aircraft that was missing had dropped its bombs too close to the ground. It was destroyed by the blast. Air Marshal Harris, delighted by the results, had ordered his staff to plan a second sortie. This formation was not as fortunate. Slightly off track, they flew directly over a fighter airdrome. Eleven out of the twelve were shot down. The leader was the only skipper who managed to bring his aircraft back to England.

The Eighth Air Force of the US Army Air Corps had arrived in England. They had been preceded by the Corps of Engineers, who, to the amazement of the English, constructed air bases for them in three months. These bases included runways longer than any of those on the Stations in Bomber Command; interconnecting taxi-ways and hard stands for aircraft; living quarters, hangars and sundry out-buildings to American specificatons. As this first rumble of American know-how and military capability was attracting England's attention, I made myself unpopular by reminding the English boys that it had taken the union-restricted Works and Bricks Department more than six months to build a twelve-by-twelve brick 'shit-house.' When the Corps of Engineers blew the whistle, the war-weary English were treated to the encouraging sight of squadrons 'of B-17s and B-24s in formation like fighter squadrons flying and landing twelve aircraft on their beautiful new runways in about as many minutes. Overnight, it seemed everybody was complaining that you couldn't move in London because of the Americans, with their brindle tunics, pink pants, metal wings above a chest full of ribbons. You couldn't get a taxi. The drivers seemed interested only in generous-tipping Americans. The Poles, Canadians and Australians, having previously been the targets for snide remarks, were replaced by the Americans.

At the beginning of July, there was a bizarre occurrence which rocked Fighter Command. A Luftwaffe pilot landed a FW 190 intact on a South Coast airdrome. Up to this point we had thought that in the 190 the Germans had sacrificed armour and armament to improve performance. Now we discovered that not only did it have four cannons and two machine guns, but a sizeable amount of armour plate. Having regretted his action, the Luftwaffe pilot offered to take on a half a dozen Spitfires in a dogfight. His offer was refused. At Duxford, we had just received the latest model of the Spitfire, Mk IXB. It had the Merlin 61 engine supplying 1400 h.p. with a two-stage two-speed supercharger and intercooler that automatically provided this horsepower at twenty thousand feet. It had a four-bladed prop and twelve seconds of cannon fire. This was the answer to my dream, and I had devoted as much time as possible to studying its peculiarities.

AFDU would be doing the testing of the 190, and I was chosen as the 190 test pilot. I was just about to leave for Farnborough for the trials when a signal arrived from Air Ministry stating that they were sending Jamie Rankin to fly the 190, and that AFDU was to supply a Spitfire VB, a Spitfire IXB, a Mustang P-51 and a pilot for comparative trials. I was disappointed, but I couldn't think of anybody who deserved the privilege more than Jamie. As it turned out, the task I got was infinitely more advantageous. I flew the Spitfires and the P-51 against a pilot who flew the 190 like a Hun.

Farnborough was a hive of activity, full of strangely modified aircraft and overrun by 'boffins' and visiting VIP's. A temporary building was used as a dining room. With the constant influx of visitors it was difficult to find a seat. The arrival of a famous fighter pilot like Jamie Rankin went unnoticed. Everybody was preoccupied with some top priority project.

With some disappointment, I found that the 190 had already had its black crosses and swastikas replaced by British rondels and a hastily applied coat of RAF camouflage. In the few places that had been missed the beautifully smooth original finish could be felt. The 190 was a perfect example of precise German design and workmanship. Unlike our Spitfires, the panels were so well fitted that they looked like one piece. Ingeniously designed finger-operated locks opened the panels to reveal an engine that had been designed for easy maintenance. To reduce drag, the space between the spinner and the outer cowling was reduced and the turbine impeller on the same axis as the prop, rotating three times as fast, sucked air in to facilitate cooling. It had a wide sturdy undercarriage and a cockpit that was a fighter pilot's dream. All engine, undercarriage and flap controls were neatly arranged for finger-tip control beside the throttle leaving the right hand free to manoeuvre the airplane and fire the guns. The one-piece perspex top came down half-way to the elbows on either side and gave almost perfect visibility to the sides and the rear. The two inner twenty millimetre cannons in the wing roots and the two machine guns over the nose were synchronized to fire through the prop arc. This gave the 190 a narrow cone of lethal density from its guns along the line of sight from about fifty yards out to well beyond six hundred. The Spitfire, by comparison, with its guns all outside the arc of the prop, produced its lethal density along the line of sight only between two hundred and four hundred yards.

We were allotted a piece of grass on the field to park the aircraft and just about the time we were preparing for the first trial Jamie was told to muster all his personnel beside the aircraft in preparation for a visit from VIP's. A gaggle of Air Vice Marshals and Group Captains arrived squiring American Generals and one Russian Colonel. I was instructed to answer any questions about the Spitfires. The new Spitfire IX generated the most interest. When the others moved on to inspect the 190, the Russian Colonel hung back and began quietly plying me with questions.

'How fast does this Spitfire go?' he asked me.

'It depends on the height, sir!'

'You are being insolent. Answer my question. How fast does the airplane go?'

I was irritated by his truculent dictatorial manner and suspicious of his motives.

'If you want to get the performance figures on the Spitfire IX, sir, why don't you ask the Air Vice Marshal over there? He probably would be happy to give you the handling notes.'

His face turned white with fury as he said, 'In Russia we do not tolerate such insolence. Men have been shot for less than this.'

Refusing to be intimidated, I said,

'I'm terribly sorry, but you'll have to ask the Air Vice Marshal.'

With a scowl, he stomped off after the others.

With no further interruptions, we got down to the trials. I started with a Spitfire VB and found that at fifteen and twenty-one thousand feet the 190 was five to ten miles an hour faster. I hadn't a prayer in catching it in a dive. The Mustang, on the other hand, was faster in the dive than the 190, but couldn't keep up with it in a full throttle climb. But the things that I discovered about the comparative performance of the Spitfire IXB proved invaluable to me in the next two years. In level flight and high speed the 190 flies slightly nose down. With a higher wing loading than the Spitfire, the 190's maximum rate of climb was attained at an air speed of about 240 miles an hour. The Spitfire IXB's maximum rate of climb was attained at 160 miles an hour. Thus, if you were foolish enough to try to follow the 190 in full throttle climb at the same angle, you would soon find out that he was above you. On the

156

other hand, if you pulled away and held the Spitfire at an air speed of 160, you would climb at a much steeper angle and end up with a height advantage. Below twenty thousand feet in level speed runs there wasn't much in it either way. But once above twenty thousand feet, the Spitfire IXB's second blower kicked in, giving it the advantage. The Spitfire could not compete with the rate of roll of a 190. As a result of these trials, the clipped wing Spitfire VB came into service with the object of giving it a cheap increase in rate of roll. If Jamie followed the favourite German technique of flicking over on his back and going straight down, he would pull away from me in the first two or three thousand feet. After that the Spitfire IXB could gradually catch him. Jamie never bothered trying to turn inside me in my Spitfire. Both of us knew that it wasn't possible. That was one advantage that all British fighters enjoyed. At the end of the trials, when I added up the pluses and the minuses, I came to the conclusion that I would still prefer a Spitfire IXB.

My next assignment was fighter liaison with the Eighth Air Force of the US Army Air Force. For a pilot used to the RAF it was an experience. These well-trained crews had just come over and had been held down to an intensive training programme. They had had no contact with the RAF and had never seen a Spitfire. Their warmth stimulated me to make an error that almost cost me my life. I was sent to the US Base at Alconbury, the home of a B-24 Squadron. The runways and taxi-ways were so long that my radiator temperature was off the clock before I found a place to shut down. Unbeknown to my American admirers, I was flying an old Spitfire II with all the guns out. Despite the patched bullet holes and the paint flaking off, without the weight of the guns and ammunition it was light as a feather and fast. Before I could get out of the cockpit I was surrounded by the entire Squadron. They fingered every part of the aircraft like excited schoolchildren, and took turns sitting in the cockpit. They were soon joined by their Commanding Officer. He introduced himself, and shaking my hand warmly, thanked me profusely for taking the time to come. Then, turning to the others, he shouted,

'All right, men, our visitor is a busy man. We mustn't waste his time. Everybody into the Flight Office on the double.'

After he had proudly watched his men scampering off, he led me in their wake. There was nothing trifling about this man; he was all business. He gave me a short introduction, then handed me the floor. To an attentive audience I gave my sales pitch on the corkscrew technique. Their standard formation was well designed to provide maximum cross-fire from their gun turrets. When I expressed doubt about the feasibility of corkscrewing a whole formation, the Colonel interrupted me.

'Well, let's get into the air and try it, and see what you think. Okay, men, all crews be prepared to take off in fifteen minutes.'

I was a witness to an extraordinary bit of formation flying. Twelve B-24's took off so close behind one another that there were always three aircraft in motion on the runway at the same time. At some distance from the field, the leader began a gradual turn to port and all subsequent aircraft did an immediate turn in the same direction so as to get to their stations. By the time the leader had completed one circuit of the field, his twelve aircraft were in tight formation. While I did simulated attacks, the Colonel proceeded to corkscrew the entire formation, a feat which I frankly didn't think he could do. At the debriefing after lunch I was able to show the camera gun films that I had taken of them. I gave them full marks stating that I felt sure they would have shot me down with such a concentration of turrets firing point 5's. After thanking me, the Colonel called for a round of applause. In all my travels I had never enjoyed such enthusiasm. Their desire to establish good relations with the RAF and their admiration for what it had done was very evident.

As I prepared to climb in my cockpit and take my leave, the Colonel said,

'As the Commander of this Air Field, sir, I would like to make one last request. My men have never seen a Spitfire; would you honour us with a shoot up?'

'In the RAF, sir, that is a court martial offence.'

'To relieve you of any responsibilities, permit me to make that an order.'

There was a loud cheer behind him as I said:

'Yes, sir.'

I taxied my aircraft to the very end of the runway and took off. I held my wheels on the ground until I had ample flying speed then snapped them up, staying at the same level until I reached the end. I pulled straight up into an upward roll, and proceeded to do a half a dozen such manoeuvres increasing my height and diving speed with each. As a finale, I came straight across the field towards the crowd in front of the Flight Office, rolled over and flew over them inverted. Just as I went by them, I relaxed my forward grip on the stick and for a second my nose dropped down below the level of the roof of the Flight Office. I instantly jammed the stick forward so as to climb above the obstacle and gain enough height to roll out. With my hands shaking, I climbed straight ahead to a safe altitude, waggled my wings and set course for home. On the way I chided myself for my stupidity. My ego, intoxicated by the accolades, committed me to an orgy of dangerous aerobatics that had nearly cost me my life.

These cooperative sorties with the USAAF Bomber Groups

continued and at each Station I got an equally enthusiastic reception. After the B-24 squadrons. I visited the B-17 squadrons and finally the Mitchell B-25 squadrons. The pilots flying the B-25 twin-engine medium bombers all seemed to be frustrated fighter pilots. They were just as proficient in formation flying, but were much more anxious to dog-fight. A Major, one of their best pilots, challenged me. During this joust, another tragedy was narrowly averted. This time, it was not due to my miscalculation. The Major manoeuvred his B-25 with remarkable skill, but understandably was no match for a Spitfire. Finally, from ten thousand feet directly over the airdrome, he half rolled and went straight down. I followed him long enough to get in an adequate burst with my camera gun and pulled out. He continued on down. Finally with condensation trails streaming from his wing tips he pulled out just over the top of the trees. I was most impressed and followed him in to land. When I went over to congratulate him, I found him white-faced and shaken. The long dive had been unintentional, his tail had stalled out. When he returned the stick to the neutral position, the aircraft pulled out by itself.

At Duxford one day a U.S. Army Captain arrived unexpectedly with a P-38. Like the other Air Corps pilots, he had no battle experience and asked if he could get somebody to dogfight with him in a Spitfire IXB. Flight Lieutenant Clive, implying that he was in charge, said he would be glad to cooperate. He would fly the Spitfire himself. We were all a witness to the P-38 outmanoeuvre Clive even turning inside him. When they landed, Clive came into Dispersal sweating profusely and stated that the P-38 could outmanoeuvre the IXB. The Captain asked if he could have that in writing to show his Commanding Officer.

'Certainly,' said Clive, 'I'll have it ready for you by lunchtime.'

I was convinced this was wrong, and pleaded with Campbell-Orr to let me fly against him before issuing any report. The Captain supported me in my request, and off we went. I was able to show that there was no way he could come anywhere near me in the Spitfire. To demonstrate the turning ability, I let him get on my tail. In two complete circles from this position, I was able to be in firing position behind him. The Captain was not a bit upset, he had come to learn the truth. I told him I thought a good pilot in the 109F would give him a lot of trouble.

On August 19th, Operation Jubilee was launched. Units of the Canadian Army made a sea-borne landing in Dieppe harbour. The defending German Army inflicted incredible losses upon them. Out of 5000 men over 3000 never returned: A thousand were left dead on the field. The bombers and fighters of the Luftwaffe were out in force. There was an air battle comparable to some of the heaviest in the Battle of Britain. We lost 98 aircraft at a cost to the enemy of 93 destroyed and 180 probably destroyed or damaged. Thirty of our pilots were rescued from the sea.

News of the landing spread instantly through the RAF. Itching to get into it, I took off from Duxford in a Spitfire IXB with the excuse that I was going to see how high I could get it. Climbing to the South Coast, I got to 42,500 feet.* By the time I reached mid-Channel I felt as though I was going to burst. The only thing I could see in the direction of Dieppe was smoke. I dared not take a chance on becoming engaged. I was flying a top secret airplane. With a deep sense of frustration I turned back and dived back to Duxford. Later I learned that contemporaries of mine, Lloyd Chadburn and Sydney Ford, had led their Squadrons with great distinction and that Canadian pilots had accounted for a large percentage of the German aircraft destroyed. These were the kinds of losses that the joint Chiefs of Staff who planned the invasion were prepared to expect.

At the end of six months with AFDU, I informed the Wing Commander that I was ready to go back on Operations. I requested any RAF Squadron in Eleven Group that was slated to be equipped with Spitfire IXB's. I was told that if I were patient, he would see what he could do. Conscious of the fact that this period of rest had slowed my reflexes, I launched myself on an 'increase the twitch' programme. If I found myself outside with nothing to do and heard the drone of an aircraft, I would spin my head around and try to pick it out as quickly as possible. When flying, I would imagine I was fifty miles inside the French coast, alone, and had to see every aircraft in my vicinity. I did a mock attack on everything that came within range, firing my camera gun and checking my accuracy on the assessment machine.

Pregnancy brought a noticeable change in Connie's outlook. She had lost interest in bantering with the boys in the Mess. She was knitting bootees. The nesting instinct had taken over. In Scotland, the excitement was running high. Her Aunt Jessie had contacted Dr. Maxwell who had delivered Connie, and he put her on his list for the end of June. As soon as I was posted back on Operations, Connie was to leave for Scotland and await the arrival of the baby at her uncle's. On the second of November, a signal arrived that I was posted to 401, now stationed at Kenley. I put in for the seven days' leave that I had been saving to enable me to close up my digs and move Connie to Scotland.

The seven days at Castle Douglas I found very unsettling. With the anticipation of return to operations, the hackles had already started to rise: The slow-moving tempo of a Scottish farming community was a ludicrous contrast to such preoccupation. While I was reliving dogfights,

---

* At 40,000 feet the pressure is so low that even breathing pure oxygen the brain will suffer from anoxia. Body gases in the stomach and the bowel expand, pushing the diaphragm into the chest and making it difficult to take a full breath.

I listened to discussions of the latest market prices for sheep and cattle. I had little to say as plans for Connie's confinement were under discussion because I would not be there for the event; but it was a comfort to think that she was safe in good hands.

On the fourth of November there was some encouraging news: General Montgomery had beaten Rommel at the Battle of El Alamein and driven his Afrika Korps out of Egypt.

13

THE SECOND TIME ROUND

I was glad to stretch my legs with the walk to the Mess, at RAF Station Kenley. In spite of the comfort of a first-class compartment, the train from Glasgow was crowded and I had to be content with a middle seat. I never got used to sleeping sitting up. We stopped for hours at Carlisle, and to pass the time I had walked up and down the platform with a cup of luke-warm NAAFI tea and a bun. I felt really grungy. With the Glasgow train a half hour late at Euston, to make my connection at Victoria I had to grab the first taxi I could get. With my two-suiter canvas zip-up bag in one hand, and a parachute bag and Spitty straining on her leash in the other, I had my hands full.

It was lunchtime when I kicked open the blackout doors of the Mess. In front of me stood a tall Group Captain and a heavily decorated Wing Commander, both jauntily sipping pink gins. In front of them sat a huge Great Dane and two Bull Terriers. Seeing Spitty, with ferocious growls the dogs attacked, the Bull Terriers running in number two and three position on the Dane. With all my strength I kicked the Dane in the face. There was an audible silence as the two officers eyed me quizzically. Finally, the Group Captain said:

'As you have already made the acquaintance of my dog, I think I should introduce myself. I am the Station Commander. Who, may I ask, are you?'

'I'm Flying Officer Godefroy, sir, reporting to 401 Squadron for a second tour.'

'Seeing he's one of yours, Brian, I won't press charges. Godefroy, meet your Wing Commander Flying, Wing Commander Brian Kincombe.'

'Very pleased to meet you, sir. Terribly sorry about the dog, but I didn't know what else to do.'

'I prefer my pilots to reserve aggression for the enemy,' said the Wing Commander with a smile.

Brian Kincombe, an ace in the battle of Britain, was an aesthete. His aura of detachment was interrupted periodically by a facial tic. When he smiled, his features took on a wry twist.

I sensed that they had tired of my company, so I excused myself to 'freshen up.'

162

I found that the only pilot left who had been in the Squadron when I had gone to Duxford was George Murray. George had been a Sergeant Pilot when I last knew him, now he was a Flight Lieutenant and had earned himself a DFC. The Squadron was under the command of Squadron Leader Keith Hodgson, an RMC graduate, who had started his Air Force career instructing in Training Command.

To my great relief, within a day one more familiar face was added. Dean MacDonald showed up, having done his rest as an Instructor at an Operational Training Unit. He had found it deadly dull and was very anxious to get back into action. Dean and I soon found ourselves discriminated against. They obviously thought we were clapped out. At twenty-three, I found this a bitter pill to swallow. Like sprog pilots, we got nothing but the 'Joe' jobs. I did convoy patrols and the flight and gun tests on eight different aircraft after major inspections before I got on a sweep. Then to my chagrin, Keith Hodgson put me in the middle of the formation as his No. 2, to see if I had lost my nerve. When I passed this test, I was delegated to No. 4 position.

Dean MacDonald got the same treatment.

We both knew that the Rhubarb or low-level strafing attack was dangerous unless planned and flown with navigational precision. To relieve some of the boredom at Duxford, whenever I was alone I had practised navigating at zero feet. We went to Monty Berger, the Intelligence Officer, and asked for a list of authorized Rhubarb targets. We spent hours studying the latest flak charts looking for weak spots in the Coastal defences. We got permission from Keith Hodgson to fly together and went out and back on all our defensive patrols at zero feet.

Finally, on January 4th, 1943, we were given permission to attack the Wehrmacht hutted camp at Balbec. The flak charts indicated a weak spot in flak at Yport, so we chose this as our point of entry and departure. At five o'clock I felt Monty Berger's hand on my shoulder.

'The weather's "go" for your Rhubarb; I'll wake Dean. Meet me in the Intelligence Office in three-quarters of an hour.'

I was instantly wide awake, with my stomach churning. Throwing off the covers I sat on the side of the bed for a minute reflecting. It was 'on.' Do it now, or you're dead. I thought of my conversation with Chuck McLean at Biggin. He had told me that every time he went on a sweep, he went through the same ritual he did when he was playing football for McGill. He talked himself into a frenzy of hate for the other side. I had to hate a little more. I jumped up and dressed and went down for breakfast. Monty had alerted the kitchen and, with the Mess to ourselves, Monty drank a cup of coffee while Dean and I ate eggs and bacon. When we were finished, we went straight to the Intelligence Office.

'Monty,' I asked, 'are you sure that wind speed's right? We've got a hundred miles of water to cross without a land mark, and if it's wrong, you'll have us going over a heavily defended flak area.'

'I've had them check it four times, Hughie. That's all I can do.'

'Okay, Dean, let's go.'

We taxied out with our navigation lights on and took off on the main runway. With Dean nearly bolted on my starboard wingtip, I set course. The air was smooth as silk and, in the inky darkness, our navigation lights seemed bright as a Christmas tree. The sound of my engine was a faultless purr and the exhaust stacks a blue glow. Gradually, the light improved, and I could see that the sky was obscured by solid cloud with good visibility below. Ahead was the outline of the South Coast with the sea beyond. There was Rye. We would be going out just west of it, I thought, right on course. We got a slight bump from the air when we crossed out over the sea and as we dipped down over the wave tops, I checked my directional gyro once more against the compass. If we were to make our land-fall at Yport, I had to fly a perfect course for twenty-five minutes. Flying over the wave tops made one conscious of speed. The twenty-five minutes seemed to last an eternity. Gradually, with the coming of first light we could make out the outline of the coast of France, and as it came closer and closer, I could distinguish the cliffs but nothing that would give me a clue as to our point of entry. I looked over at Dean. He nodded his head slowly and deliberately as we rocketed along. Gradually the cliffs got higher and higher, then suddenly we were upon them and, pulling the stick back, I went over the top. The moment of truth. Looking down, there it was, just as the picture showed it. Yport! We were right on target. In no time, we were beyond the flak belt. Not a shot was fired. There was the railroad which we were to follow to the west looking for trains. We reached the canal without seeing one. The canal was full of barges, and, as I peppered them, out of the corner of my eye I saw Dean's cannon shells exploding on the rolling stock on the rail line that ran along side. There was the lock-gate at the end, and as I pounded it, a man on the top jumped into the water on the other side. By my calculations at this point, if I pulled up and made a sharp turn to port, the Army camp should be right below me. I looked down, and there it was. I plastered it from one end to the other. Forty-five degrees to port and two miles, from low down I should soon be able to see the radar station. Silhouetted against the sky, rotating aerials, it couldn't be anything else! The last of my cannon shells exploded all over it. Straight ahead should be Yport. I looked for the cement pill-box. It could give us trouble going out. A flat roofed rectangular cement building different from the rest, to the right, a steel helmeted German soldier looking out to sea.

That's it. I cut down the soldier with machine-gun fire, rocketed over the pill-box and dipped down onto the sea beyond. Dean was right beside me. We both looked back. There was not a single flash to be seen. Out of range of the shore batteries, Dean came in close, pulled down his mask and with a broad grin shook his fist in triumph. At last we had accomplished something the way we had planned it.

Being the only pilots in the Squadron who put in for Rhubarbs, we found our comrades looking at us with a little more respect. However, we were still made to fly 'at the back of the bus.' On my thirteenth sweep, I almost bought it.

Brian Kingcombe had been sent off on a rest, and Wing Commander Nobbie Fee, DFC, a Canadian, had taken over as Wing Leader. We were escorting Fortresses and as usual had been instructed to limit ourselves to keeping fighters away from the bombers. As Nobbie put it, 'None of this farting around and chasing Huns.' With these limitations, this 'Rodeo' (as it was called) was about as rewarding as a convoy patrol. I was flying Red 4 behind Keith Hodgson in the lead section. On our way back Westhaver and Ibbitson in Yellow Section, who had been allowed to chase some 109's away from the bombers, were down below us. Keith Hodgson waggled his wings and asked Ibbitson if he could see us. He replied that he was five thousand feet below and climbing back up. Looking back, I saw a lone aircraft climbing up dead astern from below. It had dihedral wings and two radiators on the underside like a 109, but so did a Spitfire IX. It must be Ibbitson, I thought. Don't report it, or they'll think you're windy. Nobody else seemed to be concerned. I forced myself to ignore the hackles that were beginning to rise with something on my tail. I forced myself to look ahead. Suddenly, Keith Hodgson shouted, 'Red Section, break!'

The first one to get it in Red Section would be No. 4, and that was me! That wasn't Ibbitson, it was a 109. With all my strength I pushed my left foot down and pulled the stick back. At 220 m.p.h. I spun into a series of flick rolls. When I released my grip, I came out with such a snap that, in spite of my Sutton harness, my head hit hard against the coup top. I wondered if my tail had broken.

'Are you all right, Red 4?' Keith Hodgson inquired.

Gently, I tried my controls. To my amazement, they seemed to be working.

'Yes, sir,' I answered with relief.

'Well, you'd better keep your eyes open, that one just about got ya.'

When I landed at Kenley, it was like old times, three holes in my tail. I sat down beside Dean in Dispersal to bring my log book up to date.

'What's the date, Dean?' I asked.

'The 13th, Hughie,' said Dean, not looking up.

165

Some days later, under Nobbie Fee's leadership the Wing was to cross the Fench coast at Le Touquet and patrol the St. Omer to Dunkirk area at twenty-six thousand feet. At this altitude, the temperature was 53 below. We had all the clothing we could get on and still fit in the cockpit, including flannelette pajamas. At 'Angels 25' the whole Wing was making smoke trails. We were visible for miles. Just inside the coast, I saw fifteen 190's circling high above us. The issue brown leather gauntlets with the silk interliners were inadequate protection at this temperature, and I kept rubbing my fingers together trying to keep them from turning numb. In spite of the heavy Red Cross stockings pulled well up over my knees, the sides of the cockpit seemed to be drawing the heat out of my upper legs, turning them to ice.

In accordance with the plan, Nobbie Fee turned 90° port and headed for Dunkirk. This put the gaggle up sun and behind us. In spite of the cold, I started rubbernecking and switching my tail like a cat with a dog in the house. Out of nowhere tragedy struck. The moisture in our breaths began freezing in the oxygen masks, shutting off the supply. One after another, aircraft lazily began sliding out of the formation, the unconscious pilots slumped over the controls, falling away like falling leaves. Down twanged the 190's on these helpless victims of circumstance to blast them into the great beyond. Aid was not ours to give, for the 190's held a considerable height advantage. With anguish we watched our planes turned into balls of fire.

At Dunkirk we turned port again, and in the turn my windscreen frosted up completely. I couldn't even see the man in front. In my ear I heard, 'Snack Bar Leader, eight 190's diving down twelve o'clock.'

To make myself a difficult target, I kicked my aircraft into flick rolls. When I snapped it out, just as suddenly the frosting cleared, and I found myself looking into streams of tracer from three 190's attacking head on. I had time for a one-second burst before they went by me like meteors twenty yards off my port wing. They continued on and disappeared inland. Our return journey was uneventful.

There were six pilots missing. As soon as we refuelled, we went straight out again and scoured the sea off Dunkirk. We stayed until dark. The only thing visible was the wheel of a Spitfire floating in the waves.

Our request for another Rhubarb was authorized, but this one was a different story. Dean and I had the same long Channel crossing, but the wind was strong and irregular and put us several miles from our point of entry. We crossed in over a heavily defended flak area and were greeted by long streams of tracer and showers of orange balls of 40 millimetre. The sound of the guns alerted the flak positions inland. As I was the lead aircraft, they always opened up on me first. The flak positions were so well camouflaged I couldn't see where the fire was coming from. At one point an open field became a fountain of tracer. As I weaved madly, I could see the stuff coming up between my wings and tail. Expecting to feel the sear of bullets any second, I was startled when suddenly it all stopped. Looking back, I saw the reason. Dean had turned and was plastering the gun positions, drawing the fire. Our target was rolling stock but we saw none. We got flak all the way and, even when we came out over the sea, the shells were dropping around us in the water. Once we were out of range, feeling sure we must have been hit, I sought some altitude in case one of us had to bail. When we landed, to our utter amazement we found they hadn't put a mark on either of us.

They let me fly No. 3 position at last. While patrolling behind Dieppe, I asked permission to knock off a train. With my request granted, I dived at 90° to the train and pounded the engine until it was enveloped in steam, then raked the train from one end to the other.

Our efforts at train busting were reported to be causing considerable havoc, and so Eleven Group encouraged us to strafe whenever we were unopposed. On 17th January the Wing was dispatched to the Evetot area with instructions to knock out anything on the ground that moved. Nobbie Fee led our Squadron, and once again I was in No. 3 position in Yellow Section. Seeing no fighter opposition, Nobbie sent the entire Wing down to strafe, keeping only Red and Yellow Sections up to act as cover. The strafers merrily went about their business, one pilot cheerfully reporting a soccer game in progress in the village. Suddenly the top cover was attacked by a gaggle of 190's. The R/T chatter changed abruptly.

'190's, Red Section break.'

In an instant the air was full of 190's and Spitfires in the dogfight above the soccer field. I saw them early enough to turn, but three of the four aircraft in Red Section were hit immediately. Nobbie Fee calmly reported that he was damaged, but was going to try to get out. I turned on the last 190 in the formation, took careful aim and fired. Immediately it streamed a long trail of smoke. Another 190 was trying to get on Gib Coons, my No. 2's tail. I had to turn quickly and lost sight of my original target. As most of the strafers were out of ammunition, Keith Hodgson instructed all aircraft to make their way to the Coast and withdraw. Gib Coons stuck to my tail like glue, as we fought our way to the coast. With nothing on my tail, I found a 190 patrolling the shore. He tried to turn into me, but I gave him a two-second burst and saw two large orange flashes exploding at his port wing root. I left him diving inland. In spite of having been taken by surprise, we had destroyed four planes and damaged nine, not to mention the damaged trains. We had lost three. Unfortunately, one was Nobbie Fee.

Keith Hodgson was promoted to Wing Commander Flying, and to my horror, 401 Squadron was to be posted to Twelve Group for a rest. They were to be replaced by 403, the Wolf Squadron. When Dean MacDonald heard the news, he came to me almost in tears.

'Hughie, for God's sake, we've just come back from a bloody rest.'

'Come on, Dean,' I said. 'Let's go and speak to Keith Hodgson.'

We found Keith at his desk doing paper work. He looked tired. He'd had a long tour. His rugged face broke into a grin when he saw us, and leaning back in his chair, said impishly,

'I can't imagine what you boys are after.'

'Sir, I think Dean and I are going to die, if we have to go back on another rest. I know Sid Ford in command of 403. He and I were in the same flight at ITS. I understood he's the only experienced pilot in the outfit. I feel sure he would be glad to have us, if you'd let us go.'

For a long time, he just looked at us with a wry smile.

'Please, sir,' Dean pled.

'Okay, fellas, if you can talk Ford into taking you, I'll let you go.'

'Thank you, S-i-r!' we snapped in unison, and, shaking his hand vigorously, we dashed out.

Air Marshal Harris had launched his first thousand-bomber raid on Berlin. The night bombing of London was intensified in reprisal. I always felt stifled without my window open, so I had got permission to take my blackout curtains down. I was trying to get some sleep that night in spite of the bombs and the ack-ack, when I heard the characteristic pulsing drone of a Ju-88 coming straight overhead. There was a sharp rattle of cannon fire followed by the sound of the 88's engines built up to a scream as though he was divebombing the Mess. He pulled out just over the roof-top and for a second I saw him go by my window a flaming torch. He hit the ground with a sickening thud, and for a while the guns fell silent, their flashes replaced by the flickering flames of the burning aircraft. I closed my eyes to the sound of exploding ammunition. In what seemed no more than a few minutes, I was wakened by Monty Berger.

'It's another day, Hughie, and you're Orderly Officer. The guards have got one of the crew of that aircraft in the brig at the front gate. Get dressed, we have to go and see about him.'

As I donned my uniform and strapped on the Orderly Officer's arm-band, I vowed inwardly that I was going to make this just as unpleasant as I possibly could for this fellow. When I walked into the guard room, the RAF Regiment Guard snapped me a salute and pointed to the corner.

'The Interrogation Officer is on his way, Sir.'

Lying on the floor against the wall with a half unzipped coverall flying suit was a boy who didn't look a day over sixteen. A WAAF Nursing Orderly was dabbing a cut on his hand with iodine. When he looked up and saw me, his faced turned white as chalk. He began to shiver and his lips to tremble.

'He wants a cigarette, sir. Can I give him one?' asked the Nurse.

'He's to be given nothing,' I snapped.

'But he's just a boy, sir, and he's in shock.'

'You heard me, that's an order.'

The boy looked absolutely terrified. I felt sorry for him, but orders were orders. I couldn't help myself. I shot the lad a wink and told the WAAF to let him lie down in the brig.

Ten minutes later the guard room door was flung open, and in walked a short, stocky RAF Officer with battered cap pulled well down over his right ear and his greatcoat collar turned up. He had a greying moustache and two days' growth of beard on his chin. He looked in his middle forties.

'Where's the prisoner?' he growled.

'We've put him in the brig,' said the Sergeant.

'Give me the key,' said the Interrogation Officer, shooting out his hand. When he unlocked the door, the boy was lying down on the straw on the floor sobbing quietly.

'Achtung!' barked the Interrogation Officer.

With one bound, the boy was on his feet and standing stiffly at attention, his eyes looking up at the ceiling. The Officer put his arm on the boy's shoulder and in a soft soothing voice began speaking to him in German.

He came out and led the lad to the two guards who waited for him at the front door. As he passed me, he said, out of the corner of his mouth:

'There's no doubt I'll get everything there is to get out of this bastard.'

Then began the grisly job of visiting the crash and insuring that the wreck was properly guarded so that it could be inspected by the technical people in the morning. The distorted broken bodies of two crew members, their eyes open in death, like discarded puppets, lay in a jumbled heap.

We were short of pilots, so I was taken off Orderly Officer's duties and put on first readiness. Dean and I were scrambled immediately for a patrol from Beachy Head to Shoreham. After an hour and forty-five minutes we returned to Kenley only to be told by George Murray that as soon as we were refuelled we had to go straight back out again.

'Not again, George,' said Dean. 'I'm starving.'

'Get yourself a bun, Dean. There's the NAAFI tea-wagon.'

Grumbling to himself, Dean stumbled over to the NAAFI wagon and got himself two sugar-coated buns. He ate the first one, and carried the second along to eat on patrol.

Dean flew with his mask down, munching away on his bun. I headed for Beachy. Five minutes away from Kenley we heard:

'Snack Bar 19, Snack Bar 19, sixty plus 190's have just crossed in over Beachy Head, heading for London. They should be about five miles east of you.'

I saw Dean cram the rest of the bun in his mouth and close his mask, shaking his head excitedly. Turning 90° port I dived down just on top of the trees to be able to see the intruders against the sky. Sixty 190's over England, in daylight! At least we're going to be able to fight them over our own ground.

'Snack Bar 19s. They've just passed over Kenley and now appear to be making for Beachy. Steer 190 and Buster.'

Jamming my throttle through the gate I turned onto the vector. Just on top of the trees we headed for the coast. The course put us dead on Beachy Head, and as we passed over it, we got a shower of tracer from our own defences.

With the coastal defences still shooting. I weaved my way to the west. Suddenly, there they were, pouring like a tidal wave over the coastline in a shower of ack ack.

'I see them, Dean. I'm going in. Head straight south from Beachy, and you should cut them off.'

Just above the wave, I headed for the gaggle. Even though I joined the formation, not one of them moved. They were all nose down and going balls out for home. With 190's behind me I closed to three hundred yards on the aircraft on the flank. Taking careful aim, I gave him a long burst. Cannon shells exploded on his wing and fuselage. Out of the corner of my eye I saw something to port — it was Dean barelling in from the east. Evidently, he still hadn't seen them. He almost collided with a 190. They both took evasive action. I looked back for my target, and it was gone. The rest of the 190's still didn't move, as Dean settled down behind one in the middle of the formation. As he seemed not to realize that there were other 190's behind him, I pulled up so as to keep an eye on his tail. While he was concentrating on pounding his target, one of them behind him slid over to get into firing position. I warned him, and he pulled up. The culprit didn't follow but continued on with the others. Dean let a few of them go underneath him, then settled down behind another while I gave cover. Again I witnessed him scoring strikes. The 190's were faster at zero feet, and, with no chance of catching them now, we reluctantly turned back towards Beachy. With our fuel consumption at 135 gallons an hour at full throttle, we were short and landed on the

20 Spitfire VB of 401 Squadron in flight
21 Sgt. Omer Levesgul force-landed this
   401 Squadron Spitfire near Wellingor
22 F/L Ian Watson and F/O W.F. Napier,
   401 Squadron

21

22

24

25

23 P/O H.C. Godefroy's Spitfire YO.R
   over Kent, February 1942
24 Winter at Biggin Hill (February 1942,
   401 Squadron)
25 Winter at Biggin Hill (February 1942,
   401 Squadron)

26 P/O G.W. Northcott, 401 Squadron
27 P/O H.C. Godefroy and his puppy

28 P/O H.C. Godefroy and captured
   FW.190
29 F/O H.C. Godefroy, 1943
30 S/L C.M. Magwood DFC, CO of
   403 Squadron 1943
31 W/C Sid Ford, DFC and Bar

30

31

32 P/O Dean H. Dover and
Sgt. Utley (killed May
1943) 403 Squadron
33 Bud Handley working
on Spitfire of 403
Squadron

34

34 P/O W.T. Lane showing enemy damage to his 403 Squadron Spitfire, 1943
35 P/O E.L. Gimbel, DFC of Chicago, (Missing April 1943)
36 P/O W.T. Lane, 403 Squadron, (missing April 1943)

37 G/C Fenton, DSO, DFC, W/C Johnny Johnson, DSO, DFC, (Wing Commander Flying 127
Wing), A/M Sir Trafford Leigh-Mallory, KCB, DSO, S/L Bolton, DFC, S/L C.M. Magwood,
DFC (C) 403 Squadron), S/L Milwood (Controller)

38 403 Squadron pilots in loose formation, 1943

top of Beachy. As I taxied over to the Watch Office, I felt utterly frustrated. I had seen scores of hits on my target and had got him to the point where he was swaying like a drunken sailor, but I still hadn't seen him hit the water.

As I shut down, two men in Army uniforms jumped on the wing and said,

'Are you the fellas that attacked the 190's?'

'Yes,' I said dejectedly.

'Which of you was the first to attack?'

'I was,' I said.

'He sure hit the sea with a hell of a splash.'

'Did you see him go in?' I asked excitedly.

'We sure did. Didn't you see him?'

'No,' I said, 'I took my eyes off him for a second, and when I looked back, he was gone.'

'Well, don't you worry, sir. We can confirm it. That one's in small pieces at the bottom of the Channel.'

A great peace came over me. At last I would have a confirmed victory. The feverish compulsion had left me — the hunting-dog had brought back his first bird. The jinx was broken. Now I could be patient and wait.

By the end of January, the news broadcasts were full of Russian triumphs. Marshal Chukov had held out all summer thwarting every German attempt to take Stalingrad. On 23rd November he had surrounded an entire Army at the gates of the city, and by the end of January, cut off from supplies, the remainder of the Army surrendered. Over a hundred thousand German soldiers, half-frozen and starving, had been taken prisoner, including a Field Marshal, and over eighty thousand Germans were left dead on the field. Hitler in his madness had sacrificed an irreplaceable number of first line soldiers. The tables were beginning to turn.

Gleefully the Wolf Squadron arrived at Kenley. Their exuberance reminded me of the first time Dean Nesbitt had taken us to West Malling. Sid Ford, DFC and bar, looked a little older than I had remembered him. His hairline had receded, but as before, cool and self-assured. Leadership had made changes however. Gone was the carefree ready smile. He seemed preoccupied. He listened to my request in silence. After a moment, he turned and, looking me straight in the eye, said:

'I'll be glad to have you both, Hughie, but you have got to understand that I am responsible for these kids, and I show no favouritism.'

'Sid, I can assure you we don't expect any.'

He pulled a Benzedrine inhaler from his pocket and took a long sniff in each nostril.

'I understand you two fellas have been flying together. I'm going to have to break you up. Hughie, I'd like you to fly behind Terry O'Leary in A Flight, and Dean, you will be in B Flight under Charlie Magwood. I won't *stop* you flying Rhubarbs together. I'd prefer that you slow up on them a little bit until I get some experience into these young fellas.'

'Okay, Sir, whatever you say,' said Dean.

In the months of January and February, 1943, Sid Ford was feeling us out. I wasn't just because he had earned a DFC and bar that he had been promoted to Squadron Commander. He ran a tight ship and insisted on implicit obedience. In 403, Dean and I enjoyed more respect from the pilots. In the month of February we got off on another Rhubarb. Just as we were about to cross in over the French Coast, we received an order to return. No explanations were given.

The Spitfire Mk. XII had arrived at Duxford for testing. I got permission to fly up and have a look at it. The boys at AFDU were glad to see me and let me fly it. The Spitfire XII had the Griffon engine and was designed to give maximum performance below fifteen thousand feet. I was impressed with its speed at low level, but for the work that we were doing at Kenley I was glad that I was on the spitfire IX B.

The Germans had an armed merchantman in Dunkirk harbour and in the middle of the month we escorted several formations of Bostons attempting to bomb it. The efforts were consistently frustrated by poor weather. Expecting it to break out, the Navy sent MTB's to patrol the coast, and we were called to cover them when they returned. On one of these sorties, 403 Squadron lost its first pilot. Flying Officer Connacher vanished.

27th February found us on a sweep at twenty-five thousand feet covering the withdrawal of bombers from the Dunkirk area. I was flying in the No. 3 position behind Terry O'Leary. At the end of an uneventful patrol of the Coast, we were returning to Base from the Ostend area when I saw twenty-five 190's coming up behind us dead astern. 190's didn't usually come out over the sea this far. As the Squadron was short of fuel, Sid Ford decided to continue on and just keep an eye on them. To our surprise, they attacked. The lead aircraft came right up behind our Section and at 1000 yards I called a 'Break.' For some reason, Terry O'Leary was slow in responding and the leader knocked him down. Immediately the whole formation of 190's turned and dived straight back to their own coast. As soon as we had refuelled, Sid Ford ordered the Squadron back out over the sea to look for Terry. We scoured the sea for an hour and a half in vain.

To my delight, Ford asked me to take over B Flight. After two years, this was my first true leadership rank in a fighter squadron. One by one the pilots from B Flight came to offer congratulations, and each in his own way left me in no doubt that they were ready to follow me.

As more and more units were added to the US Eighth Air Force, we found ourselves continually escorting the inexperienced gaggles of B-17's. At first they were perpetually late for the rendezvous and had difficulty in navigating to their targets. To stay with them, we were always running short of fuel. To help us tolerate the frigid temperatures at twenty-five thousand feet, we were issued electrically heated gloves so our trigger fingers wouldn't go numb.

The first escort I flew as Leader of B Flight was on 8th March. It was designated 'Operation Ramrod' to St. Lo escorting fifty Fort-resses. What with the bombers being late for the rendezvous over Dungeness and the zig-zag approach to the target, it was a long cold trip. With the order limiting us to keeping the Huns away from the bombers, frustration was an added discomfort. On the return leg flying on the port side of the bombers I saw a single Focke-Wulf 190 sneaking up from below. I was afraid to move, lest the flash of light reflecting off my wings would scare him off. I waited until I was up-sun, then dived down. With my Flight in tight formation behind me, I closed to three hundred yards, took careful aim, and pressed the firing button. In a second the 190 was covered with orange flashes. As my cannon shells exploded over the cockpit and wing roots, slowly a black pall of smoke began pouring from his tail. With the expectation of no other opportunities I kept right on firing. As the shells con-tinued to explode around the cockpit, I found myself pressing even harder on the button. I was as though mesmerized. Suddenly I realized I was closing fast. My vision faded as I entered the smoke. Oil covered my windscreen, and I flew through a hail of bits and pieces flying off. I pulled the stick back just in time to miss the tail. Throwing my air-craft into a steep turn so as to see through the side panel, I was just in time to see the 190 blow up. A fiendish ecstasy enveloped me. I bit my lip and my mouth was filled with the blood. The spell was broken by the high-pitched voice of Harry Dowling:

'Magnificent, Skipper, magnificent!'

13th March was an unlucky day for the Squadron. It was a wonder that any of us got back. The sortie was a 'Ramrod' escorting sixty Fortresses. Rendezvous was over Dungeness. They were twenty minutes late. To add to our concern, instead of flying straight to Amiens, the Fortresses flew first to Dieppe then Rouen then Beauvais before bomb-ing the marshalling yards at Amiens. Then they made a wide turn to admire their bombing and came out over Abbeville in the Somme Estuary. Sid Ford was the only one to get a shot. He destroyed a Focke-Wulf 190. By the time we reached the French coast on the way out, all the No. 3's and 4's were short of fuel. Pilot Officer Cummings and Sergeant Dunbar decided to turn back into France, rather than risk a watery grave in the Channel. Sergeant Morrow, a teenager on his first sweep, was flying No. 4 in my Section. When we reached the Somme Estuary, he said in a hesitant high-pitched voice:

'I've only got seven gallons!'

'Okay, Blue 4,' I said, 'don't panic; disregard formation, set your throttle at plus four boost twenty-six hundred and fifty revs and lean mixture and let down one hundred feet a minute. Head straight for Dungeness, we'll stay with you.'

At these settings, the Merlin 61 consumed one gallon a minute. As I watched Morrow drop out of the formation, I could just imagine that boy looking at that cold blue water.

'Six gallons,' he said.

'Five gallons.'

'Four gallons.'

'Three gallons,' with his voice pitched just a little higher.

'Two gallons.'

Two minutes went by with the background static on the R/T seeming particularly loud.

'There goes my engine!'

'Okay, Blue 4, pull your revs straight back, glide at 140 for the tip of Dungeness.'

Zig-zagging above, I watched him glide for the coast with George Aitken, his Section Leader by his side. The minutes ticked by in noisy silence.

'I'm over.'

'Okay, Blue 4, pick a good field and stay high enough so you can slip off the last bit of height and get in.'

Slowly he turned to the west and aimed for a field. There were trees on the near side. In a shower of leaves he went straight through the tops and ground in on the dirt in a cloud of dust. I winced. I remembered too well the sound of metal tearing apart.

'I'm down.'

George Aitken was also desperately short of fuel. He did not make it to an airdrome and had to crash land as well.

It was a disgruntled group of pilots who attended the debriefing. Sid Ford was hopping mad. Emphatically he stated that he couldn't afford to lose good pilots because of late rendezvous and poor navigation. He asked Keith Hodgson to inform Eleven Group that if this ever happened again, we would instruct the bomber leader to abort the mission or go on alone.

Our next big escort job was a trip the Eighth Bomber Group would not forget. On 28th March, a sortie with the code name 'Circus' was launched. We were to escort 100 Fortresses deep into enemy territory to bomb a target not far from Paris. Once again the bomber formation was late. We chased away all the enemy aircraft that threatened the formation to start with, but, with the delay, it was obvious that we couldn't possibly stay with the bombers to their target and hope to fight our way out again. Keith Hodgson called the leader of the bombers and said that if he wanted fighter escort, he would have to turn back. There was a long delay before there was any reply, and then we heard on the R/T.

'Hello, Sunrise Leader, Roger, we enjoyed it, y'all come back. We're going on.'

Keith Hodgson turned back for the coast. We weren't more than ten miles away from the formation when I saw a flock of 190's approaching them head-on. With their wings flashing in the bright sunlight like a school of fish, they flicked over on their backs and attacked inverted. The last man in the box flying behind the leader began undulating his aircraft wildly up and down as though riding the waves. Cannon shells twinkled all over him, then, very slowly he rolled straight over on his back. We had a horrifying view of this huge aircraft tumbling lifelessly out of formation. A thousand feet below it exploded. Underneath I could see a cluster of parachutes floating gently down. A voice on the R/T said:

'My God, did you see that?'

We were too far away to help. In silence we made our way home. The bombers were never late again.

So it went on. Each day found us on a Ramrod, a Rodeo, or a fighter sweep, but for Keith Hodgson time had run out. Since the loss of Nobbie Fee, Keith had led the Wing for two months longer than a normal tour. He was sent on a rest. Sid Ford was promoted to Wing Commander and sent north to form another Canadian wing. Charlie Magwood replaced him as Commander of 403 Squadron, and we were informed that we would get an RAF Wing Leader, Wing Commander J. E. Johnson, DFC and bar.

Group Captain Fenton, the Station Commander, brought him in at lunch time, and with Squadron Leader Bud Malloy's help introduced him around. He made a positive first impression. When he spoke, it was firm and decisive. He was a wiry sort of fellow who walked with almost a cocky swagger. There was none of that fishy eye aloofness about him. He looked at the person talking to him as though he was paying attention. His face broke into a smile which emphasized the chip out of a top tooth.

He called the Wing into the Briefing Room for an introductory orientation. Using short crisp sentences and slow, almost Churchillian, emphasis, he stated that he expected implicit obedience to his flying orders. Flying discipline was the only discipline he was interested in;

he didn't give a tinker's damn what we did on the ground. He favoured the 'fluid 4' formation to produce better cross cover. He stated that he expected it would take a little time for us to get used to each other, but that he looked forward to leading a Canadian wing.

'Any questions?'

There was dead silence.

'Okay, chaps,' he said with a broad grin, his eyes twinkling. 'Give me a chance for a quick squirt, and I'll see you in the bar.'

There was a roar of laughter, and as the gathering broke up, it was evident that he had won the pilot's respect.

About this time, it was announced that the Windmill Girls of London would put on a show for us at the Station theatre. In spite of the bombing, the Windmill Theatre had continued to put on its variety show. The troupe had become a legend. The British laws of censorship allowed women to appear on stage nude as long as they didn't move. The Windmill took full advantage of the privilege.

Mindful of my experience at the Cafe de Paris, I chose a seat four or five rows back, mid stage. I was sitting beside Ibbitson. I had not gone to the show in London, being used to the crude strip-tease acts in Toronto. I had assumed that the Windmill performance would be the same. To my great surprise, the show was delightful. The choreography was high grade and faultless, the skits full of light-hearted humour devoid of crude suggestion, and the women m-a-g-n-i-f-i-c-e-n-t! Scattered throughout the performance were turns in which the curtains would part to reveal these gorgeous women totally nude and motionless posing like Greek statuary. On one of these occasions a particularly beautiful blonde with a smooth peachy complexion and beautifully rounded bosoms stood as the centrepiece. As the show progressed, Ibbitson beside me slid further and further down in his seat. All that was visible from the front were two beady little eyes standing as though on stems. Ibbitson was pitifully shy. He would rather have faced a dozen Messerschmitts than be left alone with a good-looking girl.

'What's the one in the middle look like, Hughie?' he whispered.

'Well,' I said, 'she's got large beautifully rounded breasts with prominent erect pink nipples.'

'No, no, I can see that — her face!'

The show got a half a dozen curtain calls, plenty of whistles but none of the lewd remarks I had heard from the audience at the Gaiety in Toronto. The troupe was invited to the Mess afterwards for drinks. The girl who had been the centrepiece was just as beautiful at close quarters as she had been on the stage. She wore a silk print blouse open at the neck loosely covering a bosom that nobody could now doubt was real, a tailored skirt, and high-heel spectator pumps that complemented her gorgeous legs. Ibbitson thought he couldn't stand

176

it. He said he was going to go upstairs for a cold shower. Ibbitson's self-appointed protector, Westhaver, refused to allow it and got him a double scotch to quiet his nerves. By the time the second drink was coursing through his veins, he was malleable, and we marched him up to meet her. She caught on at once and to the delight of the assembly began to tease him. Given a chance to talk to these girls at close quarters, we quickly realized that these were fine people. They were a dedicated group of professionals with social graces equal to their looks. Knowing the pilots, I couldn't help but worry that somebody would make a suggestive remark. Nobody did. They were all on their best behaviour. The troupe left as a body having earned the respect of everyone. Poor Ibbitson didn't have long to think about his 'blonde bombshell.' A short time later, on a dark and rainy night, he died by the side of the road in the arms of his friend, Westy. He had been crushed beneath his overturned jeep.

As a leader Johnny Johnson was like the Pied Piper. We found ourselves bounding out of bed repeating his catchy phrases, 'Okay, chaps, get into 'em!'

The events of 17th April I remember vividly. In the morning Johnny led our Squadron on a Wing sortie. It was a 'Ramrod' escorting Fortresses to the Abbeville — Caveay area. We escorted the bombers unopposed to the target and just after they had dropped their bombs twelve 190's came diving in. Johnny led us on to them immediately, but before anyone could close to fire, they all half rolled and went straight back into France. Then he ordered the Wing to split up into sections of two and disperse ourselves around the formation. As we approached the coast, I saw three tiny specks ahead at our level, and as there seemed to be nothing else about, Johnny gave me permission to investigate.

With Paul Gray as my No. 2, I went after them. I identified them as 190's in Vic formation climbing hard towards the coast. As I approached them from dead astern and below, I felt sure they must have been able to see me. They didn't move. When I had closed to a range of four hundred yards, they began a gradual turn and the man on the port side of the formation flicked over and dived away. But for the others it was too late: With the bead of my gun-sight on the nose of the leader at three hundred yards, I opened fire and kept my finger on the button until I was buffeting in his slipstream. His port cannon magazine exploded with a tremendous flash, and, as the cannon shells poured into him, great chunks flew off like chips from a woodman's ax. He spun for about a thousand feet, then exploded in a ball of fire. I could not take my eyes off it and watched until it hit the water twenty thousand feet below. It left a smoking green hole on the Channel. The spell was broken by Paul Gray's excited voice on the R/T,

'I got him! I got him! I got him! He's going to hit right beside yours. I got him! J-e-s-u-s C-h-r-i-s-t!'

Reproaching myself all the while, I said,

'That's enough Yellow 2, line astern!'

He paid no attention, but gyrated around the sky ecstatically. After the Wing had landed, a lone Spitfire dived into the circuit and did a series of upward rolls. It was Paul Gray. Paul came over to me afterwards much subdued.

'I'm sorry about that, Hughie. I couldn't help it. I've been waiting a lifetime for that to happen.'

After lunch we were off on another Circus, to the Le Havre area. Again we were heavily opposed. I bided my time watching the melee until I saw a lone 190 dive down and swoop back up again below the formation.

'Sunrise Leader, the bandit climbing beneath the formation is mine,' I said.

I dived down and closing fast from 5° off dead astern, and with the nose of the 190 pointing at the bead of my sight and half-way to the edge of the ring, I waited. I wanted a range of three hundred yards. At the edge of my field of vision I suddenly saw something directly above me. Looking up I saw the belly of a Spitfire. I snapped the stick back in my guts and for a second I heard the roar of his engine and my aircraft shuddered as our tails slapped each other. For a while my aircraft seemed to vibrate, but I couldn't be sure whether it was me shaking or the aircraft. My teeth were on edge. It had been an awfully close call! The 190 flicked over on his back and went vertically down. He must have miscalculated his height above the water and never pulled out. With a tremendous splash he went straight in. I had not seen the letters on the other Spitfire. I vowed that when I returned to Base I would find out who the clot was. On the ground nobody in the Squadron would admit to being the culprit. Knowing it must be one of them, I carefully examined the elevators of the aircraft for a matching dent. I found one. It was a desperately keen new Sergeant pilot I had hit. He hadn't owned up for fear of being grounded. With eyes lowered like a naughty little boy, he listened as I lectured:

'We don't mind keenness, laddy, but for God's sake keep your eyes open. You damn near killed us both.'

The Squadron was credited with one destroyed.

I had a forty-eight hour leave coming up, but with Connie in Scotland I didn't want to take it. Until recently, I had been very concerned about the survival of all these keen young pilots. They were so impetuous that you had constantly to hold them down. I felt much more secure when Walter Conrad was posted to my Flight. Walter had done a full tour in the Western Desert, been shot down fifty miles behind the lines and crash-landed his Spitfire in the sand. When the two German pilots in 109's saw him get out of the cockpit, they took to straffing him, first from the nose, then from the tail. Wally just ran from nose to tail hiding behind his engine until they ran out of ammunition. He was picked up by the famous Special Air Service (SAS) which operated in jeeps behind the German lines. He had some fascinating stories to tell of the daring displayed by this small group of men and his impressions of their fearless leader, Major David Stirling. He described him as a tall, rather foppish-looking fellow with a large handle-bar moustache, dusty battledress and beret and a cluster of DSO's with his belt dripping with hand grenades. He sported a German Luger on one hip and a Commando knife on the other. He and his men had destroyed upwards of ninety aircraft on the ground behind the lines. Once they had driven up to the German Officers' Mess in Tobruk, thrown in a couple of hand grenades, and finished off the survivors with a tommy gun.

Conrad fitted in beautifully. He added to my flight that bit of restraint which comes with experience, and had all the requirements for leadership. With him as a backup, I didn't feel any hesitation about taking some leave. Charlie Magwood suggested that I just go up to London for an 'oil change.' Instead I asked Johnny Johnson if I could fly up to Scotland. He said he would only consider it on the condition that I go on up to Inverness afterwards and pick up the pair of Churchill's he had left there at the end of the grouse season. In the morning there was Form 'D' from Group Headquarters.

'You won't be able to go, Hughie. I'm going to need you. We are taking Fortresses to Antwerp. Maybe after that, I can spare you.'

After we got back from Antwerp, I ran around looking for Johnny. I found him in the bar. With a broad grin, he said:

'Look at him, he can't stop salivating, the lecherous bastard. Okay, Hughie, 'way you go. Don't forget my guns, laddy!'

I dispensed with lunch, threw a few essentials in my parachute bag and got airborne. After a 'max' climb to twenty-five thousand feet and fast cruising revs and boost, in an hour I was circling Dumfries airdrome four hundred miles away. I taxied in and shut down by the Watch Office.

'How could I get some transport? I've got to get to Castle Douglas,' I asked the Duty Officer.

'Service transport out of the question; I can call a cab to the Main Gate for you if you like.'

'Please do,' I said. I'll walk out there and wait.'

A half an hour later the cab arrived.

'Take me to Castle Douglas, please.'

'I'm sorry,' said the driver. 'Government regulations restrict me to five miles, but I tell you what I can do. If I can phone MacFadyen in Buittle, he could meet us and take you the rest of the way.'

Having done the four hundred miles from Kenley in one hour, it took me two hours and fifteen minutes to travel the fifteen miles to Castle Douglas.

My visit was a complete surprise and caused great excitement. Definite changes had taken place in Connie. Being five-foot-three, there was no doubt about her 'condition.' Her face had a shining healthy outdoor look, and to my relief she seemed quite secure and now was anxious to get it over with. She had never looked more beautiful. Our private moments were absorbed in answering her questions. In my total ignorance of childbirth, the prospect of her having to endure 'labour' filled me with uncertainty.

The next morning to my great relief, Connie spared me the tears. In stoic silence she straightened my tie, kissed me and whispered,

'Look after yourself.'

Without another word, she turned and went inside. It was I who shed the tears as I rode through the countryside of Galloway. She was the brick; she knew the odds after a year working in the Ops Room at Biggin. It had come to me very clearly of late how much easier it is to take a risk yourself than send a friend to take one. Now with the anticipation of a baby, more then ever before she needed me alive. But she had done the big thing. She had forced herself to curb her emotions so as not to weaken my resolve. I was grateful to have to concern myself with getting the weather report for my flight.

It would be overcast fifteen hundred to a thousand feet with scattered rain showers, but nothing that should prevent me from getting to my destination. I filed a flight plan to go over the sea to the west of Ayrshire to avoid the hills, and then straight up to the Caledonian Canal. I would fly up Loch Ness to Inverness on the Moray Firth.

I flew close to the shore of Ailsa Craig to look for signs of life. There were none, so I set course for the Canal. Below, fifteen hundred feet over the water, the visibility was good. Above was solid overcast. At the entrance to the Canal the ceiling was down to a thousand feet and light rain peppered my windscreen, reducing visibility to about a mile and a half. As I followed the Canal, the ceiling became lower and lower. By the time I reached the bridge of land that separates the Canal from Loch Ness it was raining hard. The ceiling was down to a hundred feet with the mist reducing the visibility to less than half a mile. Cursing the Weather Office, I pressed on, afraid to turn around now lest I run into the mountains that rose straight up from both shores of the Loch to as much as four thousand feet. If I ran out of visibility, I had only one recourse, climb straight up and bail out. From my experience in planning Rhubarbs, I had memorized the position of Inverness airdrome. If the map was accurate, I had to go into a gradual turn to port, and I should go right over it. My course took me straight over the grass field. I pulled my throttle back, did a tight turn, put the flaps and wheels down, and landed. By the time I stopped rolling, the fog was so thick I couldn't see to taxi. An erk finally ran out from the Watch Office, took my wing tip and guided me to a place to shut down. The flight was a frightening reminder of what the Coastal Command boys had to put up with, operating from this area. I got a lift to the Hotel where Johnny had stayed on his grouse shoot. Needless to say, they remembered him well. They even recalled that he had taken his guns with him.

'Our roast grouse with a good bottle of wine and a few Drambuies has made the best of men forget a few things,' said the innkeeper.

I asked if I could stay to dinner. The innkeeper said he would be glad to accommodate me, but they were a bit crowded, and I might have to wait. The dining room was jammed with people mostly dressed in tweeds. I had been standing in the queue for about half an hour when the headwaiter slipped by the couple in front and asked me if I'd object to sharing a table.

'Certainly not,' I replied.

As he showed me to the table, he said:

'The gentleman in question, seeing you were alone, said he would share his.'

My dinner companion was a man who looked in his early sixties with a neatly trimmed full moustache, iron-grey hair and a well-tailored dark grey business suit. When I had introduced myself and thanked him for letting me share, the waiter handed me the menu, and I placed my order.

'Are you stationed in this part of the world?' he asked.

'No, sir,' I said. 'I was sent up here on a wild goose chase. Our Wing Commander Flying sent me to pick up a pair of Churchills he thought he'd left here last summer. The innkeeper informs me that he took them with him.'

'Are you on fighters, or bombers?'

'Fighters, sir.'

'What part of Canada do you come from?'

'Ontario,' I said, 'Toronto, to be exact.'

'You know, I have a lot of friends in Canada, and I know Toronto well. It's a big city, but by any chance did you ever come across a Canadian pilot by the name of John Weir?'

I was so thunderstruck that for a moment I was speechless.

'If you mean John Gordon Weir, sir, he and I have been inseparable friends. We were at school together in our early teens.'

'Were you really? Gordon Weir, John's father, has been a close friend and business associate of mine for years. In the last note I had from him, some time ago, he told me that John was missing. I haven't heard since.'

'I was posted directly from Canada to the same squadron as John,' I said, 'and we flew as a pair right up until his last sweep when he got shot down. He's a prisoner of war. I've had a letter from him. He was pretty badly burnt around the face, but sounded very much alive in the prisoner camp Stalag Luft III.'

'I'm so relieved. I had never heard, and I didn't have the heart to write and ask.'

He was a stimulating man to talk to, reminding me very much of Colonel Weir, except for his Scottish brogue and the tendency to feign uncertainty carefully choosing his words. Pleasant company made all the hazards and frustrations of this diversion worthwhile.

By first light, an area of high pressure covered the whole of the British Isles. In a cloudless sky I retraced my path, flying straight down Loch Ness and the Caledonian Canal with the snow-capped mountains glimmering in the bright sunlight on either side and landed at Speke. I was invited to play knock rummy by a WAAF Officer before lunch. When I took off for Kenley, I was richer by 2 pounds 4 shillings and sixpence. As soon as I reached Kenley, I pounced on Johnny in the bar.

'They said you took your guns with you, Johnny.'

'Did they now; well, well, I can't think what the bloody hell I did with them then. Let's hope that between now and the glorious twelfth I'll remember.'

During the month of May, 1943, we began encountering larger and larger formations of fighters on the Western front. Intelligence estimated that there were five hundred in our area, and we saw many formations of 109's still with their desert markings. Escorting eighty Fortresses to Meaurspts, I managed to get behind one of them and knocked great chunks off him. I had to leave him smoking and diving inland as I had two others on my tail.

Dean McDonald and I had started a competition as to who could destroy the most aircraft. When he saw mine go down, he scurried around until he got one.

In the early hours of May 13th, I had another of my memorable dreams. Dean and I had both been shot down and captured. We were sitting in a room talking as we usually did each night following a hard day. I said to Dean:

'There's no point in our fooling around, we've got to get out of here.'

The bed in my room at Kenley was right beside the window. Under the spell of my dream I sat up and drove my fist through the glass. I woke up with blood gushing from my forearm and, realizing what I had done, I went to the bathroom and sat on the john to think. Charlie Magwood, wakened by the sound of breaking glass, came in. When he saw me streaming blood, his face went white as a sheet. Thinking that I had gone berserk and cut my wrists, he ran out and got Cam McArthur. Irritated by all the fuss, I explained to Cam from the lavatory that there was no reason to be alarmed and that I would be grateful to him if he would just get on with getting the bleeding stopped.

'Come with me,' he said, as Charlie Magwood came over to take my arm.

The last thing I remember was following Cam out of the bathroom. When I regained consciousness, I found myself lying on top of Magwood who was wriggling around trying to get out from under me. As a result of this, I was scratched from the morning show.

The Squadron was heavily engaged; Charlie destroyed one and damaged one, but unfortunately he lost his No. 2, Sergeant Uttley, a nineteen-year-old boy in my Flight. Uttley was a likeable lad. Because of his tender years, we had nursed him carefully. He had just begun to get some confidence in himself.

In spite of Cam's objections, I went on the afternoon show, escorting forty Fortresses to the Courtrai area. The 190's were out in force, and I got in behind one carrying what looked like a torpedo or a bomb slung from his midsection. After a six-second burst, he was pouring black smoke. I got his oil smeared all over my windscreen again. He began to spin and with a tremendous flash crashed seven miles south of Ostend. Dean MacDonald's voice came on the R/T:

'You're not getting ahead of me — watch this.'

Looking around, I saw a 109F with a Spitfire in hot pursuit. Cannon shells twinkled all over it, and it went down on fire.

But the exultation that came with our successes was mixed with the anguish of costly losses. The next day we were on a Ramrod to the Poix and Cavaux area. It had seemed like a particularly long and tiresome trip, with groups of 190's feinting attack, trying to draw us away from the bombers. On the withdrawal, I was patrolling behind the formation as it crossed out over the water. Our fuel tanks were low, but I estimated that we could all get home. Suddenly Dean MacDonald's voice came on the R/T, high pitched and full of alarm:

'Can anybody give me a hand? I've got twelve 190's on my tail, and they've just shot down Willie!'

'Where are you Blue 1?' I barked, turning inland.

'Over the Somme, Angels 25.'

I climbed to twenty-six thousand feet, and with my Section in line abreast headed up the Somme. There was nothing to be seen.

'Where are you now, Blue 1?' I said, noting some smoke trails forming over Boulogne. There was no answer.

'Blue 1, Yellow 1 calling, are you receiving me?'

A transmitter snapped on, and for a minute we heard the sound of heavy breathing, and then Dean's voice, grunting with every word:

'I don't think . . . I don't think they can get me now. I'm at 42, and I'm crossing out over Boulogne . . . they don't seem to be able to climb any higher.'

I turned around and headed for the Coast.

At Kenley I taxied over the the Dispersal Hut, shut down and walked over to Dean's aircraft. He was still in his Mae West talking to his rigger. When he saw me coming, he threw down his gloves, stuffed his hands in his pockets, and shaking his head, walked away. By the time I caught up to him and put my arm on his shoulder, his face was wet with tears. We all loved Willie Lane, who found humour in the simplest things. We walked together for a while, Dean sobbing quietly. I found it difficult to know what to say.

'It's not your fault, Dean. That's the way the ball bounces, boy.'

'Son of a bitch,' he said, biting his finger.

'Come on, Dean. Let's go back to the Mess and get cleaned up and have a drink.'

He stopped, and for a moment stood vacantly staring at the grass.

'Ya, I better do that. I've got to change my drawers — anyway.'

I left him walking slightly bowlegged towards the Mess.

At first, Dean didn't come to my room that night at bedtime, and I was grateful. I didn't think there was anything more I could say. About midnight I was wakened by a hand on my shoulder.

'Are you awake, Hughie?'

'Yup. What is it?'

'I can't sleep. Can I talk to you for a minute?'

'Sure, boy,' I said. 'Put up the black-out and I'll turn on the light.'

For a while Dean sat at the end of the bed staring at his hands. Finally he said,

'You know in the daytime, Hughie, I'm keen as mustard and can hardly wait to get on the next sweep. But at night my mind keeps going over the things that have happened, and it scares the hell out of me. You know, Hughie, I haven't always done right; I've never got anybody into trouble, but I've screwed around a lot. Hughie, do you believe in God? Back home, we were always made to go to Sunday School and Church, but I didn't listen much; and now, even if I could think of what to say, I don't know whether it would do any good to pray.'

The air felt cool as I sat slowly up in bed and faced his enquiring eyes. With his simple directness, he had penetrated the armour that I

184

had built for myself. At sixteen when the juices of manhood had flooded my veins, such thoughts had shattered every prop I had had. Up to then my mind had been content with the placid dreams of boyhood. All at once I found myself galvanized by the frightening awareness that I was becoming a man. I had started my searching for some meaning to life. Caught between the simple Presbyterian faith of my mother and the almost agnostic science-oriented views of my father, I had found myself in the limbo of doubt. It was unthinkable that one day all these feelings would be extinguished like the lighted match hitting the water. Unable to sleep, one night I had gone to my father. He seemed to me to know everything. I asked him if there was a God. He had thought a long time, too, before he answered:

'Hughie, something is altering the laws of natural selection. Changes do not take place as a result of chance alone. Science cannot call it God, nor can it deny that something is there that is unequivocally altering the course of things in an extraordinary way. I am sure of it, but I don't know what "it" is.'

For my father, this was a departure from his preoccupation with the laws of mathematics and measurements. It gave me a glimmer of hope; even he had admitted that there was something else.

I had tried to close my mind to everything, as though in death, but I couldn't. This world was real, I felt, only because I could see and feel and touch and smell it. It could not disappear when these senses of mine ceased to be. That night with my father I acquired what was to me the comfort of a sixth sense, the awareness of an unrelenting immeasurable force that, for lack of a better word, I called my 'God.'

Now, faced with Dean's openness, and his troubled enquiring eyes upon me, I realized what he needed was a simple answer.

'Yes, Dean, I believe in God, and I cannot believe that he would be so cruel as to give you the drive to be a man and then punish you for acting like one. Go to bed, Dean, and sleep.'

Next morning, I saw Dean at breakfast before the first sweep, chomping on his bacon and eggs.

'How are you doing, Dean?' I said quietly.

He gave me a shy grin and said:

'Ready to go!'

In the air, Johnny Johnson was Greycap Leader, cool, commanding and as aggressive as a bull terrier. But when the sun went down, he didn't mind being called Johnny. He was one of us. His responses seemed Canadian, pure and simple.

'What we need is a pissup. I've had my fill of liver and onions. Monty!'

'Sir!'

'Call the Red Lion at Redhill and tell them to kill the bloody fatted calf. We're on our way. Come on, lads, fill up the vans and follow me. Hughie, you'd better come in mine. I may need a second pair of eyes on the way home.'

Chuckling with anticipation, everybody grabbed their caps and piled into the vans. As expected, it was a hair-raising ride. What with the masked headlights and my poor night vision, I didn't see obstructions until we were almost upon them.

'Get out of the bloody way, you stupid bastard!' Johnny would shout, as he suddenly overtook a vehicle.

'Clear the road, the Kenley's are coming!'

'That's original, Hughie, I rather like that.'

'Look out, Johnny, there's a man in the middle of the road!'

'Bloody Canadian, you obviously haven't learned to drive in England yet!'

I was greatly relieved when we pulled in the parking lot of the Red Lion.

'There we are — my kingdom for a pint of Guinness.'

To the amusement of most of the regulars, we took over. There was plenty of beer, games of darts and skittles. Johnny, with the help of Walter Conrad, led a sing-song around the piano with old favourites like 'Roll out the Barrel,' 'Waltzing Matilda,' and the South African Zulu war dance, 'Hey zinga, zumba, zumba, zumba.' There was food for those who wanted it: smoked salmon and excellent steak-and-kidney pie.

When the proprietor shouted:

'Time gentlemen, please!' there was a chorus of:

'A-w-w-w-w-w-w-!'

'Time gentlemen, for one more for the road!'

'Right you are,' said Johnny. 'Okay, lads, you've 'ad it. Bottoms up! There's work to do in the morning.'

I offered to drive.

'What?' said Johnny. 'You drive in your present state of public drunkenness? Not bloody likely! What we need is a sober man at the wheel. Look, some stupid clot has boxed me in. I'll show the bastard!'

With a crunch, Johnny backed the van into the car behind, driving it a good six feet to the rear.

'That's better. All aboard, chaps.'

When the van was full, we were off in a cloud of dust. But now, with a few pints of ale under my belt and the steak-and-kidney pie, somehow it didn't seem to matter. After a while, in the dim light of our shielded headlights, I saw half dozen women walking on the right side of the road. With a squeal of tires, Johnny slammed on the brakes.

'There they are chaps, same level, twelve o'clock, get into them and don't let any of them get away!'

Tittering with laughter, Johnny led us in pursuit of the women who now had broken into a trot. Johnny caught the hand of a young lady straggler and as he spun her around she butted her cigarette in his left ear.

'Ow-w-w,' he said, 'you nasty little bitch!'

The ladies in front stopped, and from their midst we heard a querulous voice say,

'Nobody calls my daughter a nasty little bitch. I say, what's all this in aid of?'

'They've got us outnumbered, return to Base!'

To the sound of Johnny's giggling laughter, we all piled back in the truck again and took off. It was a happy light-hearted evening, full of harmless fun, and in the Johnson tradition punctuated with the unexpected. There wasn't a man who didn't waken refreshed and ready to follow him in the morning.

Bud Handley, the Canadian rigger in charge of my aircraft, and the rest of the lads on my ground crew, considered themselves part of a team with me competing against the others. Even with two sweeps a day, my Spitfire never left the ground before every speck of oil had been washed from its belly and the perspex cleaned and shining like a mirror. I had put 150 operational hours on it, and on the last sortie I had chased a 109 straight down through fifteen thousand feet until my aircraft was shuddering so hard I couldn't shoot. At full throttle, I expected I might have damaged the engine and shaken more than one rivet loose. In the light of present knowledge, I may have dived through the sound barrier. After careful inspection it was discovered that the only thing wrong with it was that the paint was flaking off. It was still as fast as any aircraft in the squadron. But RAF Regulations demanded that if an aircraft survived 150 hours operational flying, it was slated for the bone-yard, taken to pieces, never to fly again. The older and more experienced I got, the more I found I resisted change. A comfortable pair of shoes I would get resoled until the tops were falling off. I felt the same way about my KHF. Despite my objections, it was taken to the hangar and dismantled. To add to my uneasiness, Spitty had been missing since the night 'wing thrash' at Redhill. I had left her with a pilot confined to bed, and he had let her out for a squirt just before the raid started. I never saw her again. I had come to look forward to the ecstatic welcome she always gave me each time I returned and had got used to her warm furry body across the foot of my bed each night. This was not the sort of casualty that I was prepared for. I diverted my feeling by concentrating on inspecting my new aircraft. I had to admit, that for a Spitfire, the paint job was outstanding and the panels fitted much better than the average kit coming off the line. The engine wasn't as smooth as my old one, but acceptable, and the cannons fired on the first test when I flew inverted. On my first sweep in her we got bounced by forty 190's and during the dogfight one of them took a wild shot at me and put five holes through that beautiful new finish. I thought Bud Handley was going to cry, but after careful inspection he informed me that no vital support structures or cables had been damaged and that he could patch it and make it look like new.

Nobody in the Squadron could possibly forget Athol McQueen; Arse-hole, as he became to be known affectionately. This hollow-chested round-shouldered kid made everybody aware of him from the moment he opened his mouth. With naive directness he voiced his every emotion on anything for that matter that came into his head. He expressed the thoughts and feelings that most of us had but wouldn't admit to.

At one of the briefings Johnny Johnson read a complaint from Eleven Group Headquarters. Too many pilots when they were hit were reporting their misery on the operational frequency instead of switching over to button 'D,' the emergency frequency, and giving a May Day. 'From now on,' the directive read, 'all pilots in distress will make all such transmissions on Button "D." '

Most of us had heard this coldly worded order many times before. There was no comment. When the Pilots had all returned to Dispersal for final preparations, Charlie Magwood gave the Squadron Commander's briefing and made last-minute changes in flying orders.

'Are there any questions?'

The silence was broken by Arse-hole.

'Okay, you guys, get a good look at that yellow streak down my back. I might as well tell you I'm too chicken for this button "D" business. You can be damn sure if I ever get hit, you're gonna hear me on button "A." I'm counting on you guys giving me a hand. You notice who's flying arse-end-Charlie in Blue Section, don't ya?'

There was a roar of laughter, and then Charlie Magwood said with a chuckle:

'Arse-hole, if you can keep your nose up Dean Dover's jacksey and your mouth shut, we won't have to worry.'

With a big grin, Charlie did a little shuffle and then feinted a kick at McQueen. We donned our parachutes and prepared our aircraft for the Wing takeoff. As it happened, this was an uneventful sortie, and nobody had to use button 'D.'

In the early hours of the morning of June 19th, I was awakened by a hand on my shoulder.

'Are you asleep, Hughie?' I heard a voice whisper.

Thinking it was Mac, without opening my eyes, I said with some annoyance,

'Not now, of course. What is it?'

'It's Maggie, Hughie. I've got something important to tell you; let me put the blackout curtain up and turn the lights on.'

With me sitting bolt upright in bed rubbing my eyes, Maggie sat down on the bed.

'Hughie, you have just been made CO of the Wolf Squadron.'

Every nerve in my body began to tingle. I must be dreaming. I shook my head and rubbed my eyes. When I opened them, I looked into the sombre face of Charlie Magwood. It wasn't a dream. Maggie had said that. His face reflected the sort of loneliness that comes when you are told that you are through. But for him, it was infinitely more traumatic. A fighter pilot's dream, command of a Squadron, and now he must relinquish it.

'You must be kidding, Maggie.'

'No, Hughie, I'm not kidding. Here's the signal.'

He pushed it into my hand. My wildest dream had been answered:

'To Commanding Office 403 Squadron stop Squadron Leader Magwood to relinquish command Stop Flight Lieutenant H. C. Godefroy J3701 promoted to Squadron Leader War Substantive stop 13 June '43.'

Slowly I became conscious of the full weight of its implication. For what seemed like years I had complained about leadership, but now that the torch had been thrown I would have to show what I could do. I was in full command of the highest scoring Squadron in Eleven Group.

'Congratulations, sir,' I heard somebody say, and looking up saw Larry, the Squadron Intelligence Officer. It felt funny to have Larry call me sir, and as I reached out to shake his hand, I felt myself blush. I heard the heavy thud of bare feet running down the corridor. I knew it was Dean. Sure enough, around the corner he came in his pajamas, a broad grin on his face. At first his mouth twitched as though he were searching for words, and then he said:

'Congratulations, sir.'

That did it.

'MacDonald, now you're bloody well gonna have to smarten up; I'm not putting up with any dead-beats in my Squadron.'

With a bound he was on my bed.

'There's gonna be no living with you now, Godefroy. I'd better beat the hell out of you while I've got the chance.'

The sounds of the scuffling and merriment awakened others, and soon several faces appeared at the door.

'What's going on?'

'I'm just beating up your new CO, and I'm finding him pretty dead beat.'

'Congratulations, Boss, when did it come through?' asked Dean Dover.

'It's just as much a surprise to me as anybody. Maggie just handed me the signal, Dean.'

'Good old Yellow Section, MacDonald, get some bloody time in!' said Harry Dowding.

Soon my room was filled with pajama-clad members of the Squadron all jabbering excitedly. It gave me a warm sense of reassurance that they all seemed genuinely happy with the change in Squadron's leadership.

'I've got some bad news, too, Hughie,' said Maggie. 'Sid Ford got it today attacking E-Boats.'

Gradually, the jabbering stopped with someone asking:

'What did he say?'

'Sid Ford bought it attacking E-Boats.'

'Oh, Christ.'

In silence, they hung their heads, and one by one went back to their rooms.

Blessed with full cooperation, command slipped easily into my hands. With two outstanding Flight Commanders in Dean MacDonald and Wallie Conrad, there was no question about flying discipline. The Wolf Squadron was a beautifully co-ordinated flying team. The Wing was now composed of three, ourselves, 421; the Red Indian Squadron; and 416, the Wild Cat Squadron. For a while, Johnny kept us doing top cover, and although I had always led the Squadron when Charlie Magwood was away, now I concentrated on keeping my unit properly stationed on the Leader in full view above and down sun.

After a while, it became our turn to be Lead Squadron, and, as such, I became Deputy Wing Leader. I flew as Johnny's No. 2, Ramrod 95, escorting forty Flying Fortresses to the Bournay and Lisieux area. Behind Johnny, I felt relieved of responsibility, and watched my Squadron in perfect station in the wide, line-abreast formation. At twenty-five thousand feet, twenty miles inside France, far ahead of us I saw a cloud of tiny specks.

'Greycap Leader, Red 2, twenty plus . . . two o'clock same level.'

'I can't see them yet, Red 2. Lead me to them.'

'Greycap, they've got a top cover of another twenty plus at least.'

I slipped out in front and, climbing to get the height advantage, I headed towards them.

'Right you are, Red 2, I see them. It's about chaps, tanks away!'

Since belly fuel tanks were not self-sealing like our mains, we dropped them, empty or not, before going into action. On all sides, tanks went sailing down, as Johnny eased his throttle open until we were balls out. When the bottom enemy formation was just about on our starboard beam and below, Johnny rolled over and dived, leaving the upper formation for our top cover. They saw us coming and began a slow defensive circle to port. Johnny attached himself to the end of the chain, and around we went. With each turn we got closer and closer to the last aircraft, but the lead 190's got closer and closer to us. As the range closed, my head was rotating from back to front. Who would get there first? Johnny cut inside the last 190 and left him for me. At 350 yards I took one last quick look behind. I could still see only the upper surface of the 190. From that I knew he could not give me enough deflection to hit me. I concentrated on my target. It was a $15°$ deflection shot. With the bead just in front of the tip of his spinner, at 300 yards I opened fire. There was a twinkling of cannon shells all around the cockpit and engine and as large pieces flew off, the propeller looked as if it was going to stop. Pouring black smoke, it pitched sharply forward and went spiralling down. I tightened my turn and got back in behind Johnny and just as I got into position, all the 190's half-rolled and divided. Looking up, I saw four Spitfires going straight down after them, streaming white puffs, as they fired. For us, the battle was over, and Johnny began a slow climb, gave his position and ordered the Wing to reform. After escorting the Fortresses back to the Coast and seeing nothing about, Johnny dived the Wing towards England. When we crossed in over our own ground, Johnny waggled his wings and the Squadron slid into tight formation of three lines of four. As we dived across the airdrome, Yellow and Blue Sections on the flanks broke away in upward and outward climbing turns in a perfect rendition of the Prince of Wales' feathers. Later, Johnny confirmed that he saw my 190 crash and, besides the one he got, Dean MacDonald was credited with one probable, and Wallie Conrad and Trapper Bowen each credited with one damaged. Bowen was one of the few Canadians in Johnny Johnson's old squadron. Johnny had arranged his transfer to the Kenley Wing. As his nickname indicated, Bowen had been a fur trapper before joining the Air Force. He was resolute and cool.

Wallie Conrad, Dean MacDonald and I had all experienced the evaporation of a unit's morale because dead men's shoes had been filled by inadequate or inexperienced men. We had a lot of green pilots of good tough fibre, and we took pains to nurse them into a state of confident awareness. On the next sweep in which the Squadron was flying top cover, Johnny engaged an enemy formation which we estimated at between 70 and 100 190's. Johnny deployed the bottom two squadrons in the attack, leaving us above to cover them. As we watched the battle, we saw an enemy straggler, and I dispatched Flight

Sergeant Shouldice and Flying Officer Marshall to get him. Shouldice chased his man aggressively and sent his first 190 down in flames. Unfortunately, in the process, Marshall was hit, but not badly enough to prevent him limping back to Base. Shouldice was safely out of the nest.

I was somewhat startled when Johnny out of the blue said,

'Hughie, I'm gonna nip up to town for a thrash. I want you to lead the Wing.'

'Okay, Johnny,' I said with more confidence than I felt. I had just become comfortable with my responsibilities as a squadron commander.

Johnny hadn't been gone from the Mess in his Morris Minor a half-hour when Monty Berger came up to me.

'There's a Form "D" in, Hughie. It looks like a big one. The Hornchurch Wing will be joining us. You will be leading. You'd better come over to the Ops Room and have a look at it.'

I followed Monty over in silence, full of self-doubt and uncertainty. I had never been good at reading anything. The only way I had ever been able to express myself had been extemporaneously. Monty handed me the Form 'D,' the printed Eleven Group orders for the Operation. It was about five feet long. The thought of having to brief the whole Wing while reading the fine print on this frightened me.

'Monty, I have heard a lot of people haltingly stumble through a briefing. I would prefer not to do the same. I believe a good briefing can add a lot to the success of an operation. Could you give me any ideas that would enable me to do it properly?'

'Hughie,' then hesitating for a few moments, he continued, 'I should call you "sir," but it doesn't come easily. I've called you "Hughie" too long. I've put the briefing information on this wall hundreds of times, but you're the first one to ask me for help. I've been tempted to offer some suggestions, but never did. I'm flattered that you asked. O.K., here's the situation: In this corner I have put all the weather information. Open with a general description of the type of operation — Sweep, Ramrod, Rodeo, with the types of bombers that are being escorted, and the height. Then deal with the weather information at that height and below as to how it will affect flying conditions and your plans as the Leader. Now move to the map and deal with the actual operation itself. I think it's of importance, for example, on this show, to bring to everybody's attention that when you reach the target area the Biggin Wing and the West Malling Wing will be behind you and will be in a position to give any stragglers a hand on the withdrawal. Then you should make your own plan as to how you will fly the sortie and how these various factors have influenced your plan. Does that seem to make sense?'

192

'It certainly does, Monty. That's the way I'm going to do it. Thank you very much.'

With Monty's help I was able to do my first Wing briefing without a stutter. With a plan to follow, I felt confident. I was able to deal with the question period with ease.

After the briefing, Monty walked to my aircraft with me. I admitted to him that I thought six squadrons in one gaggle was going to be unwieldy. I remembered only too well the confusion of the early sweeps with ten to fifteen squadrons and one Stirling bomber. I told him I would do the best I could.

In the air the Hornchurch Wing joined us right on time for the climb to the Coast.

It was a little tricky leading two Wings, but I gave a full minute's warning before changing throttle settings or direction, so the Squadrons would have a chance to maintain their proper stations.

Once I had crossed in over the French coast, I dispatched the closest unit to engage enemy formations as they arrived. This reduced the size of the formation and gave it more mobility, while maintaining a visible marshalling point for the attack units to return to. It seemed to be going well until Dean MacDonald, having been sent on an errand, ran into an overwhelming force of 190's. They nibbled away at his Section until they shot down his No. 4, his No. 3, and then his No. 2 man, in that order. Arse-hole was his No. 2. On fire and trapped in the cockpit, he went down from 25,000 feet. We heard his terrifying screams until he hit the ground. I felt as though I was dying with him. When we landed, Dispersal was like a morgue. One after another, the pilots came in, put their parachutes and Mae Wests away, and without a word left and went back to the Mess. I was glad to see Johnny Johnson in his Morris Minor coming up from the main gate.

Not all our losses were so poignant. I remember one in which there were no regrets. It was the result of a curious situation: In the early years of the War, as the Air Training Scheme was mushrooming, many good pilots were lured into Instructors' School with the promise of rapid promotion. All those who lobbied to become instructors were commissioned and went there directly. An elite Officer Class dominated Training Command, and Sergeant Pilot Instructors ceased to exist. Pilots like Andy McKenzie and Hart Finlay were trapped in the System for a while. Finding their primary objectives frustrated they refused to conform, and raised so much hell that they were classed as unsuitable and sent overseas. They fitted into squadron life painlessly.

By 1943, when Canadian squadrons were coming into their own, increasing numbers of instructors of Flight Lieutenant and even Squadron Leader rank arrived in England. Some of them thought that they would be handed a flight or a squadron of experienced flunkies who would protect them while they ran up a score.

One such individual was sent to the Wing and in no time had generated enormous resentment affecting the even atmosphere of the Mess.

The situation resolved itself. On an otherwise uneventful sweep he failed to return. Nobody had seen what had happened to him, and nobody seemed particularly curious. The thorn was gone, and overnight the mess became a different place. Replacements were screened much more carefully from then on. I have always wondered who shot 'Cock Robin.'

I was walking around the perimeter track towards 403 Squadron Dispersal, when I noticed a man sitting on a chair behind one of our Spitfires, sketching. I was overcome with curiosity. I had to go and look over his shoulder. After I had been standing there for a while, he turned around and said:

'I hope you don't mind. I'm Edwin Holgate. I've been commissioned by the RCAF to do some paintings. I'm doing a field sketch — what do you think?'

My love of art, drawing and painting had been inhibited as I adapted to the life of a fighter pilot. As a result, my perspective had narrowed. The tail of the Spitfire in his drawing looked disproportionately large and the position of the port cannon... 'Well, there's one thing you'll have to change: a cannon in that position would blow the tips of the prop off. It has to be out farther.'

'You're right! I would hever have noticed that. Thank you!'

Edwin Holgate stayed at Kenley more than a month, during which time we became fast friends.

(See Appendix Holgate I and II.)

On the 29th of June, Johnny was leading 421 Squadron, and we were top cover. Eight-tenths cloud covered the South coast, but France was reported clear. What we didn't know was that there was a thunderstorm imbedded in the cloud over England. When the Wing left Kenley, 403 Squadron was the last to take off. When the Lead squadron entered cloud, the other squadrons continued on the same vector penetrating after it. Everybody climbed at 1,000 feet a minute and 160 m.p.h., so as to end up in the same relative position on top of the cloud. I entered with my squadron in the usual 3 sections of 4 aircraft line astern. Trapper Bowen was Leader of Yellow Section on my port side. The Leaders would fly on instruments while all the other aircraft in the Squadron formated on him. If a Section Leader lost sight of the lead aircraft, he was to go on his instruments immediately, turn 15° left or right away from the Leader, fly for one minute, then turn back on the original course. Usually he ended up in the same part of the sky, on top. In the cloud it began getting darker and darker, the air became turbulent, and it rained so heavily that fine droplets entered the cockpit around the hood and peppered my face. I hunched down over the instruments and stayed on course. Suddenly my aircraft gave a violent shudder, and there was a sound of tearing metal. When I looked up, the tail of a Spitfire was on the end of my spinner. In the next instant, the whole tail section flashed by my port side, and my instruments were tumbled. I tore back the coupe top to bail out. Before I could pull the quick release, I popped out of the cloud, half inverted. Finding that I was able to level the aircraft, I looked around to estimate the extent of damage. My engine sounded very rough and high pitched, and a good foot-and-a-half was missing from the blades of my wooden prop. The panel was gone from my port cannon which was flapping gently in the wind. With my coupe top open, I flew straight and level and pulled back the throttle. My air speed indicator was still functioning. The aircraft was still controllable at 100 m.p.h. It had been prearranged that, if I had to return for any reason, Dean MacDonald would take over and lead the squadron. I called the Controller and announced that I was returning to Base. My gyros were still tumbled, so I flew around looking for a hole. Towards the south I found one and dived through it with my throttle pulled right back. I wondered who the other poor sod was. Estimating that the accident occurred at 5,000 feet, I felt sure that without a tail he wouldn't have time to bail out. Over Kenley I called the Airdrome Control Officer. This man was stationed in a truck parked at the downwind side of the runway. A bubble on the truck's roof allowed him unrestricted view. I told him I had collided with someone and asked him to see if my wheels were down. He told me they looked down but asked that I delay my landing until the crash truck was in place. I decided to land without flaps in case they were damaged. I brought it in fast, tapped the wheels down to make sure I had a bounce and wheeled it on. By the time I stopped rolling, I had the crash truck on one side and Cam MacArthur in a jeep on the other. Before I could get out, Cam MacArthur was on the wingtip screaming:

'Why the hell did you bring that aircraft in on the wheels: you know perfectly well you should have come in on the belly.'

'I wanted to try and save the aircraft, Cam.'

'To hell with the Goddamn aircraft! If you'd blown a tire, you might have killed yourself.'

He was so mad there were tears in his eyes. Cam couldn't fly, but he knew as much about emergency procedures as many pilots. He had listened to the shop talk and come to every briefing. He was a difficult man to argue with on points of flying judgment. He stopped shouting at me only when an erk came out to tell him that he was wanted on the telephone.

'Who is it?' he asked in annoyance.

'It's some hospital, sir. They say they have one of our pilots who's just bailed out.'

Cam looked exasperated as he strode off. The man I had hit was Trapper Bowen; he was alive and already in bed in a hospital. He had a badly fractured left arm. Cam took off straight away. When he returned, we got the full story. Trapper openly admitted that he had made the worst mistake in formation cloud flying. The cloud had become so thick that despite our flying with our wings overlapping he had lost sight of me. Instead of obeying the rule to go on instruments and turn $15°$ away from me, he tried to find me again by skidding towards me. Why the men flying line astern on us did not collide with each other was a mystery. Trapper knew his tail was gone because the control cables whipped forward and wrapped around his foot. When he slid back his canopy, the slipstream caught his left arm and snapped it between the elbow and shoulder. Somehow he had managed to get out and pull the ripcord. He had taken one swing in his chute and landed in an enormous tree on the front lawn of a hospital. While he dangled in his harness twenty-five feet off the ground, the hospital personnel formed a human pyramid to try to pull him down. Trapper made the only sensible suggestion: He told them to call the fire engine and get him down on its ladder. The bone of his arm was in splinters. His flying days were over, and before I had a chance to visit, he was sent back to Canada.

In the month of June, the Biggin Hill Wing recorded its thousandth victory. Everybody agreed it merited a celebration. A committee was formed, with Spy, Biggin's Chief Intelligence Officer, at its head to make the arrangements. Spy, renowned for his organizational wizardry, did not disappoint us. Grosvenor House in London was commandeered for a ball, and every room in the hotel was reserved. Every pilot who had flown in the Wing received an invitation, as well as the top brass of all active Services. There were sixteen hundred invitations issued, and it looked to me as if they all attended. The renowned RAF Dance Band was commissioned to provide the music. Biggin Hill's Catering Officer, a celebrated scrounger, promised his best.

Some of the most beautiful women in London were there. There were Service representatives from all the Commonwealth countries, America, and our European Allies. It was a colourful affair. If the Luftwaffe had hit Grosvenor House that night, the war might have been fought differently. Champagne flowed like water. The buffet table was bedecked with flowers and groaned with glazed hams, garnished boiled salmon, pheasant in full plumage, and platters of shrimp and shiny pink lobster. The only detail that Spy neglected was the inclusion of an Accounts Officer on his committee. Astronomical debts accrued.

Afterwards a fund-raising campaign was required. Requests were sent to every Station in Fighter Command to help pay for it.

On the 1st of July, I missed the opportunity of a Squadron Commander's life-time. With the acuteness of my distance vision, I found that I was able to pick up enemy aircraft sometimes as much as sixty miles away. Johnny would get me to lead the way to them, and then he would attack himself. I began to find it a little tiresome finding the bone and then watching another dog feast on it. My Squadron was top cover on a sweep to the St. Omer area. Johnny led the Wing on a course parallel to the coast in a westerly direction. I saw a gaggle of tiny specks at twelve o'clock at my level. With Johnny a couple of thousand feet below me, I felt justified in not reporting them. I gradually opened my throttle and headed in their direction. Soon I was able to see that it was a gaggle of 109's climbing in the same direction as ourselves. I continued to ease my throttle open until I was full bore. I noted that all my Squadron were right with me. I started a shallow dive until I was well below them. They were flying in a wide V formation. I called Johnny.

'Greycap Leader, Sunrise Leader calling, twelve 109's twelve o'clock.'

'Lead me to them!'

'They're too close, Greycap, and too far above you; I'll have to go in.'

With my Squadron in V behind me, I had two choices: I could attack the end of the formation with the likelihood of getting two myself, or go for the Leader and leave the others for my Squadron to shoot at. I chose the latter. I climbed up in the centre of the V and closed in on the lead aircraft; I passed right by the ones on the flanks. They didn't move. As I approached firing range, I became increasingly uncomfortable and spun my head from back to front watching the 109's behind me. They still didn't move. I knew I should be shouting orders to 'pick your man and don't let him get away.' I was so mesmerized by the circumstance that I was speechless. In silence I bore down on the leader. At 350 yards I took careful aim and gave him a two-second burst. Cannon shells burst all over the cockpit and the engine. He seemed to be knocked two feet into the air. Then slowly he began to turn to port. Knowing my vulnerability I did a sharp break in the same direction and looked back. I had stuck my neck out too far: a 109 on the flank was right on my tail laying off deflection. With a clear view of the barrel of his cannon that fired through the spinner, and his belly radiator looking like an open shark's mouth, I braced myself. He couldn't miss. Before my eyes, his engine exploded, and the aircraft was enveloped by fire. Sergeant Shouldice, my No. 2, had not let me down. Looking back for the leader, I was just in time to see him tumbling like a falling leaf to the ground. Instead of twelve,

197

we got three. Flying Officer Fowlow, a section leader, sent one down in flames. The rest of the squadron pilots had followed their leader.

About this time, I received a refreshing addition to my Squadron, two American lads, Danny Brown and Hank Zary. They had been trained by the Commonwealth Air Training Scheme and had had one tour in the Western Desert. They had turned down the higher pay and the fast promotion promised by the US Army Air Corps because they found the life in the RAF amusing. They were perfect foils for each other. Danny was an exceptionally handsome dark-haired boy while his friend provided ludicrous contrast, with his sharp beak-like nose and beady inquisitive eyes. Intelligent and well-informed, they were the promoters of countless debates, invariably siding with the unpopular view. They denied having the slightest interest in personal advancement, claiming instead that they believed in the promotion of every form of bizarre conduct. For a start, Brown, a Flying Officer, decided that it was his duty to try to seduce the Station 'Queen Bee,' the Flight Officer in command of all WAAF's on the Station. The fact that she was several years his senior, relatively matronly and proper, seemed to do nothing but add to his ardour. They openly admitted that they preferred to cheat at dice or cards and had had plenty of practice. When the conversation got dull, they would promote a debate on some controversial issue like the charms of homosexuals. Their claim to be interested only in their own skins was not borne out by their behaviour in the air. They were reliable, aggressive fighter pilots. Like a couple of cockleburrs, they constantly made their presence felt.

One day, in a sweep near Ostend, Wallie Conrad and Shouldice, his No. 2, were chasing a 109 down from 25,000 feet. Shouldice, in his eagerness to get a shot in, collided with Conrad. Wallie had just announced quite coolly that he would have to bail out, when Danny Brown's voice came on the R/T:

'I bags his typewriter!'

Before he jumped, Wally just had time to say:

'Like hell you do, Brown, I'm coming back!'

Watching from 25,000 feet, to our horror it appeared Wallie's parachute did not open completely but candled. Shouldice, the man to whom I owed my life, reported that his aircraft was still flyable and that he was going to try to make it back. He was never heard from again. Several months later we were in the bar at Kenley with Brown and Zary holding forth as usual, when a strangely familiar voice said:

'Okay, Brown, give me my typewriter.'

Everybody spun around and looked into the smiling face of Walter Conrad.

Walter's escape could only be classified as miraculous. He had landed in the centre of a Belgian two-storey haystack, the only one within a radius of five square miles. He was knocked senseless by the impact, but suffered no broken bones. When darkness fell, members of the underground dug him out. He was housed in the tiny dwelling of the local commander of the underground, a former Belgian Army officer who had lost both his legs. This maquis leader allowed nothing to interfere with his operational objectives. On the night before he dispatched Walter on a train for the Spanish frontier, he insisted that Walter sleep in the only double bed in the house with his wife, an exceptionally beautiful younger French woman. Walter recounted that he did not rest well.

He travelled on the train with a French-speaking companion and within plain view of the Spanish frontier the train was stopped and all passengers checked by the Gestapo. He had been ordered not to say a word to anyone. The companion producing forged identity papers, stating that Walter was deaf and dumb. He was placed in the hands of a Basque guide who made his living conducting escapees over the Pyrenees. Walter's physical stamina was stretched to the limit by this first-ever mountain climbing expedition. At the point of exhaustion, he plodded on against howling winds in bitter, penetrating cold. One of the other escapees was unable to go any further. He was left by the guides without a qualm to freeze to death. Across the Spanish frontier, he was captured by the Guardia Civil, the Spanish Police, who threw him into jail. He experienced some very rough treatment from his captors. Finally, the British High Commissioner negotiated his release, and he was taken to Gibraltar and flown back to England.

With the increasing success of the underground in smuggling pilots back to England, we were encouraged to lay on escape exercises during periods of bad weather. Groups of pilots were given an escape kit and a map, and stuffed into the back of a truck with the canvas flaps closed so they couldn't see out. Knowing only that they would be somewhere within the fifty square mile area on their maps, they were dropped individually. The Army Defences were alerted and ordered to search for them as if they were enemy. The pilots enthusiastically participated, some displaying surprising ingenuity. None of them was ever captured by the Army, and each had a different tale to tell on arrival at Kenley. Even the RAF Regiment which guarded the airdrome was on the alert in the hope of capturing them before they got back to the Mess.

One lad, dropped in a corn-field, crawled on his belly to the protection of a hedge-row nearby. When he looked on the other side, he saw a grass field with Typhoons dispersed around it. Spitfires were the only fighters he had ever flown. Seeing nobody about, he crawled over and got into one of the Typhoons. He read the starting procedure printed on the cards in the cockpit, started it up, and took off; fifteen minutes later he landed at Kenley. Another, seeing a roadside pub in the distance and feeling thirsty, started sneaking towards it. Outside the entrance he saw an Army truck with the driver sitting at the wheel. Seeing nobody about, he slipped up, opened the door, stuck his service revolver in the driver's ribs and said:

'If you make a sound, you're dead!'

Still keeping the driver covered, he got in the seat behind him, crouched down and waited. Soon an Army officer came out of the pub, wiping froth from his moustache. He climbed in the seat beside the driver and ordered him to carry on. The next thing he felt was the barrel of a revolver at the nape of his neck. He got the same warning. The pilot ordered them to drive to Kenley. Finding the barrier down at the main gate with the alerted guards carefully checking each vehicle before allowing it to enter, the pilot ordered the driver to park, but to leave his engine running. As soon as he saw the guards raise the barrier to let a vehicle in, he ordered the driver to follow the vehicle past the barrier as fast as he could. At gunpoint, he marched the Army officer and his driver into the Mess. The officer had to buy drinks all around.

On rainy days there were lectures on how to conduct yourself in Europe so as to avoid suspicion. The habit of holding a cigarette between the index and middle fingers could give you away. Special fleece-lined escape flying-boots were issued, with tops that could be cut off with a pocket knife hidden in the lining, leaving a good pair of walking shoes. Mistakes escapees had made filtered back to England.

We all knew the risks the underground was taking on our behalf and what the Gestapo would do to anybody helping a combatant. Early in the War, this was brought home clearly when a pilot shot down over Holland became impatient hiding in the attic of a house. Disobeying explicit instructions, he walked outside and ran straight into the arms of the Gestapo. They shot every man, woman and child in the village.

The record time for a downed pilot to be returned to England was twenty-four hours. This lad was put in the Lysander that had just dropped an agent. Two days later he was back on operations.

Early in the month of July, Johnny Johnson called me up.

'Hughie, I've just had a call from RCAF Headquarters asking me if I would take George Beurling. You've heard all the stories about how difficult he is to manage. Are you interested in taking a shot at him?'

'I've never met the fellow, Johnny, but he must be a hell of a good fighter pilot. He's got 29 destroyed, hasn't he? I never judge a man on second-hand information alone. If he is willing to come and fly like any other pilot in the squadron, I'll be pleased to take him. However, I would want to hear him agree to these terms without reservation.'

'Okay, Hughie, I'll tell them to send him down, and we'll have a chat with him.'

We had been concerned with the inaccuracy in shooting displayed by some of the combat films. We had set up a ground training device in the briefing room in the hope of improving it. It consisted of a chair with a ring and bead sight in front of it. Accurate models of enemy aircraft were impaled on a support attached to a ball joint. This was mounted on a tripod to be moved along a track in the line of sight. Marks on the floor that were shielded from the pilot's view were scaled every range from 150 to 600 yards. When the tripod was placed opposite these marks, the model would look the size of a real aircraft at that range. The model could be turned to any position, and the exact angle of attack could be read off on a circular scale by a pointer. Beurling would be the ideal man to be put in charge of this programme, we thought. Beurling was a tallish slim fellow with a dishevelled crop of blond hair, sharp features and deep creases down each cheek. He was given to chewing gum slowly and deliberately with his mouth open. He had large ice-blue eyes that rarely blinked. With George there was no place for preambles. I went straight to the point. I outlined the conditions under which I would accept him into my Squadron. He listened in silence, his face an expressionless mask. Johnny then pointed out that we needed experienced leaders with his capability and that he wanted him to take charge of the Ground Gunner Programme. There was a long pause while we both waited. Finally he said:

'Yep, I'll do it!'

'Okay,' I said, 'go on down to the Dispersal Hut and meet your squadron mates and familiarize yourself with the Spitfire IX. You'll find it a lot different from the V's that you flew before.'

Without a change of expression he turned on his heels and strode out.

'Friendly chap, isn't he?' Johnny chuckled.

Buck McNair, who had completed a very successful tour in Malta, was in command of 421 Squadron. He was a handsome blond Westerner renowned for his outspoken criticism of Headquarters personnel. His fearless aggressiveness as a fighter pilot and his natural ability to lead forced the higher-ups to tolerate him. His squadron was the most important thing in his life. He insisted on implicit obedience to his flying orders which included following his example of bulldog aggressiveness in battle. Anyone he found hesitating he turfed. Those who stood behind him he would defend even though he was threatened with Court Martial. He believed in the merit system, and he had no use for promotion based on seniority. On one occasion when he was away on a forty-eight-hour pass, a signal arrived promoting one of his pilots to Flight Commander. Buck had not authorized this change in leadership. With his face white with rage, he picked up the telephone and called Air Chief Marshal Leigh-Mallory at Fighter Command Headquarters. He was put straight through.

'Leigh-Mallory here.'

'McNair here. If you want to run this squadron, you come down here and lead it. As long as I'm in command, I'm gonna decide who gets promotion. Do you understand?'

Without listening for an answer, he slammed down the receiver. The Air Marshal spent the next half hour trying to find out who had called him. Fortunately, he was unsuccessful. Buck made his own choice for the Flight Commander vacancy and the appointment was changed quietly at a local level.

When day gave way to night, he became a different person. He absolutely refused to talk shop. He mixed with everyone on an equal basis. If anything, alcohol seemed to increase his tolerance, and he drank just enough to enjoy such carefree moments to the full. He was generous with women, claiming that he was incapable of watching them suffer. For a while, a striking-looking plotter in the Ops Room received most of his attention but not with serious intent. Unbeknown to anyone, the continuous bombing in Malta had opened a chink in his armour. A raw nerve had been bared. One evening in the bar a pilot touched that nerve. This lad was a new replacement in Buck's outfit and was fascinated by his Commanding Officer. He hung on Buck's every word. While standing beside him, during a lull in the conversation, he began to whistle imitating the sound of a falling bomb. Buck's smile evaporated. With a lightning right to the jaw, he knocked the lad to the floor. Then slowly and emphatically he said:

'I don't find that a bit funny — never do that again.'

In the early part of July Johnnie took seven days leave and told me to lead. In leadership matters Buck gave me full support, and I drew great benefit from his counsel. We became as close friends as circumstances permitted.

On July 10th Canadian, American, and British forces landed in Sicily. The trap was beginning to close. On the same day I led the Wing in support of 200 Fortresses on Ramrod 128 to Paris. The target was obscured by cloud. The mission was aborted. But for us it was not a fruitless journey. We destroyed one and damaged two.

On the 13th we repeated this mission. They were ready for us and engaged us in great numbers. A massive dogfight developed early in the sortie. We used up so much of our fuel I had to withdraw the Wing before the time anticipated. The bomber force had planned to do the last part of the journey unescorted in any case. Once again, just after we left, we saw three of these enormous aircraft go down in flames. All my aircraft but one got back to Kenley safely. Pilot Officer Bob Pentland ran out of fuel over the field. He undershot and crashed into some oak stumps. Ground crews seem to go crazy when they see a crash. Ignoring the fact that the aircraft was likely to burst into flames at any minute, they jumped on it and jerked Bob's unconscious body from the cockpit. Unfortunately, he had suffered a broken neck and was paralyzed. He had been one of the most outstanding athletes in Western Canada.

That night I felt particularly depressed. A light comedy was showing at the station cinema so I decided to go hoping that it would cheer me up. It was so light it was dull, but with nothing else to do I sat through it. With the Form D in for another Wing Ramrod to FéCamp I didn't feel like listening to jokes in the bar or playing knock rummy. I went straight up to bed. I had just turned the light off and taken the blackout curtain down when my phone rang. It must be Monty, I thought, they've probably changed the time for take-off.

'Godefroy speaking.'

'Sir,' said the operator, 'I have a telegram for you. Shall I read it?'

Thinking that it was from Eleven Group Headquarters, I said:

'Hold on, let me get the light on and a pencil, and I'll take it down.' I returned to the phone with paper and pencil.

'Okay, carry on.'

'Squadron Leader H. C. Godefroy RAF Station Kenley stop You have just become the father of an eight-and-a-half pound baby girl stop.'

Suddenly all the telephone operators on the Station came on at once and said in unison,

'Congratulations, sir!'

'Oh, my God,' I said. 'That was the furthest thing from my mind.' I put a call straight through to Castle Douglas. Auntie Jessie in great excitement gave me the whole story. Connie had had a long hard labour, and Dr Maxwell finally had to use forceps to deliver the baby. Connie was awake, very sore and tired, but doing well. The baby had a forceps mark on her forehead but was a 'fine healthy wee lass'. I told her I would come as soon as I could.

I slept fitfully and woke next morning tired. With the requirement to prepare my briefing, I soon found myself totally absorbed. We did our job without losing a bomber, and as I circled Kenley, I felt relieved that the mission had been accomplished without loss to ourselves. I was about to leave my aircraft when Cam McArthur came up.

'Dick Denison has crashed. He's dead. I'm going.'

Dick and I had flown together in 401 Squadron on our first tours. He had flown me to Duxford in the 'Maggie.' Before coming back for a second tour, he'd had one month at home in Canada. He had told me about it in full detail. I had been delighted when he came back to this Wing, but, with my responsibilities, I hadn't seen much of him.

'I'm going with you!' I said.

It was a horrifying experience, but finding that Cam was just as upset as I was somehow made it easier. But seeing the waxy blood-stained body of my friend, his glazed eyes open in death, emphasized the maddening pointlessness of this bloody war. For me, this was not Dick Denison, it was a ghastly caricature. Dick Denison was the warm happy personality who would remain in my memory for ever.

With our Station Commander, 'Iron Bill' McBrian's, permission, I handed over leadership of the Wing to Buck. An hour later I landed at Dumfries. Again it took me two hours and fifteen minutes to get to 31 Crossmichael Road in Castle Douglas. Uncle Archie had been watching for me from his chair by the front drawing-room window. He came out to meet me at the gate. With his face masked in seriousness, he said:

'Well, Hugh, ya canna deny this one, lad!'

His face broke into a shy smile, as he led me inside. I went straight upstairs. There was Connie looking pale and particularly 'wee' in the large mahogany double bed. She assured me that she was fine, just a little tired. The baby had been delivered in this very bed, but she preferred not to talk about it.

'Have you seen Isabel?'

'Isabel? Is that what you've named her? That's my aunt's name.'

'It was my mother's name, Hughie. Go and see her.'

Experienced Canadian fighter pilots were filtering back in increasing numbers for a second tour. Dal Russel, who had earned himself a DFC in the Battle of Britain, was leading a new Canadian Wing stationed at Redhill. No. 401 was one of his Squadrons, now under the command of Jeep Neal. Ian Ormston was back. Like Jeep, he, too, had got married on his month's leave in Canada. In my Squadron I got Buck Buckham, a cool, second-tour Fighter Pilot from British Columbia. After tours in the Middle East and Malta, came such outstanding Fighter Pilots as George Keefer, Wally McLeod, and George Hill. Under the administrative command of Iron Bill McBrian who was promoted to Group Captain, a rugged Canadian force began to assemble.

In the Desert Campaign the Air Force had been operating as close support to the army, and each Unit was organized for mobility to move with the battle lines. Instead of Navy, Army and Air Force Headquarters running their operations independently of each other, a combined Operational Headquarters had been created with the Heads of each Service operating under one roof. In preparation for the assault on Fortress Europe, a similar Headquarters would be established. A mobile tactical Air Force was to be created with the prime object of acting as close support to the Naval and Ground Forces. In preparation for such a state of mobility, it was rumoured, we would be losing the comforts of a permanent Station, be equipped as Mobile Units and move on to temporary air strips and live in tents. Improving the fitness of the pilots was to be emphasised. Group Captain McBrian with his RMC and previous training command orientation had definite ideas on the subject. In his eyes, the deportment of the pilots seemed totally undisciplined. Along with a fitness programme, he would like to have seen more emphasis on drill and ground discipline. After living with us for a while, he was made to realize that he would have to be satisfied with good flying discipline. With our present heavy commitment of escorting high-altitude heavy bombers daily, there was no time for jogging through the countryside playing hares and hounds. Competitive sport that could give vigorous exercise in a short period of time, like squash, was possible. Each permanent Station had squash courts, and we all began to play. I knew how to handle a tennis racket, having been trained by my father. As a university student, he had been almost good enough to make the Dutch National Tennis Team. Bill McBrian soon taught me that squash was a different game, thrashing me consistently whenever I played with him. After learning something about the game from him, beating Johnny Johnson should have been a piece of cake. What Johnny lacked in ability, he made up by the furious application of his competitive nature. He was all over the court, running into you or stepping on your feet. It was dangerous to get in front of him: You either got hit in the arse with the ball or crowned with his racket at the end of his follow-through. If he missed the ball with his racket, he was just as likely to do a little dance and try to kick it up with his toe or his heel. The only thing I didn't see him try was heading the ball. I found him a hard man to beat.

Bob Pentland had been a stimulus to athletics when he joined us. He had been active in organizing games of one kind or another and could always give you a good workout on the squash court. Cam MacArthur had given us hope that there was still a possibility his paralysis would not be permanent. A group of us got together and went down to see him in the hospital. Having remembered what a fine physical specimen he was, I was horrified to see how much the muscles of his arms and legs had wasted away in just these few weeks. His hands, like bony claws, lay motionless on towels at his side. His head was held in a nest of pillows and small beads of perspiration dappled his forehead. All he could do was follow us with his eyes, and he spoke so faintly that you had to get close to hear what he was saying.

'You guys are the only ones that would understand, for God's sake help me. Do *something*! Cut my throat, shoot me in the head! For God's sake have mercy! I can't stand it, this is a living death!'

As we stared at him in silence there wasn't one of us who didn't feel tempted to comply. Fortunately they only let us stay for a moment. The Pentland story was not ended. It was the story of two people — the girl who nursed him with tender devotion and helped him have the courage to carry on. She married him and took him back home to the West. When I last heard of him, he was working as a sports announcer giving daily radio broadcasts from his wheelchair.

At this time, what had been a rumour now became a reality. All the Canadian Wings ceased to be a part of Eleven Group and became part of the Second Tactical Air Force under the Command of Air Vice-Marshal Dixon. The Kenley Wing became 127 Airfield. This exciting change was the first inkling that definite preparations were being made for the invasion of the Continent. With the Luftwaffe's reaction at Dieppe, we presumed that the greatest air battle of the War was yet to come. Nobody wanted to miss it, and those of us whose operational time was beginning to creep up began juggling figures so we would be there. Destiny would dictate that some would not make it. George Aitken, as he got closer and closer to a hundred, began losing weight. He was one of my most reliable aggressive pilots and regularly took his place at the head of the Section. When a No. 2 was shot down behind him, his reaction became one of combative emotion. He wanted to go straight back again and wreak his vengeance. After some discussion Cam MacArthur and I decided that this was a dangerous attitude. I grounded him and sent him back to Canada. Replacements seemed plentiful, some with interesting backgrounds. I got a young Pilot Officer, for instance, who went by the name of Peter Logan. I was informed that his real name was Pierre Lacoque. Just before the War, Peter had been sent by his family in France to school in Canada to perfect his English. His family was caught in France, and as soon as he was of age, he joined the Royal Canadian Air Force. To prevent Gestapo reprisal on his family in the event of his true identity was discovered, his name was changed to Peter Logan.

Johnny Johnson decided that before they moved us into tents we should have one last 'glorious thrash' at Kenley. He phoned Air Vice Marshal Dixon and got permission for the Wing to be stood down for twenty-four hours. With great excitement arrangements got underway for the big 'wing ding.' Invitations were sent to all the Wing Leaders in the South, the top brass at RCAF Headquarters, and 2nd TAF. For a few days, the meals in the Mess deteriorated, but nobody complained because we all knew that the Catering Officer was away scrounging. The RAF Dance Band was booked, and all the unattached invited the most beautiful girls of their acquaintance. Johhny warned us that everybody had to be on their best behaviour, as Paula, his wife, was coming. The last show before the party, happily, was not a long escort job. It was a simple Fighter sweep of the Ostend/Dunkirk area to mop up fighter opposition.

'Okay, chaps,' said Johnny at the briefing. 'It's an easy one. Let's make it nice and tight and see if we can bring back a brace or two for the party.'

The Wing seemed to fly particularly good formation. We crossed in at Ostend just above twenty thousand but below the level of making smoke trails. As usual, we were welcomed by black puffs of heavy flak at the Coast. Johnny ignored it, penetrated about ten miles, then turned starboard and followed a straight course towards Dunkirk parallel to the Coast. We were right over the heavy flak belt and the black puffs increased in number astern, exactly at our level. With the Wing looking like three skeins of geese, we followed Johnny as the black puffs got closer and closer behind. A high-pitched voice broke R/T silence:

'Greycap Leader, Red 4. Flak at six o'clock, and it's getting Goddamn close!'

'To hell with the fuckin' flak, we're after fighters!'

Johnny had no sooner finished speaking when a shell went off behind and to port of him, blowing him almost over on his back. There was a pregnant silence as we all watched him come back straight and level. For a second his aircraft dodged around a little bit like a bird that had experienced a near miss. Finally he came on the R/T:

'Makes you bloody think, dun it!'

It was a magnificent party, and with evident regret the Air Vice-Marshal followed his AOA away from the jubilation, before the hour was up. His presence had not been allowed to subdue the company — the dancing and frolicking continued into the small hours of the morning.

We all felt that the AOA who had looked so disapproving at the party was responsible for the Form D that arrived at 6 a.m. We had to get up to escort a gaggle of Mitchells on a low level bombing attack.

The Padre at Kenley had been particularly well chosen for the job. Like Cam, he made himself an integral part of the Wing. He would take a drink, play poker, crap, knock rummy and bridge like an expert, attend the briefings, and spent most of his time with the pilots. I was startled to discover that he was a Jesuit Priest. As far as he was concerned, there wasn't a 'maudit Protestant' in the outfit. His non-denominational Services would satisfy the most discriminating 'Wasp.' I was most impressed with the way he handled an awkward situation: A married Protestant lad, who'd been away from home for several years, in his cups one night took up with a toothsome Cockney girl and got her pregnant. A short time later, he was killed. A month went by, and a short scruffy little man appeared on the Station and asked to speak to the Padre. After announcing that he was the father of the girl in question, preening his walrus-like moustache, he said:

'Think this whole affair should be worth a few quid. If it's not forthcoming, I'll be obliged to get in touch with the family.'

The Padre, fixing him with a cold eye, rose from his desk and silently walked over to face him.

'The Royal Canadian Air Force assumes full responsibility for the delivery of your daughter's child. If you should dare to write to this officer's family, the Air Force's Legal Department will descend upon you and sue you for malicious slander. Do I make myself clear?'

The man squirmed in front of the Padre, then said in a high-pitched voice:

'I didn't want to make any trouble, mind you; you can't blame a chap for trying.'

The Padre settled the matter without the knowledge of the next of kin.

Our Chief Engineering Officer, Squadron Leader Alex Hamilton, an essential cog in the wheel, was another tireless dedicated worker. Whenever faced with an urgent request to replace some aircraft, he never said, 'I can't.' He said instead: 'How long have I got?'

He never bitched and grumbled; he faced each crisis with a smile and got the aircraft back on line even if he and his men had to work all night.

With the relentless build-up of operational time among the leaders in the Wing, some juggling had to be done. Johnny had not had a proper rest since the Battle of Britain. The Canadian Government had a ruling that no Canadian was allowed to do more than two tours. Bill McBrian approached me and asked if he sent me on an extended leave, would I be willing to come back and take Johnny's place as Wing Leader. Dean MacDonald had secretly married a girl from Wales. McBrian wanted to send him back to Canada for a month's leave and, on his return, put him in command of one of the Squadrons of 126 Wing. Buck McNair was fresh and would become the Wing Leader of this Unit at Biggin Hill. With Bill McBrian's powerful connections, the whole thing was arranged with RCAF Headquarters. As I was preparing to go on leave, Dean MacDonald was packing his bag happily for his flight back to Canada.

Several of us were in Dean's room as he was making these preparations. While we watched him close his bag, he turned and with a grin said:

'When you bastards are munching marmite sandwiches and picking the bones out of your kipper, think of me, won't you? I'll be up at the lake eating steaks, homemade apple pie and ice cream.'

With a flourish, he slapped his cap onto the side of his hand, grabbed his bag and said: 'Have a jolly time, fellas. Canada, here I come!'

14

DARKWOOD LEADER

I spent the month of August in Castle Douglas. The first week I was nervous as a cat. Bill had told me to stay in Scotland until he called and during that week I kept worrying something would happen to make him cancel his plan. I very nearly called him to ask him how things were going.

Domestic affairs for Connie had undergone an unexpected change. When she had felt strong enough, to placate Auntie Jessie, she had dismissed the nurse. Triumphantly, her Aunt took over complete charge of the baby. When Connie found that she couldn't nurse her child, even that job was taken away from her. The only way she could see to get out of her dilemma was for me to announce that I would need her in the South when I went back on Operations. She much preferred to put up with the bombs than continue like this. She stated that if I didn't find her a place, she would take the baby to Tom's house in Tunbridge Wells and find one herself. She was prepared for the fact that I would not be there to help her, as I would not be allowed to live off the Station. She was fully confident that she could cope alone. When I hesitated, thinking the thing through, I found myself faced with a flood of tears. There was no other choice. With some uncertainty, I complied. The announcement was received in silence by Auntie Jessie.

This done, Connie happily proceeded with the plans for Isabel's christening. The hand-embroidered family christening robe was brought out of mothballs, and Aunt Jessie set to making the preparations to entertain the guests.

The mark on Isabel's forehead had completely disappeared, the black hair that had been present at birth was gone, and a fine blonde fuzz had begun to appear. She had large blue eyes that occasionally would cross. With all the attention she'd been getting she had already learned that if she cried, somebody would pick her up. A social consciousness had started to develop, and at the christening she seemed to sense that she was the centre of attraction and competed loudly with the Minister. When she was put back in her cot, she responded by holding her breath and straining with all her might. With her face

209

purple with the effort, nobody was in any doubt as to what she was doing to the christening robe. Everybody agreed that she was a fine spirited wee lass.

In the next two weeks, Uncle Archie kept me busy on men's business. Each day we walked down the road to inspect the two heifers while he did his routine of giving each of them a 'sweety.' We attended all the sheep and cattle auctions, which I found a fascinating experience. Seated in the third row of seats surrounding the covered ring, we watched the animals as they were herded in for inspection. The active farmers lined the railing of the first row, eyes on the auctioneer shouting, 'thirty-three and six, thirty-three and six, thirty-three and nine.' Despite paying strict attention, I never was able to discover which of these canny Scots with their expressionless faces was bidding and putting the price up. After one of the sheep auctions, I was amazed to discover that Uncle Archie had bought a half a dozen. In listening to him converse afterwards, I could only conclude that as a result of unsuitable weather and poor prices, none of the farmers was going to make a penny. While we were strolling home, I began deploring the circumstances that these men seemed to have to face.

'Agh, you can't believe a word they say. They're all making pots of money, but they'd never own up to it if their life was dependent on it. Ya might as well save your sympathy.'

With the anticipation of having to try to find a place for Connie, at the end of three weeks, I took the train to London. The counties of Kent and Surrey were within fairly easy driving distance of Kenley, and anywhere in this area would be relatively close to Tunbridge Wells. I contacted an estate agent and got a list of places to try. For several days I wandered through the countryside investigating possibilities. I was just at the point of phoning Scotland to report my singular lack of success when the agent reported he had found what he thought was 'just the thing.' It was a Tudor style cottage in Sussex, only a short bus ride from the shops of East Grinstead. It was one of many such cottages designed and built by a Swedish architect who had bought the land, meshing the area with a series of interconnecting roads without cutting down the beautiful trees. I went to investigate at once. The address was Pepys Cottage, Domewood, Copthorne, Sussex.

It was a bright sunny day when I walked into Domewood, the birds singing and the bees busily working the flowers. I walked through a maze of winding gravel roads for half an hour before I found anyone who could help me. At a cottage set well back from the road, 'The Holt,' I saw a woman weeding a floral border.

'Excuse me,' I said.

When she looked up and saw me, she smiled, and wiping some strands of grey hair from her eyes, came over and said,

'I detest weeding, but we have to do something. The bloody things are taking over the place. Much too nice a day to waste doing that sort of thing, don't you think?'

'I fully agree, but your garden looks awfully neat and tidy to me,' I said.

'Infested, absolutely infested with these nasty little things,' she said, showing me a handful as she pulled off her well-worn gardening gloves.

'I'm sorry. I always get carried away. Can I be of help?'

'Yes,' I said, 'I have spent the last half hour looking for a place called "Pepys Cottage." Could you direct me to it?

'Pepys?' she mused. 'I don't know how you missed it. Do you know where the Thornes live, just around the next corner? Of course, you don't. How stupid of me. I'll tell you what. I'd love an excuse to stop what I'm doing — I'll take you there.'

So it was that I made the acquaintance of Mrs. 'Peg' Harding. She knew the owners of Pepys well, even to the point where they hid the key. It was a lovely little single storey white stucco house, outlined with brown-stained wood in the Tudor style. It was fully furnished with two bedrooms, a small kitchen, bathroom with modern-looking fixtures, and a large living-room — dining room area that stretched from back to front. In the middle of the inside wall was a fireplace with a copper, trumpet-shaped canopy. The house was built on about half an acre of ground. It was a charming little dwelling and the perfect size for us. I was able to get it on a month-to-month basis. Connie was delighted when she heard the news and said the moment she had her things together she would move.

Ian Ormston had come across a lady with a litter of German Shepherds. Dal Russell, George Keefer, Ian and I had all reserved one. As I had some time on my hands, I went and picked mine up. At six months, his ears were standing up perfectly, and he looked to be almost fully grown with a lovely heavy black-and-tan coat. I named him 'Radar.'

The Wing had been moved to a temporary airstrip near Maidstone, carved out of an estate by the Army's earth-moving contingents. It had been equipped and fully established as a completely mobile Unit from the Aircraft Maintenance Section down to the cooking and catering. The House on the Estate had been commandeered as a Mess. Bill McBrian was the only one who wasn't roughing it. He had commandeered the small guest house the original owner of the Estate had used to entertain lady friends. By the end of the first week of September, Connie and little Isabel were settled in at Pepys Cottage, and I had erected my tent amongst those of my Squadron Mates.

A Mobile Ops Room had been established under the control of a

Squadron Leader by the name of Hunter. They had set up camp just inland from the cliffs of Dover so as to be as close to the French coast as possible. This unit was an example of what British ingenuity could do when it put its mind to it. Packed with expert personnel, especially chosen for their ability to work together and meticulously adhere to detail, this unit produced a quality of accuracy that was a fighter pilot's dream. They made the people at Fighter Command Ops Room look like a bunch of bungling amateurs. They could control only one Wing at a time, and without high batting average, Squadron Leader Hunter enjoyed working with us. The accuracy with which he directed us was demonstrated by my very first trip back on Operations. It was a pure Fighter sweep, and with a series of vectors Hunter manoeuvred Johnny to the perfect tactical position up sun and above an enemy formation. At the very last he came on the R/T and said,

'Greycap Leader, look below your starboard wing, and you'll see twenty plus.'

We looked, and there they were. Hunter was able to produce this grade of accurate control 150 miles from his station. It was a single unit effort, and when Fighter Command split up to try to produce many such units, none of them was able to do anything like it again.

Bob Buckham, one of the Pilots in 403, had had an unusual upbringing. He had been raised near the Japanese Community in Vancouver. They had trained him like one of their own and taught him Judo. He was a black belt. To those who were interested, he was happy to demonstrate the art. At about five feet eight and a hundred and thirty-five pounds, he was more than a match for the biggest man in the outfit. Although cool and aggressive in battle, he maintained an Oriental placidity in outlook back on the field. He loved children and all wild creatures. One day we were sitting together on the patio of the Estate's House enjoying a cigarette after lunch. In front of us, two steps led down to a formal garden with floral borders and a central pond edged with lilies. A wood duck had taken up residence in the pond and become tame enough to be hand-fed. Buck never left the dining table without taking him some scraps. 'Buzz' Beurling strolled out of the dining-room and stood for a moment in front of us on the top step surveying the scene. To our utter amazement, he pulled his Webley revolver from his holster, took aim at the duck and proceeded to shoot feathers out of its tail. Before he could fire the third shot, Buckan was beside him and with a lightning chop knocked the revolver from his hand. With his eyes burning like two coals of fire, he said very slowly,

'Buerling, if you ever shoot at that duck again, I'll kill you with my bare hands!'

Buerling just looked at him with those cold blue eyes, then slowly his face broke into a grin as he said:

'Okay, Buck, I wasn't going to hurt it.'

On the 11th of September, Johnny Johnson was sent to Fighter Command Headquarters for a rest. I took his place as Wing Commander Flying. Monty showed me a list of approved Wing Leader call signs, and from it I selected 'Darkwood.' From that moment by necessity my life changed. Like Squadron Leader Hunter's unit, this Wing was the test bed of the Canadian fighter effort. From it would be drawn experienced personnel with leadership potential for the establishment of the squadrons and wings that Canada would provide for the Invasion. As a Squadron Commander, one could still be a member of a small closely knit unit. A Wing Commander Flying could have no favourites among the squadrons; the Wing had to be 'the thing.' This was the highest rank one could hold in the Air Force and still lead men into battle. A mistake on my part would not just cost me my life, but possibly the lives of thirty-six others. For me to emulate Johnny Johnson was unthinkable. Johnny had accomplished what all of us had hoped. He had brought out the true potential of this Canadian fighter wing which now had an established reputation. But the eighty plus that we had shot down under his leadership had not been without cost. With the further drain to provide leaders for new wings, I saw my role as completely different from the one which Johnny had had to play. Building up a record of personal victories was of no importance. I had a good chance of leading 127 Wing on D-Day and my whole energy had to be devoted to fielding a side that would be equal to that supreme test. The first sortie that I flew in my new official capacity was Ramrod 216 on September 11th. I was escorting thirty-six Martin Marauders to Beaumont Le Roger. I was satisfied that all the aircraft in the formation returned safely and the Wing was able to claim one destroyed by Harry Dowding.

Before leaving the Wing, Johnny Johnson had decided he needed a new car. After some dickering, I had offered him 35 pounds for his Morris Minor, with the understanding that he replace the two back tires. After I took delivery, I discovered the new tires had come off a 127 Wing battery cart, and that it had an irritatingly temperamental engine. I had just become comfortable enough in my new job to be able to devote some time to working on my car, when I was made aware of a different problem: Domewood was a pleasant enough little community in daylight, but when darkness fell, alone with the baby in the blacked-out cottage, it could be terrifying. It was on the Luftwaffe's bombing run to London and was a favourite place for the night fighters to intercept. The wood was surrounded by a heavy ack-ack battery and the guns sounded as if they were being fired from the front lawn.

At midnight one night Connie phoned in tears saying there was a terrible raid in progress and I would have to come. I said I would if I could get the Morris to start. To my surprise, it started first time.

Silhouetted in the continuous flash of the guns and the air singing with shrapnel, I reached Doomwood. Mrs. Harding met me at the door in a fur coat.

'My, don't you look smart,' I said.

'This is the only thing I own that I give a tinker's damn about. It was a present from Peter. I thought Connie might be frightened so I came over. We're under the bed!'

So far, Isabel had slept quite serenely through the raid. She had stirred momentarily when a stick of bombs had come down. There was no question of us trying to sleep, so I poured three drinks from the bottle of whisky I had brought. Connie produced some cheese and crackers, and we all sat on the bed and had a little party.

They had heard one aircraft come down, and the thought that some of its crew might be out there in the darkness terrified them. When the raid was over, I instructed them both in how to load and fire my Smith and Wesson .45 that I would leave with them. Before first light I left my two girls tucked in bed, with Radar happily asleep across the foot, my revolver on one bedside table and a shillelagh on the other.

At the Airfield at Maidstone, I got a letter from my brother, Bill. For the past three years he had been stationed in Newfoundland. In the Algonquin Rifles, he had risen to Company Sergeant Major. He was now at Sandhurst taking his officers' course. He sounded desperately keen to get into action. The thought of him as a Field Officer in the 'poor bloody Infantry' landing on the beaches of Fortress Europe made me shudder.

As Wing Commander Flying, I received a daily Operations Report from Combined Operations Headquarters. This summarized the activities of all Allied Services in every theater of the War. Air Marshal Harris was launching the full weight of Bomber Command in nightly thousand bomber raids into the German heartland. In the hope of overwhelming the German nightfighter force, he sent them in a stream like an enormous school of fish. He was losing as many as ninety aircraft each night.

On one of the days that the Wing was stood down, I was having tea with Connie and Isabel on the front lawn at Pepys. I had just finished telling Connie about the frightful losses Bomber Command was suffering when I noticed a young Sergeant Air Gunner walking on the road in front of the house. To our surprise he turned in the driveway and walked towards us. To my amazement, I recognized my youngest brother, David, barely eighteen. I thought he was still at school at Upper Canada. Mother had sent him my address, and that's how he had managed to find us. Connie had never met any of my family, and after the introductions, I was able to get the full story. David had left school, joined the Air Force, and volunteered for any active job that would get him overseas. He had been sent to Gunnery School, teamed up with a Lancaster crew that had now finished its operational training. They had been released on a forty-eight-hour pass before joining the Goose Squadron. He was the rear gunner, the most dangerous job he could have. He had a good 'skipper,' and they were all dying to get into action. As I listened to him, barely dry behind the ears, and thought of the recent losses, I felt sick. With this boy's two older brothers committed to front line active duty, I resented the Canadian authorities accepting him when he was under age, especially when Canada still did not use full conscription. But there was nothing I could do about it now. To tell David what he was about to face could only shake his determination. If he were to panic, his whole crew would be lost. It had taken most of his forty-eight-hours' leave to find us, and he had to go straight back.

After we had finished tea, we all wedged ourselves in the Morris Minor for the ride to the bus at East Grinstead. This town was where the big Air Force Plastic Surgery Hospital was located. It was here that the renowned surgeon, Dr. Archie MacIndoe, was performing his extraordinary feats of plastic reconstruction. Every third person on the street was a hospital inmate, convalescing from one of his many operations. The whole town was dedicated to rehabilitating these men. Nobody paid the slightest attention when passing these horribly disfigured airmen, their mouths twisted by scar to reveal their teeth, or their eyes bulging from their head because of the lack of eyelids; others with two large slits in the middle of their face where their nose had been. There wasn't a mirror in the town. David was shaken.

Even in September, the ground was cold and damp in the early morning, and the grass was always wet with a heavy dew. Above twenty thousand feet it was below freezing. We always kept our clothes wadded up in the bottom of our sleeping bags to keep them warm and dry. I briefed the Wing in front of a portable blackboard on the field. Only in the afternoon shows, when the dew had dried from the grass, could the pilots sit down to listen.

The Huns had again changed their tactics. They rarely flew in small numbers, preferring the security of larger formations. They were hesitant to do battle, and the moment one turned towards them they would dive away. On the 19th of September, on Ramrod 233, I was escorting a dozen Mitchells to bomb the marshalling yards in Lens. A formation of 109's appeared on the scene above me, then made a wide sweeping turn and came in to attack. As soon as I turned into them, they pushed their noses forward and streaked for the ground. Buck

Buckham was leading Yellow Section in the Wolf Squadron. He was the closest to them and gave chase. He pursued them right to ground level where he shot down one, while his No. 3, Hank Zary, knocked down another.

One of the fringe benefits of being a Wing Leader is that you are provided with a new aircraft emblazoned with your initials rather than the standard Squadron markings. When I looked at it I felt a surge of pride. For the first time I found myself treating an aircraft as though it were mine. On the 24th of September, on the second sortie of the day, on Ramrod 243, I was escorting seventy-two Marauders to bomb the Beauvais Tille Airdrome. This was a Fighter Base, and they turned out in force. A dogfight reminiscent of old times erupted, and I led the lead squadron in the attack on the main formation. They were all 190's, and Buck Buckham and I shot down one apiece in the initial attack. Buzz Beurling gave a nice exhibition of marksmanship by taking a 90° deflection shot at one and knocking his port wing off. After the show, in all seriousness, he grumbled that he was out of practice or his line of sight would not have been off. I could hardly share his disappointment, for the Wing had destroyed three without a loss. In the first few days of October, the Luftwaffe became more aggressive. Operating in the Woensdrecht and Schipol area, we became heavily engaged. The Wing destroyed five for the loss of two. Pilot Officer Cook shared in the destruction of one of them with Pilot Officer Carl Linton, but then Cook was badly shot up and had to bail out in enemy territory. Once again our escape exercises paid off. Six weeks later Cook was back in the Mess in England.

By the 15th of October it got cold enough to make us really miserable living in tents and flying two sorties a day at sub-zero temperatures. I was allowed to take my Wing back to the comforts of Kenley. Up to this point we had had to satisfy any desire for cleanliness by taking bird baths over the canvas basin in front of our tents. To us, a hot shower was a luxury. The bar was filled with a sea of cleanly shaven faces, all in their best blue with buttons and boots shining. We agreed that this was a much more civilized way of fighting a war. On the next show, we expressed our appreciation by chasing the Huns right back to their home base, and Carl Linton shot one down in the circuit.

At this point, I received a letter from the Central Chancery of the Orders of Knighthood, St. James' Palace, Southwest One. At the top in large print, underlined, was the word 'CONFIDENTIAL.'

'Sir,' it stated, 'the King will hold an investiture at Buckingham Palace on Tuesday, the 9th of November, at which your attendance is requested.' This was the second such letter I had received, the first arriving sometime after I had been awarded my first DFC when I was a Flight Lieutenant. At that time I had been obliged to send my regrets owing to prior operational commitments. Bill McBrian thought that this time I should show up. Connie insisted that neither my grey thread-bare T. Eaton Company uniform, nor the poor-fitting one that I had bought from Gieves, was suitable. She wouldn't allow me to meet the King without a new one. I took a forty-eight-hour leave, picked Connie up from Domewood in the Morris.

Finding a decent room in London at short notice could be difficult. Luckily because of a cancellation I got a room at the Savoy. Once again we were treated as though we were the most important guests in the hotel, and after much snapping of fingers for attendants, we were ushered into one of the rooms with the glorious view of the Thames.

I had booked a table for the dinner dance at the Mayfair. Here, also, the service was first class and the menu offered a surprisingly wide choice. In spite of the long siege of the British Isles, the restaurants of London still produced wine. How it got there may always remain a mystery. I selected a dry white wine. It always seemed a little more festive. It felt like years since we had danced together, and it was with some hesitation that we took to the floor. After the first turn, I stopped wondering if she could still follow me. It seemed no time before they were playing the last waltz. I tried to hail a taxi but none would stop. We settled for the bus like married folk. A raid was in progress, and with the strengthening of the ack-ack defences, the shrapnel was particularly noisy. Of late this had been quite a problem, several people being killed by it every night. It was a relief to reach the protection of the Savoy. The Hardings were looking after Isabel, but even though we knew that she couldn't be in better hands, we still worried. We passed an unsettled night.

Not to be dissuaded from the purpose of our trip to London, Connie marched me down to Saville Row. Unknown to me, this quiet little section behind Regent Street was to London tailors what Harley Street was to the medical profession. With hands behind my back, I wandered around the street looking at the various establishments. Neither one of us knew one from another. Finally we decided on Huntsman and Sons and timorously went inside to have a look. As though he had been expecting us, a dapper middle-aged man, with a handsome full moustache turned up at the corners, welcomed us inside. Packer was his name, which he repeated with deliberate emphasis when I made the mistake of calling him Parker. He assured me that Huntsman and Sons was quite used to arranging its priorities to meet the demands of Investitures. I didn't know what he meant when the tailor asked what side I dressed on, and when he saw me looking confused, he went ahead and found out for himself.* The subject of money was never raised, which made me suspect that this was going to cost a King's ransom. I stifled my curiosity, assuming that it would be bad form to ask. By the time I had finished, I could have used one of the rum cocktails at the Salted Almonds. To curtail expenses we settled for coffee and sandwiches at the Chicken Inn in Lower Regent Street. We had two tickets to the matinee of Jack Hulbert's Variety Show at the Palace in Cambridge Circus, so our afternoon was already paid for. We had an early dinner and decided to turn in for an early night. We had just begun to snuggle into our luxuriously soft bed when the siren went. The flashes of the guns made the skyline jump, so I closed the curtains. The raid lasted only about fifteen minutes, but in its intensity it seemed like hours. Behind the thunder of the guns, I could hear the characteristic drone of Junkers 88's. The building shuddered and shook, as one stick of bombs followed another. Just as suddenly the guns stopped and the all-clear blew, always a blessed relief. When I realized there was only one thing on my mind, sleep — I knew I was getting older. We were wakened by the waiter in the morning.

As I drew back the curtains and let in the morning sun, I looked out across that vast city, expecting to see bomb damage. There wasn't a sign of it. Unperturbed, the people of London were going about their work; the buses, taxis and lorries crossing the bridges in an endless stream. But the Luftwaffe could not drop that number of bombs on this city without killing some of its stout-hearted people. Out there, Air Raid Wardens, Police and concerned passers-by would be digging through piles of brick and mortar. Since the blitz of 1940, day after day, these people had endured Hitler's vengeance. Death and destruction were so much a part of life that to them it was no longer newsworthy. Their unshakeable courage was a shining example to the world.

On the morning of November 9th, Connie, her sister in law Kathleen Helm and I left Pepys Cottage for Buckingham Palace. We had to be at the gates not later than 10:15. Even though we were ten minutes early, two enormous queues had already formed across the inner court of the Palace out to the gate and along the sides. One was made up of those who were being invested; the other and larger queue were the guests. Buck McNair and Bob Buckham were also being presented with decorations. Having no family in England, they had given their tickets to Bobby Page and Cam McArthur. Bobby, an ex-Captain in the Royal Flying Corps, owned and operated The Kimmul Club in Burleigh Street. Throughout the War, Bobbie had extended his hospitality to

---

* For those who do not know, the term to dress on the left or right side refers to the thigh on which the penis normally rests.

fighter pilots, even putting them up for the night. Cam and Bobbie escorted the ladies to the guest queue. The Air Force, being the junior Service, came last. We were impounded in a large rectangular room with a high gilded ceiling. The walls were lined with stiff tall-back chairs. It was noon before we saw any indication of progress. A dapper-looking man in a morning suit, carrying a sheaf of papers, came in through the heavy entrance door. I presumed this was Major Stockley, who had signed the letter I received from St. James' Palace. After calling for order, he began reading out names to place us in order of rank. I came first, followed by Buck McNair. While he was still in the process of getting us in order, the massive door opened and in walked an Admiral. He seemed to fill the doorway. He stood straight as a ramrod, his chest a blaze of decorations, and the gold stripes on his sleeves went halfway to the elbows. Dark bushy eyebrows shielded deep-set gimlet eyes, and fuzz covered his cheek-bones like hoar frost. He surveyed us critically, grinding his teeth, while in silence we cowered.

'I presume you have all observed the dress regulations,' he said with measured emphasis. Noticing a man with gloves on, he shot him a disapproving glare and continued: 'Gloves will be carried, not worn. By the time the King is finished with you people, he will have presented some two thousand decorations. He is very tired, and you must follow the instructions to the letter. When I call your name, you will take two paces forward, which will put you in front of the King. You will turn left, bow to His Majesty, and then take one long pace forward to receive your decoration. This is of the utmost importance, so as to prevent the King from having to reach out. If His Majesty should choose to ask you a question, your answer should be brief. You will take one pace to the rear, bow, turn right, and as quickly as possible, get off the ramp.' He paused, surveying his silent audience haughtily, then said,

'Any questions?'

There was dead silence. He took one last glower at Stockley, then strode from the room.

At last the great doors were opened, and we were instructed to join the line behind the Army. Shuffling along at a snail's pace, we gained admission to the corner of a huge rectangular room. A platform stretched the full length of one long side and in the middle of it stood the King. On the flanks stood the Yeomen of the Guard and clustered on either side of His Majesty, high-ranking Officers of the three Services. In front of the platform row upon row of seated guests stretched from one end to the other. While we waited, Buck and I passed the time searching through the sea of faces for the girls. We found them well back almost hidden behind women with large brimmed hats. Connie caught my eye and gave me a nervous little wave with her gloved hand. Gradually, I became lost in my own thoughts. I tried to remember the wording of the Royal Proclamation — 'King, by the grace of God of Great Britain, Ireland and the British Dominions beyond the seas, Defender of the Faith, Emperor of India.' I recalled a vision of my grandfather when the Prince of Wales passed standing stiffly at attention on the balcony overlooking King Street, with his grey Homburg clasped over his heart. In spite of the nervous flippancy we had recently engaged in, it was an honour that could not be taken lightly. I was awakened from my reverie by the Admiral barking,

'Wing Commander Goad-e-froy, DFC and bar.'

Suddenly my heart was in my mouth, and my knees weak as water. Overcome with self-consciousness, I took two stealthy steps forward and turned left. Thinking only of the long pace that I must take for the convenience of the King, I forgot to bow, and took such a long pace forward that I was but a few inches away from him. I heard Buck McNair say in a loud whisper:

'My God!'

For the first time I realized the King was very short. His nose was about the same level as my second tunic button. Determined to show respect, I bowed where I was and the King obliged by bending gracefully backwards. To my great relief, I discovered that he was smiling with considerable amusement and allayed my nervousness with a reassuring remark. As he pinned on my medal, I thanked him, took one long pace to the rear, where I had space to give him a low bow. Just short of the double, I made my way down the ramp. At the bottom, an Attendant grabbed my medal from my breast, slapped it in a box and handed it to me. I was just in time to hear Buck's penetrating voice say:

'Just fine, Sir, how's the Queen?'

I was out of ear-shot and didn't hear an answer.

After it was all over, Bobby Page insisted on having us all to lunch. Bobby was at his most charming, and with the company's spirited repartee, I soon got over my mortification.

As planned, Buck McNair was promoted to Wing Leader of 126 Airfield at Biggin Hill. Walter Conrad took over command of 421. Ian Ormston, Dean MacDonald, and George Keefer were put in command of the Squadrons in Buck's Wing. They were equipped with Spitfire IX A's which had the same Merlin engine as ours, except for the blower. Buck's aircraft had a blower that gave maximum performance between ten and twenty thousand. They were equipped with Stromberg carburetors made in the States that could handle a hundred and twenty-five octane fuel. The bugs had not been worked out of this combination. A series of engine failures over enemy territory was the result.

As Gunnery Officer of my Wing, Buzz Beurling was doing a fine job, and, without consulting him, I put him in command of a flight.

As soon as the signal came through confirming his promotion, he stomped into my office and said:

'What are you trying to do? I'm not interested in Administration.'

I was flabbergasted.

'Administration? As a Flight Commander, you don't have to do any administration; all I want you to do is lead your men and lead them well. I told you when you first came here that we needed men with experience. Now you've done a good job as Gunnery Officer, and if you do just as good a job leading your Flight, you'll probably be the next man to be put in command of a squadron. Now get on with it; you'll find that all the administration is done for you.'

For a long while he stood staring at me in glum silence. At last he said,

'Okay, I'll try it!'

With his hands in his pockets, he slowly wandered out.

Monty Berger had heard the conversation and, with his face a mask of disbelief, said:

'My God, he's a hard fellow to understand; you'd think you were giving him seven days CB.*

Unknown to me, by this act I had lost Beurling's cooperation. The Wing Tiger Moth, which we used for running errands from one airdrome to another, was established for maintenance in his Flight. In bad weather he began taking up various members of his ground crew and showing them how well he could perform aerobatics. The new inexperienced pilots in our outfit were fascinated by him. They practiced furiously on the ground shooting device trying to match his quality of accuracy. Every day that the weather was bad, I would see him from my office window, in the Tiger Moth doing precision aerobatics over the airdrome, below eight hundred feet. After the third or fourth time, I took him aside in the bar and said:

'Beurling, I don't mind your practising in the Tiger Moth, but you know as well as I do that aerobatics below a thousand feet over the airdrome is a Court Martial Offence. If you want to do aerobatics, get away from here where the rest of the pilots and I can't see you. If I let you do it, some of these young pilots will see no reason why they can't do it, too, and probably kill themselves. Can't you see that?'

He just looked at me with a wry smile, then, without saying a word, shuffled off.

Prolonged periods of bad weather hung heavily on everybody's hands. The pilots got edgy, accentuating minor differences that existed between individuals. Some would drink too much and maybe take umbrage at some comrade's snide remark, and a fight might start. On

---

* Note: C.B. — confined to barracks.

one of these days, Andy MacKenzie had spent the day on second readiness. He had done everything he could think of to keep himself busy. He'd helped his Ground Crew wash down his airplane, spent hours with a polishing compound shining the perspex. Frustrated and fed up, before dinner he had settled down in the bar and got himself in a happy boisterous mood. Buck Buckham had recently been made aware of a domestic problem. He had been over in England some three years, and his wife was getting sick of it. While she sat twiddling her thumbs, the best part of her life ticking away, her unattached friends were living exciting, gay lives. She knew that other pilots were coming home between tours, like Dean MacDonald, Ian Ormston and Jeep Neal, and she had begun to think that Buck had ulterior motives for staying so long in England. On the contrary, Buck had lived an exemplary life, but like me he felt that a leave at home would have a dangerously softening effect upon him. He had discussed the issue with me, and I had been able to offer no sensible suggestion. He had just finished writing a letter home and was walking down the corridor towards the bar with his hands in his pockets, when Andy MacKenzie danced out. Seeing Buck, he decided that a good-natured wrestling match was in order. With a gleeful shout of 'Tally Ho' he made a rush for Buck like a big playful puppy. Buck was in no mood for play. Using the momentum of Andy's one hundred and eighty-five pounds, he pulled him by the lapels, rolled with him on his back, and with his two feet in Andy's stomach, shot him like a cannon ball fifteen feet down the corridor. Without even turning around, Buck put his hands back in his pockets and sauntered into the bar.

Walter Conrad, in command of 421 Squadron, had three pilots who were getting a little too boisterous for his liking, so he sent them off on a forty-eight-hour pass. These lads, Patterson, Rogers, and Blackie Campbell, went up to London and during a lunch-time session in the bar of the Regent Palace, decided to play a trick on Walter. They all went to a hairdressing salon and told the barber to dye their hair white. They were then going to go back to Walter and show him what his aggressive leadership was doing to them. Unfortunately, the scheme backfired. The dye succeeded in turning all their hair a brilliant orange. There were hoots of laughter when they all showed up in the bar and told the story. They had to get the Station Barber to shear their locks, and for the next little while their heads stayed covered with an orange fuzz.

It was a great relief when the weather broke and we were able to resume offensive operations. With broken cloud over France, the weather was unsuitable for bomber missions, so I took the Wing on a fighter sweep once again under the control of the Forward Ops Room at Dover. Between towering cumulus clouds, Squadron Leader Hunter

222

vectored me onto a large formation of 190's, and I dived to the attack. Beurling was leading the Section on my port side, and when I was about a thousand yards from the formation, I saw Buzz out of the corner of my eye roll right over on his back and then go straight down. Instructing the rest of the Squadron to get into them, I pulled up to see what was going on. While watching Danny Brown knock one down, I heard Beurling's unmistakable voice on the R/T:

'I've had it!'

I called him and asked what the trouble was. There was no answer. I reformed the Wing and with nothing more about, took them all back to Kenley. Half an hour after the Wing landed, a lone Spitfire came into the circuit. It was Beurling. He did a very cautious turn around the field, put his flaps down and came in and landed. The whites of his eyes were nothing but two pools of blood. Beurling had seen a single 190, thousands of feet below. Instead of attacking the ones in front of us, he had decided to get the one underneath. He had dived straight down from twenty thousand feet and not realizing how the Spitfire IX would build up speed, he had got going so fast that his elevators had frozen up. Just after he had said, 'I've had it,' he had turned back the elevator trim and his aircraft had pulled itself out, blacking him out completely. Massive subconjunctival haemorrhages had resulted from the excessive G. His aircraft was a complete write-off, with all the rivets on the underside pulled from their mountings. The Wing had one destroyed and three damaged, but Blacky Campbell did not return.*

Cam McArthur grounded Beurling from operations. With the continuation of poor weather, Beurling resumed his aerobatics in the Tiger Moth. Once again he put on a show over the field. With considerable annoyance, I warned him that if he didn't stop, I'd have no alternative but to press charges. Feeling fed up at having to spend my time doing this sort of thing, I took off forty-eight hours and went down to Pepys Cottage.

I made a fire in the fireplace, and we had just finished having supper around it when the phone rang. Connie answered and told me that Bill McBrian wanted to speak to me. Wondering what on earth could be wrong, I went to the telephone.

'Hughie, I've got some bad new. You know they've had a series of engine failures in 126. Ian Ormston had his engine cut out on takeoff, crashed into a cement pillbox. He's in hospital with a broken back. Buck McNair had his engine cut out over France but was able to glide

---

* Years later, I got the first-hand story of Blackie's experience. After bailing out, Blackie was picked up by the Gestapo and exposed to a long period of interrogation. When his orange hair began coming in black at the roots, the Gestapo felt sure that he must be a spy and had given him a very hard time.

it back and make a safe landing. Dean MacDonald's engine cut out on the other side, and two of his squadron flew with him while he glided back. On a vector from Control, they found themselves over ten-tenths cloud at four thousand feet. They were told that below the ceiling was fifteen hundred feet and that if he glided down through the cloud, they thought he'd be over land. When they got through the cloud, they were still over the sea. Dean tried to bail by pushing the stick forward to throw himself out over the top. The two fellows who were with him said he landed astride the aircraft, impaled on the radio mast and rode it into the sea. Somebody has got to call his wife. You know her better than I do. Would you phone?'

Without answering Connie's inquiry, I put through the call before I had any more time to think. The cruellest thing would be to hold out any hope. Dean was dead, and I might as well tell her. I haven't the slightest idea now what I said. All I know was that I was frank. She must have sensed what emotions I was suppressing as I spoke, for she listened in silence, and then in a soft understanding voice, thanked me and hung up the receiver. When it was over, I couldn't help myself. I cried bitter angry tears; the pointless injustice of it all denied understanding. I was sitting in front of the fire with my head in my hands feeling absolutely wretched when a rap came to the door. It was Peggy Harding. When Connie whispered to her what had happened, she came straight to me and offered condolence. I felt mortified to be caught displaying emotions. Besides, it wasn't I who deserved the sympathy; it was Peggy MacDonald. This gentle, shy little Welsh girl had just had all her hopes and dreams shattered. There was only one consolation: he had died where he wanted to be, leading his own Squadron. Finally I got myself together and asked Peggy Harding if she'd have a drink.

'No, my dears, I really must go. But before I do, Hughie, maybe you could help me with something. I just got this telegram, and maybe with your knowledge you could tell me how I should interpret it.'

She handed it to me, and I read:

'Regrettably, Lieutenant Peter Harding has been listed as seriously wounded. Further progress will be reported.'

I looked up into the expressionless haggard face of Peggy Harding, and her eyes searched mine for a glimmer of hope.

'Do you think that he has a chance?'

I didn't have the heart to tell her what the classification of seriously wounded meant and found myself answering:

'Peggy, where there's life there's hope.'

Peter recovered, was sent back into action, and a short while later the Hardings got another telegram stating that Peter had been killed in action. During this period, Buck McNair's engine cut out twice more over enemy territory. The first time he was again able to glide back and make a safe landing; but the second, his engine caught fire halfway across the Channel, and he had to bail out. He was burnt around the eyes, and by the time he got close to the water they were so swollen that he could hardly see. Thinking that he was just about to go in the water, he jetisoned his 'chute and fell from about three hundred feet into the sea. He was picked up by the Air-Sea Rescue boys. As soon as Buck's eyes were opened wide enough, he insisted on returning to lead his Wing.

With the Sicilian campaign over, the high-ranking triumvirate of this Campaign were recalled to England in preparation for the Invasion. From the Army came Generals Montgomery and Patton. From the Air Force came Air Marshals Tedder and Coningham and Air Vice Marshal Broadhurst. Tedder put Coningham in charge of the Tactical Air Force, and Air Vice-Marshal Broadhurst replaced Air Vice-Marshal Dixon, who had guided the 2nd TAF through the teething stage. All were under the Supreme Allied Commander General Eisenhower. The Field Commanders brought their personal caravans and set up Mobile Command Posts around them. Eisenhower provided each one with a personal staff car marked with the appropriate number of stars of the equivalent American rank. Each had their Staff Officer's pennant fluttering from the front fenders. Broadhurst loved driving his Cadillac convertible. It was a common sight to see him at the wheel, his personal assistant Burgess beside him, with the driver in the back seat. One day he found himself held up by a large slow-moving convoy of American trucks. The last vehicle was filled with bored American GI's who began shying refuse at the Air Vice-Marshal. The enraged Broadhurst got in front of the truck at the first opportunity, stopped, and told Burgess to get out and take their names. Not only did the GI's refuse to cooperate, but they pulled his cap down over his eyes and roughed him up. Broadhurst had no choice but to complain to Eisenhower. GI's didn't take orders from anyone but Americans.

As soon as his Field Headquarters was established, Broadhurst started weekly conferences for all the Wing Leaders under his command. Broady, as he was referred to, had led a Wing in the Battle of Britain and subsequently made a name for himself as an efficient Staff Officer and a hard-nosed Field Commander. He openly admitted at first that he had little use for Canadians and Buck McNair in particular. Buck had flown under him at Hornchurch before he had left for Malta. As far as Buck was concerned, the feeling was mutual. I distinctly remember the first Wing Commanders' conference that Broady called in his Headquarters. In desert tradition, the meeting was held in a long rectangular field-tent furnished with a mobile conference table, field maps and collapsible chairs. Broady chaired the meeting from one end of the table, and by chance Buck McNair occupied the chair at the other end. Through the meeting Buck sat with his chair pushed back, his arms folded, with a disgruntled frown on his face. The meeting had no particular purpose, except to give the Air Vice-Marshal an opportunity to tell us exactly what he expected of us. His remarks required no comment, and instead of asking if there were any questions, the Air Vice-Marshal hunched forward in his chair and, glaring at Buck, said:

'McNair, I'm disappointed in you. This is the first time I have seen you sit there without opening your big mouth. Are you ill?'

There was a long silence as Buck measured his gaze without blinking an eye. Finally he said with a smile:

'These meetings of yours are interfering with my social life, Sir.'

For a second Broady's jaw stiffened, and he glowered down the table at Buck. Just when the tension was getting unbearable, Broady suddenly threw his head back and laughed uncontrollably. Nervously the Company followed his example.

I was sitting in my office on the field on another dreary day with the ceiling overcast at eight hundred feet, catching up on paper work. Hearing the sound of an engine, I looked out through the window and saw the Tiger Moth just about air-borne. With its wingtip just off the grass, it turned towards me, flew straight at my window and zoomed over the rooftop. In a minute or two I saw it again doing aerobatics. I picked up the phone and called Dispersal.

'The Wing Commander here; who's flying the Tiger Moth?'

'Beurling, sir.'

'As soon as he gets down, tell him to report to my office.'

I was seething. Beurling had purposely disobeyed me. I had just posted a general order forbidding low aerobatics in the Tiger Moth. An hour later, when I had cooled down, Beurling slumped into the office with a sly grin on his face. He stood in front of me with his arms folded.

'Buzz, why did you purposely disobey my orders?'

'The Tiger Moth's in my Flight; I'm going to fly it when and how I want to. You can't tell me what to do.'

'All right, Beurling. You've had fair warning. Go back to your quarters. You're under open arrest.'

Throwing his head back to get the hair out of his eyes, with a wide grin on his face, he sauntered out.

Within an hour of sending the signal for Court Martial, I got a phone call from RCAF Headquarters. It was Air Marshal Breadner, the RCAF's Commander-in-Chief.

'Godefroy, what's this I hear about you putting Beurling up for Court Martial?'

'That's right, Sir!'

'We can't do that. Mackenzie King did everything but crown him before he was sent back over here.'

'As long as I'm Wing Commander Flying of 127 Air Field and he's on this Station, I will proceed with Court Martial. I couldn't care less if you decide to override me, but I will not allow him to fly again in this Wing, and he will be replaced as Flight Commander.'

'I don't blame you, Godefroy. Tell him to pack his bags and report to RCAF headquarters.'

A short time later, I got a call from Buck McNair:

'Hughie, Breadner tells me you've turfed Beurling,' he said, laughing. 'He asked me if I would take him. What do you think?'

'Well, Buck, you heard me bragging about what a good job he did as Gunnery Officer. The mistake I made was giving him a Flight. You know as well as I do you can't let one pilot purposely disobey your orders. If you limit him to being in charge of gunnery and fly like any other pilot in the Wing, maybe he'd be happy. But for God's sake, don't let him fly the Tiger Moth.'

'With all the trouble I've had, Hughie, and all these new pilots, I could use some experience. I think I'll have a go at him. Cheers!.*

Monty Berger came in the office smiling.

'Here's a chance for you to do something that's a little more pleasant. Listen to this. From Field Commander Andrews Field to Wing Commander Flying 127 Wing Second Tactical Air Force: The Officers of Andrews Field would consider it a privilege if you and two Pilots of your Wing would attend the Mess dance to be held October 24th, 1900 hrs.'

---

* In December 1947 I was in the Laurentians above Montreal skiing. At the end of a day we went into Grey Rock's Inn for a hot drink. I saw a familiar face: George Beurling.

He seemed glad to see me and came straight over and inquired about my activities since last we'd met. He told me he was going to the Middle East on the invitation of the Israelis. They had P-51's, and he would be doing dive bombing and strafing against no fighter opposition. He invited me to come. I would get $1,000 for crossing the Atlantic, and after eight weeks' flying, I could come home with a net $8,000. As I thought about it, he watched me with those ice-blue eyes of his. Finally, with a slight smile, he said:

'There's only one hitch, Hughie. This time you'll be flying behind me!'

I told him I would think about it.

When I related the conversation to Connie, she said she would take the children and go back to Scotland if I went!

On May 21, 1948, the front page of the *Montreal Gazette* reported that George Beurling and his friend, an American fighter pilot, Len Cohen, were dead. His engine cut on take-off, and in a desperate attempt to get his Norseman back on to the field he spun it. Sabotage was suspected.

Technically, I consider George one of the greatest fighter pilots I have ever known.

'Where's Andrews Field Monty? I've never heard of it.'

'I've looked it up on the map. It's a big U.S. Marauder Base on the other side of the Thames about twenty minutes flying from here.'

Big changes had had to be made in aerial maps of England in the last year. To accommodate the U.S. Army Air Force, the American Corps of Engineers had built dozens of airdromes in the Midlands. This would be an excellent opportunity to establish closer ties. I accepted.

Used to the reserve of the English, I found their reception overwhelming. The arrival of three Spitfires was to them unusual. Our aircraft were surrounded by a crowd of curious airmen. They inspected everything. We were rescued from the endless questioning by the Base Commander in his staff car. As we drove to the Mess, none of us was in any doubt that the Marauder crews appreciated the escort that we had been giving. The easy-going informal atmosphere was a sharp contrast. The Base Commander seemed to address everybody by his first name. After getting a series of salutes from hatless personnel, I felt obliged to explain to the Colonel that our regulations allowed saluting only with caps on. The first thing he did was take me to his quarters where I was to occupy the spare bedroom. After removing his tunic, he presented me with two cartons of American cigarettes, a box of cigars, and poured me a large scotch and soda brimming with ice. He didn't seem a bit anxious to go on to the party and took his turn asking questions. He kept repeating how much it meant to them when they knew that they were being escorted by Spitfires. He assured me that if there was anything I or my boys wanted, to let him know. If he couldn't find it in their depots in England, he'd see that it was shipped over from the States.

Finally, he put on his tunic, and we went to the dance. A full orchestra in uniform played the latest American jazz. Seats and a table awaited us, and the bar steward came straight over with some more drinks. The dance was in full swing to the accompaniment of orchestral renditions that reminded me of recordings of Benny Goodman and Tommy Dorsey. I found my foot tapping to the music. A Captain was giving an expert demonstration of the Big Apple with a very pretty girl.

'Oh, you'd like to dance!' said the Colonel standing up and beckoning to the Captain:

'Captain, the Leader of our Escort would like to dance. Would you introduce him to the lady?'

Without hesitation the Captain introduced his partner and stepped to one side. With some embarrassment I led the girl to the floor. I was incapable of competing with the Captain's performance, but the girl was a good dancer and easily followed me through my simple routines.

The rest of the couples made room for us on the floor, making me feel even more conspicuous. It was not only because of this that I found myself not enjoying the dance; for the first time I realized what it must be like when the Madame of a brothel gives you one of her 'girls.' No foreplay, no titillating signals of sexual attraction — the chase had been eliminated. I had been handed the prize, and without regret I delivered her back to the Captain. It was a grand party, distinctly different from anything I had attended — abundant hospitality that gave us a taste of home.

I hadn't thought about where the American bombers came from before, but now I began looking on the Form D's for the boys from Andrews Field. It wasn't long before I found myself escorting them to Schipol Airdrome. For me, this sortie had additional significance. They were bombing a Luftwaffe fighter base not far from The Hague where my father's family lived. I took a more personal interest in my charges this time. They were in perfect formation, and approached the Dutch Coast like a regiment of Coldstream Guards. On their run-in on the target, they flew through an incredible barrage of flak. The sky around them was a conglomeration of black puffs and twinkling explosions. Seemingly oblivious, the formation ground straight through it. Several of the aircraft began to drop back, smoke trailing from engines; but even these limped behind their leader to the target. All at once it looked as though the formation had dropped its bombs at once. A ladder of bombs like a great curtain dropped horizontally from the formation. As they fell, all their noses turned together and went straight down. The whole airdrome disappeared in a huge ball of smoke. Slowly and deliberately, the great formation turned out to sea, followed by their stragglers. With some satisfaction I found a 190 and sent him down in flames. I wondered if any of my family could be watching and wanted so badly to shout: 'That's a present from me.'

At this time, I received a rather unusual replacement, Pilot Officer Claude Weaver, DFM. He had been shot down on a strafing expedition over Sicily when stationed at Malta. He had been interned in an Italian Prisoner of War Camp. The Italians treated their prisoners without the slightest respect for the Geneva Convention. Disregarding the fact that it is the duty of a captured combatant to try to escape, the Italians brutally beat Claude after his first two attempts to gain his freedom. At last he escaped and made contact with the advancing

Note: In 1953, I made my first return visit to Holland in a British European Airways jet and landed at Schipol. As we circled the field, I noticed the grass was dappled with round patches of a different colour. Ten years had elapsed, but the places where the Maraunder bomb craters had been were still visible from the air.

Allied Troops in Italy. Claude was an American trained by the Commonwealth Air Training Scheme, who wanted to stay in the RAF. Having heard of the treatment he had endured at the hands of the Italians, I fully expected to meet a very subdued character. When he presented himself at my office, I found myself faced with a tall blond keen-looking fellow in his early twenties. He had a neatly trimmed moustache, bright eyes, and his uniform, buttons and shoes were in impeccable order. The only sign of past Military experience was the DFM ribbon below his wings. It was evident in talking to him that he wanted to get back on Operations as quickly as possible. I delegated him to 421 Squadron and told him to get checked out on a Spitfire IX and fly around and get familiar with the country.

On the day he did his first solo, the Wing was grounded by bad weather. Just after tea, I got a phone call from Alex Hamilton, the Engineering Officer.

'Hughie, have we had anybody flying operational today?'

'No, Alex, there's just been the odd fellow doing local flying. Why?'

'One of the aircraft in 421 Squadron came back with the spinner missing from its prop. It's obviously been blown off by a cannon shell. Who is this guy, Weaver?'

'He's a new second tour replacement; was he flying the aircraft?'

'He was!'

'Have them send him up to my office immediately!'

Twenty minutes later, Claude Weaver came into my office looking a little sheepish.

'Weaver, I told you to go local flying. Where did you go?'

'It didn't take me long to get familiar with the area, sir, so seeing that I was up, I went over to France and did a little strafing.'

'If that's the kind of thing you're going to do, Weaver, you might as well pack your bags and go back to Air Force Headquarters.'

For a moment, I thought he was going to cry. In pleading with me to let him stay, he did everything but go down on his knees.

'Okay, Weaver, I'll give you one more chance. From now on I will decide if, and when, you venture over enemy territory. Do you understand?'

'Yes, sir, I promise — I promise!'

This was not the last time I would have to deal with Claude Weaver. Inwardly I was delighted with his keenness; and, with his reaction to the threat of being turfed, felt sure that he wouldn't play this trick again.

During the first and the last days of the month of November the weather was fine, and we did two sorties a day, escorting bombers. We visited targets from the Cherbourg peninsula to the Dutch Islands. In the early part of the month I led the Wing to Idsley, near Lands

End for refuelling. We were to escort 162 Marauders to Martinvast. To my great surprise, I found that the Station Commander of Idsley was one of my former Squadron Commanders, Squadron Leader Douglas, DFC. My last relations with Douglas had not been pleasant after I had criticized the Biggin Hill Wing Leader. He had left me in no doubt that he thought that I was an undesirable influence. Understandably, I felt a sense of satisfaction in his presence, having redeemed myself somewhat. He rekindled the respect that I had once had for him by offering me warm and genuine congratulations. Only big men are willing to admit when they have miscalculated.

In the latter part of the month I led my Wing to the very border of Germany. Here I was reminded how thin was the thread that binds a fighter pilot's security. Beyond Nijmegan, while preoccupied with issuing commands and directions, my engine cut. Gliding over the Third Reich with a dead engine soon takes the starch out of you. I didn't know which to do, head in or out. After an eternity, it started up again, and I was able to make my way home.

The strafers' bullets, the bombs and the shrapnel were not the only hazards that threatened the life of the civilians in England. In the early days of December, shortly after takeoff, my forty-five-gallon drop tank came off. Without this extra fuel reserve, I had to hand over the leadership to my Deputy and return to Base. On my arrival I found that my tank had killed a civilian.

The Luftwaffe fighter forces were limited by fuel shortages, and it wasn't until the 20th of December that they gave us some action. I took the Wing on a simple fighter sweep to the Lille area, leading the Red Indian Squadron. Because of the last few weeks I despaired of seeing anything. Away in the distance I saw fifteen plus aircraft. Without much sense of optimism I went to investigate. As we got closer and closer, I began to feel my scalp tingle as I recognized the long noses, the thin wings and the black crosses of Messerschmit 109's. As though reflecting my own excitement, a high-pitched voice came on the R/T and said:

'They're not Spits; they're 109's!'

As I went in to attack, the enemy formation broke up, so I gave the order to attack individually. The Red Indians didn't have to be told twice. They went after them, cutting inside me in the process. Outpositioned, I pulled up and was a witness to a magnificent dogfight. Silhouetted against the cloud were 109's twisting and turning in every direction with Spitfires in hot pursuit. A 109 did a series of horizontal flick rolls just above the deck of cloud below with cannon shells twinkling all over him from the guns of the Spitfire on his tail. They both disappeared into the cloud. A short time later I saw two Spitfires in line astern come out of the cloud below. To my horror a few seconds later, I saw two 190's come out of the cloud right behind them.

'The Section that just climbed out of the cloud — BREAK. There are two 190's behind you,' I shouted, diving to the attack.

As I went down vertically, the two Spits turned sharply, condensation trails streaming from their wing tips. A string of white puffs trailed from the tails of the 190's as they fired. The lead Spitfire did a series of flick rolls, and before I could get into range, they all disappeared back into the cloud. I pulled out of the dive feeling sick. I was sure one of my boys had bought it. Angry, I searched for something to take out my vengeance on. A lone Focke Wulf 190 popped out of the cloud. I dived to the attack. As I manoeuvred to fire, I found that I was not alone. Three other Spitfires were boring in on my target from different directions, one attacking head-on! When I found myself flying into the hail of bullets from this aircraft, I pulled up. I patrolled the area for another fifteen minutes, and seeing nothing I waggled my wings, ordering all aircraft that saw me to reform to return to Base.

Back at Kenley, counting heads, I found that Jim Lambert was missing. The two aircraft I had seen coming out of the clouds with the 190's on their tail had been Ed Gimble and Andy McKenzie. They had ended up underneath the cloud still with their two 190's, and each of them had shot one down. Jim Lambert was seen to shoot one down in the initial attack, so the total Wing score was seven destroyed and one damaged. One each destroyed by Carl Linton, Decoursier, Gimble and Lambert, while Andy McKenzie got three. For this fine effort under difficult circumstances, I put Andy in for a DFC.

Once again the Luftwaffe stayed on the ground to lick their wounds. Two days later on a similar type of sortie, after encountering no opposition, I dived the Wing to eight thousand feet and did a circuit or two over a Fighter Base near St. Omer. As I circled the field, I saw a lone Junker 87 (the Stuka) taxiing out to the main runway. To my amazement, he turned into wind and took off. Initially, the pilot must not have known that we were above him. As soon as he was airborne, he must have switched on his radio and been warned of our presence by the Ground Station. He did a very sharp turn and attempted to come in to land again. Claude Weaver was leading Yellow Section of 421 Squadron and at that moment was inside me and below as I circled the field. His request to attack the Stuka was granted. As the Stuka levelled off to touch down, Claude's cannon shells were exploding all around him on the runway. Understandably, he went around again. Twisting and turning, the 87 was chased by his pursuers away from the airdrome while I circled above him at three thousand feet. The Stuka pilot gave an admirable performance of defensive flying against overwhelming odds and just over the top of the ground turned inside his pursuers repeatedly as they attacked. Ignoring my feeling that his performance had earned him a chance to live, I called Claude Weaver and said:

'Yellow One, if you guys don't put that fellow out of his misery in another minute, I'll go down and do it for you.'

My message had been like waving a red flag to Weaver. Leaving the rest of his Section to keep the Stuka busy, he dived away from him on the treetops and came back at him from below. Attacking on a tangent to the Stuka's orbit for the first time I saw cannon shells exploding all over the aircraft. As though in slow motion the Stuka, pouring smoke, sliced into the ground with his port wing and, with his engine on fire, ground along in a cloud of dust. Claude Weaver reported that at the very last, the pilot stood up, the cockpit a cauldron of fire. He put him away with a merciful burst of machinegun. The Stuka pilot had gained the respect of everyone, but the time in the War had passed for chivalry — Hitler had one less pilot for the final battle.

On the 22nd of December I had the Wing released from offensive operations for Christmas. Both my brothers were coming to Pepys Cottage for the celebration, and Connie was frantic wondering what she could find to feed them. I mentioned her dilemma to the Captain of the Salvation Army Post at Kenley. Before I left for Pepys Cottage, the Captain presented me with a magnificent ten-pound Canadian Swift's ham.

'I hope you all have a Merry Christmas,' he said.

We decorated Pepys Cottage with holly which we found nearby in abundance. Dried fruits and raisins were not too difficult to obtain, and, with her sister's recipe, Connie made her first plum pudding and hard sauce. There were plenty of strong arms to help with the stirring. The pudding broke coming out of its mould, but that took nothing away from its festive flavor. My brother Bill had almost finished his Course at Sandhurst. It had whittled him down to one hundred and thirty-five pounds, the poundage he carried when he won his weight in boxing at Upper Canada College. The presence of baby Isabel, her head a halo of blonde fuzz, her big blue eyes full of limpid curiosity, rekindled childhood memories of Christmas. On the last day, as I watched my two brothers playing black jack in front of the fire, the thought occurred to me that maybe I would never see them again. In the Infantry, brother Bill's chances of getting through the hail of bullets that would meet him on the beaches were poor. If he survived that, he would join in the task of driving one of the greatest armies of all time, street by street and house by house, out of Europe.

For David, war was no longer a great adventure. He had completed five trips as part of Air Marshal 'Bomber' Harris' night offensives. From his rear turret in a Lancaster that had penetrated the incredible flak defences of the Ruhr, he had shot down one 109. He had twenty-five more trips to go. I felt torn between two pressing responsibilities. Connie prayed for the day that I would be taken off. She needed me as a father to help raise our child. She had accepted her part of my duty to fight, but she could not hide the frightened looked whenever I kissed her goodbye. But now, even more than before, my experience as a fighter pilot would be needed. Every German fighter we shot down was one less that might send David and his crew down in flames. I had to stay and fight.

In a job which demanded total commitment, the memory of our Christmas reunion soon became part of the past. I was jerked out of such preoccupations by the following letter:

Cobalt, Ont., 3/2/44
P.O Box 625

Mr. Hughey Godefroy,
England.

Dear Hughey:

Very glad to receive your interesting and welcome letter.

Things have changed a great deal since you were here years ago. The death of your dear Uncle Hugh caused me a heartfelt shock, and I still miss him a great deal. I have wandered a few times towards the small cabin on that point of rocky ground at the east end of the lake. The vandals pilfered somewhat, taking a couple of panes of glass out of one window and removing another in its entirety. The rest was O.K. I had nailed galvanized iron sheets across both windows, and they did not disturb that, so the snow does not penetrate in there and cause the floor to decay.

No, Hugh, I do not migrate in the winter, as you surmise. I have lived in the old Cabin since 1921 steadily, but I frankly admit I am getting fed up with the lonesome and isolated life. Age, I suppose, has a lot to do with that feeling. I crossed the divide of 70 and tumbled head-first into 71 on the 4th December last. I am not as healthy as I used to be. The old ailment Bronchitis is recurrent occasionally, but I can beat it by using oil of Eucalyptus for a few days. Was very sick four years ago. Was prepared to enter the unknown but managed to pull through. Gastritis, Lumbago and Bronchitis plotted together and tried their best to floor me, but no soap. The greatest souvenir of their dirty work is a set of false teeth, which I consider the greatest affliction thrown my way. Have short spasms of Rhuma in the right and left fore-arms, — note the handwriting not so smooth and flowing as in the past.

So you married and are the proud father of a lovely little girl!

234

It takes guts to marry in such critical times, but I suppose a short while of happiness is ample reward for the sacrifices to be faced. Glad to hear your two brothers are in England, and you all had the pleasure to be together at Christmas eve.

I wonder if your Uncle Hugh made a will. Those two claims at the end of the lake are worth attention, — one never knows! Any undeveloped claim is considered a wildcat by me: still they may turn out O.K. later on. I would suggest that you advise whoever is the legatee to pay the taxes regularly; $5.00 an acre is the fee at the Gillies limit and a 20-acre claim costs only $100 yearly. I am interested in 10 claims all in a group. Will do my utmost and try to make a deal the coming Spring, even if I have to sacrifice. What is the use of hanging on to them when I have no near relatives to think about. One of my partners is dead; the other is far gone, being 73 and crippled with rheumatism. Ewan Cousins, the Ottawa fellow, was in Alaska with me four years. Like me, he had an itchy foot: My intentions are if I make good with my properties in the near future to take a trip to Alaska again, — you know I spent eight years in that country when it was a wild and perfect wilderness. . . Would also like to visit a cousin in Los Angeles, Calif., and a Marine pal who is in Ohio. He was attached to my Regt. Staff as a steno, — a fine boy he was, clean and straight. He is the only one of those of my regiment I have corresponded regularly with since demobilization in 1919. We had a severe siege of influenza lately, and, of course, it would pass me up. O.K. now, but the old virility and staunchness of the past are starting to elude me. But the heart is still dauntless, and when one has that, he can fight without flinching.

Best regards to you, your brothers and family. . . Come back to us, Hugh! The little cabin will always be ready to welcome you.

Ever the same,

little Albert Napoleon Gauthier

As I read, I could see Albert writing at his table by a flickering coal-oil lamp, and smell the musty odour of his cabin, a combination of dried sweat and wood smoke.

With pride he insisted on sharing his simple fare of fried salt pork and beans laced with black-strap. With company he would allow himself the luxury of a pipe after supper, lit with a great flourish with a twig from the wood stove to save matches. I could see him sitting back and blowing a cloud of smoke in the air, then exclaiming something like:

'Hughie, never trust a man that can't look you straight in the eye.'

He had been the one who had re-established our correspondence. He had seen my picture in the paper and had written to congratulate me on being awarded the DFC. He had addressed it to Flight Lieutenant Hughie Godefroy, Wolf Squadron, England.

Uncle Hugh had been his kind of man, tough, straight and independent. And Uncle Hugh had been my idol; it was through him that I had met Gauthier. As it was to Albert, his death had been such a shock to me that I had not allowed myself to think of it. It was men like these who had shown me solid principles by which to live. Their diverse ethnic backgrounds had not mattered. Independently, they had acquired the dauntless spirit of real Canadians.

It was typical of Albert to assume that I would return and have to see about Grandpa's silver claim. I promised myself, if he was right, I would go and see him.*

---

* My first assignment on repatriation was as visiting lecturer for the War Bond Drive. I chose the Ontario mining district so as to get to Cobalt. At the post office I discovered that he was well-known and loved. They had become concerned about him out in the bush and convinced him that he was needed to keep order at the Liquor Commission. They gave me the address of his room in town.

It was late morning when I rapped on his door, and it was some time before I heard a stir and the sound of shuffling feet coming to answer. How incredibly small and bent he looked as he squinted up quizzically in the bright sun. Surprised by a man in uniform, he first looked me up and down. Finally he said:

'Are you a Mountie?'

'No,' I said.

'You're not. . . . You're not big Hughie?'

'Yes, Albert, it's me!'

Tears poured down his wrinkled cheeks, and he threw his arms around me. 'I knew you'd come back. . . . I knew you'd come back!'

As he struggled to regain his composure, I, too, was close to tears. With a lump in my throat, I said:

'They tell me that you're working at the Liquor Store, Albert. That's good!'

He wiped the tears from his face with his sleeve, then frowned and said:

'Yes, but I'm going to have to quit.'

'Why, Albert? That's a good job for you!'

'Hughie, everybody knows Albert Gauthier, and they all want me to have a drink. That's not good for me. I'll have to go back to the cabin, Hughie, where I can face my Maker with a clear mind. That's where I belong. I don't want to die this way!'

15

THE BEGINNING OF THE END

1944 was the year of invasion fever. The year of painstaking contingency planning at the Staff level. It was the calm before the storm. Increasing evidence began to accumulate that Hitler's threat of devastating secret weapons was not an idle one. Along the French, Belgian and Dutch coasts the Germans were building rectangular cement ramps, and they were all pointed at London. Intense aerial surveillance by our PRU (Photographic Reconnaissance Unit) aircraft indicated that these structures were designed to launch something. A technique was devised to use Spitfires as dive bombers, and a directive describing it was sent out.

The target was to be approached at eight thousand feet. When it was opposite the wing tip, the aircraft was to be turned and dived at an angle of sixty degrees holding the bead of the gun-sight on the target. At three thousand feet a gradual pull-out was to be executed and on the count of three, the bomb dropped. As a footnote to the instructions, a word of caution was included. The bomb should not be released in the dive, only in the pull-out, lest it should hit the prop and blow you all to hell. Norm Fowlow, one of my former pilots in the Wolf Squadron was given command of a squadron of his own. While leading his men in a dive-bombing attack on the launching pads, his aircraft was seen to disintegrate. It was assumed that his bomb must have hit the prop.

It wasn't long before we discovered that this technique of dive bombing was extremely inaccurate. One could only take a guess at what was a 60° dive. Without dive brakes, Spitfires dived so fast that the hands of the altimeter went around in a blur. Pulling out at exactly three thousand feet with the use of an instrument that lagged was impossible.

Squadrons went out individually, twelve aircraft at a time. I took my turn leading these sorties, and on one occasion I led my old outfit. I was told to bring the bombs back if I found the target obscured by cloud. The tail of the bomb was approximately an inch from the ground on takeoff or landing. In spite of the experts' assurance that the bomb would not explode unless the arming switch had been pressed, none of the pilots was anxious to see what would happen if it fell off. I dutifully read this order with tongue in cheek. I hadn't the slightest intention of bringing the bombs back.

As we approached the target twenty miles away, I could see that it was obscured by a cloud. We were flying up the Somme, and we were welcomed by a furious barrage of heavy flak. Looking down, I saw a large round heavy gun emplacement emitting a series of flashes from its eighty-eight millimetre gun.

'Echelon port!'

Instantly the Squadron slid underneath me and stationed themselves on my port wing.

'Press arming switches and prepare to attack!'

When the bunker was opposite my starboard wingtip, I rolled over and went straight down. There was nothing I could think that deserved a bombing more than a flak battery. I pulled out as close as I could to three thousand feet and on the count of three dropped the bomb. When I cocked my starboard wing up, I was just in time to see my bomb explode in the centre of the bunker. The rest of the Squadron's bombs hit all around it. The flak ceased. I ordered the Squadron to regroup and was relieved to count twelve aircraft. As we flew home, a voice on the R/T said:

'Sheer unadulterated bullshit luck, Skipper!' I maintained a discreet silence.

With the Luftwaffe rarely opposing us on Wing Fighter sweeps, I would move down to eight thousand feet searching for ground targets. Trains and rolling stock received so much of our attention that the Germans began operating flak trains composed of nothing else but camouflaged cars bristling with light flak. They were impossible to distinguish from ordinary freight trains. On one of these sorties I was leading 421 Squadron. Claude Weaver was leading the Section on my starboard wing. In the first half hour we saw nothing. Suddenly Claude said excitedly:

'Darkwood Leader, Yellow One. There's a train down below at nine o'clock. Can I go down and get it?'

'Okay, Yellow One. Be careful! It may be a flak train.'

With careless abandon, Claude peeled out of formation with a sweeping wing over and dived to the attack. Because of the camouflage on the upper surface of Spitfires, in no time it was impossible to see him against the ground. Suddenly the sky above the train was filled with streams of tracer and arching balls of bofors flak. Through this cloud I saw Claude's cannon shells exploding on the engine, which emitted clouds of steam. Exploding cannon shells then ran the full length of the train. For a second I saw him flash over the train, white puffs trailing from his wings.

'Yellow One, Darkwood. That's a flak train, leave it alone, return to formation!'

There was no answer.

'Yellow One, Darkwood, are you receiving me?'

There was still no answer. In a moment the streams of flak started again. This time I saw cannon shells hitting the rear of the train and running the full length up to the engine. Again I saw Claude flash over the top of it, going in the opposite direction.

'Yellow One, Darkwood, leave that damn train alone.'

'Aircraft calling Yellow One, your transmission is garbled.'

Once again the streams of tracer from the train started as Claude Weaver attacked a third time.

'Okay, Yellow Section, line astern!' With a sigh of relief, I saw the four aircraft climbing back up to join me.

At the debriefing, I said to Claude:

'Weaver, after your first attack, didn't you hear me tell you to leave that train alone?'

His face was a mask of surprised innocence as he said:

'I sure didn't, sir. There must have been something wrong with my radio!'

I was convinced that Claude Weaver didn't understand the meaning of the word 'fear.' Despite our doing everything we could to protect him, sometime before 'D Day' Claude disappeared.

Through the grapevine I heard that Buck McNair had become particularly hard to get along with of late. Beurling had been forbidden to fly the Tiger Moth, so he had taken his frustration out racing station transport around the tarmac. Buck had told him that if he didn't pack up and get off the Station within the hour, he would beat him up. But Buck was not impatient just with Beurling — apparently nobody seemed to be able to get along with him. It was noticed also that every time he came in to land he would level off about ten feet above the ground. Underlings are always hesistant to question the Wing Commander's flying, particularly one who had become almost unapproachable. Squadron Leader Arnold Jones, the Medical Officer, however, had never been renowned for shyness. He went straight to Buck and asked him what was the matter. Begrudgingly Buck admitted that he had lost the sight of one eye. He had privately consulted an ophthalmologist in Harley Street. Buck had suffered a haemorrhage in the visual centre of the brain. The haemorrhage had been the result of his dropping from three hundred feet into the sea. He had no binocular vision anymore and was unable to estimate his height above the ground when landing. Buck was grounded, and George Keefer took over 126 Wing. This courageous fighter pilot had flown his last trip.

I received notice from 83 Group Headquarters that the Wing would be equipped with a new gyrosight and that the inventor himself would come and explain how it worked. On the appointed day I called all the pilots to the Briefing Room. Alex Hamilton came in with a short pudgy man, carelessly attired in baggy civilian clothes. He had a pasty complexion, widely separated eyes, magnified by thick glasses. As he sat down, he adjusted his rope-like tie. Alex Hamilton introduced him and gave him the floor. With some hesitation he proceeded to describe how to use the gyrosight. He had a sample in front of him on the table. It looked like a large piece of radio equipment that had a clear plate of glass mounted on top, slanted at an angle of 45°. He explained that the instrument had a dial on which was printed all the various German aircraft we would encounter. After identifying our target, we were to turn the dial until the pointer was opposite the appropriate aircraft. When the sight was switched on, a luminous ring would appear on the glass with radial lines at the four quadrants. These would converge on the central bead of the sight when the twist grip that would be attached to the throttle lever was turned. The bead of the sight was not fixed but would move when it was exposed to the G forces in a turn. Thus, to use the sight, one kept the bead on the target, turned the twist grip until the radial lines just touched the tips of its wings, tracked it for two seconds and then fired. The instrument automatically made allowance for range, slip or skid on the part of the aircraft or its target, the angle of attack, and computed the correct deflection. A pilot without any ability as a marksman following these instructions would destroy a single-engine fighter with a one-second burst. When he finished, he was deluged with questions. When he answered the last one, he sat down to a babble of conversation. Being curious to meet this boffin, I stood up and went to the platform. As I did so, the pilots fell silent. When I turned around, one of them was on his feet:

'Sir, we've been discussing this sight. We have all agreed that we'd just as soon not have it.'

The boffin stood up, his face a mask of disbelief:

'Would you be kind enough to explain why not?'

'Sir, if one of our lads gets shot down and the Huns get their hands on this thing, we've had it.'

The pudgy face slowly broke into a broad grin.

'Gentlemen, for three years I have worked on this day and night. I have designed it in such a way that it will take the Germans three years to discover how it works. If Mr Churchill's calculations are correct, in three years you won't have anything to shoot at.'

There was a babble of laughter. With no further questions, the meeting broke up.

To be frank, I was too long in the tooth and set in my ways to change. I kept the gunsight shut off where the bead would stay in the middle and shot just the same as I always had. But this extra-ordinary device worked; an inexperienced pilot on his first operational sortie shot down five in as many minutes. I certainly could have used it three years before.

During the early months of 1944, I had my first and only exposure to dealing with 'lack of moral fibre.' It was precipitated by an incident that occurred the week before. I was leading the Wing, and we were some thirty miles south of St. Omer when my engine began to splutter and would put out only quarter power. On this particular day the Luftwaffe had decided to oppose us in strength. My No. 2 was a young but very capable Pilot who had five sweeps under his belt during which he had seen no action. I announced that I was having trouble with my engine and turned over leadership to my Deputy. I instructed my No. 2 to come with me. I put him wide line abreast. With my engine still spluttering erratically, I had reached a point about twenty miles from the coast over the Somme when my engine began to run as smooth as silk and was capable of full power. The Wing had been vectored on a large formation, and from the R/T chatter I could hear that they were being heavily engaged. I instructed my No. 2 to go into line astern as I was going back to join them. Knowing my Wing's altitude, I climbed in their direction in the hope of gaining a height advantage. Looking behind me, I saw twelve 190's diving on our tails. There was a continuous chatter on the R/T, so I said nothing. Gradually I opened my throttle until it was through the gate and began a shallow dive to gain speed. The 190's followed. Finally I pulled up in a sharp climbing turn and let my speed drop to a hundred and sixty miles an hour. The 190's stupidly followed me. At this rate of turn and speed, they all began dropping below except the leader. My No. 2 had failed to keep underneath my tail. The leader of the 190's with each turn began to gain on him. At a gap in the R/T chatter, I said:

'Red 2, Darkwood, you've got twelve 190's up your arse, and if you don't look sharp and get in underneath me, they're going to shoot you down.'

The lad had not seen them. After a quick look around, he zipped up underneath my tail like a scared rabbit. In this position, the 190's couldn't touch him, and when I had reached a point where I was about a thousand feet above them, I half rolled and attacked. The whole formation flicked over on its back and went straight for the ground. I let them go and continued on to join my Wing. By the time I took over command, the battle was over.

A week later I was in my office when McArthur came in.

'We've got a problem, Hughie,' he said.

'What is it, Cam?'

'I'm going to have to send one of your pilots back to Canada. He's lost his nerve. He's been drunk every night in the Mess, and he came to me today and said he doesn't think he can ever fly across the Channel again.'

It was the young Sergeant Pilot that had been with me as my No. 2.

'Go get him, Cam, and bring him over here, and let's have a chat.'

This strong healthy-looking young fellow swaggered into the office with the suspicion of a grin on his face.

'Squadron Leader McArthur tells me that you refuse to fly across the Channel again. Is that correct?'

'That's right, sir. I just can't go across that water any more. When I volunteered, I didn't think it was going to be like this. I just can't take it.'

'From what I can understand,' I said, 'you have done six sweeps. The last one is the only one that you've ever seen anything but flak. Even on that occasion nobody even took a shot at you. I can hardly classify that as frightening.'

Unconcerned, he looked straight ahead and said:

'I can't take it any more. You'll have to send me home.'

For a long time I sat without saying a word, just looking at him. He showed none of the signs of stress and didn't look a bit contrite. In fact, to me he seemed quite pleased with himself. It had taken a long time to build the type of morale the Wing had now. An all-for-one and one-for-all unwritten pact had been formed, and it was respected even by those who were faint of heart. The Wing was made up of ordinary people who knew the meaning of fear. I could not let one man chicken out the first time things got tough.

'Do you realize that what you've just said merits a charge of 'lack of moral fibre'?

He folded his arms, and said:

'They can't do that to me; I'm a volunteer. I've had enough of this; I want to go home!'

As I watched him in silence, my mind went back to Dean McDonald the night he had sat on the end of my bed. Like hundreds of Canadians now he was dead. He had been afraid, but he had done his duty. His last moments on this earth had been spent riding his aircraft to his death. If I let this boy slither out of it, Dean and many more like him would turn over in their graves.

'Cam, instruct the Station Administrative Office to put this man on open arrest and charge him with 'lack of moral fibre.''

[The Court Martial proceeded from the inquiry stage to the final hearing which came before Air Vice-Marshal Dixon. By this time the lad realized that he wasn't going to get away with it and was willing to accept a compromise. Luckily for him, Air Vice-Marshal Dixon was a kindly fatherly man. In his Summation he said:

'Under ordinary circumstances I should proceed with sentencing, but I take it upon myself to give you one more chance. Young man, if you are willing to go back and finish a tour of Operations, I will dismiss all charges.'

The boy eagerly accepted. He was sent to another Wing and successfully completed a tour of Operations. He saw me as head of the welcoming contingent that met his boat-train in Canada. He rushed over to me and proudly told me what he had done and thanked me for making him do it.]

With the evident build-up in preparation for the invasion, rumours circulated everywhere. Where would they choose to land? Bar room experts had their own idea as to what was the sensible, logical thing to do. When I received the order that the Wing would be getting Hotspur gliders, and that all the pilots were to be made operational on them, a new series of predictions started. 'We are going to land on the Norwegian coast — for sure!'

The Hotspur glider, like all aircraft of its type was a high wing monoplane with a single cockpit and eight passenger seats. It had no wheels, just a central skid. Several of our Spitfires were modified for glider towing, and the training programme began. Day after day a glider-towing Spitfire would be seen taking off with a Hotspur in tow. I got on with my own work. In what seemed like no time the Officer in charge of Glider Training came to me and said:

'Sir, you are the only pilot in the Wing not operational on Gliders.'

'Okay, I'll do it now.'

We walked out on to the field where the glider-towing Spitfire was parked with its towing line hooked up to the glider. Around the glider was a group of ground crew who wanted to go as passengers. As we walked to the glider, a young Public Relations Officer fell in step with us listening to our conversation. When he discovered that I would be flying the glider he said:

'Sir, I have never been in an airplane. Do you think there would be room for me?'

'Certainly, come on. Get in the back, and I'll take you up.'

I got into the cockpit. The Glider had conventional stick and rudder pedals, a three-notch hand-operated flap lever and a needle ball and airspeed on the instrument panel. I did a standard check of all controls. The young Public Relations Officer and seven others strapped themselves into seats. The Spitfire pilot started his engine, taxied forward to tighten the tow rope, and off we went. We were airborne long before the Spitfire, and with adequate elevator control I pulled the stick back and got out of the Spitfire's slipstream. For a pilot used to the buzz of a sixteen hundred horsepower Merlin engine, being airborne in comparative silence was intoxicating. At towing speed we climbed to three thousand feet. There was nothing more disturbing than a high-pitched whistle. When I pulled the tow release, the silence seemed unearthly. Completely oblivious of my passengers, I glided around in the wind like a gull, fascinated with the exhilaration of powerless flight. It was with reluctance that I concentrated on making a landing. Kenley was no place to make a miscalculation for it was surrounded on all sides by wooded valleys that were dotted with houses. I turned into wind at a height that would cause one to overshoot without flaps. As I approached the field, I played with the first notch of flap, pulling it on and off, changing my angle of glide. I was curious to see how much distance was required on the ground to bring it to a halt. When I was sure I wouldn't undershoot, I pulled on full flap. To maintain air-speed I had to dive the aircraft at about forty-five degrees. We touched down smoothly and almost at once we were stationary, and the port wing gently dropped to the ground. As we all got out, I noticed that the Public Relations Officer looked a little green. I was joined by the Officer in charge of Glider Training, and as we walked back to my office together he said:

'Well, Chief, now that you've soloed the glider, I can send off the signal that the Wing has completed its training.'

The Public Relations Officer's face paled.

'Sir, was that your first solo in the glider?'

I had been lost in my own thoughts and, completely preoccupied, said:

'That's right!'

Without another word he turned on his heel and strode off.

[Six years later Connie and I joined Bob Morrow, an ex-fighter pilot friend, at a restaurant in Montreal. We had reservations for dinner. Service was running late, and the Maitre d' asked us if we'd care to have a drink in the bar while we waited. Bob Morrow was hailed by an acquaintance, and in due course he introduced him to us. He was a reporter. When he heard my name, he said:

'Are you Wing Commander Hugh Godefroy?'

'Yes, I am. Have we met?'

Closing his eyes, he burst out laughing.

'Why, you son of a bitch, I've been trying to get my hands on you since 1944. I was the Public Relations Officer who took his first flight with you in the hotspur glider, and you on your first bloody solo!']

With the coming of spring I moved my Wing back into tents on a satellite airdrome near RAF Station Tangmere. Close by was the old town of Chichester. The South of England was like an armed camp. Every road was jammed with Army convoys, and all the Channel ports were stuffed with ships. As the months ticked by, Invasion fever mounted, but so did my operational time. I kept it a carefully guarded secret. More than anything else I wanted to be at the head of my Wing in the big battle. Knowing that every unit in the Invasion Forces. was ready, we braced ourselves each month when the tide was favourable. For only three days in that period was it high enough for the landing craft to get close enough. I gave Iron Bill McBrian a wide berth and tried to look as inconspicuous as possible.

On the 13th April, having just returned from leading the Squadron to bomb V-1 launching pads, I was walking with my head down toward my tent feeling hot and tired. Looking up, I saw Bill McBrian. He stood in my path, his legs wide apart and his arms folded. On his face was the sly smile I had seen so often just before he tapped his ring on the table in knock rummy. Instantly I knew what he was going to say.

'It's got to come sometime, Hughie. I've decided it's got to be now. That was your last sweep.'

In silence he listened to me pleading to let me lead my Wing at least on D-Day. It was all to no avail.

'Sorry, Hughie! This may be some comfort to you,' he said, handing me a piece of paper. I read:

'From — Rear Headquarters 83 Group — to Wing Commander H. C. Godefroy, 127 Wing Headquarters, April 13 — Message from Air Officer Commanding begins. . . Congratulations on your well deserved award of the Distinguished Service Order.'

I knew what this news meant to Connie. When I phoned and told her, I could hear her crying silently on the other end. To her this meant that I would have a desk job.

I was flattered to discover that Air Vice-Marshal Broadhurst wanted me on his staff. The appointment was Advisor for Tactics and Flying Personnel. When I reported to him, he did not confine me to a desk. The job did not demand that I fly operationally, but in his view I would be more useful to him as an Advisor if I would fly the various Units in 83 Group from time to time so as to be able to report first hand on the quality of leadership and changes in flying tactics. At AFDU, I had flown all the types of aircraft in the Squadrons of 83 Group. Established to act as close support to the Army, it had Spitfires, P-51's and Typhoons. My new job was a plum.

Life at 83 Group with the demands of a hardnose like Harry Broadhurst was a far cry from being on Operations. Broadhurst insisted on all out devotion to duty, and in the first forty-eight hours he gave me my first 'rocket.'

With nothing much to do at 'pink gin time,' I jumped in the Morris Minor and took off for Pepys Cottage. It had been several weeks since I had visited, and our household had undergone some change. With the Luftwaffe's intensified night bombing, as Mrs. Harding put it, 'Things had been pretty bloody.' Until recently she had spent most nights under the bed with Connie and the baby. Through a friend, the Hardings had heard of a young woman who found herself in difficult circumstances. Her husband, a former businessman, had been conscripted into the Army and was now somewhere in the Middle East. His Army pay as a Private was pitifully small. They had one child, a seven-year-old girl. As I was away so much, Connie had invited them to move in with her. The arrangement had worked out satisfactorily. Joyce was a tall dark English girl of Amazonian proportions. She was an intense, rather dominating personality with an earthy philosophy. I was pleasantly surprised to see how well Connie accepted her liberal views. It was evident from the onset that she enjoyed male company, and during dinner out of the blue she said:

'Do you believe in spirits?'

Somewhat taken aback, I replied that I had had little experience with them but had an open mind on most things. She informed us forthwith that she believed in the supernatural, was a clairvoyant, and regularly conducted seances. I could see from Connie's reaction that this was a side of Joyce she had never seen. She nervously got up and carried some dishes to the kitchen. I turned to Joyce and said quietly:

'Connie has been brought up with a host of Scottish superstitions, and hence she's afraid of such things. I think we would be wise to drop the subject.'

She promptly changed to sex. Now, with me feeling uneasy, she proceeded to inform us that she and her husband were of one mind: Though completely adequate to each other's needs, they believed that sexual freedom strengthened a marriage. Celibate living was unnatural and muddled the mind. Their marriage vows apparently allowed them to respond instinctively whenever they had the urge. As I wisely remained silent, Connie filled the void by remarking that she found it a novel arrangement. Professing to feeling 'tired,' I excused myself. I was relieved of washing up duties.

Well rested, I arrived back at 83 Group Headquarters at about nine o'clock. When the Air Vice-Marshal saw me, he said angrily:

'Godefroy, I hold a daily breakfast conference at 7:30 each morning, and I expect my staff officers to attend. From now on you be there. You are accountable only to me. When I come over from my caravan for a drink before dinner, I want a full report of your day's activities.'

At regular intervals Combined Headquarters held conferences, and I became a permanent member of Broady's entourage. Each of these meetings was chaired by one of the Chiefs of Combined Operations, and each had his own way of conducting it. General Bernard Montgomery with his Spartan habits started with the following instruction:

'During this Conference, Gentlemen, there will be no smoking, and if any of you want to cough, do it now.'

Montgomery, taken to fraternizing with the rank and file under his command, ruled his officers, on the other hand, with an iron fist. They all seemed terrified of him. He was up at dawn, and, regardless of what was happening, retired at nine o'clock. Only in the most extraordinary circumstances would anyone dare to disturb him after this hour. During the desert campaign, Montgomery's Eighth Army headquarters at one point was located in a small village. About 9:30 one evening, one of Rommel's flying columns was found to have penetrated to its perimeter. This was one crisis in which the Chief of Staff felt obliged to wake Monty.

'An armoured flying column has penetrated the village, sir!'

Furious, Monty replied:

'You know better than to disturb me with trivialities. You know they shouldn't be there. Get them out, and give me the details in the morning.'

A Colonel who had found life 'unbearable' on Montgomery's staff in England breathed a great sigh of relief when the General was sent to North Africa to command the Eighth Army. Liberated from Monty's grip, he had got himself organized. He was just beginning to enjoy life and to wangle some comforts, when he found to his dismay that he was posted to Eighth Army Headquarters in the Middle East. With fear and trepidation, he presented himself to Montgomery.

'Sir, I had the honour of serving under you in England,' he said nervously, 'and I will feel privileged to do so again here.'

'I remember you well,' Monty replied. 'You were on my staff two weeks in England. Here, it will be one.'

Montgomery's analysis of the task that lay ahead was influenced at that time by his view that every German soldier was worth five Allied soldiers or three Russians. He was prepared for massive casualties, but at Dieppe he thought some of them were unnecessary. In the short time that the Canadians had been ashore at Dieppe, eight of them became casualties from VD. Montgomery did not find in this any cause for levity.

At his Conferences, he did the talking. You could hear a pin drop. It was always a great relief to stand up as he left the room.

With Admiral Mountbatten, the Conference was conducted most casually. When we rose to our feet as he entered, he asked us to be seated as soon as he could be heard. Instead of speaking from behind the long conference table, he came around in front and sat between his hands in the middle of it. He seemed content with the state of preparedness, and proceeded to tell us of some of his experiences with Monty during the Sicilian Campaign. They had driven together in an open jeep, and he had been fascinated by the magnetic effect Monty had on his troops. News of his presence seemed to precede him, and as they passed groups of soldiers on the wayside, all tore off their hats waving them in the air and shouting 'Hi, Monty.' With mild amusement, he warned us not to try doing the same. By the time the Admiral had finished, I had acquired a great respect for this charming brilliant leader. He did not have to try to impress.

With the Air Vice-Marshal's permission I attended a dinner given in my honour by 127 Wing at the Unicorn, an Inn in Chichester. Lloyd Chadburn, whom I'd known since flying together at Digby in 1941, had taken my place as Wing Leader. Lloyd had done an outstanding job as a Squadron Commander, excelling himself during the Dieppe Raid. His easy-going manner and confident leadership endeared him to everyone.

It was the first time I had ever been the guest of honour at anything. My self-consciousness was soon dispelled by the warm affection with which my pilots welcomed me. Knowing that I had turned over to a supremely capable leader, I was able to relax and enjoy them man-to-man. Bill McBrian chaired the dinner, and when the brandy came around, he rose to his feet. After a few introductory complimentary remarks, he summoned Danny Brown. Danny placed in front of me an exciting-looking blue Mappin's box tied with ribbon. With great curiosity I stood up and carefully opened it. From the tissue paper I extracted a magnificent five-piece sterling silver tea service. On the teapot was engraved: 'To H. C. Godefroy from the Officers of 127 Wing, April 1944.' I was flabbergasted. This was the last thing I would have expected from this group of Canadians. They could not have chosen anything that I would cherish more. Having expected I would be called upon to say something, I had come prepared. I had intended to expound on the merits of Lloyd Chadburn, calling for them to give him the same loyalty they had me. With this in front of me, the content of my speech evaporated. I was determined not to be maudlin. To the obvious amusement of everybody, I mumbled away trying to express my gratitude. Finally at the last I remembered some of the things I had intended to say, and used them in my conclusion. As I sat down, utterly dissatisfied with my performance, I thought of all the things I should have said.

At five o'clock on the fifth of June, I was visiting Wing Commander Davoud's airfield. While sitting in his office chatting with him, he received a phone call.

'Davoud speaking.'

As I watched him, he listened without saying a word. Finally he said, 'Thank you, sir,' and hung up.

'Let's go outside, Hughie; I feel like getting some air.'

With his hands in his pockets, hunched over and staring at the ground, Paul walked with me towards my aircraft. When we were well out of earshot of anybody, he jerked up his head, and said:

'For the last three days I haven't been able to close my eyes. I have been privy to the most top secret piece of information in England. Hughie, it's on! Tomorrow is D-Day!'

'Are you sure, Paul?'

'There's no turning back now, Hughie. Eisenhower has just blown the whistle — we are invading Normandy!'

'Normandy? My God, they've got a hundred miles of rough water to cross. If an unexpected storm comes up, the poor bastards will be so sick they won't be able to stand.'

When I thought of the magnitude of this decision, I shivered. Had the planners of this massive operation considered every contingency? In the history of mankind no single Military Operation had been as important. Every operation that the Army Commander undertook had benefited from Air Force and Naval thinking. The Air Force fought its battles in more than two dimensions. It was still difficult for me to forget the caricature of the British General — florid frown beneath an Earl Haig moustache — red flashes on the lapels — chestful of ribbons — brain dulled from quinine and gin consumed in the Bengal Lancers, the charge of the Light Brigade or the thin red line, oblivious to the carnage visible through his field glasses as his men go over the top. To beat Rommel, Von Rundstedt and the weather, as Churchill put it, 'There could be no surer road to disaster than to imitate the plans of bygone heroes and fit them to a novel situation.'

I left Paul wandering back to his office and ran to my aircraft and took off, Grey murky clouds hung over the South coast as far as the eye could see. I went straight for the Isle of Wight where the ships had been lying at anchor for such a long time. Yes, they were moving. Two columns of ships were heading out to sea, and all the rest were steamed up and ready to go. Landing craft were buzzing. The Navy was on its way, and 'England would expect every man to do his duty.' In these ships were the poor bastards of the first wave. Whether they realized it or not, many would not survive the first charge. Over their dead bodies would step the men who would invade the Continent. These would be the young, the eager and the vigorous, the cream of our youth, who had been hammered into hardened soldiers.

Turning inland, I set course for 83 Group Headquarters. Looking to the north, I saw at my level what at first appeared to be a dark cloud. When I got closer, I realized that it was a solid line of aircraft. Hundreds, 'My God, maybe a thousand.' Halifaxes, Stirlings, and DC-3's in an endless line that stretched to the horizon, towing enormous gliders. These were the men in the wooden horse. Within the hour they would land behind the German lines with the objective of taking and holding the ground regardless of cost. They were to be

relieved by the men from the beaches. I flew up close beside the formation, waggled my wings furiously, then did a series of victory rolls.
For an hour after I landed they still kept coming, and I stood and
watched them until I could see no more. All through the night the air
was filled with the drone of heavy engines. Bomber Command was on
its way for the saturation bombing of the beach defences.

I couldn't sleep that night. I was too excited. With no one to wake
me, I slept longer than I had planned. I went straight to my aircraft
and took off. I headed out across the Channel in the direction of
Caen. From the Isle of Wight to the shores of Normandy was a solid
stream of ships all shapes and sizes. The sky was overcast, but the
visibility was good below. I hadn't gone very far before I ran into an
American Fighter Patrol, and from then I was never out of sight of
Allied aircraft of some kind. At the beach-head, just off shore, among
the cargo vessels, were several huge battleships broad-side on all guns
pointed inland. I recognized HMS Rodney that I had visited in the
Firth of Forth. Her great sixteen-inch guns fired a broadside, which
made the outline of her hull become hazy for a moment as it shuddered
with the vibration. As though a pebble had been dropped in the water,
an elliptical series of waves radiated from her water-line. The guns sent
black doughnuts of smoke-rings rolling towards the shore. A barge-like
vessel with its deck bristling with rockets like the quills of a porcupine,
nosed in onto the beach. The next instant, volleys of flaming rockets
seconds apart streaked for the beach like flights of burning arrows.
A rectangular pattern of explosions first appeared at the water's edge,
then rolled up to the base of the cliffs, up the face and over the top
like a giant carpet. As the rocket ship pulled back, the whole area
was enveloped in smoke. A great waterspout rose just beyond a destroyer lying broadside. It was a shell from a shore battery. In a few
seconds another waterspout straddled the vessel. Fascinated, I held
my breath knowing that the third was sure to come. There was a
tremendous explosion amidships. It broke in two, jack-knifed in the
middle, and in no time disappeared below the surface.

There were so many squadrons of Spitfires patrolling the beach
that I decided not tó add to the traffic and set course for England.
I landed at Ford, where Johnny Johnson's outfit was stationed. He
had promised to let me fly on one of the morning patrols. He had just
returned from the first sortie. In an hour and a half they hadn't seen
a single German aircraft. The absence of the Luftwaffe suggested that
initial surprise had been accomplished. But I respected the enemy and
felt sure that on the next sortie we would find them. I flew as a wing
man in Dal Russel's Squadron. We spent two hours patrolling the
beach-head without seeing anything. The only hazard was the traffic.
It was on such a patrol that Lloyd Chadburn was killed. He collided

head-on with the No. 2 man to the leader of a Spitfire squadron patrolling in the opposite direction.

For the fighters of 83 Group, D-Day was uneventful. I had nothing to report to Broady except that I would fly with the Typhoons in the morning. He asked me to go with Squadron Leader 'Bunny' Rose of 184 Squadron.

I flew a Typhoon giving Fighter cover for the rocket-equipped aircraft. Flight Lieutenant 'Dutch' Holland was leading. He had a free hand to choose his own target. Southwest of Caen we came across a marshalling-yard with tanks on flatcars. To my consternation, Dutch first did three circuits of the yard looking at it.

'Okay, chaps, I think this will do. Let's have a go,' he said languidly.

The moment he rolled over, the sky was filled with flak. He dived into a stream of tracers and balls of 40 mm. White streams trailed from his wings as his eight rockets streaked down. A cannon shell exploded on his nose, and instantly a long stream of glycol poured from his radiator tracing the path of his pullout. As he rolled over on his back, we heard,

'Red One, bailing out!'

The moment No. 2 got his rockets away he was hit and streaming glycol pulled out and went up into a loop. The No. 3 suffered a similar fate, and, having fired his rockets, crashed straight into the ground beside his target with a tremendous flash. The No. 2 continued on around his loop, then dived straight into the ground. I was so fascinated by the carnage that I failed to notice the flak bursts around me. Coming to my senses, I took sharp evasive action. I took over the lead and brought the survivors back.

I was anxious to see how some other Typhoon boys were making out and dropped in on Group Captain Gilland's airfield. One of his squadrons had been given the job of knocking out the radar stations in Boulogne Harbour. The operation called for eight rocket Typhoons. A single aircraft without rockets was to fly 2,000 yards ahead of the main force. He was to draw the flak to give the others a chance to knock out the radar stations. They called for volunteers to take the lead. One pilot volunteered.

The light flak in the harbour was concentrated in three places: One on the end of the jetty, and two more large batteries on the surrounding hills.

On the attack the lead pilot silenced the battery on the jetty but was hit in the process. He flew on attacking the batteries on the hills and was hit again by both batteries. The seven rocket Typhoons were able to knock out the radar station without having a shot fired at them.

Despite having one arm and one leg almost blown off, the lead pilot flew back and crash landed in England. At that point it was too early to say whether he would survive.

As Gilland was proudly telling me about it, I could see that he would have loved to lead. Gilland was a very highly decorated pilot who had made a reputation sinking ships in a bomb-carrying four-cannon Hurricane. His technique was to start firing his cannons on the attack at 1,000 yards. His shell would kick up a spray in front, shielding him from view. He flew into the spray until he saw the masts, then pulled up and dropped his bombs. He had had remarkable success.

When he finished his tale, I told him that I thought the lead pilot qualified for the Victoria Cross. Group Captain Gilland did not agree. He felt that everybody should be willing to do the same. To my knowledge nobody in Fighter Command was ever awarded this decoration.

On D-Plus 3 the first landing strip at B-2 in Normandy was ready. Air Vice-Marshal Broadhurst, Flight Lieutenant Burgess, his P.A. (Personal Assistant), and I flew over. The landing strip from the air looked a little short. Burgess and I gave the Air Vice-Marshal cover as he put his flaps and wheels down. I landed second. To my surprise I used up only half of the runway.

The Canadian Air Field Commander, 'Father' Brown, was there to welcome us. There was something triumphant about stepping down on French soil. For such a long time I had flown over this occupied territory. If I had done this four days ago, I would have found myself a hunted man. Burgess and I went for a stroll. We walked in silence, kicking up dust from the ground — bared by the Army's earth-moving equipment.

Two Sherman tanks were making their way up a rise in the ground of a corn field, the caterpillar tracks squeaking noisily as they went. Now widely separated, Burgess and I struck out through the tall corn in their direction. Suddenly I fell flat on my face. I found myself lying on the distended, blackened corpse of a German soldier. It was alive with blowflies and maggots wriggling from his nose and eyes. On his belt buckle was stamped: 'Gott Mit Uns.'

When we returned to our aircraft, Wing Commander Brown had produced a jeep, and he took the three of us on a tour.

We wound through several dirty-looking villages. The townsfolk just stood and stared at us vacantly. Used to German oppression and reprisal, they seemed reluctant to show any feelings. They weren't at all sure that the German war machine was not capable of pushing us back into the sea. We came upon long convoys and from an airman's point of view, I could not think of a more unhealthy place than in a large convoy in broad daylight ten miles from the German lines. The Army seemed to have long since forgotten about an air threat. They took no interest in anything above their own level. I did not share their peace of mind. I watched the sky.

We came to a crossroad where a red-capped Service Policeman was directing traffic. We stopped. Two soldiers were dragging past with their rifles slung over their backs, and one cockney said to the other:

'We must be well back of the lines now, 'Arry. There's a bloomin' S.P.!'

In the course of our inspection we passed a straight bit of road where a small company of soldiers was resting in the ditches. It was a spot where heavy fighting had taken place and large quantities of German equipment were strewn along the roadside. Above the heads of the soldiers several pairs of German jackboots protruded from the grain field. We stopped to stretch our legs, and Burgess and I went for a stroll. A three-ton lorry rumbled up to us and ground to a stop in a cloud of dust. An Army captain stuck his head out the window and said:

'I say. Can you tell me where the stiffs are?' The PA was nearest and answered:

'I'm terribly sorry, old man, we can't help you; we were just out for a stroll, and until you arrived we were rather enjoying it.' The truck trundled off down the road, and we were able to see his cargo: The rear was piled high with German corpses, their boots dangling over the lowered tailgate. Along the road we came across some Tommies, and we inquired if there were any German helmets about. One of them pointed to a field and said:

'There's dozens there, but I would't go after them if I were you — it's mined!'

We continued on our way back to the airdrome. Burgess and I went to chat with the airfield construction men. They were all in good form and looked tanned and healthy.

There was a whine of a bullet overhead, and I asked where it came from.

'Oh, that's just our friend, the sniper in the village over there. He's been there as long as we 'ave, and they can't seem to find 'im. 'e gets one over about every hour, but it's usually wild.'

The Air Vice-Marshal was not ready to leave yet, so we borrowed a motorcycle. I got into the driver's seat, and away we went. We had gone only a short distance when we almost had a head-on collision with an Army truck. I had forgotten we were on the Continent, where one drives on the right-hand side of the road. Heading for the beach, I came to a village. It had seen a lot of fighting. The village spire had a gaping hole in its side. We were told by the soldiers that it had housed snipers who had held up the advance. The Navy had come to the rescue and fired two shells. The second one went straight through the spire. Most of the village was reduced to rubble. The houses that still remained standing were scored and pitted with bullets. Outside the village in the ditch beside the road we came across a pile of stones with a stick wedged between the rocks. On the crossbar was printed:

'B.E.R. PRINCE S.R.A. 913893, JUNE 6, 1944.'

Passing on, we came across a field surrounded by a wooden fence. On each of the fence posts was a black sign with a white skull-and-cross-bones painted on it. Underneath was the printed word: 'MINEN.' The Huns had had to depart so quickly they had forgotten to remove their signs. The road ahead was blocked with transport, but on a motor-cycle we were able to weave between the trucks. I could not help but wonder what this would have been like if the air had not been filled with the throb of our Spitfires but instead with the scream of Stukas and the chatter of cannon and machine-gun fire from 109's and 190's.

The road was taking us straight towards the sea, and as we reached the crest of a hill, we saw the Channel. It was full of ships of every size and description. Each was flying a balloon like a silver banner. Behind were the great battleships lying at anchor. At intervals, their rugged outline would disappear behind a cloud of smoke and flame. After a few seconds the very ground shook with the roar of their guns. Heading in were the little landing craft pushing up white bow waves as they churned their way ashore. Just a few hundred yards off were a dozen ships neatly sunk in a row to provide a breakwater. Jutting out from the shore was a makeshift quay running to their centre. The unloading was proceeding according to plan.

We passed on and drew near yet another village. On the right was a pasture where the grass was covered with huge chunks of parched earth. It looked rather unusual because these bits seemed to have fallen from above. We dismounted to investigate. Some distance from the road, behind a roll in the ground, we came across several enormous shell-holes. The very bowels of the earth seemed to have been un-covered. These were the footprints of the modern Mars. In the fullness of time they would become mill-ponds where the grazing cattle would come to drink. They would also serve to remind this quiet village of the day of June the Sixth, 1944, D-Day. As we made our way back across the Channel in our Spitfires, my heart was full. I wondered why more of my countrymen whose families had come from Normandy did not share our determination to liberate their homeland.

Two days later I visited Wing Commander Eric Habjorn, the famous Norwegian Typhoon Pilot. On D-Day, Eric had done three sorties. Each time he had been hit and had to bail out in the Channel. Eric was a tall blond gentlemanly fellow with a retiring disposition. He was one of the great Typhoon Wing Leaders of the RAF. In the afternoon Eric's Wing was called upon to attack a heavy railway gun that was shelling the ships. He took three Squadrons, and he let me come along as fighter cover in one of the Typhoons without rockets. His Wing flew perfect formation. These aircraft with their rockets slung under the wings looked like a bunch of great bulldogs thundering out to sea. Eric went straight to the spot on his map reference, and well before reaching the railway tracks he gave the order to echelon port. He picked the difficult target up immediately and led his three Squadrons down in a continuous stream. He dived through a hail of flak, but his attack had come so quickly that the ground gunners were inaccurate. After the first Squadron fired its rockets, there was a huge mushroom of black smoke from the target, and the rest of the aircraft had to fire into the smoke. Their hits appeared as flashes exploding beneath it. In just a few minutes Eric reformed his Wing and set course for England.

On D-Plus Eleven, the 17th of June, I took off for France with my personal effects. I landed just before dusk at B-2 and went to look for 'Father' Brown. I found him in his tent, already in his camp-bed buried in a fox-hole a foot below ground.

'Father Brown,' I said, 'don't tell me they've got you sleeping in a hole?'

Propping his head on his elbow and looking very tired, he said to me:

'Okay, smart arse, you arrived over here too late to get a tent for yourself. You can sleep right over there, and by tomorrow I guarantee you'll be laughing on the other side of your face.'

I had had supper so with darkness I rolled out my sleeping bag and climbed in. I had just closed my eyes when I heard the familiar drone of a Ju 88. One after another, they came all night. They didn't just drop sticks of bomb; they dropped what we called 'breadbaskets.' They consisted of cylindrical canisters, which opened up to spew out hundreds of little anti-personnel bombs. They exploded on contact beating out a tattoo of deafening explosions. Each little bomb would cut the grass an inch or two from the ground.

After the first 'breadbasket,' 'Father' Brown stuck his head up out of his fox-hole, his tin hat jauntily cocked over his ear, and said:

'How are you getting along up there, Hughie? Cozy, isn't it?'

The place I was given to erect my tent was full of rocks. It was impossible to dig a hole, so I commandeered some bales of hay from a nearby farmhouse, dug holes for the feet of my camp-bed and surrounded my bed with the bales. I calculated that the bales would stop a piece of shrapnel, if nothing else. I took 'Father' Brown's advice and got into my bed a half an hour before sundown. My steel Tommy hat was heavy, so I put it aside. The Luftwaffe gave us a return visit, but I was asleep. I woke up with my 'Tommy' over my ear.

On the 19th June, Broadhurst sent me back to England to carry a report to the Air Ministry. As yet, no communication system had been established with the beachhead. Before leaving, he told me to get him some fresh bread and a few bottles of Guinness. I landed at Northholt, the home station of the Polish Wing. I delivered my messages and wangled a Jeep to drive to Pepys Cottage. I had not made contact in weeks. In the interval Hitler's V-1 flying bombs had been raining on London and the surrounding area. In spite of all attempts to destroy them, they penetrated by the hundreds. Knowing that some of the launching sites were aimed so their missiles would pass over Domewood, I was ridden with trepidation as I drove through the night. I parked on the road and walked up the path to the front door. I raised my hand to knock. Before I had a chance, the door opened, and there stood Joyce in her negligée.

'I knew you were coming; I divined it.'

I was thunderstruck and stood there for a moment agape.

'Where's Connie?'

'You'd better step inside or the Air Warden will be after us.'

Once inside the door, I handed her my raincoat, walked into the living-room and repeated my question. Joyce came into the living-room and sat down.

'Since D-Day the buzz bombs have been frightful. We have had one over the house every fifteen minutes day and night. The ack ack batteries and the fighters have been doing everything they can to shoot them down before they reach London. So many of them have been falling around here Connie decided the safest thing to do was to move Isabel back to Scotland.'

'They're both safe?'

'Yes, she phoned me. She's staying with her sister at Bathgate.'

'Well, what are you two doing here?'

'We have no other place to go, my dear.'

Jumping up and walking towards the kitchen, she said:

'Let me get you a whiskey and soda. I know you need it.'

While she was away, I did a quick appreciation. Connie and Isabel were safely in Scotland, and, knowing Effie's hospitality, she was being well cared for. I would have to go back to France in the morning; if I phoned her, she would be disappointed that she had missed my visit and worry even more. I had delivered Broadhurst's messages, posted his letters, bought his bread and Guinness, and if I wasn't mistaken, I could hear a bloody buzz bomb coming directly overhead. Joyce was right. I deserved a whiskey and soda — a double.

When I got to Northholt in the morning, I felt better than I had in several weeks. I was well rested and had breakfasted on egg and bacon, for a change. I opened the gunbays of my Spitfire and stuffed in the bread and Guinness. I pulled out my parachute, and in strapping it on, I noticed for the first time that I had made a mistake. It wasn't my parachute. It was far too big for me — it obviously belonged to the PA. He was longer in the body. Oh, well I thought — nothing to do about it now. When I had done my cockpit check, I put thumbs up to the Polish erk who started the battery cart. I pressed the starter button, and my engine started with a roar. I noticed that the oil pressure didn't go above 50 pounds per square inch. It should have been 95. I shut down, climbed out, and told the erk to call his Flight Sergeant. When he arrived, I reported the trouble and told him to call me at the Mess when he got it serviceable.

While looking for a cup of coffee, I ran into a Polish Wing Commander. He graciously asked me if there was anything he could do. In no time he saw to it that my coffee materialized. He had ordered one for himself. After hearing that I had just returned from France, he plied me with questions. I filled him in while he pensively cleaned his nails with a penknife.

For a moment we sat in silence. There was something sad and empty in this man's face.

'Are you married?' I asked at last.

It was a long time before he answered:

'I was — my wife and children all died in Warsaw.'

Turning to me and pointing the knife in the air through narrowed eyes, he said:

'When I get to Germany, I will kill every man, woman and child I see.'

The Bar Steward came over and said my aircraft was ready. I shook hands with the Wing Commander and thanked him for the coffee and took my leave.

My aircraft started as before, but this time the oil pressure was at 98. When I was air-borne, I called Eleven Group and gave my destination. He departed from R/T procedure and wished me luck. As I approached the Isle of Wight at five thousand feet, I checked the oil gauge. It still read 95. There was a high thin overcast, and in the bright patches the sea was blue, the white caps a dazzling contrast — ten miles out, I checked the oil pressure. It was down to 70. 'The engine sounds normal,' I thought to myself. 'It must be the bloody pressure gauge.' I called the Controller, and, hearing no side tone in the earphones as I transmitted, realized that my radio was dead. Broadhurst would never swallow the story if I turned back and had to spend another day. I opened the throttle, climbed to ten thousand feet and transmitted on Button D, the mayday frequency. There was no side tone. The oil pressure was down to 50. The Merlin 61 Handbook stated that at 45 pounds per square inch the Merlin 61 would run for two minutes.

'If it gets to 45 and the engine is still running, it must be the gauge.'
I was halfway across when the oil pressure reached 45. I checked the
clock. In two-and-half minutes there was a spluttering hissing sound,
and two white streams of glycol came pouring out of the exhaust
stacks. I immediately lost power. 'This just couldn't happen to me.
I've been over this Channel a thousand times, and here I am with no
radio and fifty miles from land in any direction.' The temperature was
off the clock, so I pulled the throttle back and started gliding. I noticed
a little ship pounding through the waves. The cloud had thickened and
the sea was now an icy green. I would have to bail, and here I was
wearing the P.A.'s parachute that hadn't been packed in at least three
weeks. Maybe it wouldn't open! The straps of this parachute were very
loose. If the Parachute Man was right, the loose leg straps could act
like a guillotine and castrate me. As my altitude decreased, I thought of
Dean McDonald; we were the same size. I was not going to try his
technique. I would walk out at five thousand. I slid back the coupe
top, took off my helmet, and trimmed the plane to glide at 110. Un-
buttoning my Sutton harness, I stood up in the cockpit holding on to
the windscreen. It wasn't too difficult. Planning to dive between the
port wing and the tail, I let go of the windscreen. The wing caught
me and spun me around. My left heel caught between the armour
plate and the edge of the cockpit. For a moment I hung suspended
dangling. With all my strength, I pulled on my knee and kicked wildly.
The instant I was free I felt a painful blow on the left knee. The sudden
silence was unearthly as was the sensation of weightlessness. I was
tumbling in space as if in slow motion, and sky and sea rotated around
me. The rip cord, pull the bloody rip cord. Without looking, I clawed
for it with my left hand and found nothing. Looking down, I saw the
harness almost around my back. I jerked the cord and for what seemed
an eternity I stared at it in my hand. At last, I felt a jerk, and I was
swaying beneath the parachute. Weightlessness had left, and, looking
down at the cold sea, I realized I wasn't far up from the water travelling
fast across the waves down wind. I grabbed the straps above me and
spun the chute so I was looking down wind. No sooner had I done this
when the waves seemed to rush up at me, and I was in. I had just
bobbed to the surface when I felt a jerk. The next thing I knew I was
being pulled through the water, my parachute acting like an enormous
sail. The water pressure on my arms pinned them to my sides as I was
pulled along on my back. At each crest of the waves I disappeared
beneath the surface. I turned the wheel on the parachute release box
and with both hands compressed it. It was jammed. Holding the box
in my right hand, I took a furious swipe at it with my left. With my
waist below water the blow was reduced to a light tap. With the effort
of struggling and my head below water at ten-second intervals, my

vision began greying as though I was blacking out. I wasn't breathing properly. If I didn't concentrate on breathing, I would soon be unconscious. I relaxed every muscle in my body, and in the valley between the waves took big deep breaths. My vision began to clear, and my mind with it. There must be a way out, I thought. I continued breathing deeply in the valleys and holding my breath through the crests. Slowly the panic left me. I tried arching my back and rounding it like the bow of a ship. I found that I glided up on the crest and only for a second was my head below water. With my strength returned, as I glided up on a wave, I raised both fists in the air, arched my back, and brought them down on the release box. It snapped open. The parachute straps on my left leg bound around my foot, and I was towed backwards. Holding my breath, I pulled in my foot and separated the straps. I was free! For a long while I lay drifting, gasping for breath as the waves crashed over me. My dinghy! I had to get into my dinghy! I found the cord that attached it to my Mae West and reefed it in. As I pulled open the snaps, I remembered the instructions, flattened it out on the water before turning on the compressed air tap.

'Short bursts at first or you will burst the dinghy.'

I turned it on just for a second. One side blew up, so I stopped. I turned the dinghy around in front of me to flatten it out, then felt for the compressed air bottle. It was gone. With a feeling of utter hopelessness, I threw my arms on the inflated part of the dinghy and let the waves drive me. From the time I left Northolt, everything had gone wrong. How was it that the engine lasted only long enough to get me to mid-Channel? Was it not strange that my radio packed up about the same time? A Polish Airdrome surely was the easiest of the RAF Stations for a spy to penetrate and sabotage its operation. Nobody knew I was missing. Broadhurst probably thought I was sitting in the Park Lane Hotel drinking pink gins. It might be a month before the authorities would list me as 'missing' and send the dreaded signal.

It seemed like hours that I drifted, the past four years passing before my eyes like a silent movie. Suddenly I saw the bow of a ship. It was bearing down on me from up wind. A man on the bow shouted and waved his arms. The little ship turned broadside putting me in its lee and flattening out the water around me. The railing was lined with men with lines. A shower of ropes shot in my direction each of them short. I could hear the Captain on the bridge cursing.

'If someone doesn't get a line to that man, I'll put you all in irons.'

A big seaman picked up a cork life-belt with a line attached and hurled it at me. It hit me on the head. I grabbed for it, locked my arms and held on. When the men on deck saw I had hold of it, they rushed to the line and pulled. With my clothes and boots sodden with water, I was water-logged, and they almost pulled the life-belt out of my grasp.

As the little ship bobbed up and down in the rough waves, I felt strong hands grab my clothes and drag me onto the deck. I lay there breathing hard, too weak to stand.

'Take him down to my cabin,' shouted the Captain.

The men had been standing staring at me. With that they sprang into action and carried me down a steep gangway and deposited me on the floor. For the first time since hitting the water, I felt cold, colder than I had ever felt in my life. Every muscle in my body began to shiver uncontrollably. A wave of nausea swept over me. Before I could raise my head, I vomited. As I lay there gasping for breath, a voice from the corner said:

'Don't tell me you've been sick. I can't stand it.'

A slim pale-faced American officer got out of the bunk, ran up the steps, and disappeared. A minute or two later he returned and began removing my wet sodden clothing.

'I'm sorry about that,' he said. 'I've been on this damn ship for two-and-a-half weeks and been seasick the whole time.'

When he got my clothes off, he rubbed me down with a towel. At this point I didn't care if I lived or died. He helped me to my feet and put me in the other bunk and covered me with half a dozen blankets. It didn't make the slightest difference. I still shivered. There was the sound of heavy seaboots on the steps, and the ship's mate appeared with a large tumbler of brown liquid.

'Here, drink this,' he said, sticking it under my nose.

I smelt rum.

'Don't be a fool man. I've just thrown my guts up, and that'll make me throw up again.'

'Drink it!' he said roughly.

'Okay, you fellas, I can't help you with the cleaning up. Here goes!'

It took me a half a dozen swallows to get it down. To my great surprise it stayed there. Almost immediately, warmth began spreading throughout my body, and closing my eyes, I slept.

I was wakened by a tap on my shoulder, and I opened my eyes to see the smiling face of the mate once more, with a mug of tea in his hand.

'Good morning, sir. I hope you didn't think I was being disrespectful last night. You can't tell the rank of a naked man. Even if you are a Wing Commander, at that point you needed to be told what to do.'

I sat up, and sipping the hot tea, said:

'You don't have to make any apologies. That rum saved my life!'

'How do you feel?'

I had to think for a minute. My right ankle was sore and I had a pain in the pit of my back. My left knee ached but otherwise I felt pretty well.

I feel pretty fit,' I said. I'm even hungry.'

'I'm sorry, but I can't offer you anything very exciting to eat. We've been anchored off the beachhead for two weeks and were on the way back to Portsmouth to replenish supplies. The only thing I have to offer you is hardtack. I'll get you some.

While the Mate was away, I noticed my clothes across the foot of my bunk. I reached down and felt them. They were warm and dry. I threw off the blankets and began getting dressed. The only thing that I was missing was the separate collar to my shirt and my black tie. Once again, I heard heavy seaboots on the steps. This time the Captain appeared, with two cakes of hardtack. He was a chunky, leathery-faced man in his middle fifties. I saw from his sleeve that he was a two-striper in the Merchant Navy.

'Good morning. The Mate tells me you're hungry. Sorry about this, but here is all I can offer you,' he said, handing me the two cakes of hardtack. 'You'll find them pretty hard to choke down without something to drink. I brought you another mug of tea.'

I took a bite of the hardtack, and chewing hard, looked up to see the Captain watching me.

'Tasty, isn't it?' he laughed.

It took every bit of moisture out of my mouth, and before I could answer, I had to take another swallow of tea.

'I must admit, it can't compete with Scottish shortbread, but at this point I would settle for anything. I'm famished.'

'You'll soon get something better to eat. We're about an hour out of Portsmouth. When you've finished, if you feel like it, come up and join me on the bridge.'

Accustomed to the darkness of the Captain's cabin, when I got up on deck, I had to squint; the sun was brilliant. A few scattered puffs of cumulus cloud drifted by, and the sea was light blue again, as our little ship pounded into the waves. I could see the outline of the Isle of Wight and beyond the coast. A steady stream of ships passed us on the port side. The salt air felt clean and fresh. I put my hands on my hips, closing my eyes, and began deep breathing through my nose like my father used to make me do in the morning. The cobwebs were gone. I couldn't get over how well I felt. In front of the entrance to the Captain's cabin were two blanket-covered stretchers. From each of them protruded two very white feet.

Two men sat on the deck in Army battledress. One was staring vacantly out to sea; the other was sitting with his head down, his arms locked around his knees, a wool sock on one foot and nothing on the other. They were a pitiful sight. I walked over and spoke. Neither one of them seemed to hear me. As though through blind eyes, the one kept staring out to sea, the other at the deck between his feet. I left them alone and climbed to the bridge. Besides the Captain and the helmsman, there was a young seaman beside the Aldis lamp. He squinted as he watched a signal flashed from shore. When the flashes stopped, the Captain turned to the signalman and said:

'What did he say?'

The lad looked uncomfortable. Screwing up his face, he said:

'I didn't get it, sir!'

The Captain pushed himself away from the railing with exasperation and turned to me and said:

'I've been two-and-a-half weeks at sea, and he hasn't been able to read a single message. This is the sort of thing I've had to put up with. The Mate and I are the only seamen on board. The rest of the crew are half-wits like this and a contingent of American soldiers. The American officer in my cabin is supposed to be in charge of them: he's been no use to me. He's been seasick from the moment he stepped on board. I wish I had never let them talk me into coming back.'

In subsequent conversation I discovered he had been retired and later induced to take command of this little ship, the *Peggy Nutten*. Prior to being refitted as a smoke-laying vessel, the *Peggy Nutten* had been holding a balloon down in the Thames Estuary. He had sat off the beachhead for the past two-and-a-half weeks but with no air attacks he had never had to lay smoke. On his return passage, he had picked up the two corpses and three survivors.

As we got closer to Portsmouth, things became more congested. A message came from a little vessel at the harbour entrance. With his nose wrinkled up and eyes blinking, the signalman stared at the flashing light. The Captain was leaning against the railing once more, staring down dejectedly.

'What did he say?'

The same pained expression came over the boy's face.

'I didn't get it, sir!'

Wearily the Captain turned around and looking at me, raised his eyes to the heavens, and gave a deep sigh.

After a while, the little vessel that had been signalling came alongside. It was the Harbour Master. With a bullhorn he roared:

'Are you blind? Can't you answer a signal?'

Angrily, the Captain grabbed a megaphone and striding to the side bellowed:

'With a signalman who can't read, what do you expect?'

'Go in and tie up at Quay No. 6, *Peggy Nutten*.'

The Captain waved his arm in acknowledgment and, ringing up half speed, approached his berth. As we made our way in slowly, the Captain's seaman instincts took over. He barked to the mate to muster all hands on deck. Half a dozen American doughboys shambled up from below, and the mate dispatched them to various positions for docking. The Captain watched their activities critically. On the bow, an American soldier was standing one hand on his hip and a coil of light rope in the other. With the tide, the stern seemed to be coming in first, and lines had already been thrown to secure it. The Captain roared at the man in the bow:

'You there, throw your bloody line!'

With an injured look on his face, the American soldier looked up at the bridge and said:

'I can't; the back end isn't in yet!'

In utter exasperation the Captain threw up his hands and raising his eyes to heaven said:

'What can you do!'

No sooner had the ship been secured than a shore-based crane lowered a great net amidships. The two corpses on their stretchers were placed in the middle, and deposited on the quayside. The two men on deck had not moved. Once more the net returned to the deck, and the two men, seemingly oblivious to their surroundings, meekly let themselves be led to the middle of the net, where they were made to sit down. Up went the net once more, this time with the living, and gently deposited them beyond the stretchers.

Feeling a little sick, I made my way below to the Captain's cabin. The Captain was already down there, preparing his bag to go ashore. When he had finished, he offered me a cigarette and lit one for himself. For the first time in three weeks he said he felt as though he could afford to sit and chat. He told me how I was picked up. The lookout on the bridge had been watching my aircraft and called the alarm when he saw it pouring smoke. Shortly thereafter the aircraft burst into flames. When they saw my parachute open, the Captain called all hands. At full speed he made for the spot where he thought I would hit the water. He estimated the wind at strength seven to eight. I landed far downwind. With the chute dragging me, he found that I was getting away. HMS *Peggy Nutten* had a maximum speed of six knots. He estimated mine at eight. When the chute finally collapsed, he took a bearing on his last sighting and headed for it. He had chased me for about an hour. Apologizing for the delay, he said he had never picked up an airman before.

At the end of the gangplank I was met by an officer who conducted me up the hill to a long building commandeered for a casualty clearing station. The Mess Hall was filled with collapsible tables and benches. Sitting at one end of the tables were the two soldiers from *Peggy Nutten*. In front of them was a large plate of food, a knife, and a fork. The two men sat immobile, staring at their plates.

'My God, man,' I said. 'These two men are in deep shock. They can't eat. They should be put in the hospital at once.'

The Officer, cocking his head to the side, said condescendingly:

'We have our routine, sir; after they pass through stores, they'll be going to hospital.'

I was offered a plate of food, but I had lost my appetite. I ate some of the meat. I, too, was put through stores. I turned down the running shoes. I took the shaving kit, the toothbrush, and toothpaste, the soap and the handkerchiefs. The next thing I knew, I was in the back of a Staff Car and on my way to the hospital. The Medical Officer didn't pay the slightest attention to my objections: I was relieved of my clothes, given a hospital bedsmock that opened down the back, tucked into bed, and a thermometer stuffed in my mouth. When the matron plucked the thermometer from my mouth, I asked:

'Why do I have to be in bed?'

She didn't answer until she finished scrutinizing the thermometer and recording my temperature on a chart.

'You are suffering from shock; the Medical Officer will decide when you are fit to leave.'

She hurried off in a rustle of starch.

It took me several days to get out.

All the bedmates in my ward were in serious shape. Whenever the Doctor did his rounds, I told him that I felt fine. He kept me anyway.

When I got out, I went straight to Gatwick to the 83 Group Transportation Flight. It was here I met the thoughtful Equipment Officer who wrote off everything I had been issued since 1940. I drew a watch, flying helmet and Mae West, and a parachute. I scrounged three loaves of bread, half a dozen bottles of Guinness, and commandeered another Spitfire. This time I was very finicky about the ground and radio check. I made it to B-2 Normandy without a hitch. I can't say I enjoyed the crossing.

The Air Vice-Marshal was in his caravan behind his desk looking out through the open door. He was scowling at me as I walked towards him.

'Where the hell have you been? I gave you forty-eight hours, not a fortnight.'

By the time he had listened to my story the scowl had faded. At the end, he threw his head back and roared with laughter.

'Serves you bloody well right. Go on with you. I'll see you at dinner.'

It wasn't long after 83 Group Headquarters was set up in France that all the squadrons were stationed at airstrips like B-2. My trips to England became fewer and fewer, and my liaison work was done by motorcycle. I had a Harley-Davidson Big 4. At first it was a common sight to see me hunched over the handlebars, bouncing along the rough roads, looking very much out of control. As time went on, I acquired the swank and reckless abandon of the trained dispatch rider. The dust and the dry weather were only equalled by the mud and the wet, and between the two, our blue battledress began to look like the grey German uniform. This didn't matter a great deal as long as we didn't stray away from the British Sector. The American soldiers, however, were not familiar with the RAF battledress. If you weren't careful, you might be shot on sight.

The experience of an RAF Radar Officer bore this out. He was sent to do a job in the American Sector. In the course of his travels, he came across a platoon of American infantry. He narrowly escaped being shot and was taken prisoner despite his insistence that he was on their side. The American platoon had some fox-holes to dig, so he was given a shovel and put to work, carefully supervised by a burly Top Sergeant. All his complaints were to no avail, and as far as the Top Sergeant was concerned, he was lucky to be alive. He had been accompanied by another RAF Officer, who had managed to make his escape. He reported the incident to his Headquarters. A Major chosen for his command of American colloquialism was sent to his aid. He was able to convince the platoon Commander of the Radar Officer's true identity. It was stories like this that kept me within our own Sector.

One day, visiting one of our Mustang (P-51) Wings, I was standing talking to some of the pilots outside their tents. My ears were accustomed to the drone of our aircraft, but while we were talking, I became conscious of an unfamiliar sound. It was the ever increasing noise of a diving aircraft, something about its pitch made me feel uncomfortable, and I glanced upwards. I found myself looking to the gun barrels of four 190's and two 109's.

'Look out — 109's!' I shouted, running for a ditch.

There was a chatter of cannon and machine-gun fire, and bullets ripped through the trees over my head. It seemed as though they were all firing at me. They were gone as quickly as they had come; and as their sound faded, Pilots began to reappear from different points of vantage. We counted heads and found that nobody had been touched. It was easy to laugh now. We began to compare exactly what we had seen and what we had done. Most of my companions had found themselves in nettle bushes. Gradually I became aware of a familiar unpleasant odour — 'Shit!' My uniform — my boots — were covered in shit.

A crippled Spitfire came in for a landing at one of the strips. It was Flight Lieutenant Mackelroy. He reported that he couldn't control his aircraft below a speed of 160. He would try to bring it in on its belly on the grass beside the wire. When he hit dirt at a hundred and sixty miles an hour, both wings and his tail were torn off; the fuselage skidded on its side in a cloud of dust. We all rushed to the airplane. Mackelroy, strapped in the cockpit, was motionless. There seemed no immediate threat of fire, so cautiously we decided to ease him out of the cockpit while holding on to his head in case his neck was broken. When we touched him, he began to move. Slowly he raised his hands to his face, then more quickly touched his arms and legs. Then in obvious amazement exclaimed:

'I'm alive! Christ, I'm ALIVE!'

Another event was recorded by the Typhoon Wing. They were knocking out tanks and transports with rockets. One of the pilots who lacked experience dived to attack some transport, and when he pulled out sharply, his aircraft 'mushed.' At 400 m.p.h. he hit the ground. Fortunately for him, he hit on a long flat area without obstructions. After skidding for about a mile, he came to rest and stepped out of the aircraft unhurt.

When Bill McBrian told Buck Buckham that he had been relieved of flying duties, Buck accepted the decision without a word, but when he told him to pack his bags and fly back to the Communications Flight of 83 Group, he said:

'Bill, I'm not flying across the Channel one more time. You will have to send me over in a boat.'

It had been impossible to tell Buck had been under any sort of tension. He was always there, ready, willing to go, his aggressive spirit never faltering. He told me afterwards that he had long since given up all expectation of coming out of the war alive.

[Buck was with me on the RCAF Staff Officers' Course at Toronto. It was here that I got to know the gentle side of his nature. He stayed in the Service. In bad weather he flew into the side of a mountain and was killed. Thus another great Canadian was lost.]

Air Vice-Marshal Broadhurst had some more things to deliver to Air Ministry. This time, he gave me forty-eight hours' leave. As soon as I got down at Gatwick, I phoned Connie. I was greeted with a flood of tears. She had received a brown 'On His Majesty's Service' envelope addressed to me, and, of course, opened it. Inside was a handwritten letter from the Captain of HMS *Peggy Nutten*. It included the water-stained separate collar of my shirt, and my black tie. She read me the letter. He hoped that this found me well and free of complications from my swim in the Channel. My collar and tie had been found in his bunk, and he was happy to be able to return them. From the date of the letter she had surmised that this had all taken place some time ago. She had been frantic. She had been in contact with RCAF Headquarters which apparently did not know any more about it than she did. Like Connie, they thought that I was off operations. She cried bitterly over the telephone, saying that she did think that I had had enough, and she felt now that I did deserve to go back to Canada like the rest. She was sick and tired of the bloody War, and if we were ever going to go back to Canada, she wanted to go now.

I felt wretched. What a brick she had been through it all. I could not see how the Germans could push us back into the sea now. The hardest battles had been won. With Lloyd Chadburn dead, RCAF Head-quarters would never let me go back on ops. My staff job would be the best I could do, and there were lots of people eager for the spoils and accolades of final victory who would be glad to replace me. My cup was full; it was sheer gluttony to ask for more. The Personnel Officer at RCAF Headquarters had asked Connie to tell me to call Head-quarters immediately. I promised I would.

I couldn't bear to do it right then, so I called the Hardings at Dome-wood. Peggy was delighted to hear from me and invited me to stay. We had dinner at the Duke's Head, their favourite pub nearby. Eagerly they questioned me about Normandy. Tub Harding, in the Home Guard, listened with such envy it was pitiful. At the last a thought came to me:

'Tub, how would you like to fly down with me tomorrow in the Anson for a look at the South Coast?'

His eyes wide with excitement he said:

'I'd love to, Hughie, but how can you arrange that?'

'I tell you what you do. You come with me in the morning in your Home Guard uniform, and I'll tell them you're my driver.'

The plan worked perfectly. We got straight through the gate at Gatwick and over to the Communications Flight. I introduced Tub to the Flight Commander as my driver and told him I needed the Anson. It was serviceable, and off we went. I gave Tub Harding the job of winding up the undercarriage. It took about a hundred and twenty turns on the crank. It was comical to watch how vigorously he did the job. We flew down to Portsmouth and out over the sea. A line of ships continued to the horizon in the direction of Normandy. Tub was thrilled and pointed out the various types of ships like an excited child. When I swung around towards the Isle of Wight, he turned to me and in a pleading voice said:

'Hughie, please take me over to France. I can fight, you know. I'm tough as nails. Let me avenge Peter! Once I'm over there I'm sure I can talk my way into getting into the line. Please, Hughie, *please*!'

I was in full sympathy with his feelings, and knowing Tub Harding I had no doubt that if he got there, he would give a very good account of himself. But I could not get away with landing the Anson at B-2.

'Tub, if I landed this old Anson at B-2, Broadhurst would have me shot on the spot. He's had trouble enough with me now. I can't do it.'

We returned to Gatwick and without further incident made our way back to Domewood. As promised, I called RCAF Headquarters. As soon as they heard who was speaking, they asked me to hold for Air Vice-Marshal Breadner.

'Godefroy, I've been hearing all sorts of things about you. What's this about you ending up in the Channel? You're supposed to be flying a desk. I want to send you back to the Staff College in Canada. You will take the course first and then become a member of the Teaching Staff. The next course starts the first of September, and I want you on it. Do you hear me?'

'Yes, sir, I hear you.'

'Okay, get in touch with the Immigration Officer and get cracking.'

Before doing anything else, I went back to Gatwick and took off for B-2. I had developed a genuine affection and profound respect for Broady. I had to tell him first. Broady had been good to me. The only other Canadian on his staff was Group Captain Gordon McGregor. He had given Gordon a secondary Organizational Appointment making him responsible to the Air Officer Administration. It had been difficult for Gordon to find out what he was supposed to do. He had been very unhappy. As for me, the petty politics of peace time militarylife in Canada had little appeal. But Connie had done less binding and complaining than most women. She had earned a break.

It was with a heavy heart that I walked towards the Air Vice-Marshal's caravan. He was writing at his desk. Without looking up, he said:

'Come in, Godefroy. How was England?'

'I'd like to have a word with you, sir. Is this a convenient time?'

'Yes, what is it?'

He listened to me in silence, and when I had finished, he said:

'What do you want to do, Godefroy?'

'I can't think of anything I'd rather do than stay here under you, sir, but my wife has put up with a lot, and I feel her efforts deserve some consideration.'

For a long time, he just sat there looking at me. Finally he said:

'Godefroy, I think you would be a fool to let your wife or any domestic consideration interfere with your career.'

'Sir, if I thought that you really needed me, nothing would prevent me from staying.'

'Godefroy, nobody on my staff is irreplaceable. If you want to stay, I can countermand Air Marshal Breadner's orders without the slightest difficulty. The job is there.'

A wild thought suddenly came to me.

'Sir, if I were to take my wife home to Canada and get her settled, would you take me back?'

'If you can arrange it, I will find a place for you.'

'In that case, sir, I would like your permission to take them back to Canada.'

The month following my return from France was Hell. The buzz bombs were raining on London by the hundreds, and there was one over the house every fifteen minutes. My first visit to London was to RCAF Headquarters to see the Immigration Officer. In the hall a bunch of Admin. Officers recognized me. I was chatting with them when the air raid siren went. I turned my head towards the nearest window to listen, and when I turned back, I was alone. My companions had evaporated. There was a thunderous explosion which shook the building, followed by the All Clear. I continued up the hall to the office of the Immigration Officer. It was empty. I sat down and waited. Soon he appeared, and I asked him to arrange passage for myself, Connie, and Isabel.

'You will be going back by yourself, and we will send your wife and child later.'

'Oh, no, you don't! The only reason I'm going home is to take my wife and child out of England. We go together, or we don't go at all.'

'You've been posted back to Canada, not your wife. We can take you in ten days.'

'I'll see about that,' I said, jumping to my feet and strode out of the office.

I went over to Canada House. I had met Vincent Massey, the Canadian High Commissioner. As the runt of the school, I had presented the flowers to his wife two or three times on prize day.

When I asked to see the High Commissioner, I was told he was out. His Secretary was in and would see me. The Secretary was an Army Colonel in his early fifties. He welcomed me most cordially. I told him my story. I said I would accept Air Vice-Marshal Broadhurst's offer and return to my Staff job rather than go home without my family. He listened in silence, smiling in mild amusement.

'You're mad, aren't you?'

'Bloody mad, sir!'

'All right, settle down, laddy. I think we can do something for you. I feel sure the High Commissioner would be more than happy to use his influence, particularly if you are able to do something for him.'

'What on earth could I do for him?'

'You can tell us what happened to his son Hart. The High Commissioner got a report that he was wounded. Do you know anything about it?'

I threw my head back and laughed.

'Yes, I know what happened. First of all, tell Mr. Massey not to worry. Hart is all right. He was standing on one of the airfields talking to the pilots when a German fighter dived out of the cloud and strafed them. Two of the machine-gun bullets creased his temples just cutting the skin. How do you like that for luck?'

The Colonel looked most relieved and thanked me for the news. He took down my telephone number at Pepys Cottage and told me to go home and wait and do nothing until I heard from him.

The next morning he telephoned me to confirm that it was all arranged. The boat would be leaving in about three weeks, and I would be informed later about final arrangements.

For the next two weeks I kept running back and forth to London RCAF Headquarters Pay Office, Canada House, the Immigration Office, Lloyd's, Bank, and my tailor in Saville Row. It seemed incredible the number of things that had to be done before we left. Then I was faced with the ghastly job of packing for the trip. I spent several days in London looking for somebody that could pack breakables. Finally, I found a man in East Grinstead. Connie left Isabel with Effie and took the train to London to help me with what she called the 'flitting.' I had scrounged some steel trunks formerly used to pack parachutes. The day before Connie arrived was sunny, and I had the trunks out on the front lawn, painting our name on them. I heard the pulse of a buzz bomb. Was it coming straight overhead or to one side? The sound steadily increased so I knew it was coming straight overhead. I put down my paint brush and stood up to watch it go by. It was about to come into view, when the engine stopped. I could distinctly hear the whistle as it glided down. I dived at the trunk of an oak tree, threw my arms around it and held on. There was a deafening explosion. The concussion transmitted through the ground thumped my chest, almost taking my breath away. My arms were torn from the tree trunk by the blast, and I was rolled across the grass like a piece of paper. Mrs. Harding came running over.

'Are you all right? Thank God!'

It took us a half-hour to find where the thing had hit. Three empty houses, close together, had been reduced to rubble. Fortunately, I had most of the windows of the cottage open, so none was broken.

Peg Harding and I sauntered back, lost in our own thoughts. After a while, she said:

'They are devilish things, aren't they? Blast them. I must say that shook me. Oh, well, it could have been worse, We've put up with it this long. I guess we can put up with it a little longer.'

Her words triggered a chain of thoughts. I would not have to put up with this much longer. I was going home — leaving these isles maybe — never to return — never to see Tub and Peg again. They had become as close to me as my own parents, closer in some respects. I would miss the English, all of them. Studiously extreme, the sloths and wheedlers utterly repulsive, the indomitable superb. Even the brown-nosers

I had to admit had a certain style. I would remember them at their finest hour.

Connie had been very excited at the thought of Canada. Her head danced with visions of a vast new world rich with natural resources. Dwellings shining with modern appliances, shelves groaning with joints of beef, fresh laid eggs and butter. But when the time came to leave her family, heart-breaking tears were shed. The troopship was jammed with wives and children of servicemen, and Connie was faced with her first disappointment. She and Isabel were to be placed in a cabin with three other women and their children, and I at the other end of the ship. I went straight to the Purser.

'Are there any officers on board in private cabins?' I asked.

'Yes, sir. There's a Colonel and his wife in a private stateroom.'

I took out my pocketbook and extracted the last five-pound note I had in my possession and handed it to him.

'I am the next most senior officer on board, I take it. I know that you have at least one cabin unoccupied. I want it . . . now!'

I told Connie not to move a thing. Half an hour later, we had our cabin.

The trip could hardly be classified as a cruise. The refitted liner had been stripped of all non-essentials. The only good thing was the bread, rolls crusty and white as snow. I realized I hadn't tasted white bread in four years. After the frenzy of making preparation to move, inactivity was an unsettling anticlimax. There was nothing to do but wait and think. To pass the time I recounted my happy memories of childhood. We would be arriving in time for the glorious fall colours, and before long we would be in the grip of the Canadian winter. I longed to smell again the cold crisp air on a winter's morning and hear the wind sighing in the twisted pines on a rocky shore. The street lights would be on, and there would be no more air-raid sirens.

As I got closer and closer to my country, the full impact of starting a new life with a family descended upon me. I had done nothing to prepare myself for such a task. I had thought only of war and read nothing but operational orders. I had behind me only unfinished studies in Engineering that had not inspired. I had drifted through adolescence without a goal or viable prospects. I didn't have a job to go back to, and little money. To waste my life and vitality on pointless parades in a peacetime service was unthinkable.

After being involved with moving my family with all the irritating little domestic jobs that had to be done, I realized that I couldn't drop Connie and skip gaily back to France.

What would I do? For the first time I felt an overpowering sense of moral fatigue.

There was one glimmer in the darkness: With a challenge I had learnt to do one thing well. I needed another goal. I had seen perseverance result in triumph in spite of what at first looked like impossible odds.

With a challenging goal I would find a place! In war I had stalked through the valleys and the shadows; surely it would give me the armour to brave the peace.

On our last day at sea, we were leaning over the railing on the promenade deck listening to the bleating of the ship's foghorn and watching the seagulls glide by us on the wind. Whiteness enveloped us on all sides, and, as we watched, a soft breeze cooled our faces and lighter patches appeared in the swirling mist. As the wind freshened, these grew brighter. Whiteness gave way to form and colour. Finally, we saw a green shore, and a small church, with its tall spire looking out to sea.

APPENDIX

HOLGATE

Edwin Holgate's work gained wide acceptance, rewarded by one-man shows in The Canadian National Gallery. Modesty prevented him from telling me at Kenley that he was a member of the famous Group of Seven Canadian painters. The work of these men had always been a source of inspiration to me. As a boy, I had been particularly thrilled by the boldness of Lorne Harris. Howey Harris, one of his sons, had been a chum of mine at Upper Canada College, and had proudly shown me his house designed by his father.

Edwin Holgate's daughter married Chris Hare, a classmate of mine at Initial Training School at Regina. After distinguished service as a pilot during the War. Chris was killed in a flying accident. It was through Chris that I received the following letter:

Morin Heights, Qué.
February 8, 1960

Dear Hugh:

You will be surprised to hear from me — seventeen years after my visit to Kenley during a rather agitated period of our history.

Chris Hare has told me of meeting up with you again and carried a message to me to the end that if I had any drawing made at Kenley recalling those days, you would be glad to possess it. Here then is my reply, but bear in mind that this is *not* a picture; it is a 'field note' — giving me the information to be used later in more developed form, and it must be regarded in that light. The notations and corrections are left untouched, and I believe that it may be more interesting in that state. Recently I was looking over an accumulation of such drawings and notes and felt *this* to be the one of most interest to you. I hope that you will like it.

Seventeen years sounds like a long time — but my memories of Kenley are the warmest and most vivid of my experiences on any of the stations I visited. Buck McNair I saw fairly frequently as he was at Lac St. Denis about four miles from here and where I was an honorary member of the Mess — Wally Conrad. I have not seen him again, though I have heard of him. 'Chad' I shall always miss.

And now you are an M.D. — a logical reaction from knocking them down to building them up!

If you are ever up in these parts — look me up. I am not hard to find.

I hope that the drawing will please you.

With best regards,

Sincerely yours,
Edwin Holgate

Edwin's field sketch is one of my most valued possessions.
Edwin died in his 80's in 1977.

Absender:
Vor-and Zuname: P/O C. W. Floody
Gefangenennummer: J 5481, R.C.A.F.,
Lager-Bezeichnung: Dulag Luft,
DEUTSCHLAND

Kriegsgefangenenpost
Mit Luftpost
Gebü brenfrei!
An: P/O Hugh Godefroy,
    R.C.A.F., C/o Canada House,
    MH 29/12
Empfangsort: Trafalgar Sq.,
StraBe: London,
Land: ENGLAND.

Dear Hugh:

A strange place to be writing you from but such is the fortune of war. I'm well and being treated surprisingly good. Whitson is with me and Hodge is also alive and well. Would you have the Adj. get in touch with the Red Cross and ship me my greatcoat, hat, underwear, shirts, socks and sweaters, also my oxfords and if there is any more room (ten pounds to a parcel) my uniform — pants anyway!

Johnny Small was killed, I believe. Hope this reaches you without any more casualties.

Also, would you tell the Adj. that I am trying to have all my pay transferred to my wife and would he look into it in case some of my cards don't reach the bank.

Give my best to the rest of the boys and have a drink on Whit and I.

Yours,
Wally.

Note — From this we knew that Whitson was alive.